Cortázar and Music

LEGENDA

LEGENDA is the Modern Humanities Research Association's book imprint for new research in the Humanities. Founded in 1995 by Malcolm Bowie and others within the University of Oxford, Legenda has always been a collaborative publishing enterprise, directly governed by scholars. The Modern Humanities Research Association (MHRA) joined this collaboration in 1998, became half-owner in 2004, in partnership with Maney Publishing and then Routledge, and has since 2016 been sole owner. Titles range from medieval texts to contemporary cinema and form a widely comparative view of the modern humanities, including works on Arabic, Catalan, English, French, German, Greek, Italian, Portuguese, Russian, Spanish, and Yiddish literature. Editorial boards and committees of more than 60 leading academic specialists work in collaboration with bodies such as the Society for French Studies, the British Comparative Literature Association and the Association of Hispanists of Great Britain & Ireland.

The MHRA encourages and promotes advanced study and research in the field of the modern humanities, especially modern European languages and literature, including English, and also cinema. It aims to break down the barriers between scholars working in different disciplines and to maintain the unity of humanistic scholarship. The Association fulfils this purpose through the publication of journals, bibliographies, monographs, critical editions, and the MHRA Style Guide, and by making grants in support of research. Membership is open to all who work in the Humanities, whether independent or in a University post, and the participation of younger colleagues entering the field is especially welcomed.

ALSO PUBLISHED BY THE ASSOCIATION

Critical Texts
Tudor and Stuart Translations • *New Translations* • *European Translations*
MHRA Library of Medieval Welsh Literature

MHRA Bibliographies
Publications of the Modern Humanities Research Association

The Annual Bibliography of English Language & Literature
Austrian Studies
Modern Language Review
Portuguese Studies
The Slavonic and East European Review
Working Papers in the Humanities
The Yearbook of English Studies

www.mhra.org.uk
www.legendabooks.com

STUDIES IN HISPANIC AND LUSOPHONE CULTURES

Studies in Hispanic and Lusophone Cultures are selected and edited by the Association of Hispanists of Great Britain & Ireland. The series seeks to publish the best new research in all areas of the literature, thought, history, culture, film, and languages of Spain, Spanish America, and the Portuguese-speaking world.

The Association of Hispanists of Great Britain & Ireland is a professional association which represents a very diverse discipline, in terms of both geographical coverage and objects of study. Its website showcases new work by members, and publicises jobs, conferences and grants in the field.

Editorial Committee
Chair: Professor Trevor Dadson (Queen Mary University of London)
Professor Catherine Davies (University of Nottingham)
Professor Sally Faulkner (University of Exeter)
Professor Andrew Ginger (University of Bristol)
Professor James Mandrell (Brandeis University, USA)
Professor Hilary Owen (University of Manchester)
Professor Christopher Perriam (University of Manchester)
Professor Philip Swanson (University of Sheffield)

Managing Editor
Dr Graham Nelson
41 Wellington Square, Oxford OX1 2JF, UK

www.legendabooks.com/series/shlc

STUDIES IN HISPANIC AND LUSOPHONE CULTURES

21. *Photographing the Unseen Mexico: Maya Goded's Socially Engaged Documentaries*, by Dominika Gasiorowski
22. *The Rise of Spanish American Poetry 1500-1700: Literary and Cultural Transmission in the New World*, edited by Rodrigo Cacho Casal and Imogen Choi
23. *José Saramago: History, Utopia, and the Necessity of Error*, by Mark Sabine
24. *The Cultural Legacy of María Zambrano*, edited by Xon de Ros and Daniela Omlor
25. *Cortázar and Music*, by Nicholas Roberts
26. *Bodies of Disorder: Gender and Degeneration in Baroja and Blasco Ibáñez*, by Katharine Murphy
27. *The Art of Cervantes in 'Don Quixote': Critical Essays*, edited by Stephen Boyd, Trudi L. Darby and Terence O'Reilly
28. *The Modern Spanish Canon: Visibility, Cultural Capital and the Academy*, edited by Stuart Davis and Maite Usoz de la Fuente
29. *The Novels of Carmen Laforet: An Aesthetics of Relief*, by Caragh Wells
30. *Humanizing Childhood in Early Twentieth-Century Spain*, by Anna Kathryn Kendrick
31. *Gómez Manrique, Statesman and Poet: The Practice of Poetry in Fifteenth-Century Spain*, by Gisèle Earle
32. *No Country for Nonconforming Women: Feminine Conceptions of Lusophone Africa*, by Maria Tavares
33. *Form and Reform in Eighteenth-Century Spain: Utopian Narratives and Socio-Political Debate*, by Carla Almanza-Gálvez
34. *Women and Nationhood in Restoration Spain 1874-1931: The State as Family*, by Rocío Rødtjer
35. *Francisca Wood and Nineteenth-Century Periodical Culture: Pressing for Change*, by Cláudia Pazos Alonso
36. *Pepetela and the MPLA: The Ethical Evolution of a Revolutionary Writer*, by Phillip Rothwell
37. *Queer Genealogies in Transnational Barcelona: Maria-Mercè Marçal, Cristina Peri Rossi, and Flavia Company*, by Natasha Tanna
38. *Hispanic Baroque Ekphrasis: Góngora, Camargo, Sor Juana*, by Luis Castellví Laukamp
39. *Contemporary Galician Women Writers*, by Catherine Barbour
40. *The Marvellous and the Miraculous in María de Zayas*, by Sander Berg

Cortázar and Music

Nicholas Roberts

LEGENDA
Studies in Hispanic and Lusophone Cultures 25
Modern Humanities Research Association
2019

Published by Legenda
an imprint of the Modern Humanities Research Association
Salisbury House, Station Road, Cambridge CB1 2LA

ISBN 978-1-78188-807-0

First published 2019

All rights reserved. No part of this publication may be reproduced or disseminated or transmitted in any form or by any means, electronic, mechanical, photocopying, recording or otherwise, or stored in any retrieval system, or otherwise used in any manner whatsoever without written permission of the copyright owner, except in accordance with the provisions of the Copyright, Designs and Patents Act 1988, or under the terms of a licence permitting restricted copying issued in the UK by the Copyright Licensing Agency Ltd, Saffron House, 6–10 Kirby Street, London EC1N 8TS, England, or in the USA by the Copyright Clearance Center, 222 Rosewood Drive, Danvers MA 01923. Application for the written permission of the copyright owner to reproduce any part of this publication must be made by email to legenda@mhra.org.uk.

Disclaimer: Statements of fact and opinion contained in this book are those of the author and not of the editors or the Modern Humanities Research Association. The publisher makes no representation, express or implied, in respect of the accuracy of the material in this book and cannot accept any legal responsibility or liability for any errors or omissions that may be made.

Trademark notice: Product or corporate names may be trademarks or registered trademarks, and are used only for identification and explanation without intent to infringe.

© *Modern Humanities Research Association 2019*

Copy-Editor: Dr Ellen Jones

CONTENTS

	Acknowledgements	ix
	Note on Translations	xi
	Introduction	1
1	*La música culta* and/as Language	26
2	*La música culta* and/as Revolution	56
3	Tango: Nostalgia and Creativity	103
4	Jazz: The Theoretical Framework	149
5	From Jazz Theory to Jazz Practice	182
6	'More Than' Jazz	214
	Conclusion	239
	Bibliography	247
	Index	260

For Heiddy, Gabriela, and Alejandro

But the water said *earth* and the water said *sky*.
We were everyone we'd ever been or would be,
every angle of light that says *You*, that says *I*,
and the sea was the river, the river the sea.
  — Philip Gross

ACKNOWLEDGEMENTS

This project started its life in a very different form some eighteen years ago. Rather than indicating glacial rates of progress, I would like to think this is more an indication of the nature of modern academia, as various projects and administrative roles take centre stage at different points in time, dominating all else for their duration. Either way, what is remarkable is that the central figures whom I must thank for their input into this book and the research that it fronts have been there from the very start: Steven Boldy and Dominic Moran, first as lecturers and supervisors, then as colleagues and friends, have been a constant presence in the gestation and realisation of my thought on Julio Cortázar's texts. Their seminal work on Cortázar has been a persistent inspiration, and their help, stretching from recent conversations all the way back to supervisions in my undergraduate days, invaluable in more ways than they can know. In particular, I should like to thank Professor Boldy for finding the time to read a provisional draft of several chapters of the present book's manuscript, offering comments that both encouraged and also alerted me to several missteps I had made.

A number of other people were also of immense help in offering to read and comment on draft chapters towards the end of the book's writing. In this vein, I would like to offer my deepest thanks to Marcela Cazzoli and Samuel Llano, who were kind enough to bring their knowledge of matters Argentine and musical respectively to bear on their reading of my work. Similarly, I cannot let the opportunity pass to express my gratitude to Graham Nelson, who must have discovered hitherto unknown wells of patience, faced with my numerous and often (exceedingly) protracted prevarications and radio silences. Much like a good Mackem, in the face of all logic, he kept the faith.

Given that I can scarcely remember what I have done from one day to the next, it is not surprising that I find myself unable to recall the myriad people from spheres both literary and musical whose work, thought, and words have influenced and helped my research over the course of the years spent preparing and writing this book. They are many, and my thanks go to each of them. In one of the most enchanting Prefaces I have ever had the pleasure of reading, C. S. Lewis once talked of the innumerable, name-forgotten giants on whose shoulders he had stood and to whom thanks were due. It is a sentiment and an understanding of how this game of thought and writing works that I now fully grasp and can only repeat here.

It would be remiss of me not to acknowledge some of the key musical figures who have accompanied me during the research for and writing of this book. In particular, and at different stages of the process, Bob Dylan, John Martyn, Joe Satriani, and Marco Sfogli have been sources of inspiration and astonishment that have kept me at least reasonably sane. At the same time, I must also thank Julio Cortázar himself, whose work led me better to know, spend time with, and appreciate the genius of musicians such as Charlie Parker, Ornette Coleman, and Clifford Brown. Like great authors and works of literature, once such musicians and their music enter one's life, one knows one will never be quite the same person again. I have subsequently, it might be said, become a new person many times over the last eighteen years.

Finally, I should like to thank my parents for their limitless love and support, always there on the end of the phone for help and advice, Heiddy for her forbearance and love, not least during the feverish last year of writing, and my gorgeous and magical Gabriela and Alejandro. Ten years ago, I thanked Gabriela for helping me to understand what life was really about. She continues to do so. And now so too does Alejandro, whilst reminding me that life is also about football.

N.R., Durham, July 2019

NOTE ON TRANSLATIONS

The approach undertaken in this study to the translation of text in languages other than English has been guided by both the availability of published English translations and the requirements of my analysis. Where no published translations exist, translations are my own. Where published translations are readily obtainable, these have generally been used. However, on occasion I have opted either to favour my own translations or to adapt the published English versions, in order to bring out aspects of the original text that I consider important, but which have not been stressed or made sufficiently present in the published translations. Translations of in-text quotations are my own where they appear in square brackets with no citation marks; where parentheses and citation marks are used, the translations are ones already published. The translation of indented quotations, all of which are in square brackets, are my own where no parenthetical reference is provided. In all cases, adaptations to published translations are indicated via the use of square brackets within said translations.

INTRODUCTION

'[La] Música [...] es algo inefable, algo que va más allá de las palabras.'
[Music [...] is something ineffable, something that goes beyond words.]
(Cortázar 2012a: 29)

That a book on music in the work of Julio Cortázar should find itself beginning by saying more about language, poetry, and ontology than about any genre, theory, or practice of music itself may seem to indicate an author who has, from a very early stage, lost sight of his point of focus. Whilst not precluding this possibility, the nature of the first pages of this introduction is, in many ways, symptomatic of any attempt to pin down Cortázar's engagement with music, precisely because that engagement only operates within and as part of the wider themes and concerns of his work and thought. Reaching the point where music can be viewed in isolation, without the extraneous 'noise' of questions of the linguistic, the revolutionary, and the metaphysical, is as impossible as the search for it is ill-advised. Such a move results in the veiling of both the significance and, just as importantly, the problematics of music in Cortázar's work.

Not that that does not mean that this is precisely what some critics have done,[1] although there have also been a number of more incisive studies, generally focusing on specific aspects of Cortázar's musical texts and encounters.[2] What is lacking thus far in the vast sphere of Cortazarian scholarship, however, is a study that looks to combine, on the one hand, an examination of all of the principal genres of music with which Cortázar engages and the ways in which he appeals to them, and, on the other, an attempt at understanding how this multiform and multivocal engagement plays into, informs, and is informed by the wider, often philosophical, debates at stake in Cortázar's writing.[3] This is the goal that the present work sets itself. In short, its aim is to explore the place of music in Cortázar's work and thought from the earliest to the latest periods of his production, considering the detail of certain key texts in order to gain a greater purchase on the implications of and motivations for his constant and repeated appeal to this art form. Thus, this study will not be comprehensive in terms of listing every time that Coleman Hawkins or Beethoven is mentioned by Cortázar, or every occasion on which he alluded to a tango by Carlos Gardel. There are already publications that have such a goal.[4] Rather, it will focus on how the practice of using music within his fiction must be seen alongside his theorising of 'the musical' (which, in itself, leads beyond the confines of Cortázar's own texts into broader theoretical ambits), as well as underscoring that any study of, for example, jazz in Cortázar's work is necessarily made poorer if it is not accompanied by an exploration of his engagement with *la música culta* [cultivated/ art music] and tango. Or, indeed, with poetry, language, and ontology.

Literature and Language

And so, somewhat circuitously, we return to the departure point of this study: the wider concerns of Cortázar, against which his use of and appeal to music must be understood. Even the most cursory of scans through the critical studies that have been published on Cortázar's work makes clear that issues of an ontological and linguistic nature are almost universally seen as lying at the heart of his writing and thought, where Cortázar's aim is a radical and total rethinking (not, by any means, an unproblematic term) of the most basic customs and tenets by which Western humankind lives and expresses itself, what Dominic Moran sums up as:

> the unstinting drive to expose, denounce and consequently escape from what he [Cortázar] perceived to be the stultifying and oppressive domain of Western metaphysics and its *supposed* ontological, socio-political, sexual and — perhaps most critically — linguistic modes of classification, organization and restraint. (2000: 1)

Put simply, being and language are, from the earliest of Cortázar's texts, the fundamental areas and problematics around which his work gravitates. And it is unsurprising that this quest for revolution should end up manifesting itself in socio-political form, most obviously in his engagement with and support for the Cuban Revolution, although, as several critics have pointed out, such a division of Cortázar's consciousness, awakened to the political through the events of 1959, relies more on its romantic appeal than the facts.[5]

Indeed, despite Cortázar's own statements regarding the difference between his (early) concern for individual liberation and his discovery of socialism and revolution, largely through the Cuban Revolution and his first visit to Cuba in 1963,[6] this 'descubrimiento del prójimo' (González Bermejo 1978: 120) [discovery of my fellow man], is, as we shall see, etched into some of his earliest, more ontolinguistic writings. Similarly, as both Steven Boldy and Peter Standish, amongst others, have pointed out, Cortázar's engagement with the Cuban Revolution, and political revolution *per se*, went hand in hand with 'his continuing focus on the personal, his insistence on individual freedom' (Standish 2001: 131), and with a persistent underlining of the importance of linguistic and literary 'rebellion'.[7] This is made clear in texts such as 'Literatura en la revolución y revolución en la literatura: algunos malentendidos a liquidar' (Cortázar 2006g [1969]) [Literature in the Revolution and Revolution in Literature: Some Misunderstandings to be Settled] and 'Viaje alrededor de una mesa' (Cortázar 2006h [1970]) [Journey Around a Table], where the need for linguistic and ontological (individual and collective) rupture and shift is emphasised in strong terms:

> La sociedad tal como la concibe el socialismo no sólo no puede anular al individuo así entendido, sino que aspira a desarrollarlo en un grado tal que

toda la negatividad, todo lo demoníaco que aprovecha la sociedad capitalista, sea superado por un nivel de su personalidad donde lo individual y lo colectivo cesen de enfrentarse y de frustrarse. (2006g: 415)

[Society as conceived by socialism not only cannot annul the individual understood as such, but aspires to develop him/her to such a degree that all the negativity, all the devilishness that capitalist society takes advantage of is overtaken by a level of his/her personality where the individual and the collective stop opposing and frustrating each other.]

Hay que ir mucho más lejos todavía en las búsquedas, en las experiencias, en las aventuras, en los combates con el lenguaje y las estructuras narrativas. [...] Hay que crear la lengua de la revolución, hay que batallar contra las formas lingüísticas y estéticas que impiden a las nuevas generaciones captar en toda su fuerza y su belleza esa tentativa global para crear una América Latina enteramente nueva desde las raíces hasta la última hoja. (2006h: 428)

[One has to go much further still in one's quests, experiences, adventures, in one's battles with language and narrative structures. [...] One must create the language of the revolution, fight against all linguistic and aesthetic forms that prevent the new generations from capturing in all its force and beauty that global attempt to create a Latin America that is entirely new, from the roots to the final leaf.]

This focus on the individual within the wider collective of society and humankind, then, bound up primarily with questions of being and language, represents a constant, underlying thematic thread that weaves its way through all of Cortázar's texts. And tangled up in this fabric as a constituent strand is music, which must be understood as an integral part of both these broad ontolinguistic questions and struggles and their socio-political manifestations.

The general principles of Cortázar's concerns and goals in regard to both being and language, in particular as found within the Western metaphysical, literary, and cultural tradition, are set out across a series of early texts. That is not to say that these issues are not developed and (re)formulated throughout the course of his life and works. And neither is it the case that the ways in which he conceives of the problems and potential solutions in terms of both ontology and language are consistent and uncontradictory. Indeed, it would be problematic if they were, not least because such logical constancy and rigidity would fly in the face of the escape from reason and structure that Cortázar desires.[8] But in early texts, in particular *Teoría del túnel* (Cortázar 2006c [1947]) [*Tunnel Theory*],[9] Cortázar sets out a number of fundamental discussions and ideas that would serve as a touchstone for his entire writing career, and this latter text serves as a useful starting point in understanding how music operates in Cortázar's *œuvre*.

Teoría del túnel is a work that deals, ostensibly, with literature and language. It begins by laying out some of the main problems with literary language and forms, as found in and exemplified by 'the Book', by which Cortázar means the literary form which reached its apogee in the novels of the nineteenth century, in authors such as Gustave Flaubert.[10] For Cortázar, such works are, above all, aesthetic objects which tend towards the uniform, with the writer being not so much an individual as an 'instrumento agente dentro de un orden que lo subordina y lo supera' (2006c: 53) [instrumental agent working within an order that subordinates and exceeds him/her]. Seeing Romanticism, in the opening pages of the essay, as the earliest movement which set itself up against this literary reality, Cortázar describes it as where the writer must 'apartarse a la vez del libro como objeto y fin de su tarea' (55) [distance him/herself at the same time from the book as the object and end of his/her task], and finally see it, instead, as 'producto de una actividad que escapa a la vez a todo lujo estético y a toda docencia deliberada, instrumento de automanifestación integral del hombre, de autoconstrucción' (55) [the product of an activity that escapes at the same time all aesthetic excesses and all deliberate teachings, an instrument of man's integral self-manifestation, of self-construction]. In short, the question of (individual) being and its relationship with the literary work becomes central, where this being is either reflected by ('automanifestación' [self-manifestation]) or created through ('autoconstrucción' [self-construction]) the written work. Moving on, Cortázar makes clear the extent to which what is at stake in such a recasting and rewriting of prose fiction (since this is primarily what Cortázar has in mind in this discussion) is the question of the language used in it, as he talks of the condition of the modern (mid-twentieth-century) writer as being one dominated by 'la duda *de que acaso las posibilidades expresivas estén imponiendo límites a lo expresable; que el verbo condicione su contenido, que la palabra esté empobreciendo su propio sentido*' (62) [the doubt *as to whether the expressive possibilities might be imposing limits on the expressible; whether language conditions its content; whether a term impoverishes its own meaning*]. Language, (individual) being, and the rethinking of literature, that is, emerge as the dominant strands here.

Faced with the necessity of this rethinking or recasting of prose fiction in order to recover (or discover) the creative being who writes, Cortázar talks of the need to find a way of writing books '*con la esperanza de que ayuden a la tarea teleológica de liquidar la literatura*' (64) [*with the hope that they might help in the teleological task of liquidating literature*]. For Cortázar, this involves a renewing of language, where 'el lenguaje vuelve a ser lenguaje puro, cada imagen tendrá que nacer allí de nuevo, cada forma prosódica responderá a un contenido que crea su justa, necesaria y única formulación' (65) [language returns to being pure language, each image has to be born anew, each prosodic form responds to a content that creates its appropriate, necessary, and unique formulation]. This is referred to as a Trojan Horse, an undermining of 'the Book' by using its very language to effect such a revolution, burrowing its way, tunnel-like, into the edifice and linguistic structures and identity of the work.

It is notable here that Cortázar should emphasise the primacy of language in this envisioning of a more authentic communication, for what is at stake, as I have intimated, is very much not just a renewal of 'the Book', but an attendant renewal of how a human being can express and communicate him or herself more 'authentically'. This focus on language rests at least in part on the fact that it is a form of expression, a tool, that is open to a wider range of people than other forms, in that it requires much less — or indeed no — special training or skill (65). More significantly, in a footnote, Cortázar adds that 'el verbo es la forma expresiva menos mediatizadora de un estado anímico que se quiera *comunicar*. Lo plástico, la danza, la música, son formas analógicas, simbólicas; el verbo es la forma más inmediata del Logos' (65) [language is the expressive form that least interferes with/mediates a state of mind that one desires to *communicate*. Plastic arts, dance, music, are analogical, symbolic forms; language is the most immediate form of the Logos]. Language is prioritised not just because it is a form of expression open to everyone, but because it is here deemed to be a particularly privileged and immediate form of 'authentic' expression and communication. And yet, at the level of its argumentation and reasoning, this statement is also, as we shall see, at odds with much of what Cortázar says elsewhere in his early texts. In addition to *Teoría del túnel*, to which we shall return shortly, several other early essays are significant in developing Cortázar's thoughts in regard to the problems of language and being. Amongst them are 'Soledad de la música' (Cortázar 1992 [1941]) [Solitude of Music], 'Elogio del jazz: carta enguantada a Daniel Devoto' (Cortázar 2006d [1948], henceforth 'Elogio del jazz') [In Praise of Jazz: Gloved Letter to Daniel Devoto], and 'Para una poética' (Cortázar 1994b [1954]) [Towards a Poetics].[11] That these three works are also pillars of Cortázar's musical engagement is not, then, a trivial detail, and, in particular in their demand to be read in conjunction with *Teoría del túnel*, they make evident music's importance in his early thought, despite the prioritisation of language in statements such as those cited above: 'Soledad de la música' appears thus as an earlier treatise on similar themes to those covered in the more extensive, later text; 'Elogio del jazz' constitutes, as Cortázar himself describes it, a piece which could well be the final chapter of *Teoría del túnel* (2006d: 204); and 'Para una poética' represents a further development of Cortázar's thoughts on poetry and poetic language, including their relationship with music. Together, these essays help point towards music as being not an adjunct or a minor strand within which Cortázar's main concerns are given a stage where they can be played out, but, rather, as a central, constitutive part of the foundational thinking upon which his work is built. Accordingly, then, in order to elucidate the axial role played by music in Cortázar's early texts and thinking, I shall first look at 'Soledad de la música', bringing out ways in which it works alongside ideas found in *Teoría del túnel*, before turning to 'Para una poética' and, briefly, to 'Elogio del jazz'. I shall also bring in examples from later writings and interviews.[12]

Expression

'Soledad de la música' begins with a comparison between poetry and music, in the process signalling the importance of the relationship between these two artistic forms in Cortázar's thinking: it subtends, in fact, his entire discourse on music, although that is not to say that the ways in which he sees the two forms as reflecting and contrasting with each other are either stable or consistent over the years. In this early essay, poetry is used, initially at least, as a contrast to music. Leaning on the ideas of the French poet Paul Valéry, the essay sets out the unfortunate position of the poet, 'obligado a construir su Obra con palabras, elementos impuros y sujetos a los peores malentendidos' (Cortázar 1992: 290) [obliged to construct his/her

Work with words, impure elements subject to the worst misunderstandings]. In short, the poet must use language, which, in a way more fundamental than the problematics of uniformity and aestheticisation found in prose fiction described in the later *Teoría del túnel*, is here defined in terms that chime with the sort of Derridean understanding of language that came to dominate late twentieth-century thought: words are impure, that is, somehow contaminated (with the trace of other words), their meaning uncontrollable and unbound, always wont to be reinterpreted and (mis)understood in different contexts and in different ways. In contrast, the musician 'alcanza la identificación de su *idea* musical con el material sonoro en absoluto estado de pureza' (290) [achieves the identification of his/her musical *idea* with the sonorous material in an absolute state of purity]. In other words, the basic difference between music and poetry (words) as set up here is that in the latter there exists a gap between Idea and expression which is not found in the former: 'Mientras lo poético en sí guarda sólo una relación de analogía con el vehículo que intenta expresarlo, la música es *una* con su expresión sonora' (290) [Whilst the poetic in itself has only a relationship of analogy with the vehicle that tries to express it, music is *one* with its sonorous expression]. The shifting terms in which this language/music debate is carried out in Cortázar's texts are thus made apparent, with this statement being reversed entirely in the later *Teoría del túnel*, as we have already seen (2006c: 65). In general, however, it is this earlier declaration that remains closest to the ongoing *theoretical* advantage that Cortázar sees music as holding over language, in particular, as chapters 4 and 5 of the present study will set out, in the case of jazz improvisation.[13] And certainly, in 'Soledad de la música', Cortázar is at pains to emphasise the importance of this oneness between the musical Idea and its expression, effectively removing 'la llamada "música descriptiva"' (1992: 291) [so-called 'descriptive music'] from the equation, that is, music which looks to describe storms or hunts or battles and the like. Such music 'despreciando el valor absoluto de los fines musicales, intenta subordinarlos a una función imitativa' (291) [with scant regard for the absolute value of musical ends, tries to subordinate these to an imitative function], a characteristic which, in the breach it opens up between the sound and its 'meaning', in effect reduces the music to linguistic principles.

Turning to the poems of Cortázar's first collection of poetry, *Presencia* (Denis 1938) [*Presence*], which appeared under the pseudonym Julio Denis, we find that music is depicted in a way that resonates with — or, rather, pre-empts — the affirmations of 'Soledad de la música'. The fact that this first published work by Cortázar should begin with a poem entitled 'Música' [Music] is not insignificant, and, at risk of labouring the point, I would suggest it constitutes a further, and not merely serendipitous, example of why music must be considered fundamental to both his praxis and ideas. Indeed, the presence of music continues unabated: 'Música II' [Music II], 'Jazz', and 'La Presencia en la Música' [The Presence in Music], in addition to a section entitled 'Músicas' [Musics], which comprises seven poems, all attest to the importance of music to this foundational work. Significantly for our present purposes the first two of these poems in particular, 'Música' and 'Música II', prefigure the ideas I have been setting out. 'Música' describes music as bringing out our inner essence ('eso somos, | libres bajo las carnes, en asomos | de lírica, de ilímite, de altura' (9) [that's what we are, | free under the flesh; emerging flashes | of lyric, of unlimit, of height]): peaks emerging from an oceanic surface, as the interior is exteriorised in a musical oneness, an exteriorisation free from the shackles of language (speech and writing) ('epifanías | en salmodia sin líneas y sin lenguas' (10) [epiphanies | in line-less, tongue-less chants]) and the ties, binds, and (Derridean *avant la lettre*) sense of loss or absence that they entail ('sin sollozos, sin lazos y sin menguas' (10) [without weeping, without ties, and without reduction]). Similarly, in 'Música II', the unfettered freedom of music in its expression of what is within is conveyed with the reference to the 'canción cantada y libre' (16) [free and sung song] and the '¡puro canto | de amaranto y marfil y luz y lino!' (16) [pure song | of amaranth and ivory and light and linen!], a polysyndeton which reiterates in successive images the sense of untainted purity and wholeness as it emphasises the whiteness of the song, thus aligning it with the Logos rather than the prismatic splitting asunder of the latter into words. In this way, the allusion to the amaranth, (etymologically) a flower that never fades, further underscores the idea that nothing of the interior-being-conveyed is lost.

Many of these early poetic ideas and elements re-emerge, then, in the opening paragraphs of 'Soledad de la música', with music's advantage being that it allows for 'una creación *absolutamente* pura' [an *absolutely* pure creation], without the loss of 'las puras esencias' (Cortázar 1992: 291) [pure essences]. But, to reiterate, what is added to the musical eulogy of *Presencia* in 'Soledad de la música' is the contrasting case of poetry, where such 'esencias' [essences] find themselves replaced by words in the verbal construction that poetry is obliged to use to express itself.[14] The repeated emphasis on this being, specifically, Paul Valéry's take, however, already suggests what will become clear in the course of the essay's subsequent discussion, namely that this clear-cut differentiation between (generic) 'poetry' and (an equally generic) 'music' will be shown to be nothing of the sort. Indeed, this opening section of the essay already hints at the possibility that poetry can, perhaps, overcome the gap that language opens up between the Poetic and its expression, positing the idea that the poet might find 'el medio de devolver a los pensamientos y a las palabras su virginidad primera, por obra de un concierto, una armonía, una recreación; por medio de una música suprema' (Cortázar 1992: 291) [the means to give thoughts and words back their first virginity, via a concert, a harmony, a recreation; by means of a supreme music]. Significantly, then, poetry can be Poetic if it can be musical. The musical poem, that is, is one where '*el verbo ya es poesía*' (296) [*the word already is poetry*], where Poetry and its verbal expression 'dejan de ser elementos diferentes' (296) [cease being different elements]. Poetry aspires to the musical. Or, to put it another way, the musical is primary, and what poetry aims to be. And when Cortázar declares that 'el idioma *nace de nuevo con un Rimbaud, con un Neruda*' (296) [language *is born anew with a Rimbaud or a Neruda*], he is thus claiming that such an aim, revitalising language in the way he desires, has already been achieved by some poets.

But if, save for these exceptions, 'Soledad de la música' places poetry in the role of music's flawed counterpart, *Teoría del túnel* problematises this relationship, in effect transforming the somewhat tentative rejoinder concerning poets such as Rimbaud and Neruda found in the earlier text into the primary way in which poetry and its potential are to be understood.¹⁵ Rather than focusing on poetry as an example of the problems of language as a vehicle and tool of expression, this later work describes at length how poetic language is precisely the means by which the language of the novel might be revived so as to render it intimately bound up with a putative essence of being. Thus, Cortázar talks of '[e]l lenguaje poético, no estético, lenguaje donde es posible burlarse de las limitaciones del verbo' (2006c: 67) [poetic, not aesthetic language, language where one can mock the limitations of the word], and goes on to set out the advantages of the poetic, repeating the claims initially made for *music* in 'Soledad de la música' in declaring that '*la poesía es, como la música, su forma*' (89) [*poetry is, like music, its form*]. In effect, Cortázar is underlining that, in a way analogous to music, poetry, properly understood as such, is found precisely at the marriage between the Poetic and its expression, as he alluded to in 'Soledad de la música', although, in contrast to the earlier text, the sense of hierarchy, where poetry aspired to be musical, is largely absent.

Some seven years later, in 'Para una poética', however, this balance has shifted once again, as the stance found in 'Soledad de la música' returns to the fore. Specifically, this later text reiterates the difference between the Poetic and the poem, whilst also addressing how these two might work together, affirming that, within the poem, the Poetic evokes and presents the essence (of being), rather than signifying it (linguistically), as we read of 'un balbuceo existencial que se agita y urge, y que sólo la poesía del poema (no el poema como producto estético) puede, analógicamente, evocar y reconstruir' (Cortázar 1994b: 278–79) [an existential babbling that stirs and urges on, and which only the poetry of the poem (not the poem as an aesthetic product) can, analogically, evoke and reconstruct]. And, importantly, what grants the poem its Poetic nature, what allows it to be poetic, that is, is described in musical terms once more:

> una posibilidad analógica exaltada, *musicalizada*, para hacerla *servir esencias* e ir directa y profundamente al ser. *La música verbal es acto catártico por el cual la metáfora, la imagen [...] se libera de toda referencia significativa para no aludir y no asumir sino la esencia de sus objetos.* (281)
>
> [an analogical possibility that is exalted, *musicalised*, to make it *serve up essences* and go directly and profoundly to the heart of being. *Verbal music is a cathartic act through which the metaphor, the image [...] is freed from all signifying reference so as not to allude to or assume anything but the essence of its objects.*]

The ability of poetry to be the essence of that which it takes as its object (that is, profoundly and essentially to be its object, which is to say, its self), is thus seen to be a question of its musicality.¹⁶ In other words, although Cortázar's writings in this period turn predominantly to poetry (even 'Elogio del jazz', as we shall see, posits jazz as an example *of* the poetic (Cortázar 2006d: 207)), his texts continually declare the nature of what makes poetry Poetic to be musical. Thus, and turning back to *Teoría del túnel*, when Cortázar talks of his desire for a destructive/constructive tunnelling into (prose fiction) language, to be carried out via the poeticisation of that language, the implications of his texts are that this equates to a call for the musicalisation of that language. The importance of music for any proper understanding of Cortázar's primary goal as a writer is thus made apparent.

Communication

Thus far, we have been addressing the issue of 'authentic' expression, that is, the relationship between an Idea and its expression. But we need at this point to dwell in a little more detail on the terms that Cortázar invokes when talking about the (musically) poetic. Particularly significant in this regard is the problematic way in which poetism is defined and described in *Teoría del túnel*, an aspect of the text which is taken up further by Cortázar in 'Para una poética'. In both pieces Cortázar describes poetism and the incorporation of the poetic into language (be it of the novel or the poem), that is, the desire noted above for the words used to be '*la cosa misma*' (1994b: 284) [*the thing itself*], as being essentially a question of '*la magia*' (284) [magic]. The poet, in 'Para una poética', is seen as cut from the same cloth as the *primitivo* [primitive one], or, more usefully, the (primordial, pre-rational) *mago* [magician]: 'Magia del primitivo y poesía del poeta son [...] dos planos y dos finalidades de una misma dirección' (270) [The magic of the primitive one and the poetry of the poet [...] are two planes and two objectives going in the same direction], whilst the novelist who writes in the poetic way that Cortázar promotes in *Teoría del túnel* is described in that essay in terms that reiterate the same magical engagement:

> Así se accede — por sendas numerosas — a un mundo de revelación incluso mágica, y siempre con la llave de mecanismos intuitivos, poéticos. [...] [P]roponen formulaciones poéticas y aun mágicas de la realidad. [...] [E]ste grupo de novelas y novelistas [...] procura un avance 'mágico' del poetismo. (2006c: 106–07)
>
> [In this way one accesses — via numerous paths — a world of revelation of even a magical nature, and always with the key of intuitive, poetic mechanisms. [...] They propose poetic, even magical formulations of reality. [...] This group of novels and novelists [...] achieves a 'magical' advance of poetism.]

Yet Cortázar then goes on to explain that such an approach to writing (and being, and the relationship between the two) brings with it an insularity in relation to what is the second of the two key interrelated aspects of his writings on both poetry and music in these works: communication:

> Pero la magia es incomunicable, engendra aislamiento y soledad. [...] Se advierte en ellos [los novelistas 'poetistas'] una creciente liberación de todo compromiso común — con la comunidad — y un avance hacia la posesión solitaria de una realidad que no se da en compañía; la magia verbal, el conjuro de las potencias de la analogía aíslan y distancian a estos escritores. (107)
>
> [But the magic is incommunicable, it engenders isolation and solitude. [...] One notes in these ['poetist' novelists] a growing liberation from all common commitment — with the community — and an advance towards the solitary possession of a reality that does not occur in company; verbal magic, the invoking of the powers of analogy isolate and distance these writers.]

For one, the fact that such individualism is not seen as desirable by Cortázar demonstrates that the seeds of his later socialist engagement are already well sown by this point. Rather, he sees the need to communicate. The 'solution' he posits is found in existentialism:

> Si el poetismo parte, en su forma más alta, de la quiebra del idioma común, el existencialismo busca comunicarse en toda forma posible, siéndole por tanto capital sostener el verbo [...] como comunicación, puente sobre el hiato del Yo al Tú y al Él. (117)
>
> [If poetism starts, in its highest form, from the breakdown of common language, existentialism seeks to communicate by whatever means possible, hence the fundamental importance for it of upholding the word [...] as a form of communication, a bridge over the hiatus between the I and the You and the He.]

Although it may seem that existentialism, as presented by Cortázar here, is enmeshed with exactly the sort of language and reason that, through the poetic, he is trying to overcome, there is still a sense that it adopts these whilst also looking to go beyond them and achieve a transcendence or authenticity of being, but one that, in contrast to (an essentialist) poetism, can only be found and potentially attained within the community. Thus, whilst existentialism is associated with an 'actitud realista, científica, histórica y social' (110) [realist, scientific, historical, and social attitude] and 'respet[a] las formas verbales, el género novela, y no nos [pide] como el poetismo la evasión de las dimensiones inteligibles' (119) [respects verbal forms, the genre of the novel, and [does] not [demand] from us like poetism the avoidance of intelligible dimensions], it, nevertheless, 'está siempre trascendiéndolo [el lenguaje] de algún modo' (117) [is always transcending [language] in some way]. But what Cortázar underlines is that this is not a question of choosing one or the other direction. Rather, he talks of the idea of an existentialism which 'marcha al encuentro del poetismo' (119) [goes off to meet poetism], and rejects the notion that the two should be opposed:

> Oponer el *poetismo* (actitud surrealista general, individualista, mágica, ahistórica y asocial) a lo que parece justo llamar con igual amplitud *existencialismo* (actitud realista, científica, histórica y social), y oponer ambas corrientes como actitudes no conciliables, significaría empobrecerlas al dejar tan sólo sus valores específicos, con total exclusión de los contrarios. (110)
>
> [To oppose *poetism* (a general surrealist, individualist, magical, ahistorical, and asocial attitude) to what seems fair to call equally broadly *existentialism* (a realist, scientific, historical, and social attitude), and to oppose both currents as irreconcilable attitudes, would mean impoverishing them by leaving only their specific values, with a complete exclusion of the opposing ones.]

This discussion on poetism and existentialism is important for a variety of reasons here, not least that it points towards the constant need that Cortázar sees for balance, for a non-exclusionary expressive and ontological practice. Part of what he rejects throughout his work is precisely the division into discrete categories, the creation of sides. As Boldy (1980: 7) sets out, the division of humankind into the represser and the repressed, leading to the creation of monsters, in the form of everything that is deemed (and labelled) taboo, barbaric, base, is an accepted point of departure in his literary practice, and constitutes precisely what much of his fiction works to expose and, potentially, transcend. This is evident from the engagement with myths of the monstrous such as Theseus and the Minotaur or Orpheus and his descent into Hades, found in many stories and novels,[17] about which much has been written,[18] to the monster/civilisation divide set up in countless stories, including 'Las ménades' [The Maenads] from *Final del juego* (Cortázar 1970a [1956]) [*End of The Game*], 'Anillo de Moebius' [Moebius Strip] from *Queremos tanto a Glenda* (Cortázar 1980) [*We Love Glenda So Much*], and 'Las armas secretas' [Secret Weapons] from *Las armas secretas* (Cortázar 1970d [1959]).[19] Such a division is, moreover, inextricably bound up with language and its operations, given that language works precisely by categorising and labelling, separating and ordering the world into discrete groups and shifters. And that this is part of what Cortázar bemoans about language is clear, one of the most notable examples of this being the opening lines of the story 'Las babas del diablo' [Blow-Up] from *Las armas secretas*, as the narrator struggles to break free from linguistic delimitations, wishing it were possible to talk of how 'tú la mujer rubia eran las nubes que siguen corriendo delante de mis tus sus nuestros vuestros sus rostros' (1970d: 77) ('you the blond woman [were] the clouds that race before my your his our yours their faces', 2013: 114).

Closing the divisions between civilised and monstrous, self and other, then, is synonymous with ending (however improbably) the constant process of meaning that operates along the endless signifying chain and its play of similarities and oppositions. The implications of such a move are most succinctly described in chapter 66 of *Rayuela*, where we are told of one of Morelli's ideas for the ending of his 'libro inconcluso' (Cortázar 2007: 531) ('unfinished book', 1966: 370), in which the line 'En el fondo sabía que no se puede ir más allá porque no lo hay' (2007: 531) ('Underneath it all he knew that one cannot go beyond because there isn't any', 1966: 370) is repeated over and over, forming 'un muro de palabras ilustrando el sentido de la frase' (2007: 531) ('a wall [...] of words that illustrate the meaning of the sentence', 1966: 370). In one of the iterations, however, the word *lo* is missing: 'Un ojo sensible descubre el hueco entre los ladrillos, la luz que pasa' (2007: 531) ('A sensitive eye can discover the hole among the bricks, the light that shows through', 1966: 370). Ending language's operations — however fleetingly — constitutes, that is, a rupture in the barrier of language *per se* that both enables and entails a fusion of ourselves with the irreducible alterity beyond its structures in a plenitude of being.

However fraught with complex binds this aim may be,[20] axial in the context of the present discussion is that such a move is predicated on the need not to exclude one of an oppositional set, or, indeed, one of any set. The need for an inclusionary, fusional praxis is at all times paramount, and the desired bringing together of poetism and (the traits he associates here with) existentialism is an example of that, putatively, we might add in the light of the above discussion, in order to end the distinction between the two.[21] In subsequent chapters, the extent to which Cortázar's engagement with music challenges, attempts to comply, and, perhaps unintentionally, does comply with this move towards an inclusionary collapsing of differences will constitute a significant element of the analysis.

Returning to the poetism/existentialism discussion from *Teoría del túnel*, what we see is that, having supplemented his affirmation of the Poetic with an attendant need for an existentialist ethic, that is, in the context of his discussion, its goal of communication 'en toda forma posible' (Cortázar 2006c: 117) [in any way possible] in particular, Cortázar's assertion that these two 'currents' should not be seen as unreconcilable is not one that implies that such a vision has actually been realised. Thus, whilst Cortázar writes relatively easily (albeit vaguely) of the possibilities of poetic expression and the successful musicalisation of language, collapsing the gap between essence (of thing, idea, writer, being) and its expression, when it comes to the other side of that 'text', the side that looks outward towards the reader — to the social —, the problems of language return all too quickly: 'la magia es incomunicable' (107) [the magic is incomunicable].

The issue of communication, and of how music and poetry compare in this regard, is, in fact, initially taken up and given its most revealing airing in 'Soledad de la música'. Anticipating the later rejection of the isolationism of poetism, Cortázar begins this part of the text by stating that in the artistic, as with the poetic, work 'toda *comunicación* de belleza exige, entre la esencia de la Obra y el que asiste al hecho estético, una posibilidad aprehensiva, una correspondencia sentimental que reproduzca en éste lo que el creador quiso plasmar en aquélla' (1992: 291) [all *communication* of beauty requires, between the essence of the Work and the one who witnesses the aesthetic act, the possibility of being grasped, a sentimental correspondence that reproduces in the latter what the creator wanted to express in the former]. The communication at stake, then, is from one person (the artist) to another (the reader/listener/viewer). Taking poetry first, Cortázar addresses the main issue that befalls it: the move of Poetry (as essence) into language constitutes a translation, shackling it to 'una historia, ya que pensamientos y palabras son historia, tradición, mácula y malentendido' (291–92) [a history, since thoughts and words are history, tradition, tainting, and misunderstanding] as he foregrounds not only the slippery nature of meaning but also the temporal and sociocultural discourses ('historia' [history]) into which this places the Poetry. The central problem, prefiguring *Teoría del túnel*'s invocation of magic, is that 'la Poesía y el Mensaje son *indecibles* y sólo arriban al espíritu por obra de una intuición ajena a todo mecanismo lógico, a toda estructura discursiva' (292) [Poetry and the Message are *unsayable* and only reach one's spirit by work of an intuition that is foreign to all logical mechanisms and all discursive structures]. The *impasse* implied by the use of language, which, however musicalised it may be, struggles to be seen as entirely devoid of discursive structure, is very much insisted upon here, and the later discussions in *Teoría del túnel* and 'Para una poética' are less than convincing in their assertion of such problems simply being overcome, as they invoke a prioritisation of 'mecanismos intuitivos, poéticos' (Cortázar 2006c: 106) [intuitive, poetic mechanisms] and state somewhat nebulously that language and the aesthetic are 'superad[os] por el hecho poético libre de mecanismos dialécticos' (91) [overcome by the poetic fact, free from dialectical mechanisms]. The move into language, into existentialist concerns (which are synonymous in their presentation by Cortázar in these texts with, amongst other things, this need for communication), surely carries with it at the very least a nod towards logic and structure. Moreover, the sense that intuitive communication *is* nevertheless possible, aside from being rather vague, additionally fails adequately to address the question of how one can know that what is intuited by the receiver is the same as what the producer intended to transmit.

The pivotal point at this stage of 'Soledad de la música' with respect to the possibility of communication is the comparison that can apparently be made with music. Initially, Cortázar sets up the same contrast that he advances regarding expression and privileges music. However, the description of music's communicative abilities is undermined by the consistent appeal to terms that speak of the mechanisms that operate in linguistic communication and of some of its problematic characteristics. Thus, the musician:

> deposita en el pentagrama <u>la notación</u> que <u>*significa*</u> la concepción sonora. En su obra no se alzan barreras de lenguaje; [...] el músico siente nacer la obra [...]. Luego, un instrumento o una orquesta <u>expresarán temporalmente</u> la obra del músico, en <u>analogía</u> que es <u>casi identidad</u> con la <u>vivencia original</u> del creador. Sólo resta escuchar, al parecer, sin problemas de significación o de conceptos; la Obra no contiene la música, sino que *es* la música. (1992: 292, underscore mine)

> [deposits onto the stave <u>the notation</u> which <u>*signifies*</u> the sonorous idea. In her/his work no barriers of language are erected; [...] the musician feels the work being born [...]. Then, an instrument or an orchestra <u>will express</u> the work of the musician <u>in time</u>, in <u>an analogy</u> that is <u>almost identical</u> to the <u>original experience</u> of the creator. All that remains is to listen, apparently, without problems of signification or concepts; the Work does not contain the music, but *is* the music.]

Clearly the manner in which this passage is written and the terms used tell us that our author is about to propose a quite different, and less optimistic, take on the communicative possibilities of music. But it is worth considering that some of the most significant problems of this extract are, arguably, found in elements that do not appear to have been used as a part of the deliberate, pre-emptive undermining of its affirmative description. The notion of the 'obra' [work], for instance, appears initially to refer to the essence, the pre-performance creation that wells up in the consciousness of the composer ('el músico siente nacer la obra'; 'expresarán temporalmente la obra del músico' [the musician feels the work being born; they will express the work of the musician in time]); yet by the end of the passage, perhaps significantly now graced with a capital 'O', the 'Obra' [Work] lends itself to an ambiguous interpretation: on the one hand, it could still refer to the work-as-essence, reiterating that this is one with the music; but, on the other hand, the spatial hierarchy found in the image of the Work which 'no contiene la música' [does not contain the music] suggests that the Work could be understood as the composed (or possibly performed) work, with the 'música', implicitly related to the temporal expression of the 'original' composition in the preceding lines, now aligned more with the essence-to-be-brought-to-the-surface, that is, with what has previously been referred to as 'la obra' [the work]. This terminological confusion could be said to indicate the very inseparability of the essence/the Idea and the musical work.

And yet it also, and perhaps more convincingly, signals how Cortázar struggles to describe the music-essence without invoking a separation and categorisation of the stages involved in its emergence, production, and communication. Indeed, a similar problematic is found in *Presencia*, where the affirmed oneness of musical expression and the interiority it exteriorises in the poems 'Música' and 'Música II' is undermined both by the title of a later poem in the collection, 'La Presencia *en* la Música' (italics mine) [The Presence *in* Music], and by its content, specifically both the opening declaration 'Tan inútil buscar sonido ausente | de tu voz' (Denis 1938: 51) [Such a useless task to seek the absent sound | of your voice] and the poet's final call to this 'presence': '¡Canta, canta, | hazte música viva, y luego arde...!' (52) [Sing, sing, | become living music, and then burn...!], suggestive of a bright burning that then fades and is lost (again), in contrast to the ever-vibrant *amaranto* of 'Música II'.[22]

Following his somewhat underwhelming defence of musical communication, Cortázar begins the subsequent paragraph of 'Soledad de la música' by asking, predictably: '¿Ocurre verdaderamente así?' (1992: 292) [Does it really happen like this?]. Equally predictably, this is quickly answered in the negative, in that, we are told, 'La barrera que distancia del poema al lector — lenguaje — existe bajo otra forma para desgajar la música de su oyente; esa barrera inevitable es la *interpretación*' (292) [The barrier that distances the reader from the poem — language — exists in another form to split the music off from its listener; that unavoidable barrier is *interpretation*]. And it soon becomes apparent that there are two principal elements to this interpretation barrier. Firstly, it responds to the fact that each time one wishes to hear, to partake in a piece of music, in the same way as one has to read a poem, so 'es preciso [...] desarrollarl[a] en el tiempo y desde el comienzo al fin' (292) [it is necessary [...] to unfurl it in time and from the beginning to the end]. Secondly, this unfurling in time of the music also works alongside the need to read the score and play what is written on a musical instrument, a task which, as Cortázar points out, is open to far fewer people than is the case with the task of reading a poem: whereas a poem is open to anyone who can read and understand what they are reading, few possess 'una técnica capaz de abrirles las puertas de la música instrumental, además de la imposibilidad de interpretar en persona las obras sinfónicas' (292) [a technique capable of opening up for themselves the doors of instrumental music, on top of the impossibility of interpreting symphonic works in person]. Although the connection between (poetic) text and musical score is only implied at this stage of the essay, such an alignment is brought out much more strongly in later interviews. In conversation with Omar Prego, for instance, Cortázar refers to both tango and 'la música llamada clásica' (1985: 163) [so-called classical music] as involving 'una ejecución basada en la partitura [...] [:] están sujetos a una escritura' (163) [a performance based on the score [...] [:] they are subject to a writing]. Certainly the musical operation that Cortázar has in mind in 'Soledad de la música' would seem to be one based on either a literal reading of a musical text (score) or one where the musician is, to use an appropriate term, offering a reading of a pre-existing musical work that (s)he knows. Either way, the terminology evidently points to music being inherently linguistic and textual in the process of its communication.

The result of this is that the communication of a piece of music comes to depend on the musician, or interpreter, a term which, as Cortázar points out, means intermediary (1992: 297). In this instance, this intermediary soon takes on an overtly religious guise, as Cortázar refers to him/her as the 'sacerdote de la música' [priest of music] (echoing Heidegger's Hölderlinian depiction of the poet),[23] where:

> sólo él tiene las llaves de la transubstanciación. Sólo por su oficio nos es dado el tránsito a los planos sonoros donde la música se goza a sí misma. [...] [Pero] cuántas veces se resuelve en mera reproducción de sonidos *sin su música, o con otra música*; porque el buen sacerdote tiene una mano en el cielo cuando alza la otra para bendecir, pero el mal sacerdote es una muralla que distancia a los fieles de su Dios. (292–93)
>
> [only he can effect the transubstantiation. Only via his function are we given access to the sonorous planes where the music itself can be met and enjoyed. [...] [But] how many times does this end up as merely a reproduction of sounds *without their music*, or *with a different music*; because the good priest has one hand in the heavens when he lifts up the other to bless us, but the bad priest is a wall who distances the faithful from their God.]

Several things are of note here, not least the recourse to the language of the very Judaeo-Christian tradition from whose metaphysics and culture Cortázar is trying to escape in his work.[24] In addition, the division of these high-priests of music into 'good' and 'bad' is fraught with problems: quite how, for example, the 'buen sacerdote' [good priest] manages to overcome, even bypass, the score in order to enable such an intuitive and 'especial comunicación' (292) [special communication] with the 'original' work is, once more, passed over in silence. This leaves us with a sense that the optimism that surrounds this more spiritually-attuned musician has a rather shakier foundation than does the dominant image of the 'mal sacerdote' [bad priest] who would unwittingly restitute the wall of language that is found both earlier in this essay ('barreras de lenguaje' (292) [barriers of language]) and in the imagery on display in chapter 66 of *Rayuela*.

Such a suspicion is then confirmed in the last paragraph of this section of the essay. After acknowledging the point he would go on to develop in *Teoría del túnel*, namely that one must consider '*socialmente* las artes y la Poesía como formas de creación que tienden a difundirse, a ser conocidas' (293) [the arts and Poetry *socially* as forms of creation that tend to be disseminated, to be known], Cortázar drops any pretence at optimism and states simply that, whereas the composer, in contrast to the poet, can express his or her emotions 'con pureza' (293) [with purity], in terms of communication, (s)he enjoys no such advantage, in that 'toda comunicación de su obra por un ejecutante es ya versión, interpretación, y no la Obra misma' (293) [all communication of his/her work by a performer is already a version, an interpretation, and not the Work itself]. Bringing up the presence of the score in this problematic, he states plainly that:

> Nada puede hacer el músico para evitar el fatal compromiso; por muy sutil que sea su notación [...] el inexpresable fluido que informa una Música, que surge del sonido plasmado por el espíritu del artista de una manera única, innominable, corre riesgo mortal en toda interpretación. (293)[25]

[the musician can do nothing to avoid the fatal compromise; however subtle his or her notation [...] the inexpressible fluid that informs a piece of Music, that surges up from the sound captured by the artist's spirit in a unique, unnameable way, runs a mortal risk in every interpretation.]

In fact, the implications of Cortázar's discussion are that, whereas poetry has to battle with the barrier of language, music's barrier is double. In the case of the former, the Idea is expressed in language — in the written text, for example —, then to be read by the reader. Yet in the case of music, the 'intérprete' [interpreter] acts as an additional intermediary: the score would be the expression in (musical) language of the Music (Idea), for this then to be read and performed by the musician, for the sounds then to be received, or processed, by the listener. Indeed, the presence of this double barrier is reinforced by Cortázar's description of the 'mal sacerdote' [bad priest] as a 'muralla' [wall], which would be in addition to that represented by the score, whose alignment with the linguistic text of the poem (and, indeed, with language *per se*) is emphasised not just by Cortázar's description of it in such terms in his interview with Prego, but by the nature of a musical score in that, as Charles Hartman points out, 'a page of music contains many times as much *information*, in a technical sense, as a page of prose' (1991: 69). This, we might note, casts considerable doubt on Cortázar's claim later on in *Teoría del túnel* that 'en la música no existe el problema de *información* y por ende de *conformación*' (2006c: 72) [in music the problem of *information*, and, thus, of *configuration*, does not exist]. Whilst it may be that, in context, Cortázar is here talking about the sounds of music, rather than the score, the discussion in 'Soledad de la música' that we have been looking at draws attention to the fact that the production of those sounds generally depends upon a score being read, either of the version being played or of previous versions on which a current version is based: the problem of information, of reading, of, in a word, language, is written into the notes of musical performance or interpretation.[26]

The 'Original'

There is, it is worth noting, some significance in my use of the word 'generally' in the previous sentence, and much will be made both in 'Soledad de la música' and in the course of this study of the exceptions to that rule: one thinks of folk music passed down orally, without the need for a score to be read, and, of course, of certain types of jazz, to name two examples. As will be discussed further in subsequent chapters, Cortázar's texts disclose that the problems he outlines are not, in fact, unique to scored music, and the seeds of this disclosure are located earlier on in 'Soledad de la música', when Cortázar identifies one of the problems of interpretation as being the unfurling of the musical piece in time. This, patently enough, is an aspect that properly speaking pertains not just to the act of reading a score (though it is, of course, part of this action), but to musical expression and musical performance *tout court*. After describing the separation from the 'obra musical' [musical work] effected by interpretation as being 'como si un cristal de silencio nos separara de ella' (Cortázar 1992: 293) [as if we were separated from it by a glass window of silence], in that 'sólo conocemos la interpretación de obras musicales; la nuestra, la ajena, la que todos aplauden o la que un paseo al atardecer puede brindarnos sorpresivamente desde alguna ventana entornada' (293) [we only know the interpretation of musical works; ours, that of others, the one everyone applauds or the one gifted to us unexpectedly from some half-open window on a stroll at dusk], Cortázar then states that only 'los creadores' [the creators] can enjoy the fruits of their work, adding that, when these try to communicate their work by performing it for a public, even they 'no siempre obtienen el sufragio de la crítica' (293) [do not always get the critics' vote]. The implied placing of the judgement of whether the essence of the music has been successfully interpreted in the minds and pens of music critics clashes somewhat with Cortázar's vehement subsequent rejection of critics and musicologists in pieces such as 'Elogio del jazz', but what is more significant here are the two examples he gives. Firstly, he points out that, of Stravinsky, 'se dice que sus obras no tienen en su batuta el intérprete que reclaman' (293) [it is said that, under his baton, his works do not have the interpreter that they demand], which, amongst other things, begs the question of how one can know that a performance, in this case conducted by the composer, does not communicate what was intended, or does not constitute what the musical piece 'deserves'. Secondly, and perhaps more revealingly, he recalls the famous, though possibly apocryphal, story regarding Charlie Chaplin, who supposedly once failed to make the finals of a Charlie Chaplin imitation competition.[27] On the one hand, this latter example seems poorly chosen, in that it has nothing to do with music. But what it calls into question is the very possibility of any expression that is not interpretation. Indeed, the idea that the problem comes when a composer wishes to communicate his/her work rather obliges one to ask where, without this playing out of the work in sonoral form, the music actually exists. It points to the possibility, then, that, despite Cortázar's distinction between (original) expression (by the composer) and interpretation, these two are one and the same: there is no 'original'. Indeed, the manner in which Cortázar summarises his argument is key in this respect. He starts by underlining that the differences and discrepancies between different versions, or interpretations, of a musical piece, are enough to 'privarnos de toda esperanza de asomarnos, alguna vez, a la Obra misma' (294) [deprive us of all hope of glimpsing, at some point, the Work itself],[28] which, given what we have just noted, thus becomes an unreachable and unknowable entity. Concluding, he maintains that this means that, even if we attempt a detailed analysis and interpretation of the music ourselves (avoiding the intermediary interpreter (*valga la redundancia*)), 'siempre seremos *nosotros* quienes recreemos la música' (294) [it will always be *us* who recreate the music]. Glossing this, he then adds that 'siempre, *entre la Idea y su expresión en el tiempo*, se alzará la dura afirmación de nuestro aislamiento, de nuestro estar solos como lo están, en su esfera, el músico y el poeta' (294, italics mine) [always, *between the Idea and its expression in time*, will rise up the hard confirmation of our isolation, of our being alone, just as, within their sphere, the musician and the poet are too]. The pretence that any musical expression is free from such apparently linguistic problematics has, I would suggest, thus been dropped: the musician-composer, like the musician-interpreter, or the listener who attempts a more 'prosaic' interpretation of a piece, is always faced with a breach between the Idea — the essence — and its expression in time, which is what music *is*, be it performed with instruments for others to hear, or — and this is a crucial implication — played out mentally. We are, then, left with a situation where, rather than communication, we have a series of *soledades* [solitudes]. The essay's very title, that is, points towards the fact that, in music, the composer, interpreters (musicians), and public are all left in their isolation, each individual destined to have his or her version of the musical Work, which, Cortázar's text implies, is, even in the case of the composer, already at a distance from that inexpressible original-Music-essence which (s)he can only unfurl in time, mentally or physically.

Much of this discussion of solitude in 'Soledad de la música' appears to pre-empt the discussion of the solitude, or isolationism, inherent in poetism in *Teoría del túnel*, which I discussed earlier. But, as ever in these early texts, we find that the same terms are used in often subtly contrasting ways, a characteristic of the essays that reflects the complexity of the relationships, problematics, and possibilities that Cortázar is trying to evince here. In this instance, we see that there is actually an essential difference between the two *soledades* in question. The solitude of Poetism in *Teoría del túnel* was one based around the fact that 'la magia es incomunicable' (Cortázar 2006c: 107) [the magic is incommunicable], thereby casting it as a solitude in which the essence (of one's self, of the world, of being) was intuited, assumed by the poet/individual in a state prior to any (communicative) expression of that essence. The solitude of music, however, whilst apparently emerging from the attempt at communication (in that we are all left with our individual versions or interpretations (expressions) of the Work), and therefore putatively being located at the opposite end of the Idea > expression > communication schema, is in fact more subversive in its implications. It suggests that any conscious intuition of an essence (Idea), any 'knowledge' or experiencing of it, any processing of it in the synapses of the individual is always already an (imperfect) interpretation.

In short, then, Cortázar's text undermines its own initial claim, repeated in subsequent texts, as we have seen, that 'la música es *una* con su expresión sonora' (1992: 290) [music is *one* with its sonorous expression]. Working through the way in which music operates, Cortázar's essay has found it impossible not to engage in discourse and thought that bends and forces a breach between the two elements, not least in the shifting meaning of terms such as 'la obra'/'Obra' and 'la música'/'Música', and in the fact that separate terms are used in the first place. We are, that is, made increasingly aware that, as Hartman puts it, 'The performance is what music essentially requires in order to exist' (1991: 69), and that this might not be such an affirmatory state of affairs. Indeed, somewhat ironically, Cortázar's earlier declaration of music's advantage over poetry, in that 'resulta dable concebir una Poesía sin palabras [...] mas no una música sin sonidos' (1992: 290–91) [one can conceive of a Poetry without words [...] but not a music without sounds], in fact either reflects the disadvantage of music or is erroneous, as the notion of a soundless Music, prior to its temporal unfurling, makes its latent presence felt throughout the essay. In this respect, tellingly, as is often the case, and as Jacques Derrida would have no doubt pointed out, it is in the footnote, in the caveat, that the key undermining of apparently clear statements is to be found. In this case, Cortázar talks, in a footnote to the statement just cited, both of Mallarmé's allusion to the *'musicienne du silence'* [*musician of silence*], which he describes as 'una de las muchas formas que en su poesía asume la nostalgia platónica de las esencias' (1992: 296) [one of the many forms that the Platonic nostalgia for the essences takes in his poetry], as well as of the unheard melodies referenced in Keats's 'Ode on a Grecian Urn'. He then goes further, declaring that 'la Idea de música, por serlo, es perfecta en su esfera inteligible [the problematic nature of this word should not go unnoticed]; todo sonido supone impureza, suena a "ici-bas"' (296) [the Idea of music, on account of being such, is perfect in its intelligible sphere; every sound supposes impurity and smacks of 'here below']. The alignment between *Idea de música* [Idea of music] > *sonido* [sound] and Word (Logos) > words is hard to resist here, and the allusion to Platonic Forms, via Platonic essences, brings to mind Jean Baudrillard's assertion that 'only the simulacrum exists' (1983: 8). In this sense, then, it is perhaps unsurprising that Cortázar himself appears to acknowledge the impossibility of ever attaining the essential, 'originary' Music, or Work, although it is notable, we might add, that this comes through a declaration towards the end of the essay that marks an abrupt shift towards a very different — and positive — approach to this ineluctable characteristic of musical engagement, as Cortázar suggests we should rejoice that we at least have versions or copies (*'aproximaciones'* (1992: 295) [*approximations/approaches*]) of pieces by Beethoven or Chopin, and be happy that 'esos artistas hayan escrito sus sueños, y que su máscara llegue hasta nosotros' (295) [those artists have written down their dreams and that their mask reaches us].

The Unrung Bell

Despite this affirmation, Cortázar ends 'Soledad de la música' by returning once more to a lamenting of the solitude in which each of us finds him or herself. Given that communication (or even expression) of the Idea, of the Music in its originary-essence, is impossible, Cortázar, in a clear appeal to Judaeo-Christian imagery and traditions, concludes that the only salvation possible is on the level of and from within the individual:

> Si el ser se ha de salvar por la belleza — camino platónico hacia Dios — la Música debe surgir, pura porque *nuestra*, desde el centro mismo de cada hombre. Cada uno debe ser *su Músico* [...]. Cada uno debe levantar su catedral. Cuando las propias manos hayan fundido la campana, dejará de oírse el doblar del badajo; el sonido no será ya el sonido de la campana sino la campana misma, en logro de Idea. (1992: 295–96)

> [If the subject/being is to be saved by beauty — the Platonic path towards God — the Music must surge up, pure because it is *ours*, from the very centre of each man. Each person must be *his or her Musician* [...]. Each person must construct his or her cathedral. When his or her own hands have forged the bell, the ringing of the clapper will cease to be heard; the sound will no longer be the sound of the bell, but the bell itself, the Idea.]

Notwithstanding the fact that the subsequent discussion in *Teoría del túnel* reasserts the necessity of a less solipsistic approach, and one where the need for the social and communication is reaffirmed, this closing passage of 'Soledad de la música' is significant for the way in which it engages once more with images of containment and the question of the location of Music (as essence). The image of the cathedral is particularly notable in this regard, a place, or, perhaps more properly here, a construction, from where songs are sung and words are addressed to reach out to the Divine, and yet also wherein the Divine dwells. It is a location, that is, which speaks to the problematic relationship between artistic construct and essence that I have been discussing, whilst also suggesting, once more, that the simple equivalency of, in the case in point, work (or musical composition) and (originary-essential) Music is open to significant question. Indeed, such a questioning is reinforced in the final reference to the bell, contained, of course, within the cathedral in the image being created, but where the cathedral is not reducible to it.

Of possibly greater importance here, however, is what Cortázar says about this bell. In talking of how, within the individual, the path to salvation, to a oneness of Idea (essence) and expression in the realm of music, is to be found, he states that this moment would be where the individual forges the bell, but where the music (as essence or Idea) would no longer be the sound of the bell, that is, its ringing, but the bell itself. On the one hand, this appears to represent a further rejection of his earlier affirmation that 'la música es *una* con su expresión sonora' (290) [music is *one* with its sonorous expression], or that it is impossible to imagine 'una música sin sonidos' (291) [a music without sounds]. But beyond that, it also engages with the Hegelian notion and treatment of *Klang* in a way which is highly revealing for what it tells us about Cortázar's conception of both music and writing practice at this stage.

For Hegel, *Klang* is the ringing (of the bell) that is the very origins of language. It is the 'ideality of materiality' that characterises 'the transition of material spatiality into material temporality' (1970: 69), which we might well see in the light of the idea of the unfurling of a piece of music in time in its performance or expression. It is, then, located at a liminal moment; as James P. Mall puts it, '*Klang* is the turning-point between light and sound, and also the threshold of speech' (1979: 95), whilst Derrida, in his treatment of Hegel in *Glas*, indicates how, in Hegel's *Philosophy of Nature*, '*Klang* was already recognized as that singular repercussion of interiority in exteriority' (1986 [1974]: 250). Yet what this final image of 'Soledad de la música' does is insist not upon that moment of opening into sonority, but, rather, upon the desirability of forgoing it altogether, of precisely not ringing the bell, that is, of not ringing in its expression or exteriorisation. The oneness Cortázar seeks here is not a oneness of Music with sound, but a oneness of Music with its potentiality prior to and from which a sound *may* occur, should one choose — to use the image employed by Cortázar here — to ring the bell and allow it to be unfurled in time. In other words, here at least, Cortázar affirms the ultimate aim not to be such an unfurling, but for the musician to have as an ideal precisely the silent potentiality of Music (one recalls Cortázar's reference to Mallarmé's '*musicienne du silence*'

(1992: 296) [*musician of silence*]). Moreover, given the alignment of *Klang* with the emergence into speech, into utterance, it is not difficult to see how the same call is being implicitly made here of the writer and, more particularly, the poet, as we both return to the start of the essay and the desirability of a Poetry without words, and are reminded of Rimbaud's (re)turn to silence, which can be read as the enactment of what Cortázar is describing here. Indeed, in his essay 'Rimbaud' (2006a [1941]), dating from the same period as 'Soledad de la música', Cortázar talks in similar terms as, referencing the case of Mallarmé once more, he talks of 'el poeta, que comprenderá su fracaso cada vez que intente la experiencia suprema, el ápice que toca ya la música, el silencio' (142) [the poet, who will understand his or her failure every time he or she tries to achieve the supreme experience, the zenith that music already touches: silence].[29]

At this point, we inevitably find ourselves turning back (or forward) to texts such as *Teoría del túnel*, 'Elogio del jazz', and 'Para una poética', where poetry and music are brought together so significantly. The contrast between where Cortázar leaves us at the end of 'Soledad de la música' and much of what these later texts tell us is striking. Whereas in 'Soledad de la música' we end with a move from expression and communication back to a solitude and an unrung, but pregnant, inner bell, in the later texts, not least *Teoría del túnel*, there is, as we have seen, a persistent sense of the need for expression and engagement with others, with the understanding that this communication needs to emerge from the poetism of solitude and isolation. It is, that is to say, an understanding of language that, with the final image of 'Soledad de la música' in mind, chimes with Heidegger's distinctly poetic envisioning of Hegel's *Klang*, whereby, as James F. Ward, discussing Heidegger's work on Hölderlin, puts it, 'what is heard [by the poet] is the "originary origin" (*ursprüngliche Ursprung*), which brings itself to stand in the poet's hearing. [...] Such hearing brings what is heard into the "sound of words" (*den Klang des Wortes*)' (1995: 227), the very musicalisation, that is, of which Cortázar speaks.

Yet what is perhaps most important here is to realise that this is not a case of this latter image superseding that found at the end of 'Soledad de la música', not least because within these later texts there are, as we have seen, equally contrasting takes on the role and nature of music and poetry (and Music and Poetry). Rather, what we have across these works are different perspectives on and understandings of the complex questions regarding the relationship between language, poetry, music, and being with which all of the texts I have been discussing concern themselves. And it is, I would suggest, precisely this sense of an ongoing, non-static discussion or turning over of these questions that proves so foundational to our understanding of Cortázar's subsequent engagement with music in the course of his life and writing. And, I might add, to the present volume.

In this spirit, it is perhaps worth ending here by taking up two putatively separate elements from 'Soledad de la música' and *Teoría del túnel*, respectively. The former begins with an epigraph, which is Blake's 'The Sick Rose'. Leaving aside the more usual interpretations of the poem, in the context of the essay we are about to read, we can see the worm that destroys the rose as being interpretation, which acts to destroy or desecrate the originary essence of Music. As Cortázar writes, regarding the word 'interpretation', '¿no condensa ya en su sentido el drama, *invisible worm*, de la música? (1992: 293) [does it not already condense in its meaning the drama, *invisible worm*, of music?]. Turning to the titular image of *Teoría del túnel*, we see a striking similarity: a burrowing or tunnelling away that destroys the fundamental characteristics of that into which it is tunnelling. Yet whereas the earlier text uses this image as way of describing how the linguistic operation of *la interpretación* irreparably alters the originary Music, here it comes to function as a way of portraying the desired irreparable altering of language by the music(alisation) of poetry. In turning to the same image to describe both the lamentable impact of language and linguistic operations on the (musical) essence and the affirmatory impact of the musical (poetic) essence on language, Cortázar underscores the ease with which different, and often apparently opposing, terms collapse into each other. But more than that: if we bring the two images together, we are left with two possible representations of it: an Escher-esque depiction of interpretation (language) burrowing away at the very 'element' (originary Music (essence)) which, in turn, is also tunnelling its way into it; or an image of eternal regress, where music is burrowed out by language which is burrowed out by music, which is then also (susceptible to being) burrowed out by language, and so on, *ad infinitum*. We are left, that is, with two images: that of a debate that goes round in circles, with each potential resolution to the questions of expression and ontology raised being undermined by those very questions, simultaneously; and that of an endless chain reaching back in search of an envisaged yet never-attainable centre which would be a locus of experiential contact with and expression of (one's/the) essence. These two images, emerging from some of Cortázar's earliest texts, constitute the bedrock of his subsequent lifelong engagement with music, and their echoes will be discernible throughout the chapters of this study.

A brief note regarding the approach taken in these pages: reflecting the mainstays of Cortázar's engagement with music, chapters 1 and 2 look at how Cortázar deals with and incorporates *la música culta* into his work, chapter 3 turns to the case of tango, whilst chapters 4 and 5 offer different takes on Cortázar's claims for and use of jazz. Chapter 6 initially takes up the issues signalled at the end of chapter 5, and is likewise focused on jazz. In the process, however, and picking up on aspects from all the previous sections, it then looks to destabilise the boundaries that the preceding chapter divisions of my own work have contributed to erecting. Accordingly, its approach will differ from that of the other chapters in being more 'porous' and allowing itself a certain poetic (or musical) licence. I end the book by examining how, at the end of Cortázar's production and this study of it, we might judge the ways in which the author and his musical texts have responded to some of the issues initially raised by his early writings, and by arguing that, above all, music in Cortázar's work must be seen to operate as a fundamental and constant challenge *to* that work and to our reading and understanding of it.

Notes to the Introduction

1. There are several items of scholarship on music in Cortázar's work which fall into this trap, to a greater or lesser extent, such as Tyler (1996), Gordon (1980), Borello (1980), MacAdam (2001), González Riquelme (2003), López (1998), Peyrats (1999), Fralasco (2005). It should be noted that, in several cases and in many ways, these publications make useful contributions to an understanding of the background to, and works/musicians cited in, Cortázar's musical allusions. In either ignoring the wider theoretical issues, or simply repeating Cortázar's claims for music uncritically, however, the complex and problematic ways in which music operates in his work remain largely unanalysed.
2. In this regard, one might highlight, amongst others: Loyola (1994), Goialde Palacios (2010), the more technical and musicological analysis found in Soren Triff (1991), and Moran's (2000: 152–59) illuminating theoretical examination of 'Lugar llamado Kindberg' [A Place Named Kindberg], from *Octaedro* (Cortázar 1974) [*Octahedron*], all on jazz; Berg (2000) and Miller (2016) on tango; and Pérez-Abadín Barro (2010) on classical music in 'Reunión' [Meeting], from *Todos los fuegos el fuego* (Cortázar 1970f [1966]) [*All Fires the Fire*].
3. Peiró (2006) constitutes an example of the former, but without enough of the latter, whilst Moran (2000) in particular focuses on the theoretical and philosophical debates and implications of Cortázar's work, but as part of a study not looking at music in its own right.
4. See Fralasco (2005) in relation to tango and Peyrats (1999) in relation to jazz, for example.
5. Standish divides Cortázar's political evolution into the Argentine (up to 1951) and the French (post-1951) periods of his life, recognising that 'the Cortázar of the Argentine phase, while not politically unaware, was certainly not politically committed or active' (2001: 122). Carolina Orloff (2013) dedicates a book-length study to the presence of the political in Cortázar's writings, arguing that politics is evident in Cortázar's work from the earliest texts.
6. Cortázar himself variously claimed that his first visit to Cuba was in 1961 (Prego 1985: 128), in 1962 (González Bermejo 1978: 120), or in 1963 (Picon Garfield 1981 [1978]: 49). His letters from this period help clarify the issue. Certainly, there is no reference to a trip to Cuba in 1961, and the invitation to make such a journey as part of the jury for a literary prize of the *Casa de las Américas* is first mentioned in a letter to Manuel Antín on 10 December 1962 (Cortázar 2012b: 327). A letter to Sara and Paul Blackburn on 16 December 1962 discloses that this would be his first trip to the island, as he states that 'all these years I have been longing to go to Cuba to have a direct experience of what is happening there' (331). The likely date of his flight to Cuba for his first visit to the island was 9 January 1963, as indicated by his letter to Manuel Antín on 6 January 1963 (340), although 10 January 1963 is also a possibility (see Cortázar's letter to Francisco Porrúa of 5 January 1963 (336)). My thanks to Dominic Moran for alerting me to this biographical misdirection on Cortázar's part in some of his interviews.
7. See Boldy (1980: 163).
8. As László Scholz (1977: 11–12) has discussed, contradiction is not only at the heart of Cortázar's thought, but is seen by him as an important part of the sort of challenge to rational thought that he advocates; thus, Scholz talks of Cortázar's 'herencia surrealista que elogia la contradicción por su esencia antirracional' (12) [surrealist heritage which praises contradiction on account of its antirational essence].
9. This text dates from 1947, but was only published for the first time posthumously in Cortázar (1994a).
10. Claudia Comes Peña (2002) offers a short but useful reading of *Teoría del túnel*, going on to link it up with a reading of *Rayuela* (Cortázar 2007 [1963]) [*Hopscotch*], chapters 10–18, which are largely centred around jazz.
11. I am not using the version of 'Soledad de la música' found in *Obras completas VI* (Cortázar 2006b), since this contains a number of important omissions, which I have assumed to be errata, since the prose loses its meaning at times as a result. Cortázar wrote this essay under the pseudonym Julio Denis.
12. I will discuss 'Elogio del jazz' in more detail in the chapters concerned with jazz.
13. With regard to jazz, for example, Cortázar described, in interview with Ernesto González

Bermejo, how 'cada músico crea su obra, es decir, que no hay un intermediario, no existe la mediación de un intérprete' (1978: 105) [each musician creates her/his work, that is, there is no intermediary, there exists no mediation by an interpreter].

14. Although not brought out as a thematic in *Presencia*, shortly before the publication of this work, in a letter to the author, and his friend, Eduardo Hugo Castagnino, on 27 May 1937, Cortázar does make clear that poetry cannot lay claim to such a oneness of Idea (or interiority) and expression, as he distinguishes explicitly between poetry in its own right and the way it is expressed (2012a: 36). He makes mention of the argument that poetic expression is 'la poesía misma' (36) [poetry itself], but says that this comes from 'el simbolismo exagerado' [exaggerated symbolism] and rejects it, calling it 'una gran macana' (36) [a load of rubbish].

15. In the later text 'No hay peor sordo que el que' (1970b: 142–59) [There is None So Deaf As He Who], Cortázar expands upon this more positive view of language, affirming that 'en todo gran estilo el lenguaje cesa de ser un vehículo para la "expresión de ideas y sentimientos" y accede a ese estado límite en que ya no cuenta como mero lenguaje porque todo él es presencia de lo expresado' (145) [in all great styles language stops being a vehicle for the 'expression of ideas and feelings' and enters into that limit state in which it is no longer mere language because it is entirely the presence of what is expressed].

16. This characteristic of poetry is also bound up with the way in which it uses analogy to bring objects together: analogy, in this poetic, musicalised sense, reaches into and refers to the essence of the objects in question, and, in the process, allows an 'understanding' of the 'participación' (Cortázar 1994b: 272) [participation] of and between things. Citing Lévy-Bruhl, and in terms that chime with precisely the sort of goal at which he aims throughout his writing, Cortázar states that 'la esencia de la participación consiste, precisamente, en borrar toda dualidad' (272) [the essence of participation consists precisely of erasing all duality].

17. Of the many examples of Cortázar's engagement with these myths, we might point to works such as: *Los reyes* (1970e [1949]) [*The Kings*]; *Los premios* (1981a [1960]) [*The Winners*]; *Rayuela*; 'Casa tomada' [House Taken Over] and 'Las puertas del cielo' [The Gates of Heaven], both from *Bestiario* (1993a [1951]).

18. Boldy, for example, deals usefully with both of these myths (1980: 64–72). Both Sosnowski (1973) and Hernández y Castillo (1981) are significant studies of Cortázar's use of and engagement with myth more generally.

19. In this latter example, the description of the 'civilised' side of the apparent dichotomy around which the story revolves underscores the association of it with neat categorisation, as the characters Babette and Roland are talked about as 'salvados por la costumbre, por los gestos mecánicos. Todo alisado, planchado, guardado, numerado' (Cortázar 1970d: 193) ('saved by force of habit, [...] by the automatic gesture. Everything smooth, ironed out, numbered and filed away', 2013: 255), in turn pre-empting the satiric exaggeration of Ceferino Piriz's taxonomy in *Rayuela* (Cortázar 2007: 693–701 (chapter 133)).

20. The theoretical complexities in relation to these aspects of Cortázar's work are discussed most thoroughly in Moran (2000).

21. Arguably, such a sense of what is required is evident from Cortázar's early letters in which he talks about his collection of poems *Presencia* and an ultimately unpublished subsequent volume, referred to with the title *De este lado* [*On this side*]. The latter, he says in a letter to Luis Gagliardi in February 1940, is the complete opposite — 'necesariamente contrario' (2012a: 78) [necessarily opposite] — of *Presencia*, before going on to explain how, in contrast to the earlier collection's focus on the musical exteriorisation of the internal and the tight poetic (sonnet) structure it employed, this new tome could be summed up in the following terms: 'el contenido, alejado de todo preciosismo y de toda "música" exterior; el verso, blanco y enteramente libre; la intención, orientada exclusivamente hacia la raíz de lo poético' (78) [the content, distanced from all overrefinement and all exterior 'music'; the verse, blank and entirely free; the intention, oriented exclusively towards the root of the poetic]. Although not presented as such in this letter, it is arguable that, rather than, as Cortázar suggests, its being simply that *De este lado* surpasses ('supera' (78)) *Presencia*, in fact both collections and approaches taken together constitute at the very least an apt metaphor for the balance of which he talks in relation to poetry more generally

in an earlier letter to Castagnino (36) and for the need that he perceives to take in both the poetic and the formal structures and exteriorisation that characterise language.

22. One might ask here whether these instances are an effect of describing music (the 'essence-work') through the problematic medium of language, or whether they speak of problems inscribed within (such a vision of) music itself. This is an issue that will re-emerge at several points in this study, but even at this early stage it is important to note that Cortázar's earliest texts bring to the fore the essentially linguistic mechanisms through which music actually operates as a form of communication.
23. See Heidegger (2001: 91–92).
24. See Moran (2000: 34).
25. As noted earlier, Cortázar's use of capitalisation in this essay suggests a differentiation on his part between an (essential) Work or Music prior to its performance and the musicalisation or playing out of such, which might thus be identifiable, contrastingly, as the 'work' or 'music'. The problematic and inconsistent nature of this capitalisation is again evident in the example cited here, however: 'Obra' appears to refer to the essential Work, whereas 'Música', here at least, could be seen to indicate a musical work informed by such an essence.
26. In 'No hay peor sordo que el que', Cortázar suggests that exceptions are possible to the problem of *intérpretes* [interpreters], talking of 'el raro intérprete musical que establece el contacto directo del oyente con la obra y cesa de actuar como intermediario' (1970b: 145) [the rare musical interpreter who establishes the direct contact of the listener with the work and stops acting as an intermediary].
27. Joyce Milton (1996: 92–93) reports this, for example, referencing as a source the *Chicago Herald* of 15 July 1915.
28. The capitalisation here once more suggests that this is to be understood as the originary or essential Work prior to or independent from its playing out in performance.
29. The essay 'Rimbaud' was written under the pseudonym Julio Denis.

CHAPTER 1

La *música culta* and/as Language

The most negative presentation of music to emerge from Cortázar's early essays is, as we saw in the Introduction, that found in 'Soledad de la música'. Here, Cortázar brandishes as evidence of music's problematic nature its unfurling in time (that is, its performance), the need for interpreters or performers in such an unfurling, and the presence of the score. This latter element most clearly underlines that the primary issue here is the way in which both the notation and reproduction of a musical work are bound to essentially linguistic operations, and these issues are brought up repeatedly in subsequent interviews. The type of music that Cortázar has in mind when making these points would appear primarily to be classical: when addressing the ways in which scored and interpreted music is in fact more problematic than language, for example, Cortázar refers to 'la imposibilidad de interpretar en persona las obras sinfónicas' (1992: 292) [the impossibility of interpreting symphonic works in person]; and towards the end of the essay the examples he names of the sort of music he is addressing are Stravinsky (293), Beethoven (295), and Chopin (295). Similarly, resonating with the discussion in this early essay, in a much later interview with Ernesto González Bermejo Cortázar refers to 'la música llamada clásica' [so-called classical music] as a music where 'hay una partitura y un ejecutante que la interpreta con más o menos talento' (1978: 105) [there is a score and a musician who interprets it with more or less talent], whilst in interview with Prego, after describing tango as a music which 'permite únicamente una ejecución basada en la partitura' [only permits a performance based on the score] and where most of its performers are thus 'sujetos a una escritura' (1985: 163) [subject to a writing], he adds, 'Digamos que el tango se toca como la música llamada clásica' (163) [Shall we say that tango is played like so-called classical music].

Given this consistent alignment on Cortázar's part of what he elsewhere terms 'la música culta' (2006d: 207) [cultivated/art music] with (the problems of) language, and, most pointedly, with writing and reading in particular, it is unsurprising to see this type of music associated in his fiction not just with language, but also with all that language and writing is tied up with in his thought, that is, the structures and strictures of Western humankind.[1,2] In the early short story 'Lejana. Diario de Alina Reyes' [The Distances] from *Bestiario* (Cortázar 1993a [1951]), for example, among the elements of the protagonist's decidedly bourgeois and regulated life of 'pulseras y farándulas, de *pink champagne*' (37) [bracelets and the showbiz world, of pink champagne] in Buenos Aires, it is notable that she is a concert pianist, whilst in the later short piece 'Louis, enormísimo cronopio' [Louis, Enormous *Cronopio*] from *La vuelta al día en ochenta mundos* (Cortázar 1970c: 13–22) [*Around the Day in Eighty Worlds*] Cortázar refers to the audience at a 'concierto de flauta y harpa' [flute and harp concert] as 'tan bien educado que era un placer [para los acomodadores]' (16) [so well-mannered that is was a pleasure [for the ushers]] .

Turning to 'Elogio del jazz' we see a similar approach to *la música culta*. Early on in the letter, contrasting *la música culta* with jazz, Cortázar states that 'la música culta se mueve dentro de una estética, mientras el jazz lo hace dentro de una poética. La música es un producto musical, y el jazz es un producto poético' (2006d: 207) [*la musica culta* moves within an aesthetic, whereas jazz does so within a poetics. Music is a musical product, and jazz is a poetic product]. Of particular significance here is the way in which the term *la música culta* simply becomes *la música*, indicating once more the intricacies of Cortázar's use of terminology and (implied) (non)capitalisation. *La música culta*, that is, is seen as encapsulating and personifying the music about which Cortázar wrote so negatively in 'Soledad de la música'. Beyond this, the identification of *la música culta* with aesthetics rather than simply language points towards both a broader and a more nuanced enunciation of the problematic associations and characteristics of *la música culta* that Cortázar is evincing here. In a footnote towards the end of 'Elogio del jazz', Cortázar sets out quite how he is understanding the term 'aesthetics':

> La razón — ordenante y tipificadora, amiga de 'géneros' y 'estilos', que son como conceptos del arte por analogía con los de la lógica —, erige sus construcciones mediatizando obligadamente, por razones instrumentales, los productos directos de la aprehensión intuitiva. [...] Considera a tales productos como materia bruta hasta que, encauzándola en cánones racionales, la 'eleva' a una Literatura, una Música, una Pintura. Estos últimos productos son lo que denomino estéticos. (214)
>
> [Reason — order-giver and category-definer, friend of 'genres' and 'styles', which are like concepts of art by analogy with those of logic —, erects its constructions, inevitably, for instrumental reasons, interfering with the direct products of intuitive understanding. [...] It considers such products to be the raw materials until, channelling them into rational canons, it 'elevates' them to a Literature, a Music, a Painting. These are the products that I call aesthetic.]

Parts of this resonate with the linguistic nature of *la música culta* set out in 'Soledad de la música', with its focus on the barrier of interpretation. But this footnote also serves to foreground other elements that work alongside language in Cortázar's general understanding of the problematic nature of Western humankind: order, categorisation, logic, pigeon-holes, and artistic and ontological straitjackets.

Moreover, in talking in terms of the aesthetic nature of *la música culta*, the discussion in 'Elogio del jazz' also points back to *Teoría del túnel*, of which, it is worth reminding ourselves, this letter 'podría constituir el capítulo final' (Cortázar 2006d: 204) [could be the final chapter]. There, we find several references to the aesthetic, none of which is particularly positive, but all of which bring to the fore a more specific type of language to which Cortázar is tying *la música culta* in his description of it as being about aesthetics. Concretely, aesthetic language here, pre-empting the definition in 'Elogio del jazz', is literary language, the language of the novel, and the affirmation of poetic language that we find towards the start of the essay is given precisely in terms of its opposition to (this) aesthetic language ('[e]l lenguaje poético, no estético' (2006c: 67) [poetic, not aesthetic, language]). More significantly still, Cortázar states baldly that the writer's 'condición humana *no es reductible estéticamente* y que por ende la literatura falsea al hombre' (69) [human condition *is not reducible to aesthetics* and that consequently literature falsifies man]. The literary, or non-poeticised, language that Cortázar is discussing here is a 'formulación estética de órdenes extraestéticos' (77) [aesthetic formulation of extraaesthetic orders], and it is against the background of these lines that we must understand his description of *la música culta* as an aesthetic product. In short, that is, the alignment of *la música culta* with the aesthetic serves to supplement the more generally linguistic depiction of it found in 'Soledad de la música' with a critique that at once reaches out to a wider range of elements of Western civilisation, whilst at the same time focusing more specifically on its synonymity with the form of language that Cortázar most roundly laments (and lambasts). Indeed, moving forwards to 'Para una poética', we see an important and revealing echo in this respect of the affirmation in 'Elogio del jazz' that music is a musical product (2006d: 207). In contrast to *Teoría del túnel*'s putatively less problematic praise of '[e]l lenguaje poético' (2006c: 67) [poetic language], this later essay differentiates between what it at one point describes as 'la poesía del poema' [the poetry of the poem] and 'el poema como producto estético' (1994b: 279) [the poem as an aesthetic product]. In the alignment of this latter declaration with that from 'Elogio del jazz' we thus see not only the equivalence of *la música culta* and poetic language, in the form of the poem itself, but a further equivalence, to the point of interchangeability, of the terms *musical* and *estético* [aesthetic] across these two texts, thus reinforcing the association between the two on which I have been focusing. Equally clear is the stark contrast between this understanding of 'the musical' and the rather more affirmative one (with a(n implied) capital 'M') found elsewhere in Cortázar's early work, as we saw in the Introduction. Put simply, when discussing *la música culta*, 'the musical' takes on the decidedly negative associations of aesthetics and language (and aesthetic language), and is thus intrinsically bound up with the sense of eliding or falsifying (the essence of) man, as described in *Teoría del túnel* and repeated in the definition of classical music found in *Diario de Andrés Fava* [*Diary of Andrés Fava*], where we are told that 'lo que se da en llamar "clásico" es siempre cierto producto logrado con el sacrificio de la verdad a la belleza' (Cortázar 1995 [1950]: 9) [what is given to be called 'classical' is always a certain product achieved with the sacrifice of the truth to beauty]. And whilst there is much to support the idea that (aesthetic) beauty is something that Cortázar came to consider arguably as being equally as important as 'the truth', I would, for instance, take issue with José Vicente Peiró's foregrounding of this line of argument (2006: 88): at this stage of Cortázar's career at least, what emerges most insistently is, as we have seen, his concern at the loss and falsification involved in this sacrifice.

Nevertheless, it would be wrong to reduce Cortázar's engagement with and views on *la música culta* to this particularly critical stance. A sense of negativity regarding *la música culta* and the separation from (the essence) of humankind it both effects and symbolises does prevail throughout Cortázar's career, as is evident from the late interviews with Prego and González Bermejo, and it is this aspect of Cortázar's thought and writing that this chapter will explore. But there is also much about *la música culta* that is affirmed by Cortázar, not least in interview with Evelyn Picon Garfield, where Cortázar states that he would choose classical music over jazz to take to a desert island, since 'es la mejor música que hay' [it's the best music there is], and 'el jazz es maravilloso pero esa música clásica es como la gran literatura, es lo más que se puede conseguir en música' (1981: 128) [jazz is marvellous but that classical music is like great literature, it is the greatest thing that one can achieve in music]. A similar sentiment is expressed in *Un tal Lucas* [*A Certain Lucas*], where we are told that, at the hour of his death, one of the two pieces of music Lucas would like to listen to is Mozart's last quintet (Cortázar 1979b: 208).[3, 4] Indeed, Mozart is frequently mentioned by Cortázar in glowing terms, with both the Austrian composer and jazz appearing as inspirations for his writing in interview with González Bermejo (1978: 108). Additionally, Mozart is elsewhere aligned with Cortázar's understanding of the structure of a short story (Prego 1985: 170), in particular how it should approach its finale: talking of how 'la nouvelle [...] a une structure très musicale. On procède par une sorte d'accumulation de tensions qui éclate vers la fin, dans le dénouement dramatique' (Olivares 1981: 56) [the short story [...] has a very musical structure. One proceeds by a sort of accumulation of tensions which explodes towards the end, in the dramatic denouement], Cortázar describes how Mozart's quintets create just such tension, before stating that 'mes nouvelles cherchent la même chose' (56) [my short stories seek the same thing]. Certainly, in reading such lines, one might be forgiven for seeing in them a stark contradiction in Cortázar's ideas on literature and literary language: both literature and *la música culta* now appear to be given a somewhat more elevated position in his tastes and thoughts than in the earlier essays and letters that we have been examining. Aside from the fact that consistency is not an obligation that befalls an author, there are also a number of more specific reasons behind these apparently ambiguous feelings towards and presentation of *la música culta*, not least the importance in Cortázar's thought and work of balancing the poetic and a (communicative) existentialist ethic, truth and beauty to which I alluded in the Introduction. The more affirmative takes on *la música culta* found in Cortázar's work will be explored in more depth in chapter 2.[5]

'Clone'

At this point, however, we return to the more negative presentation of *la música culta*. This constitutes, as we have seen, the theoretical foundation set down by Cortázar in his early writings. But what is arguably of greater interest is how these early thoughts and theories play out and are developed in the course of his career; more specifically, how are they put into the practice of his fiction and how do they — and his engagement with *la música culta* more generally — contribute to and inform his wider praxis and ideas?

A number of Cortázar's fictions, as well as a number of his more hesitatingly catalogued pieces, engage with *la música culta*, either to a lesser or greater extent: amongst his novels, *Libro de Manuel* (1973a) [*A Manual for Manuel*] and *Rayuela* stand out in particular in this regard, as do short stories such as 'La banda' [The Band] from *Final del juego* (1970a [1956]), 'Lejana. Diario de Alina Reyes', 'Las ménades', 'Alguien que anda por ahí' [Someone Walking Around] and 'Las caras de la medalla' [The Faces of the Medal], both from *Alguien que anda por ahí* (1977), 'El perseguidor' [The Pursuer] from *Las armas secretas* (1970d [1959]), and 'Reunión' from *Todos los fuegos el fuego* (1970f [1966]), whilst works such as *Un tal Lucas* are also notable for some revealing references to this type of music.[6] Several of these will be discussed in more detail in the course of this study. But Cortázar's most sustained engagement with *la música culta*, and, I would contend, the most significant and useful story with regard to the arguments drawn up in Cortázar's early texts, is the late story 'Clone' from *Queremos tanto a Glenda* (1980: 89–106), and it is to this piece that the rest of this chapter will now turn, using it as a case study of Cortázar's engagement with the problematic nature of *la música culta* in his fiction.[7]

Before looking at the detail of the story, however, it is worth commenting on one of the characteristics that distinguish 'Clone' from Cortázar's other outputs concerned with *la música culta*, not least because this is key to understanding both the importance of the story and the approach to it that I will be undertaking here. Standish argues that 'Clone' contains 'much the most adventurous use of music' (2001: 74) in Cortázar's work, and this is an accurate statement. Uniquely in Cortázar's *œuvre*, 'Clone' engages with several forms of *la música culta*, specifically Renaissance and Baroque, not just in its content, but also in both its form and the author's compositional *modus operandi*.[8] This much is made clear in the story's epilogue 'Nota sobre el tema de un rey y la venganza de un príncipe' (1980: 103–06) [Note on The Theme of a King and The Vengeance of a Prince], about which I shall say more shortly, and it underlines the extent to which this story enacts the sort of debates and discussions with which we have seen Cortázar to be concerned, intermeshing the literary, the linguistic, and the musical. Given the importance of this coming together of music and writing, and literary and musical composition in the story, my analysis will look at both the original published version of the story in *Queremos tanto a Glenda* (1980) and Cortázar's handwritten manuscript version.[9]

The Performance of the Madrigals

As we have seen, one of the main criticisms of scored and interpreted music in 'Soledad de la música' is that 'toda comunicación de [una] obra por un ejecutante es ya versión, interpretación, y no la Obra misma' (Cortázar 1992: 293) [all communication of [a] work by a performer is already a version, an interpretation, and not the Work itself]. This statement conveys the central thematic concerns of versions, or interpretations, and the notion of a putative original, where there is a fundamental aim of collapsing the breach between the two. As Cortázar proceeds to explain, underlining in his focus on the written score that this is the same problematic found in the use of language:

por muy sutil que sea su *notación* [...] el inexpresable fluido que informa una Música, que surge del sonido plasmado por el espíritu del artista de una manera única, innominable, corre riesgo mortal en toda interpretación. (293, italics mine)

[however subtle his or her *notation* [...] the inexpressible fluid that informs a piece of Music, that surges up from the sound captured by the artist's spirit in a unique, unnameable way, runs a mortal risk in every interpretation.]

The centrality of these considerations to 'Clone' is evident from the basic elements of the story, which concerns a tightknit group of eight singers. Their unity is based around their performing apparently to perfection the madrigals of Carlo Gesualdo (?1566–1613),[10] the Italian composer who murdered his wife, Maria d'Avalos, and her lover in 1590. In terms which resonate with the lines cited above from 'Soledad de la música', the singers study the music scores — significantly referred to as 'textos' (Cortázar 1980: 93) [texts] — and try to repeat the moment when the composer 'ali[ó] los poemas a la melodía' (93) ('link[ed] the poems to the melody', 1984: 44), seeking with each performance 'ese esquivo centro del que surgiría la realidad del madrigal' (1980: 93) ('that elusive center from which the reality of the madrigal was to rise', 1984: 44) rather than just producing 'una de las tantas versiones mecánicas que a veces escuchaban en discos' (1980: 93) ('one of the so many mechanical versions that they listened to on records', 1984: 44–45). Musically, that is, they are aiming at a 'direct communication' with the composer and the ideational moment of composition, Gesualdo as both man and music, as we are told, variously, that 'todo parece girar en torno a Gesualdo' (1980: 89) ('everything seems to resolve around Gesualdo', 1984: 39), and that 'ese centro era la música y en torno a ella las luces de ocho vidas, de ocho juegos, los pequeños ocho planetas del sol Monteverdi, del sol Josquin des Prés, del sol Gesualdo' (1980: 95) ('that center was the music and around it the lights of eight lives, eight sets, the eight small planets of the Monteverdi sun, the Josquin des Prés sun, the Gesualdo sun', 1984: 46).

Yet this image of the singers circling around the grounding and determining presence of Gesualdo and his music also signals the presence of an underlying linguistic model, in that it chimes with a Derrida-esque portrayal of words revolving around the Word, or transcendental signified, as the full presence and/of meaning at which Western thought (language) aims. Indeed, this is suggested more strongly still in the manuscript version, which talks of the elusive centre from which would arise 'la *plena* realidad del madrigal' (Cortázar 1982: 5: 5, italics mine) [the *full* reality of the madrigal]. For Derrida, each signifier gains meaning via a process of difference from other signifiers, hence its 'full' meaning is endlessly deferred as ever more signifiers are brought into its web of signification. The transcendental signified would be the end point of signification, closing off the process of language, or *différance*, as Derrida terms it.[11] And it is precisely an end to such a process that is highlighted by the idea of the 'clone' and its apparent attainment of the centre-written-out-by-language. One of the singers, Roberto, uses the term to describe the lack of division or difference between the group's eight members, with Lucho explaining that this refers to the fact that 'el canto y la vida y *hasta los pensamientos* eran una sola cosa en ocho cuerpos' (1980: 93, italics mine) ('singing and living and *even thinking* were all one single thing in eight bodies', 1984: 44, italics mine). In effect, then, the text implies that the words (singers) have been reduced to the indivisible Word (originary musical ideation, where composer and music are themselves 'one').

But even within the terms used to describe this unity and oneness there are already problems, not least in the insistence on the image of the eight musicians revolving around this composer/music centre. Such an image, as I have already suggested, implies an inscription within rather than an escape from the Derridean portrayal of language's workings.[12] Similarly, the very use of the word 'clone' raises a number of problems. W. J. T. Mitchell, in *Cloning Terror: The War of Images, 9/11 to the Present* (2011), talks of 'deep copying', which 'goes beneath the visual or phenomenal surface to copy the inner structure and workings of an entity' (29). This definition recalls the use of the word in genetics, both in science and science fiction, the latter being particularly relevant here, given that Roberto came across the term whilst reading this literary genre (Cortázar 1980: 93), and it reflects both the group's desire to attain a oneness with the moment of musical ideation beyond the surface of the score and the claimed indistinguishability of its members. Yet the definition cited above reveals the term to be destabilising on both fronts. Firstly, it underscores the nature of the group('s renditions) as a copy of, rather than one with, that moment or centre. The term 'clone' speaks, that is, of the group as a marker of iterability, of the move away from plenitude into the realm of replication and duplication, of *écriture* [writing] in its broadest sense.[13] Secondly, in alluding to the genetic understanding of term, it undermines the 'clone'-like oneness of the eight singers: no genetic clone is ever entirely the same as the entity of which it is a clone, as there are always differences in its development and behaviour, not least because stimuli and experiences can never be repeated exactly. On both levels, then, the use of the word 'clone' implies the sort of web of relationships that constitutes the basis of language.

Reflecting some of these problems, the story tells of the gradual disintegration of the group's unity, as there are hints of an attraction between Sandro, the group's director, and Mario's wife, Franca, both of whom are singers in the group. This disintegration is linked specifically to a loss of contact with the 'originary' essence of Gesualdo's music: as the situation gets worse, the characters see that 'todo se volverá cada vez más mecánico, se pegará impecable a la *partitura* y al *texto*, será Carlo Gesualdo sin amor y sin celos' (Cortázar 1980: 95, italics mine) ('everything will get more and more mechanical, will be impeccably glued to the *score* and the *text*, will be Carlo Gesualdo without love and without jealousy', 1984: 47, italics mine), that is, just another performance out of contact with the original Work at the ideational moment. Indeed, it is worth noting that the manuscript version of the story has 'la palabra' (Cortázar 1982: 5: 5) [the word] instead of 'el texto' [the text] here, underlining the pre-eminence of a linguistic concern at the heart of the story. And a closer look at other elements of the text's composition also reveals an increasing emphasis on this loss of an originary contact or oneness. During an early discussion by the characters about Gesualdo's life, for example, the manuscript version reads, 'ésa es la noticia de policía, el ~~informativo~~ flash de mediodía' (5: 5) [that's the police report, the midday ~~news bulletin~~ news flash], whereas the published version has 'ésa es la noticia de policía o el *flash* de las doce y media' (Cortázar 1980: 89) ('that's the police report on the twelve-thirty news [flash]', 1984: 40). This change from the symbolically-charged midday to the more mundane half-past twelve speaks of a shift away from a time associated with the apogee of light, a perfect, shadow-less time, linked with divinities from the Egyptian sun-god Re to Christ, and bound up by implication with the idea of a momentary glimpse of a prelapsarian Word.[14] Instead, Cortázar emphasises the breach opened up between such a moment and the linguistic version ('noticia de policía' [police report], '*flash*' [news flash]) we have of it. Similarly, in (what should be) the story's seventh section, when we are given details of the group's discussions of how best to perform Gesualdo's madrigals, the manuscript version's description of Lucho's call to 'dejar flotando la melodía en toda su ambigüedad gesualdesca' (1982: 5: 5) [leave the melody floating in all its Gesualdic ambiguity] is altered in the published version to 'dejar que la melodía fluya en toda su ambigüedad gesualdesca' (1980: 94) ('letting the melody flow in all of its Gesualdic ambiguity', 1984: 45). This apparently minor alteration of *flotar* [float] to *fluir* [flow] represents a concerted shift from an identification of performance as fully presencing an all-imbuing, timeless, and originary essence towards an underlining of the temporal, a move, that is, from pre- to postlapsarian being, with the attendant fall into the flow of time and language, here in the guise of musical performance.

Most crucially, however, the group's supposed unity, both internally amongst its members and with the originary music(al moment), is, from the beginning, outside the text: the story begins with the group *already* in the process of disintegration and where a oneness with the Work is only ever referred to in an indeterminate past. We read, for example, that '*alguna vez* ese centro *era* la música' (1980: 95, italics mine) ('*formerly* that center *was* the music', 1984: 46, italics mine). And the published version is notably more insistent in this regard than the earlier manuscript: whereas the latter ends (what should be) the fourth section stating: 'Sandro era el ~~mejor de~~ más músico de todos nosotros, sin él no seríamos esto' (1982: 5: 5) [Sandro was the ~~best of~~ clearest musician of us all, without him we wouldn't be what we are], the published version adds: 'Esto que fuimos, murmura Lucho' (1980: 92) ('What we were, Lucho mutters', 1984: 43). Indeed, several notable additions in the published version go further, questioning whether such unity ever was. Significantly, for instance, when Paola refers back to the supposed moment when things changed, no such moment can be located: 'Hasta que. Porque ahora algo había cambiado desde' (1980: 91) ('Until. Because now something had changed ever since', 1984: 41); and, as Roberto later asks, '¿[...] dónde empieza lo sano, dónde hay que cortar si no ha pasado nada, si nadie puede decir que haya pasado alguna cosa?' (1980: 92) ('where does the matter begin, where should it be settled, since nothing has happened, since no one can say that anything has happened?', 1984: 44), implying the possibility that the current state of affairs is the way it has always been.

Returning to the specific question of the group's musical practices, it is notable to what extent references to their performances and procedures are inscribed within terms which resonate with the critique found in 'Soledad de la música'. For a start, the story places great emphasis on the group's *ensayos* [rehearsals], with mention made of their frequency in just the second sentence. This conveys the notion of an attempt to get the piece exactly 'right', but the insistence on the *ensayos* and the idea of a correct reading of the musical *textos* (1980: 93) [texts] signals that what is at stake here is, specifically, a reading, an interpretation which is tied to, and does not go beyond, the score, whatever the claims made within the story by the singers. Indeed, this problem is highlighted by Cortázar in the essay 'Melancolía de las maletas' [The Melancholy of Suitcases] from *La vuelta al día en ochenta mundos* (1970c: 166–72), where he talks eulogistically about the practice of 'takes' in jazz recording, before underlining the difference between rehearsal and take, in that 'el ensayo va llevando paulatinamente a la perfección, no cuenta como producto, es presente en función de futuro' (172) [the rehearsal gradually takes you towards perfection, it doesn't count as a product, it's a present based on the future]. The *ensayo* [rehearsal], then, is an endless journey towards a perfect rendering of the score, in contrast to the take, which is apparently always, as this extract proceeds to underline, original. In emphasising rehearsals as the basis on which the group operates, then, Cortázar belies the claims made within the story of the group's having fallen from a past originary or perfect performance. Rather, such perfection is always deferred to the future, and, moreover, would always be determined by the score being performed.

In addition to these factors, it is notable that the story as a whole is replete not with references to unity, but with allusions to tension, division, and repression ('Estamos todos demasiado tensos, *damn it*' (1980: 91) ('We're all too tense, damn it', 1984: 41)). Far from being part of one single clone, each thinking and feeling the same way, the group appears as individuals who each read the scores and imagine their ideal production in a quite different way, a fact tied in with their individual sense of the composer himself and the emotions felt at the compositional moment ('cada uno su manera de sentir a Gesualdo' (1980: 94) ('each one in his or her way of feeling Gesualdo', 1984: 45)). As the text goes on to state: 'el *clone* se iba disgregando y cada día asomaban más los individuos con sus discrepancias, sus resistencias' (1980: 94) ('the clone was breaking up and day by day individuals appeared with their discrepancies, their resistance', 1984: 45). As noted, however, that this represents a fall from an actual state of oneness and originary performance is itself undercut by Cortázar's narrative.

The Performance of Gesualdo's Life

A close reading of 'Clone', then, reveals that rather than unity, we have a group divided; and rather than oneness with the original Work, we have performance based on an attempted 'perfect' reading of the musical score. Crucially, this revelation goes hand in hand with the realisation that the story being played out is itself increasingly aligned with the life and crime of Carlo Gesualdo, where Mario and Franca assume the roles of Gesualdo and his wife respectively and Sandro the role of the latter's lover. In other words, the writing out of the claimed oneness both amongst the group and of the group with Gesualdo as man and music is concomitant with a move towards a supposedly ever greater oneness with that man and the infamous events from his life.

Fundamental to an initial understanding of this apparent paradox is the fact that, despite the putative oneness with Gesualdo and his life that Cortázar gives us in the group's playing out of the love triangle, this enactment is revealed to be a version, rather than a perfect repetition, of the original story. The narrative details make this clear, with the group's interpretation of Gesualdo's life, as with their interpretations of his madrigals, being 'flawed': in the version played out here only the wife (Franca) is apparently killed, whereas in fact Gesualdo killed — or had killed — both figures.

I say 'in fact', but Cortázar's text leads us to ask where this fact comes from. At no point in the story are we ever given unmediated access to the 'truth' of Gesualdo's life. Our knowledge of the events being repeated by the group's members is always filtered, reported: a version. Thus, for example, the opening debate amongst the group's members as to why the composer murdered his wife and her lover is littered with different takes on the story, where 'no es tan fácil saber por qué se traiciona y por qué se mata' (1980: 89) ('it's not so easy to know why people cheat and why they kill', 1984: 39). More significantly, it is in written texts that the 'truth' of what happened can, apparently, be discovered: 'Hay mucha bibliografía sobre Gesualdo, recuerda Lucho' (1980: 89) ('There's a lot of bibliography on Gesualdo, Lucho reminds them', 1984: 40). Aside from the problematic ramifications of this turning to words to discover the 'truth', the reference here to 'mucha bibliografía' ('a lot of bibliography') discloses the existence of many different takes on Gesualdo and his life's defining events, thus underscoring the impossibility of escaping 'versions', of escaping the written text, in any attempt to get back to an original moment. Equally significant in these passages is the allusion made both in this opening section and later on in the middle of the story to these events as tangos, further drawing together language (writing) and what we have seen Cortázar to present as scored or interpreted music:

> Tuvo razón, se obstina Roberto, entonces y ahora es lo mismo, su mujer lo engañaba y él la mató, un tango más, Paolita. Tu grilla de macho, dice Paola, los tangos, claro, pero ahora hay mujeres que también componen tangos y ya no se canta siempre la misma cosa. (1980: 89)
>
> [He was right then, Roberto insists, and today it's the same thing, his wife cheated on him and he killed her, just another tango, Paolita. Your macho

nonsense, Paola says, tangos, sure, but there are [also] women [composing] tangos now and [it's not always the same thing being sung anymore].] (1984: 39)

¿Por qué la mató? Lo de siempre, le dice Roberto a Lily, la encontró en el bulín y en otros brazos, como en el tango de Rivero. (1980: 95)

[Why did he kill her? The usual thing, Roberto tells Lily, he found her in the hideout and in other arms, like Rivero's tango.] (1984: 46)

Notably, even Paola's alternative version to the tango-esque understanding of Gesualdo's life proffered by Roberto is conceived of simply as a different tango. In short, we are given a web of (linguistic and musical) versions and performances in the group's presentation of Gesualdo's life, whose defining events are not knowable in any objective or univocal form. What is more, the extent to which this represents a deliberate strategy on Cortázar's part is clear when we compare the text's published version with its manuscript counterpart. (What should be) the ninth section is particularly noteworthy in this respect. The beginning of this section as published is cited above, but in the manuscript we instead read, '¿Por qué la mató? La encontró en la cama con otro hombre' (1982: 5: 5) [Why did he kill her? He found her in bed with another man]. The reference to Edmundo Rivero's tango, identifiable as 'Amablemente', from 1963, in which a man discovers his wife in bed with another and kills her, stabbing her thirty-four times, is only added, then, in the published version, which includes the first line of the tango verbatim ('la encontró en el bulín y en otros brazos' ('he found her in the hideout and in other arms')). Likewise, a little further on in this section in the manuscript version, we are simply told that 'Roberto y Lily lo comentan entre ellos' (Cortázar 1982: 5: 5) [Roberto and Lily comment on the story between themselves]. This is replaced in the published version, however, by reference to how these characters 'se divierten en fabricar variantes dramáticas y eróticas' (1980: 95) ('have fun fabricating dramatic and erotic variants', 1984: 46). These changes disclose a conscious focusing on a multiplicity of versions or interpretations of the story of Gesualdo's life and an attendant emphasis on the narrative (Roberto and Lily) and musical (Rivero) act of composition and interpretation.

Furthermore, this sense of the inescapability of multiple versions and interpretations is not limited to the presentation of the story of Gesualdo himself, but extends to the nature of the version of Gesualdo's story being enacted in the text in front of us. The story's first sentence is key: 'Todo parece girar en torno a Gesualdo, si tenía derecho a hacer lo que hizo o si se vengó en su mujer de algo que hubiera debido vengar en sí mismo' (1980: 89) ('Everything seems to revolve around Gesualdo: whether he had the right to do what he did or whether he took revenge on his wife for something he should have taken revenge on himself for', 1984: 39). This, coupled with the presentation of the group as a whole as being a clone of Gesualdo, or, at least, Gesualdo as set down in music at the madrigals' ideational moment, leaves open the possibility that, rather than individual characters taking the roles of Gesualdo, his wife, and her lover, the story could be understood as playing out the alternative version of Gesualdo's story alluded to in this first sentence, where the breaking up of the group and the internal killing of one of its members by another would represent the taking out of the revenge by Gesualdo on himself. In other words, an understanding of 'Clone' as a single story containing several *different* versions is built into it by its opening salvo. Indeed, that this alternative version was at the forefront of Cortázar's mind in writing the piece is suggested by a comment made on the otherwise blank page opposite the handwritten text of the third-to-last section in the manuscript, where we read, 'La venganza es total, contra el <u>clone</u> que se deshará la noche del recital anulado por la ausencia de Franca' (1982: 5: 6) [The revenge is total, against the <u>clone</u> that will become undone on the night of the recital cancelled because of Franca's absence]: the revenge is not against Franca and Sandro as embodiments of Gesualdo's wife and her lover, but against the group as a whole.

The combination of the different textual versions of Gesualdo's act alluded to in 'Clone' and the variety of possible interpretations of the story's re-enactment of it points towards a text in which any notion of an originary version of the events, and, hence, perfect interpretation or performance of them, is lost. Indeed, this provides one possible reason for Cortázar's choice of Gesualdo and the story of the murders as the basis for his narrative, in that this is a story whose multifarious interpretations and 'performances' are both numerous and, frequently, divergent.[15] As Glenn Watkins states:

> The story [of Gesualdo and the murders] has been repeatedly told. It has been variously recounted in the chronicles, popularized, vulgarized, made the subject of endless poems, and later even fashioned into a novella. We have a myriad details, but a considerable amount of sorting out is required to get at the truth, and even then a few enigmas remain. (1991: 7)

An additional result of Cortázar's engagement with this aspect of the story of Gesualdo is that it further problematises the aims and claims of the group. Not only does it underline the axiomatic impossibility of any perfect performance, including their attempted rendering of the madrigals at their ideational moment, but it also, specifically, writes out any unmediated, 'correct' understanding of the events that provoked the feelings Gesualdo sought to transmute into those madrigals. Moreover, the specific allusion to Rivero's twentieth-century, Argentine tango, not as a musicalised version of Gesualdo's act, but, implied by Roberto's words, as anachronistically constituting a model for it, a basis for understanding it, underscores how any event or person is ineluctably perceived by an individual through association with texts (literary, musical, et al.) that pertain to his or her own location in place and time.[16]

In this reading of these two types of performance on the group's part — of Gesualdo's music and of his life — we thus go some way to making sense of the scenario that 'Clone' sets up. Rather than a paradox, where the move away from a perfect musical performance of Gesualdo's madrigals, associated by Lucho with a loss of contact with the composer's defining emotions of love and revenge (1980: 95), would, bizarrely, be brought about by the all-too-strong emergence of those same emotions amongst the group's members, as they enact the critical moments of Gesualdo's life, the reading set forth here suggests that the latter enactment is, in fact, entirely representative of such a lack of contact with any sense of Gesualdo's 'original' feelings of love and revenge. The performance within Cortázar's written text, that is, comprising the group's interpretation of the love and revenge of Gesualdo, is the (flawed) *textual* version of the group's insufficient *musical* performances of his madrigals (performances which are likewise devoid of his 'originary' emotions).

Yet the extent to which this story brings together the linguistic and the musical in its development of a web of versions and interpretations goes beyond both Gesualdo's music and the group's (re-)enactment of his life. A further level of interpretation and performance is at work here: that of Cortázar himself in the writing of this story. The story's epilogue details how the textual performance we have just read was constructed, and, importantly, also reveals the full degree to which the literary and the musical are fused in Cortázar's narrative. However, what is most significant about this third level of musicotextual performance is how it not only reinforces the questions regarding the notions of 'original' and copy, version, or interpretation that I have been addressing, but also goes beyond them, implying a far more complex and all-encompassing network of interpretation and performance in which characters/performers and authors/composers are caught.

'Clone' as Musical Performance

An in-part unpublished note, written on an otherwise blank page of the manuscript version of the story's epilogue, opposite what came to be its first published page, reads, 'Al final: las tapas de discos son una literatura en sí y siempre me han fascinado. Casi todo lo que sé sobre música y músicos viene de ahí, lo que permitirá juzgar sobre el nivel de mis conocimientos' (Cortázar 1982: 5: 6) [At the end of the day, LP sleeves are a literature in their own right and have always fascinated me. Almost everything I know about music and musicians comes from there, which speaks volumes about the level of my knowledge]. The second sentence of this note appears in an amended form in the published version (1980: 106). But the omitted first sentence is more significant, emphasising the intertwined, symbiotic relationship between music and writing (and, more particularly, *la música culta* and literature) that underlies both the description of Cortázar's literary *modus operandi* in which these lines participate and the story whose evolution it charts. In this respect it is also worth commenting on a revision Cortázar made within the story itself, where the line 'pero ahora hay mujeres que también *componen* tangos y ya no se *canta* siempre la misma cosa' (89, italics mine) ('but there are women [*composing*] tangos now and [it's not always the same thing being *sung* anymore]', 1984: 39, italics mine) appears in the manuscript version with 'escriben' (1982: 5: 5) [writing] instead of 'componen' [composing] and 'se cuenta' (1982: 5: 5) [being narrated] instead of 'se canta' [being sung], a revealing conflation of the linguistic and the musical, literature and scored music.

Underscoring this equating of scored music (in the form of *la música culta*) and literary composition, or, indeed, language more generally, 'Clone', this epilogue makes clear, is at once a linguistic and a musical interpretation and performance.

Cortázar describes how he set out to write the story following the model of Bach's *The Musical Offering*,[17] apparently as a way of avoiding the monotony of always writing 'como al dictado' (1980: 103) [as if by dictation].

Despite the imposition of such restrictions and rules on the act of literary composition, the choice of musical model may seem initially to be linked with the desire on Cortázar's part to get beyond the problem of the perfect performance of an original, in that Bach's piece both originated as improvisations on a theme provided for him by Frederick II of Prussia and continued to allow subsequent performers a certain amount of freedom in their own renderings, as Cortázar informs us that 'Bach no indicó los instrumentos que debían emplearse, salvo en el *Trío-Sonata* para flauta, violín y clave; a lo largo del tiempo incluso el orden de las partes dependió de la voluntad de los músicos encargados de presentar la obra' (103) ('Bach didn't indicate the instruments to be used with the exception of the trio sonata for flute, violin, and clavichord; ever since even the order of the parts has depended on the will of the musicians performing the work', 1984: 55). Yet what soon becomes apparent is that Cortázar has looked not to improvise, but to repeat — to perform — a very specific interpretation of the piece:[18]

> me serví de la realización de Millicent Silver para ocho instrumentos contemporáneos de Bach, que permite seguir en todos sus detalles la elaboración de cada pasaje, y que fue grabado por el London Harpsichord Ensemble en el disco Saga XID 5237.[19] (1980: 103)

> [I have made use of the arrangement for eight instruments contemporary to Bach by Millicent Silver, which allows one to follow the elaboration of each passage in all its details and was recorded by the London Harpsichord Ensemble on Saga XID 5237.] (1984: 55)

Matching the eight singers to the eight instruments of the Saga LP version, and having them appear in the story in the same combinations as in the musical performance, with the story divided into sections corresponding to each part of Bach's piece, 'Clone' thus pre-empts the narrative's focus on the reading of a score and the attempted perfect rendering of the original that that score putatively represents, an impression further enhanced by the methodical preparatory notes which accompany the manuscript version of the story and epilogue (Cortázar 1982: 5: 6). These notes comprise a two-page, detailed, schematic plotting of Bach's piece against the characters and structure of 'Clone' that goes beyond what appears in the story's published epilogue, as well as Cortázar's annotated photocopy of the LP sleeve.[20, 21]

Fittingly, however, Cortázar's rendering of this 'score' turns out to reflect the performance of Gesualdo's music and his life within the story, in that it too is flawed: the music of which it is the literary copy is made up of nineteen sections, following the banding of the Millicent Silver LP, whereas the story as originally published has only eighteen clearly delimited sections: Side One Bands 2 and 3 are separated only by a paragraph break in the story. This would seem to be due to the vagaries of copy editing, with Cortázar himself complaining about this printing error in a letter to Jaime Salinas on 23 October 1980, adding that, given how the story maps Bach's piece, without this break, 'su cuenta se le va al diablo y con ella el cuento mismo' (2012c: 306) [the maths of it goes down the toilet and with it the story itself]. Lamentable though this error may be, it nevertheless neatly underscores the impossibility of the perfect performance.[22]

Errors of editing/printing aside, the central point here is that Cortázar is engaged in a textual performance of the Saga LP — effectively the score which he is reading — which is itself the inscription of Millicent Silver's interpretation and performance of Bach's score. Moreover, it transpires that the actual 'score' that Cortázar used to plan and compose his story was not the LP played and read by a stylus, but, as intimated at the start of this analysis, a photocopy of the LP's sleeve and the notes written on it (Cortázar 1980: 104). In effect, Cortázar's 'Clone' is an interpretation and performance of a photocopy of a written interpretation of the engraved LP copy of Millicent Silver's interpretation and performance of Bach's written score of his interpretation of a musical theme given to him by Frederick II of Prussia. Beyond this, it is not so much that Frederick II is the final link in the chain, but, rather, that there is, here at least, no textual interpretation of where that theme could have found its basis.[23]

What we have, then, is a succession of 'clones': copies of a putative original that in each case turn out themselves to be clones, or versions, of a preceding artefact, either linguistic or musical. In this respect, Cortázar's choice of musical model is significant, in that Bach's Baroque piece is dominated by ricercars, canons, and fugues,[24] musical forms built around repetition and imitation, again underscoring the idea of variations on a theme which is itself the theme on which the varied texts alluded to in both story and epilogue are variations.[25] Indeed, the manuscript version of the epilogue is revealing here in signalling Cortázar's desire to emphasise an endless series of variations, as it discloses the author's suppression of an initial sense of closure in his depiction of the Bach piece: 'el maestro escribió y envió la <u>Ofrenda Musical</u> ~~al soberano con un mensaje donde lo donde se agotan las posibilidades~~ donde el tema real es tratado de ~~la~~ una manera más diversa y compleja' (1982: 5: 6) [the maestro wrote and sent the *Musical Offering* ~~to the sovereign with a message where the where the possibilities are exhausted~~ where the royal theme is handled in ~~the~~ a most diverse and complex manner]. Moreover, the web of versions, copies, interpretations, and variations does not stop with Cortázar's text: in 2007 the Argentine composer Antonio Zimmerman wrote an opera called *Clone*, based on Cortázar's story, in yet another coming together of scored music and literature, or language, in the unfolding narrative of this series of 'clones'. It was even performed in the possible, even probable, setting for the final performance-that-never-was at the end of 'Clone', the Colón Theatre in Buenos Aires.[26]

And yet Cortázar's epilogue does more than destabilise the notion of an 'original' text or performance. It serves, additionally, to ask whether we are ever able to move outside of the performance of pre-existing 'texts', no matter what our aims. In contrast to the other riddle canons of *The Musical Offering*, which, despite Cortázar's affirmation of their performance depending on the 'voluntad de los músicos' (1980: 103) ('will of the musicians', 1984: 55), do have a correct 'solution' that must be worked out by the performers, the riddle 'Canon a 2' is left more open, as Frederick Youens describes on the LP sleeve consulted by Cortázar:

> In 'enigmatic' or 'riddle' canons it was customary to furnish a clue to their solution by showing the notes of the theme on which the other parts should enter. In this canon, however, Bach provides no hints and simply inscribes the piece: 'Quaerendo invenietis' (Seek, and ye shall find!) There are four solutions, presented in the following order: *(a)* bassoon and violoncello; *(b)* viola and bassoon; *(c)* viola and violoncello; *(d)* viola and bassoon. (1964)

In Cortázar's story, these solutions correspond to (what should be) sections thirteen to sixteen. In contrast to Bach's open riddle and Silver's equal presentation of the four solutions, Cortázar's version leaves little doubt as to which of the passages contains the 'solution'. In the first section, beginning *'Cherchez la femme'* (1980: 97) [*Seek the woman*], Mario, in conversation with Roberto, insists there is nothing he can do about the relationship between Franca and Sandro, apparently accepting that this is simply how things are. The second section follows similar lines, only this time with Mario in conversation with Paola. In the third section Paola and Roberto discuss why Mario does not want to act, adding that Franca cannot be blamed; rather the fault lies with Sandro. None of these sections represents the 'solution' to the riddle of how the story will unfold. That is left to the fourth and final section. Here, Mario muses on why Gesualdo was so crude in his act of revenge, when he could have composed it along the lines of a madrigal ('madrigalizar una tortura de semanas o de meses' (Cortázar 1980: 99) ('madrigalize a torture of weeks or months', 1984: 51)), hinting, that is, that he has in mind an 'improved' repetition of Gesualdo's act, one set up as a (musical) performance. With the reference to Paola in the background — 'trabaja[ndo] y repit[iendo] un pasaje de *Poiche l'avida sete*' (1980: 99) ('working on and repeating a passage from "Poichè l'avida sete"', 1984: 51) — underlining the re-enactment being envisaged by Mario, this final 'attempt' thus provides us with the solution to the riddle and to the text we are reading.[27]

These sections, that is, appear to affirm a degree of authorial control and primacy for both Cortázar and Mario, and suggest, then, an escape from models that they seek to rewrite rather than copy: in Cortázar's case the non-committal rendition of this riddle canon by Silver and in Mario's case the apparently disappointing way in which Gesualdo carried out his revenge. And yet there is still an overriding sense of being bound by pre-existing texts and performances, even at these moments of apparent liberation. Cortázar's 'solution' to Bach's riddle serves to send his text down the path of performing a different preceding 'text' (Gesualdo's life), as well as being, in any case, bound by the requirement of marrying the text's denouement to the final section of *The Musical Offering*, where there are seven instruments, not eight. Indeed, more generally, Cortázar's presentation of the story's composition as a whole is built around a sense of fate or guidance which exceeds his conscious control ('todo estaba consumado desde antes' (1980: 105) ('everything had been consummated since before', 1984: 57)). Likewise, Mario's musings in effect merely underscore that his own eventual actions respond to an apparent need to live out his life in the manner of a madrigal (performance) and as a version, however 'new', of a pre-existing 'text' (Gesualdo's life). Moreover, the effect on the reader is similarly shackling, in forcing upon us a particular solution of what had been an open-ended riddle canon, and this sense of being guided and controlled, present for author, character, and reader, is reflected textually by the use of the future tense in (what should be) sections three and eighteen.[28]

The principal question thrown up by the epilogue, however, and exemplified by the 'Quaerendo invenietis' riddle canon, is: to what are the various performers, interpreters, and composers bound? The extra dimension added by the epilogue is not so much the fact that Cortázar's story is itself a version of a pre-existing performance or text, but that it brings an entirely new textual and performative strand to bear on our understanding of 'Clone'. In short, whereas the story itself appears based, as stated in its first line, around Gesualdo, both man and music, the epilogue reveals that it is also based around Silver's interpretation of Bach's *The Musical Offering*. Cortázar's narrative is driven in its content by the former, and in its structure by the latter. A correlate of this is that, likewise, not only do the characters perform the music and life of Gesualdo, but their conversations and interactions are also driven by the formal structure of Silver's interpretation of Bach that Cortázar is following. It is not just that we have multiple interpretations, versions, and performances of particular stories and texts, both musical and linguistic, but that at any one time the players, by which I refer to author, character, and reader, are engaged in the interpretative performance of more than one pre-existing text.

What 'Clone' is presenting, I would suggest, is a template for how we can conceive of the human condition when it is bound by the structures of expression and being that are encapsulated and perpetuated by the inherent characteristics of language and *la música culta*. Moreover, through the examples of both the characters' and Cortázar's own performative acts, Cortázar's story reveals that within such a template it is impossible to locate a single, 'central' text, amongst the multifarious texts, which overarchingly controls or commands the particular (textual, musical, performative) act in question. Indeed, rather than looking for a central text, or attempting to place the different texts being performed in some sort of hierarchical order, what is key is the simultaneous presence of the different performances, each of which interacts with and affects the other(s). This notion of performative interaction certainly provides an alternative way of understanding the loss of the apparent perfection of the group's musical performances as their performance of Gesualdo's life takes hold to the one I have suggested. What is more, such inter-performative impact could, in turn, also be argued to lie behind the imperfection of the group's performance of Gesualdo's act of revenge (and, with it, Cortázar's own narrative performance of Gesualdo's story). I have already noted that the version of Gesualdo's story presented here fails to be an accurate rendering of the composer's life (as transmitted via a plethora of different textual and cultural versions), in that only his wife (here, Franca) is killed, whilst her lover (here, Sandro) survives. As proposed above, this can be seen as an example of the failure of attaining an apparently perfect or 'originary' performance. But it can also be seen as a consequence of Cortázar's own attempt to perform perfectly Silver's interpretation of *The Musical Offering*, in that the final section of this requires, as noted above, that seven instruments (singers) be present, not six, as would be necessary were Cortázar to have killed off both Franca and Sandro.

In sum, we are left with a scenario whereby the story and its epilogue are replete with personae (both characters and authors) who are at once composers, interpreters, and performers of literary/linguistic and musical texts. Within this scenario, the notion of a desired perfect interpretation is shown to be illusory, in part due to the fact that any actual knowledge of, indeed, even the existence of, a supposed 'originary' is written out. But, more significantly, the implication is not only that the (creative and ontological) freedom of these personae is undermined by their reliance upon this process of interpretation and re-enactment in their performative choices (to perform the madrigals of Gesualdo; to write following the structure of *The Musical Offering*), but that their actions and, hence, lives, are governed on both a conscious and an unconscious level by these texts, or, to be more precise, these textual chains. Both levels are found in the performances of the group, of course, as the story in which their narrative is transmitted to us is, unbeknownst to them, a performance of *The Musical Offering*. But there is evidence to suggest this is the case for Cortázar as well in his description of the story's composition, not least in the epilogue's final lines, which read, 'Que [Gesualdo] mató a su mujer es seguro; lo demás, otros posibles acordes con mi texto, habría que preguntárselo a Mario' (1980: 106) ('That he [Gesualdo] killed his wife is certain; the rest, other possible agreements with my text, would have to be asked of Mario', 1984: 59). Aside from the playful *mise en abyme* here, underscoring the impossibility of escaping 'the text', these lines imply a recognition that part of the performative identity of Cortázar's text is not controlled or even known by Cortázar himself. Further still, it highlights yet again the impossibility of arriving at an original 'composer' or controlling figure, since the agency here assigned to Mario is itself undermined by the 'Quaerendo invenietis' riddle canon's disclosure of the character's desire to re-enact and 'madrigalise' Gesualdo's act.

Returning to the initial conceit of 'Soledad de la Música', we thus see how 'Clone' offers a vision of humanity where individuals — and groups — live through and according to linguistic and (interpreted) *música culta* structures. In playing up both his and his characters' common goal of rendering or performing a pre-existing text as 'faithfully' as possible — the *música culta modus operandi* — and in doing so by filling the story and its coda with examples of linguistic and musical (overwhelmingly *música culta*) texts and interpretations, to the extent that the common structures inherent in both are laid bare, Cortázar is thus using *música culta* interpretation and performance as a way of presenting the nature of the linguistic being of humanity from which he desires to break free. The implications of how this is worked through in 'Clone', however, exceed the relatively simple statements of the early essay. Rather than focusing on the human being as one who perceives and understands the world and other human beings by interpreting 'texts', in the form of words (or notes on a score, in the case of the musician), and who, likewise, has to express (and, thus, 'lose') him/herself using the same mechanisms, either as a writer (performer/composer) or an active reader (interpreter), 'Clone' shifts the attention onto the human being as a site where different texts play themselves out. It may appear at first sight, that is, that the story is brimming with performers and composers who are very much in control of and determining their textual, musical, and lived 'products': the group determines to produce putatively perfect, or originary, versions or performances of Gesualdo's madrigals; Mario, it is implied, resolves to play out Gesualdo's murderous acts in a more aesthetically perfect manner; Cortázar sets out textually to render Millicent Silver's version of Bach's *The Musical Offering* as accurately as possible; Silver herself, according to Youens, '[took] great pains to render [*The Musical Offering*] as authentic as possible by employing instruments in use in Bach's day, and [her version] is therefore free of anachronisms' (1964); Bach undertook the composition of a succession of variations on the royal theme given to him by Frederick II of Prussia. But in each case we see a hand forced, a composition determined, not just by a previous piece, but by a textual version of a putative original which is never attained. More than that, as I have shown, the double-performance in which both Cortázar's text and the group are engaged implies that in each case there are a variety of performances being enacted in each of these persona-sites, some known to, others hidden from, those personae.[29] In this sense, 'Clone' projects itself along a different trajectory from its possible 'sister' text 'Instrucciones para John Howell' [Instructions for John Howell] from *Todos los fuegos el fuego* (1970f [1966]). This earlier story has been read as utilising 'the concept of the world as a stage' (Peavler 1990: 42), showing how a sense of improvisational freedom is replaced by an awareness of 'anonymous controlling powers' (Standish 2001: 150) at work. Standish suggests that this might be seen as the 'especie de superestructura' (Prego 1985: 134) [kind of superstructure] to which Cortázar referred towards the end of his life. 'Clone', closer in time to the statement just cited, provides an alternative way of understanding such a superstructure in its presentation of the (linguistic) human condition as a passive site where a multiplicity of performances — of texts — are enacted. In short, echoing and building upon the discussion in *Teoría del túnel* surrounding solitude and its loss in relation to (the communicative ethic of) existentialism, 'Clone' leaves to one side the more concrete notions of political and legal power and organisations that undergird Cortázar's discussion of the superstructure in the interview with Prego, and speaks, instead, of the ineluctable renouncing of 'authentic' individuality attendant with the move not just into language, but into *música culta* composition and performance, whilst also removing any sense of ultimate authorial or identifiable control in the superstructure of being in its insistent focus on origin-less textual or performative chains.

But what of the two different approaches to *la música culta* that we have here? The approach of the group recalls the same logocentrism that underpins Western thought and language, whilst demonstrating that performance is always just a version of what has gone before, of a previous text/score. And, at first glance, it would seem as if Cortázar's own performance repeats this, being beset by the same fallacious goal of performing a pre-existing piece to perfection. But in his case it comes with a ludic awareness of the chain of versions, of performances, in which his text, as the opera *Clone* demonstrates, is taking its place. One might say that Cortázar's overall approach is a variation on that of the group of madrigal singers in his story. Or should that be the other way round?

Coda

The reading of 'Clone' that I have proposed is based on the importance of *la música culta* (as essentially a scored music), language, and performance both in 'Clone' and in the 'marker' text 'Soledad de la música'. Yet, just as within the text there is a sense of encroachment felt by both Cortázar when writing the story and the group on their tour, as the Prince of Verona's person and life impose themselves on both (sets of) 'performers', so too in constructing the above reading, what might be termed an 'orthodox' reading of the story has been hard to resist. And, as with 'Clone' itself, it is perhaps in the interaction between these two readings or interpretations that a fuller appreciation of this story is found.

Boldy lays bare the basic schema that operates in Cortázar's fiction, in particular his short stories, underscoring the sense of a divided humanity where what society deems barbaric, undesirable, 'other' is rejected and repressed, its existence within both society and the individual silenced and denied rather than encountered and redeemed.[30] The inner tensions within humanity, tensions made such by the very divisions operated by thought, language, and action, are brushed under the carpet, violently, only to return again in order to offer a chance for reconciliation between what are now construed as opposing 'sides' to humankind. The result, though, is usually the continuation of the cycle. The tensions that increasingly invade 'Clone', then, suggest the applicability of such a template to the story. Certainly there is a frequent sense of things being silenced or covered up, in each case appearing as an attempt at limiting any threat to the prevailing, dominant discourse of the self (in this instance, the clone). Thus, the failure to verbalise the apparent moment at which the group's unity began to disintegrate ('Hasta que. Porque ahora algo había cambiado desde' (Cortázar 1980: 91) ('Until. Because now something had changed ever since', 1984: 41)), aside from being a disclosure that such unity never was, also harbours an unspoken desire to erase from language and consciousness that which is seen to threaten the clone's unified façade. This sense of barely-contained threat, simmering beneath the cracking surface of the clone, is perceptible throughout much of the story, the repetitious emphasis on 'por debajo' ('underneath') underlining this point in the following passage:

> mirar de otra manera a Mario y a Sandro que discutían de música, como si por debajo [Paola] imaginara otra discusión. Pero no, de eso no hablaban, justamente de eso era seguro que no hablaban. En fin, quedaba el hecho de que la única verdadera pareja era la de Mario y Franca aunque desde luego no era de eso que estaban discutiendo Mario y Sandro. Aunque a lo mejor por debajo, siempre por debajo. (1980: 91)
>
> [looking at Mario and Sandro differently as they argued about music, as if underneath [Paola] were imagining a different argument. But no, they weren't

talking about that, it was most certain they weren't talking about that. Finally, the fact remained that the only real couple was Mario and Franca even though, of course, it wasn't that that Mario and Sandro were discussing. Although probably underneath, always underneath.] (1984: 41)

Significantly, this is an aspect of the narrative that Cortázar enhanced in the published version of the story. In the lines just cited, for example, the repeated 'por debajo' is not found in the manuscript version, and there is, in general, a heightened insistence in the published version on things being sensed and implied, rather than stated. As an example of this, in (what should be) the fourth section of the story, the manuscript version reads, 'Empiezan a darse cuenta' (1982: 5: 5) [They're starting to realise], but this appears in the published version as 'Empiezan a sospechar' (1980: 92) ('They're starting to suspect', 1984: 43). Similarly, whereas in (what should be) section nine in the manuscript version, the idea that the group's performances are becoming mechanical (and 'imperfect') is prefaced with the line, 'Pero Sandro ha comprendido lo que iba a decirle Lucho' (Cortázar 1982: 5: 5) [But Sandro has understood what Lucho was going to tell him], in the published version this becomes, 'Se siente en el aire que Sandro ha comprendido lo que Lucho iba a decirle' (1980: 95) ('You can feel in the air that Sandro has understood what Lucho was going to tell him', 1984: 46–47).

A reading of the story following Boldy's template thus implies that the clone is a textual representation of Western civilisation, the civilised self aligned with order, control, laws, and language throughout his fiction. Moreover, this self, on both a societal and an individual level, is, as we have seen, on several occasions in Cortázar's œuvre, associated with the world of *la música culta*, reaffirming the bringing together of language and *la música culta* as synonymous, inasmuch as they are complicit in and effectors of the move into a riven, inauthentic humanity. This identification of the clone opens up the aims and *modus operandi* of the group of performers to a different interpretation from the one I have been pursuing so far. In simple terms, we are called to examine to what extent we can see the group as engaging in acts and attitudes of repression, of the sort of rejection of *lo otro* [the other] found in so many of Cortázar's fictions. Again, the title of the story and self-applied descriptor 'clone' is useful in this regard. The term speaks of a shutting out of differences, of the exclusion of anything beyond or distinct from the self, and, certainly, this ties in with the dismay at the discrepancies and disagreements that creep into the group's rehearsals and performances. Particularly relevant here is the fact that Roberto hit upon the term when reading some science fiction (1980: 93). It is impossible to know what — if any — specific book Cortázar had in mind here, but we might consider two reasonably representative novels available at the time of writing: Aldous Huxley's classic *Brave New World* (2001 [1932]) and, as an example of more contemporary literature, Kate Wilhelm's *Where Late the Sweet Birds Sang* (1976).[31] Both present human cloning on a group or societal level (with the latter portraying groups of four to ten clones, similarly to the group in Cortázar's story) and in each case such cloning is associated with a loss of individuality, with those deemed to be exhibiting individualistic or nonconformist traits banished in order to maintain the non-differential *status quo*.

In line with this understanding of the group, I would argue that not only is its stance repressive in terms of the erasure of differences between its members (or lamenting their ineluctable appearance), but also in its approach to Gesualdo and his music. A clue to such a reading is found in Mikhail Bakhtin's depiction of the act of empathising:

> I empathize *actively* into an individuality and, consequently, I do not lose myself completely, nor my unique place outside it, even for a moment. It is not the object that unexpectedly takes possession of me as the passive one. It is *I* who empathize actively into the object: empathizing is *my* act, and only that constitutes its productiveness and newness. (1993: 15)

The group, then, apparently searching for the original of which it is to be the clone, by this reading in fact engages in an act of *self*-assertion.[32]

The extent to which such a reading is suggested, even foregrounded, by Cortázar's text, as well as an understanding of the reasons behind the clone's repressive nature here, is found by looking more closely at the person and music in question. Despite the claims made in the story's epilogue, it is hard to imagine that the choice of musical model is purely aleatory, not least given that Gesualdo's madrigals are notable for a series of characteristics that play heavily into the themes of Cortázar's text. For one, they are thematically very different from the Arcadian lyrics of composers such as Luca Marenzio and even Monteverdi, another composer whose works the group sings. Gesualdo, in contrast, composed madrigals dominated by images and feelings of anguish, pain, death, and sexual and amorous frustration. As Denis Arnold somewhat comically puts it:

> such constant misery as Gesualdo's is ridiculous, one is tempted to say. Does the man *never* enjoy love-making? The answer is — probably not. This music has an air of continuous desire and very little satisfaction […]. The constant mood is not so much […] of anguish as of 'dolore', a word which can mean pain but a continuous nagging pain rather than something sudden and very intense; and it also means sorrow. (1984: 33–34)

In terms of the music itself, several elements stand out, of which I shall mention two of the most significant. Firstly, Gesualdo was particularly given to repeating and giving variations of certain motifs and harmonic devices. Again, the words of Arnold are helpful here, as he underlines how, 'whereas his contemporaries tended to extend the melodic ideas by different contrapuntal devices, Gesualdo invents a harmonic complex, then repeats it with various alterations, usually to make the atmosphere more intense' (31). Secondly, there is a strong element of dissonance and counterpoint. Watkins, for example, draws attention to Gesualdo's 'use of prepared and unprepared dissonances' (1991: 179) and his 'genuine, essentially diatonic contrapuntal style' (183) and 'use of double counterpoint' (140).[33]

In sum, Gesualdo's madrigals are characterised by tension, repetition and variation, dissonance, and a sense of unsettlement. As well as further underscoring the insistent presence of variation on existing themes, this ties in with the image provided by the literary and musical texts of a man tortured by guilt and unease over his murderous actions, which took place before he turned in earnest to writing madrigals. The musical and lyrical traits outlined here are, moreover, particularly notable in Gesualdo's last two books of madrigals (V and VI), which are characterised by a disjointed instability of rhythm and harmony, and it is therefore significant that Cortázar should have chosen to make specific reference in 'Clone' to two madrigals from Book V,[34] 'Poichè l'avida sete' and 'O voi, troppo felici' (1958 [1611]: 51–53).[35] Most pertinently, these traits stand in sharp contrast to the group's goals of unified harmony, devoid of tension and dissonance, and we are thus left with the sense that the madrigals and, one supposes, Gesualdo's state of mind, themselves work against the ideas and aims of the group. Despite their stated aim of assuming the taut emotions at stake here (Cortázar 1980: 95), then, the group's repression is precisely of the tension of Gesualdo and his music. And whilst this can be seen as a result of the use of the score (text) in their attempt at reaching this centre, that is, the idea that 'the linguistic' is itself always already caught up in this repression, it is also portrayed as an integral part of the group's very approach to its task. Moreover, these characteristics of Gesualdo and his music also underscore that the idea(l) of breaking down the barriers erected by both language and *la música culta* to arrive at the emotional, human subject transmitted in these communicative milieux does not alter the fact that every human centre in question is precisely that: human, and thus riven by the tension and divisions effected internally on both an individual and a societal level by the structures of language, thought, and custom, through which we have our being. In their goal of a univocal centre, then, the group is at once repeating the exclusion of tensions found in the rejection of *lo otro* throughout Cortázar's fiction and drawing attention both to the problematic attempt at (re)gaining a sense of unified humanity without finding oneself slipping into the same repressive structures and approaches, and, relatedly, also to the fact that, at heart, every human is always already fractured and dissonant.

Having thus identified how 'Clone' depicts the group as an example of language, *la música culta*, and Western 'civilised' humanity's being responsible for and bound up in essentially repressive structures, the next step is to understand in what senses the story presents the return of the repressed in this more 'orthodox' reading I am proposing. Following the group's repression of Gesualdo as a human site of tension, perhaps the most obvious is found in the scenario of division and tension from Gesualdo's life returning — in the guise of the adulterous affair by Franca — to impose itself on the clone, and thus break the inauthentic, putatively harmonious version of Gesualdo that it has become. Franca's subsequent murder by Mario would thus constitute a repetition of the group's repression of *lo otro* [the other] in Gesualdo's life and music and the threat it poses to their façade of unity.

Attuned to the possibility of multiple interpretations and versions which emerged in my earlier reading of the text, however, it becomes clear that both the return at stake and the initial act of repression here are also more complex. In addition to the actions and attitudes of the group, Gesualdo himself is, of course, an example of the very type of repression of *lo otro* that so concerns Cortázar's texts. His murder of his wife and her lover is nothing if not an instance of the dominant discourse of the self (man, husband, nobleman) carrying out the violent repression of what it perceives as a threat. In seeing the group as a clone of Gesualdo, then, as I suggested in my earlier reading, the nature of the revenge or return of the repressed changes markedly. Now we see the revenge on the clone ('La venganza es total, contra el clone' (Cortázar 1982: 5: 6) [The revenge is total, against the clone]) as being the revenge *against* Gesualdo either on the part of the murdered-lover-as-the-repressed, hinted at by the fact that Sandro, playing the role of the lover, is the director of the group and is repeatedly blamed by the other members of the group for the increasing division within it, or on the part of (a more philosophically enlightened) Gesualdo himself, recalling the story's opening gambit ('si se vengó en su mujer de algo que hubiera debido vengar en sí mismo' (1980: 89) ('whether he took revenge on his wife for something he should have taken revenge on himself for', 1984: 39)).

In applying Boldy's conceptual template, what thus becomes clear is that, as with my earlier reading, the story refuses to be bound by a single, monolithic interpretation. Rather, there are, once more, several different performances being enacted, each of which play into and impact the others. Along similar lines, then, I would suggest that the two overarching readings offered here must likewise be brought together. When we do this, we see that 'Clone' offers an opportunity to revise our understanding of the repression-return-repression schema that operates in Cortázar's texts, and, in particular, in his short stories, in that the story makes it impossible to isolate such a schema from the notion of an ineluctable web of interpretation(s), versions, and variations on themes: let us not forget that Franca's killing, a primary element in my application of Boldy's template, is determined by the textual (and *música culta*) requirements of there being only seven players present at the end of the story. This story reveals, then, that the cycle of repression-return-repression is not simply a mechanism by which the other is rejected and then makes its presence felt again, only to be rejected once more. Rather, it symbolises the fact that being is underwritten by the repetition, both conscious and unconscious, of 'texts'; the cycles we see in his stories are thus, first and foremost, performances of pre-existing performances. 'Clone' discloses this by unveiling the different performances and texts at stake in this particular narrative, that is, by showing us what is going on *por debajo* [underneath] in his other stories. Moreover, the implication of such an understanding of Cortázar's fiction is that the breaking of the repression-return-repression cycle is not simply bound up with the need for a radically different response to the other('s return), but attendant with a more essential and less easily defined breaking free from the interpretative and performative structures through which we live and make sense of ourselves and the world, structures which are innate characteristics of both language and *la música culta*. In 'Clone', then, the avoidance of a repetition of Gesualdo's murderous act in response to the irruption of the other would not be so much a question of a different reaction to the affair between wife and lover, as a refusal to be bound by the structures of interpretation and performance. Indeed, the murder is repeated not, ultimately, because of a simple desire to maintain the group's façade of unity, but because Mario insists on re-performing the murder in a more orchestrated way, on *madrigalizarlo* [madrigalising it], and because Cortázar insisted on accurately performing Silver's interpretation of Bach's *The Musical Offering*, where seven instruments (voices) are present at the text's denouement.

There is one further conclusion that can be drawn from 'Clone'. For the story also asks to be understood as a comment on the wider act of reading, of interpretation *per se*. As this chapter has shown, alongside the multiple interpretations, both textual and musical, of different events, musical pieces, and stories, each of which can be classified as 'text', and as played out by both characters and composers/authors, we must add how 'Clone' addresses and guides the reader. We have seen how the story itself necessitates an engagement with a wide variety of texts: it cannot properly be understood without reference to Gesualdo's life, his madrigals, Bach's *The Musical Offering*, Millicent Silver's version of it, the emergence of the opera *Clone* twenty-seven years after the story's publication, narratives of clones and cloning in science fiction and beyond. Indeed, emphasising this point, a letter from Cortázar to Eva Vicens on 14 October 1979 reveals how the story fits in more widely to a network of linguistic and musical intertexts and variations:

> usted me envió la música que acababa de componer basándose en mi 'Zipper Sonnet'. En su comentario, aludía por dos veces a la *Ofrenda Musical* de Bach, ¿lo recuerda?
>
> Pues bien, hace menos de un año, yo escribí un relato [...] cuya estructura literaria intenta ajustarse a la [sic] diferentes partes de la *Ofrenda Musical*.
>
> O sea que usted ha escrito una música siguiendo un texto, y yo he escrito un texto siguiendo una música: pero en los dos casos existe la referencia directa a la gran obra de Bach, y todo eso se ha cumplido sin que usted y yo hayamos tenido el menor contacto epistolar o personal en todo ese tiempo. (2012c: 211)

> [you sent me the music you'd just composed based on my 'Zipper Sonnet'. In your commentary, you alluded twice to *The Musical Offering* by Bach, remember?
>
> Well, less than a year ago, I wrote a story [...] whose literary structure tries to map onto the different parts of *The Musical Offering*.
>
> That's to say you've written a piece of music following a text, and I've written a text following a piece of music; but in both cases there is the direct reference to Bach's great work, and all of this has happened without you or I having had any contact via correspondence or in person in all that time.]

'Clone', that is, is a story that obliges us as readers to operate within a network of literary (linguistic) and *música culta* texts, as sites where the performative and interpretative nature of the human is laid bare, just as the characters and Cortázar find themselves obliged to do. And, like them, we find ourselves engaging in a series of interpretations, each of which impacts the others, each of which sends us back to others, refusing any finalising or putatively perfect interpretation or version of how the story is to be understood, much like the end of the story's epilogue, which sends the story and its meaning back into the world of its multi-performative narrative. Put simply, what emerges from 'Clone' is the extent to which Cortázar's engagement with *la música culta* not only discloses the problematic nature of this type of music, as he had begun to set out in his essays and letters some thirty to forty years before, but also helps him evince and expose the textual and interpretative webs in which we, like the story's characters, authors, and composers, live.

Notes to Chapter 1

1. Scholars have generally been content to talk about Cortázar's engagement with 'classical music', and Cortázar's own use of this term is noted above. Nevertheless, the inclusion of the word *llamada* [so-called] in both the examples cited points to a dissatisfaction with the term 'classical music' on Cortázar's part, and this is made clear in an aside in the interview with González Bermejo where he refers to 'la música llamada clásica — expresión que detesto sin poder encontrar un equivalente' (1978: 105) [so-called classical music — an expression I detest without being able to find an equivalent]. Despite this claimed inability, Cortázar's uses the expression *la música culta* in 'Elogio del jazz', where it is the term of choice (see above). I would propose that this represents a more apposite way of referring to the music that Cortázar has in mind both in his declarations in the interviews quoted and in the early essays where he discusses the problems of music that is scored and interpreted. Indeed, looking at some of the specific types of such music that Cortázar mentions in his essays, interviews, and fiction, the extent to which the term 'classical music' is an inadequate categorisation into which to group them is apparent, especially considering the technical definition of the term as referring to music composed in the European tradition in the last half of the eighteenth and first part of the nineteenth centuries: not only does he allude frequently to composers such as Mozart, Chopin, Beethoven, he also references, for instance, Carlo Gesualdo, mediaeval music, and the avant-garde, in figures such as Boulez and Schönberg. In this spirit, unless there is a specific reason not to, this study will generally talk of *la música culta* rather than 'classical music' in addressing the ways in which Cortázar engages with these musical traditions.
2. Cortázar's general engagement with *la música culta* has received relatively little scholarly attention. Examples that look at it in broad terms rather than in specific works from his corpus include López (1998) and Peiró (2006: 87–101). However, such studies generally do not engage in theoretical discussion of the place of *la música culta* in Cortázar's wider thought and ontolinguistic concerns.
3. In contrast to Cortázar's own declaration that he would, ultimately, choose classical over jazz if he were limited in the records he could have access to on the hypothetical desert island, in this passage from *Un tal Lucas*, entitled 'Lucas, sus pianistas' [Lucas, his pianists], we are told that the eponymous individual would, were he to have to choose, opt for a piano solo by Earl Hines on the track 'I Ain't Got Nobody' (1928) over the Mozart piece (Cortázar 1979b: 208).
4. Mozart's last quintet was the String Quintet No. 6 in E♭ major (1791).
5. It is perhaps nonetheless worth hinting now at the most important factor in understanding this shifting evaluation of *la música culta*, namely the collapsing boundaries between it and jazz, as intimated when Cortázar talks in interview with Prego of how 'el cuento tiene que llegar fatalmente a su fin como llega a su fin una gran improvisación de jazz o una gran sinfonía de Mozart' (1985: 170) [the story must reach its inevitable conclusion like a great jazz improvisation or a great Mozart symphony reaches its conclusion]. This will be discussed in subsequent chapters dealing more specifically with jazz.
6. This is far from being an exhaustive list, but, as mentioned earlier, it is not my intention here to go into enumerative and descriptive detail of the multiple places where Cortázar engages with, in this case, *la música culta*. The musical elements and concerns of many of the texts referenced here will become apparent during the course of the subsequent pages and chapters of this study.
7. An earlier, and more limited, version of the main body of this chapter is found in Roberts (2013).
8. Several critics have addressed the particularities of this story. Earlier critics tended to focus on general commentary about the importance of music in the story (Standish 2001: 74–75; Barchino Pérez 2002: 494) and on plotting the story's structural and narrative devices (Puleo 1990: 43–44; Silva-Cáceres 1997: 127). Following Roberts (2013), which forms the early basis of the present chapter, several more nuanced and in-depth studies have appeared, notably Lachman (2014: 2–6), Pérez-Mukdsi (2015), and Ramos Ruiz (2015: 186–97). The latter in particular is a substantial addition to scholarship on 'Clone' and offers, most notably, an in-depth appraisal

of the structural and formal parallels between the story's narrative and Bach's *The Musical Offering*.

9. *Julio Cortázar Literary Manuscripts* (Benson Latin American Collection, The University of Texas at Austin), henceforth: Cortázar (1982), followed by relevant Box and Folder numbers. The manuscripts for 'Clone' are found in Box 5, Folders 5 and 6. My thanks to the British Academy, whose Small Research Grant funded a two-week research trip to study these manuscripts, and to the staff at the Benson for their invaluable help.

10. Dates will be provided for musical figures where this is deemed important for the purposes of contextualisation.

11. See Derrida (1982 [1972]: 3–27).

12. A similar image is used by Cortázar in the essay 'Algunos aspectos del cuento' (Cortázar 2006f: 370–86) [Some Aspects of the Short Story] to describe the relationship between the 'tema' or kernel of a story and the words that the writer finds to tell that story: 'un buen tema es como un sol, un astro en torno al cual gira un sistema planetario del que muchas veces no se tenía conciencia hasta que el cuentista, astrónomo de palabras, nos revela su existencia' (377) [a good theme/kernel is like a sun, a star around which revolves a planetary system of which on many occasions one was not aware until the storyteller, astronomer of words, reveals its existence to us]. The resonances with the terms invoked in 'Soledad de la música', setting out the connection between the Idea and its expression in words, are clear. All of these images speak of a central locus towards which words point but from which they are always held at a distance.

13. See Derrida (1997 [1967]: 101–40; 269–316) for a detailed discussion of how he understands and employs the term.

14. See, for example, Mercer (1949: 128); Watts (1799: 163, Book 2, Hymn XXXIII). Similarly, in Cortázar's story 'La isla a mediodía' [The Island at Noon] from *Todos los fuegos el fuego* (1970f [1966]), the Greek island of Xiros, itself bound up with suggestions of the Edenic, is only glimpsed by the air steward Marini as he flies overhead at midday exactly. Emphasising the importance and symbolic potency of this time, the story repeatedly denies any attempt at seeing the island at other times: on the return flight, the plane passes over the island at eight o'clock in the morning, when the sun glares on the window and 'dejaba apenas entrever la tortuga dorada' (121) ('you could scarcely see the golden turtle', 1979a: 93); Marini once took a photograph of the island but 'le salió borrosa' (1970f: 121) ('it came out blurred', 1979a: 93); and also gives thought to filming it so that he can 'repetir la imagen en el hotel, pero prefirió ahorrar el dinero de la cámara' (1970f: 122) ('repeat the image in the hotel, but he preferred to save the money on the camera', 1979a: 94).

15. In the story's epilogue, Cortázar portrays the presence of Gesualdo in 'Clone' as far more aleatory, in that the basic ideas and structures of the story were already in place before 'una conversación casual me trajo el recuerdo de Carlo Gesualdo [...]; todo se coaguló en un segundo' (1980: 104) ('a casual conversation brought back to me the recollection of Carlo Gesualdo [...]; everything fell into place immediately', 1984: 56).

16. Kathryn Lachman makes a similar point in relation to Roberto's recourse to science fiction in order to find a term ('clone') that describes the group. Aside from showing 'just how closely imbricated music and fiction are in this text', this textual detail underscores that 'music [may] determin[e] the course of the novella, but literature has already shaped the protagonists' perceptions' (2014: 3).

17. *The Musical Offering* is a collection of ricercars, canons, fugues, and a sonata that Bach wrote in 1747. These are dedicated to Frederick II of Prussia, who gave Bach the musical theme around which the pieces are based.

18. One of the notable features of Cortázar's engagement with *la música culta*, as is clear from his presentation of it in the essays and interviews cited in this chapter and the Introduction, is that, in focusing on the centrality to this kind of music of (a reading of) the score, attempting to attain a perfect (originary) performance, he greatly simplifies what is a more complex situation, certainly when we look at the historical sweep of *la música culta*. That is not to say that Cortázar is wrong to home in on the presence of the score and all that that entails, but in so doing he ignores the presence of improvisation or at least improvisational elements in this music, in

particular up until the mid-nineteenth century, as is exemplified by *The Musical Offering*, Bach being renowned as a highly skilled improviser. Robin Moore (1992) discusses this shift in the place of improvisation in Western art music in useful detail. It may be, that is, that Cortázar, in giving very little space to the improvisation in (the history of) *la música culta* and in his insistence on 'enacting' *la música culta* in a similarly rigid way in 'Clone', shows himself to be very much of the twentieth century in his approach to this music, as are the members of story's singing group. For more a more detailed account of the role of improvisation in the Baroque in particular, see Mattax Moersch (2009).

19. The disc in question is Bach (1964).
20. The detailed manner in which Cortázar sets out and tackles his (textual) performance of this version of Bach's *The Musical Offering* recalls the meticulous, mathematical, and cryptographic nature of Alban Berg's Chamber Concerto, details of which make up chapter 139 of *Rayuela* (Cortázar 2007: 712). It is worth noting that such careful construction of musical compositions, involving cryptograms and hidden numerological patterns, is also a feature of Bach's music. Geoffrey Poole, in the context of noting Berg's particular case, draws attention to this and other precursors (1991: 2). In this sense, one could say that Berg's composition is a further version of a compositional technique that can be traced back, amongst others, to Bach. For analysis of the construction of and patterns in Berg's Chamber Concerto, see Jarman (1979: 177–79); Dalen (1989: 141–45); and Lambert (1993). Berg also wrote a letter and a chart which set out the formal structure of this piece of music (see Reich (1963: 146)).
21. Cortázar's manuscript schematic reflects Bach's 'original' division of the work into thirteen sections, whereas the LP sleeve refers to each of the four movements of the 'Trio-Sonata' and the four solutions to the riddle 'Canon a 2' as separate 'Bands' in their own right. Side One of the LP ends at Band 8, that is, after the second movement of the 'Trio-Sonata', and there are nineteen Bands in all. It is also worth noting that, whilst Cortázar, in the manuscript schematic, determines three participants in the four movements of the 'Trio-Sonata' and the subsequent 'Canon perpetuus' (flute (Sandro); violin (Lucho); harpsichord (Lily)), the Millicent Silver version that he is 'performing' defines the *continuo*, or third element of these pieces, as the harpsichord *and* the violoncello, that is, Lily *and* Roberto in Cortázar's schematic (Youens 1964). In terms of both the division of the piece into nineteen discrete Bands and the presence of the violoncello (Roberto) and harpsichord (Lily) in the aforementioned Bands, Cortázar appears to have 'corrected' his initial schematic when it came to the writing of the story and, in the case of the *continuo*, in the schematic included in the epilogue too. In spite of this, Lachman (2014: 2) and Anuchka Ramos Ruiz (2015: 187; 230) refer to the story as having thirteen sections, or *escenas*, to match Bach's thirteen movements. Strictly speaking, and being guided by the section breaks in Cortázar's story, it is evident that there are — or are supposed to be — nineteen 'sections' to the story, to map more strictly the Saga LP being followed.
22. The 1981 Alfaguara edition (Cortázar 1981b) corrects this, restituting the line break Cortázar intended. However, further exemplifying the uncontrollable multiplication of (flawed) versions and copies that abound in and are signalled by the text, 'Clone' appears in *Obras completas I* (2003) with only seventeen sections, this time with line breaks missing between sections 6 and 7, and 8 and 9 (2003: 953–54).
23. Humphrey Sassoon (2003) notes the similarities between the royal theme and a theme in Fugue V of Handel's set of *Six fugues or voluntarys for organ or harpsichord*, composed in 1786, suggesting a possible 'origin' of the former.
24. The Handel piece which possibly gave rise to the royal theme is, as mentioned, also a fugue. Sassoon (2003) also posits that Bach himself used the Handel fugue as a model for his own composition.
25. See Ramos Ruiz (2015: 190–95) for a more detailed appraisal of the repetitive and imitative nature of the musical models used by Cortázar here, and how they are reflected in the text's form, structure, and narrative devices.
26. See 'Música: entrevista a Antonio Zimmerman' (2007).
27. 'Poichè l'avida sete' is from Book V of Gesualdo's madrigals (1958 [1611]: 67–69).
28. In a letter to Jaime Alazraki dated 6 July 1981, Cortázar expresses concern that the strict method

of composition of 'Clone' may have led to a situation where the story 'se resentía un poco y se volvía demasiado esquemático' (2012c: 372) [suffered a bit and became too schematic]. He further considers that Bach, likewise, 'pudo pensar que su obra se resentía del tema impuesto o pie forzado' (372) [could have thought that his work suffered from the imposed theme or obligatory line], before concluding that 'sin embargo le salió padre' (372) [however it turned out great], implying that 'Clone' has turned out similarly well. My analysis would suggest, however, that not only are such concerns arguably born out in other ways throughout the story, but that such an easy dismissal of them is refused by these textual instances.

29. As Ramos Ruiz notes (2015: 193), a further (re-)enactment of a prior text is intimated by the line '*Cherchez la femme*' (1980: 97) at the start of the story's 'Quaerendo invenietis' riddle canon section. These words appear to come from Alexandre Dumas's *Les mohicans de Paris* (1871 [1859]: 232), although the lines Ruiz cites — 'Il y a une femme dans toutes les affaires; aussitôt qu'on me fait un rapport, je dis: "Cherchez la femme!"' (Dumas 1889 [1864]: 103) [There is a woman in all affairs; as soon as someone gives me a report, I say: 'Seek the woman!'] —, which act as a general gloss on how this phrase is to be understood, actually come from the theatrical version. This slippage is important in pointing, once more, to the extent of the multiplicity of performative and textual chains at stake here, and, hence, of the ineluctability of the multiple (re-)enactment of textual/musical scripts. On the one hand, the line Cortázar quotes indicates that 'Clone' can be read as a further story where at the heart of the affair lies a woman, with the theatrical adaptation contributing to the general idea of the performance of pre-existing scripts. But, more significantly, the multiplicity of the Dumas origins of this line also reminds us that these words and the idea that they express did not originate with Dumas. The basic conceit is found as early as Juvenal's *Satire 6* (2014: vv. 242–43).

30. See Boldy (1980: 7–8; 41–44).

31. The choice of Huxley's novel as an example of a science fiction text that engages with the concept of the clone needs little explanation: it is a seminal and canonical novel of the twentieth century. Cortázar also referred to Huxley in several prose works, including *Teoría del túnel* (2006c: 116). Wilhelm's novel has been chosen due to its contemporaneity and due to the fact that it was the recipient of a number of prestigious Science Fiction novel awards, most notably the Hugo Award and the Jupiter Award (both in 1976), indicating its importance in the field and its quality.

32. The act of empathising is, for Bakhtin, not something that impacts solely on (the nature of) the (empathising) self: 'Empathizing actualizes something that did not exist either in the object of empathizing or in myself prior to the act of empathizing, and through this actualized something Being-as-event is enriched (that is, it does not remain equal to itself)' (1993: 15). Moreover, as Alastair Renfrew states, for Bakhtin, 'Any subject requires *another* subject, located in a relation of *outsideness* (*vnenakhodimost*), in order to acquire what Bakhtin calls "wholeness" or "unity"; the subject, person, individuality only becomes what he or she is — in a towering paradox — under the gaze of another' (2015: 33). Whilst terms such as 'wholeness' and 'unity' support the concern for and importance of the unity *of the group* in their act of 'feeling' Gesualdo, then, Bakhtin's thinking here could be seen as an affirmation of the importance of the 'other' subject (Gesualdo) in this process of rendering 'whole' the empathising subject (the group of singers). However, as Renfrew also points out, key in Bakhtin's theory of empathising 'is the sense of journeying to the position of the individual other and *returning* to oneself' (2015: 33). In other words, the empathising self and its wholeness have primacy in a schema, moreover, that suggests that the distancing between the group and Gesualdo conveyed by the sun/planets image is a necessary one for this act of empathising and subsequent affirmation of the group's unity.

33. Counterpoint is the bringing together of two or more melodic lines. These lines also have their own rhythmic and dynamic traits.

34. The reference to these two madrigals constitutes a late revision: the manuscript version talks of 'Aqui suspiro al cuore' instead of 'Poichè l'avida sete' and 'Ah dimmi' instead of 'O voi, troppo felici'. I have been unable to ascertain the origin of these two pieces.

35. Ramos Ruiz (2015: 194–95) outlines how the lyrics of these two madrigals reflect elements of the narrative and characterisation of 'Clone', as well as pointing out, amongst other things, that

both link the loved one to the figure of the sun or a star. In this way, these madrigals re-engage with the story's initial depiction of Gesualdo and his music as the sun around which the singers revolve. Once more, then, we see an example of musical and textual scripts being (re-)enacted, adding to the list of such intertwining performances on display in Cortázar's text.

CHAPTER 2

La música culta and/as Revolution

In the previous chapter, I used an extended commentary on the late short story 'Clone' to examine how the negative associations and alignments of *la música culta* were developed in Cortázar's work. But I also noted, largely in the form of a *caveat lector*, that Cortázar frequently talked about and presented this type of music in a far more positive light. Not only did Cortázar laud classical music, but, without looking to descend into grand theorisations, it is made abundantly clear on numerous occasions that he simply *liked* it. That said, it is not just a question of personal taste being allowed to overshadow the more negative ruminations on *la música culta* that we have been examining: too often do his texts suggest something more significant going on in his engagement with this sort of music for this to be the case. And, indeed, one should be mindful of the fact that the early essays dealing with the power and potential of music to revolutionise — to musicalise — language do refer to music *per se*. In other words, scattered through Cortázar's work we find hints and clues that point to a more favourable take on *la música culta*, not just in terms of its being, in one man's opinion, 'la mejor música que hay' (Picon Garfield 1981: 128) [the best music there is], but in terms of its potential, both as a narrative tool and in its own right, to offer an ontological and expressive advance of the sort Cortázar seeks in his writing. This chapter, then, will take up a series of short stories which both contain and constitute just such clues, and examine to what extent they can be seen to posit a very different take on *la música culta*, one which sees in this type of music a potential for revolution against, rather than reinscription within, the ontolinguistic shackles in which Cortázar considers us to be bound.

'Las ménades', 'Reunión', and 'Alguien que anda por ahí' represent three of the most sustained and explicit engagements with *la música culta* (and classical music more specifically in some cases) in Cortázar's *œuvre*.[1] The latter two are also amongst the stories by Cortázar that deal most overtly with (political) revolution, whilst 'Las ménades' similarly ends with outright revolt, though against what is less immediately obvious.[2] Revolution and *la música culta*, that is, are, superficially at least, tied together in these works. Given the presentation of *la música culta* in 'Clone', we might well ask why Cortázar would appeal to this sort of music for revolutionary ends, whilst also wondering, with the problematics of *la música culta* in mind, to what extent the success or failure of these stories of and as revolution is reflective of the success or failure of the way in which this music is being harnessed by them. I will attempt to tackle both of these questions in the course of the following discussion, taking these three stories as a chronological trajectory of the revolution/*música culta* thematic in Cortázar's work.

Before doing so, however, we should first briefly reflect back on 'Clone'. It is often the case in Cortázar's work that the meaning, understanding, and evaluation of people, events, and 'things' shift, depending on the perspective — or faith — with which they are viewed by a character or the reader: Robert in 'Anillo de Moebius' is either a monstrous rapist or the lifelong victim of societal repression and rejection; the eponymous island of 'La isla a mediodía' is either a locus of the other to civilisation's timetables and pigeon-holes, or the space where self and other can finally come together; and music, as we have seen, is either that which can liberate language, or that whose essence is fatally undermined by linguistic operations. Likewise in 'Clone' we can surely see the multiplying presence of versions of the same musical and textual pieces not just as a relentless copying or (flawed) performance, as I have argued; there is also scope for, alternatively, seeing it as 'affirmative' variations on themes, that is, where the focus would be on the constant differences and (hence) trajectories of freedom from pre-existing scripts, even if, finally, the story's focus on performance and interpretation determines the predominance of a less affirmative reading. With this in mind, we can assert that even in those places of Cortázar's narrative world where a particular view, in this case of *la música culta*, is forcefully foregrounded, the presence of a counter-view lies, at the very least, latent, in the interstices of the story being told: we are back, that is, at the constant hesitation and *vaivén* [back-and-forth] between apparently opposing viewpoints that I signalled in the Introduction. In short, Cortázar simply never allows us to settle into facile identification and understanding, and nowhere is that more apparent than in his engagement with different musical types, in this instance *la música culta*.

'Las ménades'

In many ways, it is this last consideration that makes 'Las ménades' such an appropriate place to start an examination of the connection between *la música culta* and revolution in Cortázar's work. Primarily, this early short story serves as a marker of the characteristics and traits of *la música culta* against which 'Reunión' and 'Alguien que anda por ahí' subsequently work, apparently paradoxically using the same type of music to do so. But we might also see 'Las ménades' as conveying suggestions that *la música culta* in fact operates in such a way as to evoke precisely the revolutionary forces and drives to which the story as a whole shows it to be antagonistic. I will consider both approaches in the course of my analysis, albeit emphasising the way in which the story fundamentally entrenches the alignment of *la música culta* with language, order, and civilisation.

'Las ménades' is a story that has received repeated critical attention, not least for its engagement with myth, as indicated by its title, a reference to the Maenads, the female followers of Dionysus in Greek mythology (the Bacchae in Roman mythology).[3] The mythic aspects of the story are indeed crucial to an understanding of it, but my purpose here will be to foreground the role of the mythic narratives and characters in contributing to the story's portrayal of *la música culta*.

The basic plot of the story is as follows: the narrator, who considers himself to be of discerning taste when it comes to classical music, is attending a concert at the Corona theatre, located, one infers, in a provincial town in Argentina. The concert is in recognition of twenty-five years of service on the part of the conductor — *el Maestro* — , who will be conducting several orchestral works. The crowd, which adulates *el Maestro*, enthuses wildly about the concert from the start, despite both the choice of music and the performance itself being, in the narrator's opinion, on the whole fairly workaday. As the concert progresses, so the fervour of the crowd grows ever greater, before, led by a woman in red, an increasingly large number start to approach the stage. This leads in turn to a scene of utter chaos where the crowd grapple and wrestle with *el Maestro* and the musicians, ripping their clothes, making off with and smashing their instruments, and, finally, it is suggested, killing several, including *el Maestro* who ends up, we infer, being eaten in a cannibalistic orgy by a group headed by the woman in red. Throughout the scene the narrator observes without participating and at the end the crowd disperses, confused.

At the heart of the story, I would argue, lies the setting up of a world of classical music (broadly understood). This world, in line with what I have been exploring thus far, is characterised by its relationship with and links to language (writing) and also by the establishment of binary terms which ensure order and apparently clear delimitations. In the course of the story, this world and these binary terms are then collapsed as the limits and rules of the *música culta* world, the world of civilised normality, break down. Both of these central aspects of the story require some analysis in order to understand what is at stake here.

In centring on a classical music concert, the text is already foregrounding the notion of sides: the concert scenario is one traditionally predicated on the division of the people present into the performers, who assume an active role in proceedings, and the audience, who receive the music passively. This division into apparently opposite sides will form the basis upon which the entire story rests, and it is one which pertains particularly to the *música culta* world, the division being literally built into the scene of its production in the separation between stage and stalls. Indeed, hinting at the delimitation and categorisation of one's place within this world, the story's opening lines refer to how 'Don Pérez me condujo a mi platea' (1970a: 53) [Don Pérez led me to my stalls], indicating not just the following of specific instructions as to where one is to be, but drawing attention to the named areas within the concert hall.[4] This focus on spatial order and structure is then continued with the details of the precise location of the narrator's seat: 'Fila nueve, ligeramente hacia la derecha' (53) [Row nine, slightly to the right]. Such a focus on ordering, numbering, and structure is typical of Cortázar's presentation of the Western civilised world (one thinks of the strict, if somewhat unrealistically well-observed, timetables of Marini's aeroplane trips in 'La isla a mediodía' or the reference in 'Las armas secretas' to the characters as being 'salvados por la costumbre, por los gestos mecánicos. Todo alisado, planchado, guardado, numerado' (Cortázar 1970d: 193) ('saved by force of habit, [...] by the automatic gesture. Everything smooth, ironed out, numbered and filed away', 2013: 255)), and we can thus appreciate how the beginning of 'Las ménades' inscribes the world and setting of *música culta* performance into that reality. Reinforcing this further, the entire text is initiated by and bound to the notion of writing, of language, that is, the principal, underlying marker of the world and being that Cortázar tackles in so much of his work, as the narrator begins by describing himself as being handed 'un programa impreso en papel crema' (1970a: 53) [a programme printed on cream paper]. This reference also reiterates the idea of a script to be followed, a writing to be read, which we have seen to be so important in Cortázar's writing on *la música culta*: the score read by the musicians is here supplemented by the programme read by the audience and adhered to by the orchestra. Indeed, the more closely one examines the detail of the story, the more aware one becomes of the prevalence of such scripts and writing *per se*: the idea of the score is referred to as the narrator describes 'los melómanos provistos de partituras' (59) [the music lovers armed with scores]; there is an article on the back of the programme about the anniversaries being celebrated through the concert, written by a Dr Palacín; and, adding a further layer of writing to the creation of the script to be followed at the concert, the pieces that appear on the programme were all chosen by request, in the form of letters, by the public (55).

If these layers of writing suggest a decidedly predetermined concert that is about to unfurl before us, with little room for unexpected or chance occurrences, then such a suggestion is bolstered by a number of further elements of the story. First, we might note that the role of *el Maestro* in educating the public with respect to their classical music tastes produces a situation whereby he 'no sólo ha formado una orquesta sino un público' (55) [has trained not only an orchestra, but also a public], and, hence, that 'también nosotros somos un poco sus músicos' (55) [we are also a little bit his musicians]. Both sides of the *música culta* scenario, that is, are predetermined in that each acts in accordance with the training and instruction that they have received, and the apparently open choice of music given to the public in terms of their requests for the concert suddenly appears somewhat more circumscribed, or, indeed, even prescribed. In addition to this, we need to consider the narrator's musings on what might be the particular design behind the order of the pieces to be played. Initially, the narrator tells us that *el Maestro* determined the order of the programme, with an 'insolente arbitrariedad estética que encubría un profundo olfato psicológico' (53) [insolent aesthetic arbitrariness which masked a profound psychological instinct]. At once his words thus imply both a deliberate ordering and a chance or arbitrary structure to the programme. The former option is preferred, it would seem, given that the narrator goes on to describe both *el Maestro*'s track record in designing his concerts and what he perceives to be the plan behind the running order of this particular concert:

> Con Mendelssohn se pondrían cómodos, despúes el *Don Juan* generoso y redondo, con tonaditas silbables. Debussy los haría sentirse artistas, porque no cualquiera entiende su música. Y luego el plato fuerte, el gran masaje vibratorio beethoveniano, así llama el destino a la puerta, la V de victoria, el sordo genial, y después volando a casa que mañana hay un trabajo loco en la oficina.[5] (54)
>
> [The Mendelssohn would get them feeling comfortable, then the generous and rounded *Don Juan*, with its whistleable tunes. Debussy would make them feel like artists, because not just anyone can understand his music. Then the main

course, the great Beethoven vibrating massage, destiny calling at the door, the V of victory, the deaf genius, and afterwards flying home because tomorrow there's an insane amount of work to do in the office.]

However, this prediction does not match up with how events transpire, an indication, perhaps, either that there was no such plan on the part of el Maestro (it is worth noting that the aforementioned design exists only in the imagination of the narrator, projected onto el Maestro), or that el Maestro is ultimately unable properly to understand his public's psychology, despite what the narrator affirms. But there is also an alternative way of understanding this breach between apparent design and the way in which the concert unfurls. Roberto Yahni describes how the Argentine author's predilection for the concert scenario in a number of his stories and other writings 'parece reflejar la preferencia de Cortázar por el enfrentamiento y confrontación de dos realidades' (1969: 56) [seems to reflect Cortázar's preference for the encounter and confrontation of two realities]. The bringing together of two sides (of the binary), namely the musicians who perform and the audience who observes and listens, active and passive respectively, that is, acts as a way of provoking a confrontation between them. This is, structurally, similar to what we see throughout Cortázar's work, where his fiction repeatedly sets up such a coming together of two apparently opposing entities, in a variety of forms. The tension that results from such a coming together leads, Yahni argues, to the appearance of 'los "intersticios de la realidad"' (1969: 56) [the 'interstices of reality'], as the insufficiency of the processes of division, repression, and categorisation of modern humankind is laid bare.

This element of confrontation in the basic concert structure is central to an understanding of why the concert in 'Las ménades' proceeds as it does. However, there is more going on here. It is not just the basic concert scenario with which we are being presented in 'Las ménades', but, as we have seen, a more thorough, and foregrounded, insistent and repeated attempt at scripting and determining the concert event, underlining in each instance how all that contributes to the staging of this concert, a metonymic cipher for *música culta* processes and performance *per se*, works (often literally) to write out the aleatory, the shocking, the ludic, the individual, and the improvisational. Much like the societal rejection of Robert in 'Anillo de Moebius' or the silencing of Michèle's rape and the murder of Pierre in 'Las armas secretas', so might we understand the irruption of the other in 'Las ménades' to be caused by, and be proportionate to, the force with which that other (in all the forms set out above) is repressed by the civilised self, here in the guise of *la música culta*. In short, it is the very order, rules, and (desired) determinism of *la música culta*, as found in the concert scene and preparations in 'Las ménades' that leads to the possibility of an encounter with that which it putatively seeks to silence. Indeed, such a suggestion — that the emergence of this other is embedded within the structures and processes of *música culta* performance — is found in the story's opening paragraph. Here, we are told that 'el teatro Corona [...] tiene caprichos de mujer histérica' (Cortázar 1970a: 53) [the Corona Theatre [...] has the cravings/ impulses of an hysterical woman], implying that the violent and bewildering scene that is about to unfold is contained within the very concert hall setting. Moreover, the narrator goes on to describe how, around row thirteen, 'hay una especie de pozo de aire donde no entra la música' (53) [there is a sort of well of air into which the music doesn't enter], a reference that recalls Johnny's speech in 'El perseguidor' in which he describes the world around him as 'todo lleno de agujeros' (Cortázar 1970d: 141) [all full of holes].[6] Both examples evince the idea of gaps, of interstices in the fabric of reality that the world of order, language, and civilisation, and, in this case, the world of *la música culta* unwittingly reveal, even as they try to cover them up.

As the story progresses, then, the other bursts forth through these lacunae, with the audience's fervour growing until it spills out into the chaos and cannibalism led by the woman in red. I shall look in more detail at various elements of this scene shortly. But first it is important to note the uncertainty of exactly to what the crowd's overflowing enthusiasm is a reaction. Antonio Planells sees the exaggerated reaction as being a result of the music's injecting into the audience a 'dosis de euforia' (1975: 32) [dose of euphoria]. Likewise, David García Pérez considers that 'la música clásica es el medio por el cual se inocula la locura' (2015: 276) [the classical music is the means by which the madness is injected]. Cortázar himself, in a letter to Planells published at the end of the latter's article, describes the origins of the story as being his own experiences of crowd fervour in concerts in Buenos Aires, talking of 'una extraña sensación de amenaza que me parecía advertir en el histérico entusiasmo del público' (1975: 37) [a strange feeling of menace that I seemed to notice in the hysterical enthusiasm of the audience], although he does not assign this hysterical enthusiasm to the music itself, at least not in such simplistic or clear terms, as he suggests that the response of the watching public had to do, more generally, with the event or performance in the broadest sense, rather than specifically the music itself (either as an essential piece existing beyond and prior to its unfurling in time, or as a purely musical rendering).

Turning to the story itself we see an even less certain depiction of the cause of the audience's reaction. The narrator, who states early on in proceedings that 'no me explicaba del todo un entusiasmo semejante' (Cortázar 1970a: 57) [I could not fully understand such enthusiasm], outlines a number of possible explanations:

> [todo] me hac[ía] pensar en las influencias atmosféricas, la humedad o las manchas solares, cosas que suelen afectar los comportamientos humanos. Me acuerdo de que en ese momento pensé si algún gracioso no estaría repitiendo el memorable experimento del doctor Ox para incandescer al público. (57–58)
>
> [[it all] made me think of atmospheric influences, humidity or sunspots, things that usually affect human behaviour. I recall that at that moment I wondered if some card was repeating Dr Ox's memorable experiment to enrage the public.]

The idea of the insufficiency of rational, scientific, and, crucially, literary explanations is thus woven into the story at an early stage.[7] And this sense of a reaction and an event that refuse to be easily understood continues as the story progresses: shortly after this, as the narrator himself begins, to an extent, to get sucked in, the cause seems to be the music itself, specifically that of Debussy's *La mer*, as he comments, 'Yo mismo me dejé atrapar por el último movimiento, con sus fragores y sus inmensos vaivenes sonoros' (60) [Even I let myself get caught up by the final movement, with its roars and immense sonorous swings];[8] yet a little further on, the identification of the music as the origins of the increasingly violent fervour is far less clear:

> ahora [...] que no se aplaudía *Don Juan* ni *La Mer* (o, mejor, sus efectos), sino solamente al *Maestro* y al sentimiento colectivo que envolvía la sala, la fuerza de la ovación empezaba a alimentarse a sí misma, crecía por momentos y se tornaba casi insoportable. (60)
>
> [now [...] that neither *Don Juan* nor *La Mer* (or, rather, their effects) were being applauded, but only *el Maestro* and the collective feeling that was enveloping the concert hall, the strength of the ovation was beginning to feed itself, growing by the minute and becoming almost unbearable.]

In short, the reaction is, initially, to the effects of the music, rather than the music itself, a statement that also leaves the interpretative door wide open as to what is meant by 'sus efectos' [its effects], and then to *el Maestro* and to the collective reaction itself. In becoming self-perpetuating, in addition to the initial focus on the *effects* of the music being applauded, the simple divide between external stimulus and internal response is thus rendered more than a little problematic. That is to say, not only should we be wary of looking to locate any definitive source of or explanation for the reaction, but, relatedly, we should also be alert to a (con)fusion of cause and effect, outside and inside that develops in the course of the story as it describes the public's response, encapsulated in the reference to the 'sentimiento colectivo que *envolvía la sala*' (60, italics mine) [collective feeling that *was enveloping the concert hall*].

In fact, this breaking down of binaries and boundaries is one of the principal characteristics of the scene that plays out before us, as the result of the exaggerated reaction on the part of the public becomes apparent. Echoing the lines discussed above, for example, the narrator at one points describes 'una sala donde el aire daba la impresión de estar incendiado pero con un incendio que fuera invisible y frío, que quemara de dentro afuera' (62) [a concert hall where the air gave the impression of being ablaze but with a blaze that was invisible and cold, that burned from the inside out], again questioning (and reversing) the relationship between the internal and the external, as well as underscoring the disavowal (or insufficiency) of a rational logic based on discrete divisions, here into concepts such as 'hot' and 'cold'. In broader terms, meanwhile, we find that the divides and roles set up by the classical concert scenario and the sense of planning, order, and decorum conveyed by the repeated and insistent references to the scripting of every aspect of the performance are done away with in the ensuing chaos. The indications of this undermining of the civilised *música culta* world are found early on. After the interval, the musicians are described as returning to their places 'desganadamente' (59) [without much enthusiasm], whereas the public is enthusiastic and already in their seats, hinting at a reversal of roles, as the active performers appear far more passive, in attitude at least, than the putatively passive audience. This reversal is, of course, developed significantly in the pages that follow, as the audience, led by the woman in red, assumes the role of protagonist, acting violently upon the passive (in the sense of being helpless) performers. Furthermore, as Planells amongst others has noted (1975: 35), the reversal at stake here is not merely on the level of the respective roles of musicians and listening public, but also in regard to gender. Thus, the audience fulfils the part of the 'la enorme hembra de la sala entregada' (Cortázar 1970a: 64) [the enormous female that is the submissive concert hall], aligned with the passivity that they are supposed to display, whilst, in contrast, the orchestra, led by *el Maestro*, assumes the role of and acts as a cipher for the masculine and all that is attendant with that in broader theoretical terms (language, the law, society, etc.), with the text describing it as 'el cuerpo masculino de la orquesta' (64) [the masculine body that is the orchestra]. In this way, the image of *el Maestro*, who, at the end of Beethoven's Fifth Symphony, 'igual a un matador que envaina su estoque en el toro, metía la batuta en el último muro de sonido y se doblaba hacia adelante' (64) [just like a matador who drives his sword into the bull, plunged his baton into the final wall of sound and bowed forwards], comes to have a distinctly sexual (phallic) resonance. And yet this image also contributes to the collapsing of the neat separation and sexual roleplaying of the two 'sides' here, ending, as it does, with reference to how the exhausted bending over of *el Maestro* is 'como si el aire vibrante lo hubiese corneado con el impulso final' (64) [as if the vibrating air had gored him with the final thrust]. There are a number of ways of reading these lines. On the one hand, they suggest a certain homoeroticism, one supported by the 'reverse' image of the baton being thrust into the wall of sound, in that, as we have seen, *la música culta* (which constitutes that sonorous wall) is inherently tied in with the male self of society, language, and law in Cortázar's work. But it also pre-empts the actions of the audience at this point, thus structurally associating the wall of sound and vibrating air (which amount to synonyms, albeit (and perhaps significantly so) through contrasting images of solidity and movement) with the 'female element' of the scene. Already, that is, confusion of identification and roles is becoming apparent, and the passage as a whole is notable for the way in which Cortázar details the female audience as it takes on the putatively masculine role, throwing off the shackles of both gender and *música culta* concert expectations, 'como si en ese jadeo de amor [...] la hembra de la sala entregada [...] no hubiera querido esperar el goce viril y se abandonara a su placer entre retorcimientos quejumbrosos y gritos de insoportable voluptuosidad' (64) [as if in that amorous gasping [...] the enormous female that is the submissive concert hall [...] had not wanted to wait for the male's climax and had abandoned herself to her own pleasure with twisting moans and shrieks of unbearable voluptuousness], before mounting the stage and attacking *el Maestro* and the musicians, as the penetrative move is now very definitely undertaken on the part of the 'female' public.

Such a reversal of roles in itself would scarcely represent an advance in terms of a collapsing of the divisions and binary divides that *música culta* performance, like language and society, sets up, of course. It is significant, then, that the focus of the description is, rather, the overriding sense of (con)fusion, such as when the narrator talks of 'los aplausos y los gritos confundiéndose en una materia insoportablemente grosera y rezumante pero llena a la vez de una cierta grandeza' (64) [the applause and the shrieks confused in a single, unbearably crude, oozing substance, though one full at the same time of a certain grandness], the reference to such a mass as 'rezumante' [oozing] being particularly important here in underlining the refusal of clear boundaries: the totality described is one which exceeds and resists any capture or definition. Moreover, as thought and logic prove increasingly incapable of grasping the scene before him ('y llegué a pensar (entre tantas otras sensaciones, trozos de pensamientos, ráfagas instantáneas de todo lo que me rodeaba en ese infierno del entusiasmo)' (65) [and I managed to think (amongst so many other sensations, snippets of thoughts, instantaneous bursts of all that surrounded me in that hell of enthusiasm]), so does the narrator return on several occasions to a description of the scene that emphasises the resistance of its elements to discrete identification and an attendant indistinguishability of apparent extremes:

> una enorme confusión de instrumentos, bajo la luz cegadora de las lámparas de escena. [...] [S]ubían hombres y mujeres de la platea, al punto que ya no podía saber quiénes eran músicos o no. (65–66)
>
> [an enormous confusion of instruments, under the blinding light of the stage lights. [...] [M]en and women were climbing up from the stalls, to the point that I could no longer tell who were musicians and who weren't.]
>
> un estrépito tan monstruoso que ya empezaba a asemejarse al silencio. (67)
>
> [a racket so monstrous that it was already starting to resemble silence.]
>
> la confusión parecía mayor, las luces bajaron bruscamente y se redujeron a una lumbre rojiza que apenas permitía ver las caras, mientras los cuerpos se convertían en sombras epilépticas, en un amontonamiento de volúmenes informes tratando de rechazarse o confundirse unos con otros. (68)
>
> [the confusion seemed greater, the lights went abruptly down, reduced to a reddish glow that was scarcely enough to see their faces, whilst their bodies became epileptic shadows, in a heap of shapeless masses trying to push each other away or confuse themselves with each other.]

Of course, in this respect the culmination of the scene, as the woman in red and her followers ingest *el Maestro* and his musicians, not only serves to underline the reversal of active male/passive female roles, but acts as a stark metaphor for the breaking of barriers and the fusion of what those barriers delineated, suggesting what both García Pérez (2015: 277) and Adrián Huici (2009: 290) refer to as the porous nature of the boundaries that are established in the story.

As stated above, much has been made of the mythic models on which the story appears to be based, and this element of 'Las ménades' plays into the reading I have been outlining. As well as pointing out the principal relevance and characteristic of the Maenads as the female followers of Dionysus, a number of critics have also highlighted their role in the myth of Orpheus as the ones who tear the god-poet to pieces. Patricio Goyalde Palacios (2001), for example, in one of the more perceptive articles on the story, sees the text as enacting a confrontation between the Dionysiac and the Apolline, much along the lines that I have been developing.⁹ Drawing attention to how the ecstatic, trance-like possession of the crowd, led by the woman in red, and the cannibalistic denouement closely align with the nature of the Maenads in Greek myth, not least in relation to their engagement in bloody sacrifice and the eating of raw meat, Goyalde Palacios focuses on the importance of both the Dionysiac rites in which the Maenads engage and the way in which *el Maestro* can be read as playing the role of Orpheus.¹⁰ Specifically, in being both a representative of *la música culta* and 'un elemento civilizador' (38) [a civilising element], *el Maestro*, Goyalde Palacios argues, is to be identified with the god-poet, 'considerado por las diferentes fuentes clásicas como un pionero de la civilización, pues además de introducir la música enseñó a los hombres la agricultura, la medicina, las virtudes de las plantas, la escritura, la filosofía' (38) [considered by different classical sources as a pioneer of civilisation, since in addition to introducing music he taught agriculture, medicine, the properties of plants, writing, and philosophy to men].¹¹ Likewise, emphasising the opposition of Orpheus to Dionysiac forces and drives, he also reminds us that the reason the Maenads ripped Orpheus to death is, according to some sources, 'por haber abandonado el culto de Dionisos en favor del de Apolo' (38) [because he abandoned the cult of Dionysus in favour of that of Apollo]. What stands out from this engagement with Orpheus, as explored by Goyalde Palacios, however, is how the apparently clear-cut divisions between the Apolline and the Dionysiac are undermined, and not solely in the turning of the crowd from a model of respectability and civilisation to a maenadic throng. He refers, tellingly, to how 'los personajes se definen por la oscilación entre ambos' (2001: 40) [the characters are defined by their oscillation between both], and suggests that, in bringing about the chaos and cannibalism through his music (a reading that, as I have made clear, I consider to be problematic), *el Maestro*, rather than being the civilising force, is in fact the one who 'incita y conduce a la consumación del ritual [dionisíaco]' (38) [incites and leads to the consummation of the [Dionysiac] ritual]. Along similar lines, Magdalena Aliau (1997: 24) and Teresa López (1998) both interpret *el Maestro* as being identifiable with Dionysus himself, leading his followers into frenzy.

Whilst these readings have the benefit of underlining the difficulty of making any hard and fast delimitations of the Apolline, or civilised, and the Dionysiac, or 'barbaric', they are less than fully convincing given the details of the story itself. In fact, whilst the myth of Orpheus is certainly present here, arguably the most important mythic allusion in the text is to Dionysus and Pentheus, as found in Euripides' *Bacchae* (2016). Both García Pérez (2015) and Alejandro Cantarero de Salazar (2014: 297–98) draw attention to the importance of this text to 'Las ménades', and there are numerous references in and aspects of 'Las ménades' that underscore the pertinence of this myth to the story, not least the presence of the blind man who brings to mind the blind seer Teiresias.¹² In addition, *el Maestro*, whilst marked as an Orphic figure, not least in his relationship with music and his ability to move people, animals, and nature (aided by the frequent descriptions of the crowd in bestial terms),¹³ can also be seen as a regal figure, a reading supported both by the name of 'his' theatre (Corona [Crown]) and by the fact that the eulogy written for him on the programme is by a Dr Palacín, a surname whose meaning is 'courtesan'. We might also recall that the event being celebrated and of which Dr Palacín speaks is the silver anniversary of *el Maestro*'s arrival, an event redolent of a Jubilee celebration.

The key figure here, however, is the blind man. In Euripides' play, Teiresias warns Pentheus, a cipher, as king, for civilisation, the law, and order, not to reject Dionysus (2016: 14–15). But a simple alignment of the seer with the Dionysiac would be precipitous: the defence he makes of Dionysus is rational and traditionalist, as well as being erroneous in its argumentation and its claims regarding the divinity,[14] and his reasons for throwing his lot in with this god figure are very much calculated and utilitarian.[15] If this all suggests an alignment with the Apolline rather than Dionysiac, then that accords with his identification both in Euripides' play (2016: 15) and elsewhere as a servant or prophet of Apollo.[16] Looking further into his appearances in Greek literature, it is hard not to be drawn to the fact that Teiresias lived as both a man and a woman,[17] implying gender reversal yet also collapsing the discreteness of these genders and acting as a pre-emptive reflection of 'Las ménades' and its foregrounding of the (con)fusion of apparent binary opposites. In short, rather than seeking neatly to define the blind man as a representative of the same 'side' as the narrator, *el Maestro*, and the musicians, or as a cipher for a certain blindness in society to the Dionysiac, as Standish suggests (2001: 71), we are called to see this character in 'Las ménades' as a central figure precisely because of the impossibility of determining who he is or what he signifies, at least in terms of the either/or schema of civilisation/barbarism, Apollo/Dionysus, and even male/female. His centrality in this regard is also a pivotal part of how we understand both the narrator and the ending of the story, as I shall argue shortly.

So far, then, we have seen how 'Las ménades' tells of the breaking down of the binaries, order, civilisation, and predictability that both the general *música culta* scenario and the specific 'scripting' of this concert in particular seek to impose and upon which they insist. But perhaps the most telling aspect of the story in this respect is the way in which the narrator continually acts to reimpose these elements. Throughout the text the narrator is identified with a number of aspects of civilised humanity that appear repeatedly in Cortázar's work. He is an observer of the scene in front of him, passing judgement on the people who attend the concerts, with what he himself tells us is his 'condescendencia habitual' (Cortázar 1970a: 55) [usual condescension], and in this regard prefigures the observational role of Bruno in 'El perseguidor' and the aloof and scientific approach of Dr Hardoy in 'Las puertas del cielo'.[18] Indeed, such a link is implied in the animalesque descriptions of the observed in each case: Hardoy, in denying such a state of affairs with his affirmation that the underclass couple whom he studies, Mauro and Celina, 'no habían sido mis cobayos, no' (Cortázar 1993a: 110) ('had not been my guinea pigs, no', 2013: 100), unwittingly reveals that this is exactly what they are to him; Bruno refers in a racially-charged manner to Johnny as, for example, a monkey and a 'chimpancé' (Cortázar 1970d: 110) [chimpanzee] on several occasions; whilst the repeated references to the throng as 'gallinitas cacareantes' (Cortázar 1970a: 56) [clucking little hens], 'como moscas en un tarro de dulce' (59) [like flies around a jam jar] and the like in 'Las ménades' support the narrator's own summary of how he 'mir[a] a esa gente desde fuera, a lo entomólogo' (58) [look[s] at those people from outside, like an entomologist]. Already, then, the principle of the binary divide between the observer and the observed is written into the narrator's character and *modus operandi*. And it is thus significant, as well as unsurprising, that he is a figure who is associated with *la música culta*. That is, whilst he may be far from a purist ('a veces me ocurre confundir Brahms con Brückner' (57) [at times I confuse Brahms with Brückner]), the manner in which he discusses both the programme and *el Maestro*'s attempts at bringing 'buena música a esta ciudad sin arte' (54) [good music to this artless city], together with his pride in what he considers his good taste in classical music, all suggests a man whom, as I have alluded to above, we can read as being synonymous with the classical music world, not least in that he sides with 'los músicos y el Maestro [que] parecían los únicos dignos. Y además el ciego [...] sin la menor bajeza' (61) [the musicians and *el Maestro* [who] seemed the only dignified ones. And also the blind man [...] nothing vile about him], despite 'inexcusablemente' (61) [inexcusably] forming part of the crowd.

As the story progresses, what stands out is the way in which the narrator, despite coming close to being carried away by the fervour of the crowd, nevertheless maintains a distance from the scene unfolding before him: his sense of decorum, so strongly tied in with the *música culta* concert scenario, consistently manages to impose itself on the emotions and desires he feels. Thus, for example, as things start to turn violent and impassioned, he states that 'yo hubiera querido ayudar, pero menudo lío es meterse en las cosas de la fila de adelante, en pleno concierto y con gentes desconocidas' (63) [I would have wanted to help, but it's such a mess to get involved with things in the row in front of you, in the middle of a concert and with people you don't know]. And as the forces grow and the crowd advances on the stage, he remains 'incapaz de moverme en mi butaca' (64) [in my seat incapable of moving]. There are, that said, several occasions where the narrator appears tempted to join in, and even a momentary sense that he has done so. Two of the most significant occur towards the end of the scene, the first of these being when, noticing that the blind man had stood up and was swirling his arms around 'como aspas, clamando, reclamando, pidiendo algo' (66) [like the blades of a fan, demanding, clamouring, asking for something], he says that 'fue demasiado, entonces ya no pude seguir asistiendo, me sentí partícipe mezclado en ese desbordar del entusiasmo y corrí a mi vez hacia el escenario y salté por un costado' (66) [it was too much [and] I couldn't keep just observing, I felt that I was a participant mixed up in that overflowing enthusiasm and I ran in turn towards the stage and jumped up via one of the sides]. A little further on, seeing a clarinettist running towards him, he tells us that 'estuve tentado de agarrarlo al pasar o hacerle una zancadilla para que el público pudiera atraparlo. No me decidí' (67) [I was tempted to grab him when he went past or trip him up so that the audience could catch him: I couldn't make up my mind]. Yet, crucially, and despite the impression initially given in the first of these examples, he does not properly participate. In both instances he ultimately ends up remaining an observer, emphasising his role as such and as someone still governed by logical thought:

> Es muy curioso pero yo no tenía ningún deseo de contribuir a esas demostraciones, solamente estar al lado y ver lo que ocurría, sobrepasado por ese homenaje inaudito. Me quedaba suficiente lucidez como para preguntarme por qué los músicos no escapaban a toda carrera por entre bambalinas, y en seguida vi que no era posible porque legiones de oyentes habían bloqueado las dos alas del escenario. (66–67)
>
> [It's funny but I didn't have the least desire to contribute to those demonstrations; I only wanted to be at the side watching what was happening, overwhelmed by that outrageous tribute. I was still lucid enough to wonder why the musicians didn't escape at full pelt via backstage, and immediately I saw that it wasn't possible as legions of the listening public had blocked both stage wings.]

Faced with the Dionysiac outpouring in the concert hall, the narrator, that is, represents the Apolline. And this is the key to the story. For as the binaries are collapsed within the story, as the script written for the concert is torn up in every sense, the narrator, linked with the civilised veneer of *la música culta* and cold rationality, repeatedly acts to ensure the active/passive, performer/observer schema of the *música culta* concert is reinscribed onto events. What is more, these barriers are reimposed precisely through the story we are reading, which constitutes the scripting of the scene being played out, as the confusion and Dionysiac drives of the events are observed, narrated, and repackaged as language. In short, recasting this in both linguistic and *música culta* terms, the scene becomes the original idea, which is written down (a 'score') by the narrator (the 'interpreter' of the events), and then received/read by us as readers. The problematic barriers of *música culta* performance, that is, are exactly reproduced and restored *by* the text even as they are apparently broken down *within* the text, as language, literature, and *la música culta* all conspire and combine to fend off the revolutionary actions and challenges made against them in the story. Indeed, in this respect it is worth noting an intriguing passage from a letter written by Cortázar to Luis Buñuel on 30 November 1962, when the latter was intending to produce a film version of 'Las ménades'. Here, Cortázar states that 'sé que en tus manos, mis ménades darían el salto total que en el cuento no alcanzan a dar, *frenadas por razones literarias* en que ya he dejado de creer y que en definitiva hay que saber violar' (2012b: 324, italics mine) [I know that in your hands, my Maenads will make that total leap that they don't manage to make in the story, *held back by literary reasons* in which I have already ceased to believe and which without doubt one must know how to transgress].[19]

And yet. At the start of this analysis of 'Las ménades' I underlined the extent to which the concert setting laid before us could be seen as containing within it the germ of the very forces and pulsations that it sought to repress and silence: the interstices found in the acoustics of the hall, the 'caprichos de mujer histérica' (Cortázar 1970a: 53) [cravings/impulses of an hysterical woman] of the Corona Theatre itself, and the suggestion that the clear-cut definitions and overt focus on language and scripting (all branches of the essential scoring of the *música culta* performance) in fact serve to provoke an engagement with the other. The act of categorising, of scoring, of dividing, inherent both to language and to *la música culta*, as Cortázar presents it in the texts I have been looking at so far, cannot but leave (or, rather, create) gaps through which the other seeps. And so it is that the gaps and seepages found in the *música culta* scenario located within 'Las ménades' are also encountered in the reimposition of boundaries, binaries, and order by the language of the text that the narrator is composing and that we are reading.

One of the principal elements in this renewed creation of such breaches is found in the text's use of and allusion to myth: as we have observed, it is never entirely clear on which mythic tale the story is based, and every time a character is identified with a particular mythic figure, there is an invariable sense of inadequacy, that something has been missed. This is the case in relation to *el Maestro*, but also, as I have argued, and perhaps most significantly, in relation to the blind man, and, in this, the narrator's response to this character at different points in the story demands some attention. Initially, he appears to identify with the blind man as one of the few decorous and 'worthy' people in the theatre, and sees in him a kindred spirit in that he is, at least to begin with, the only person who, like him, refuses to be caught up in the fervour. He is '[e]l único ser entre tanta cosa gelatinosa que me rodeaba' (62) [the only being amongst so much jelly-like stuff that surrounded me]. This is an ironic statement given that Teiresias is a figure that relates precisely to the bringing together and confusion of opposites rather than their discrete separation, and it is this uncertainty of meaning and identification that is crucial and which persists in the narrator's ongoing reactions to the character. Thus, when we read him comment on the blind man's standing up and waving his arms around, although this could be understood as indicating the latter's joining in with the increasingly maenadic throng,[20] the words Cortázar uses are in fact far more equivocal: 'clamando, reclamando, pidiendo algo' (66) [demanding, clamouring, asking for something] implies the possibility of protest against, rather than surrender to, what is occurring. Indeed, it is perhaps significant in this respect that, as we have seen, the lines following these (cited above), which might appear to support the contention that the blind man has joined in, in that they seem to show the narrator being thus inspired to do likewise, are themselves followed by a statement disclosing, as I examined earlier, that the narrator here was in fact moving into position to observe more closely what was happening: 'Es muy curioso pero yo no tenía ningún deseo de contribuir a esas demostraciones, solamente estar al lado y ver lo que occuría' (66) [It's funny but I didn't have the least desire to contribute to those demonstrations; I only wanted to be at the side watching what was happening]. Certainly we are left in some doubt as to whether this was his original intention, but it is a doubt which mirrors that which accompanies our reading of the blind man's 'participation' in events.

The most pertinent part of 'Las ménades' in regard to the confusion and slippage of alignment and meaning in relation to the blind man, however, is found towards the end of the story. Here, the narrator reveals that, upon seeing a badly injured concert-goer, 'no me dio la menor lástima, ni tampoco ver al ciego arrastrándose por el suelo dándose contra las plateas, perdido en ese bosque simétrico sin puntos de referencia. Ya no me importaba nada' (69) [I didn't feel the slightest sympathy, nor when I saw the blind man dragging himself along the floor bumping into the stalls, lost in that symmetrical forest with no points of reference. I didn't care about anything anymore]. If we take the blind man to be, as he is superficially at least in the Pentheus myth, a supporter of Dionysus and to have been a willing (eventual) participant in the mêlée, then the narrator's response here would be in line with the rejection of and desired separation from the Dionysiac outpouring he is witnessing. Likewise, if we focus on Teiresias's nature as bringing together male and female, then the narrator's lack of desire to aid the blind man would reflect his refusal of the (con)fusion before him as he works to reimpose the divide that has been putatively collapsed in the theatre that night. However, if we foreground the initial presentation of the blind man as being on the side of order, the civilised, and the decorous, a reading supported by Teiresias's rationality in *Bacchae* and his alignment elsewhere with Apollo, then the narrator's rejection becomes more problematic, suggesting the emergence of what we might see as a less civilised element within the latter. Indeed, this interpretation is bolstered by the overall sense in the passage quoted that the narrator is essentially unmoved by scenes of suffering and distress, including of an apparently defenceless blind man.

With this in mind we approach possibly the key lines of the story for the present analysis. A little further on from the passage just cited, we read:

> Yo veía todo eso, y me daba cuenta de todo eso, y al mismo tiempo no tenía el menor deseo de agregarme a la confusión, de modo que mi indiferencia me producía un extraño sentimiento de culpa, como si mi conducta fuera el escándalo final y absoluto de aquella noche. (69)
>
> [I was watching all of that, and realising what was happening, and at the same time I did not have the slightest desire to join in with the confusion, in such a way that my indifference made me feel a strange sense of blame, as if my conduct were the final and absolute scandal of that night.]

On the one hand, this indifference could be to the scene in front of him, a reference to his persistent desire to maintain a separation and to reimpose the observer/participator divide of the *música culta* concert that has been broken down. The feeling of blame he has and the idea that this behaviour is the final scandal of the night would thus be on account of his having turned down the chance for a genuinely revolutionary act, bringing down the straitjackets, divisions, and repression of Western humankind, language, and *la música culta*, in favour of the reimposition of these, an act which undoes everything that is being 'achieved' before him. However, bearing in mind the hesitation in our understanding of the preceding passage, we could also see these lines in a very different way, as indicating that, with his refusal to help those in trouble, amongst whom is the blind man, whom he has identified as being 'on his side', the narrator is indeed rejecting the Apolline, rejecting the divisions (*indifférance*?), as he casts off his civilised veneer. Or perhaps both of these possibilities are to be accepted, suggesting precisely the coming together of opposites effected by the events in the story and which the narrator putatively rejects. In short, his language — the language of the story we are reading — is a reimposition of borders that shows the insufficiency of a reimposition of borders, disclosing their inherent porosity. It is literature used in a way that undermines itself, that engages with indeterminacy and refuses easy meaning or scripting, and, as such, hints at the poetism that Cortázar envisaged in his early essays as burrowing into and bringing down the staid structures and nature of (literary) language, as set out in the Introduction to this study. And the fact that that burrowing is, as we saw, essentially a musicalisation of language is not insignificant, just as the way in which 'Las ménades' ends with arguably an overtly musical turn is not insignificant either, the final 'que sonreían' (70) [that were smiling] after the repeated reference to how the woman in red 'se pasaba la lengua por los labios' (70) [passed her tongue over her lips] acting as a final chord such as we find at the end of the concert's own finale, Beethoven's Fifth Symphony. (Indeed, it is worth noting here how the story — the re-imposition of language and its repressions and divisions — ends on an image that foregrounds the rupturing of those divisions in the ingestion of *el Maestro* and musicians by the public led by the woman in red.)

Thus we leave our reading of 'Las ménades' with the sense that, whilst language and the *música culta* world act to (re)impose and (re)script/score divisions, order, and civilisation, both ineluctably create and contain the potential for these very elements to be brought down. In the case of the numerous 'scriptings' at the start of the story that look to control the performance-event, this potential is an unwitting side-effect. But in the case of the story itself, we are given a tantalising glimpse of how it might be harnessed and actively sought by Cortázar (or by the narrator, perhaps), with the text remaining shot through, right until the final line, with tension, (con)fusion, and threat, even if, as emerges from his letter to Buñuel, Cortázar feels that the story ultimately fails properly to seek out and embrace its own possibilities. We are left to ask, then, whether, despite this, this potential, that emerges as inherent to *la música culta*, can somehow be successfully exploited and co-opted. For it may be that this type of music, its settings, and its performances work to silence and repress the pulsations, drives, and (con)fusions that irrupt in the Corona Theatre in 'Las ménades', but, albeit in a rather different and less clear way than has been suggested in the critical literature up until now, the fact is that, in amongst the various other causal stimuli, there *is* something about the music played at the concert that foments the Dionysiac in the concert-goers. Could it be, then, that *la música culta* brings with it both the Apolline in its processes and settings and the Dionysiac in the germ of 'Music' that it contains, and, as such, provides the necessary elements for an envisaged collapsing of the division between the two, again along the lines suggested in my analysis of Cortázar's early essays?

In short, we are left with the sense that that which acts to counter 'revolution' could thus be complicit in what it seeks to repress. And if that is largely inadvertent in 'Las ménades',[21] the story nevertheless does enough to suggest the possibility that this complicity may be harnessed in a more clearly deliberate manner, exploiting both the essential Music and the interstices that are found in *la música culta*. It is a possibility brought to the fore in 'Reunión' and 'Alguien que anda por ahí'.

Poetism and Aestheticism

Before proceeding to analyse these stories, taking up the question I have just posed, we need first to remind ourselves of some of the elements that Cortázar lays down in his early essays, bringing these to bear on the conclusions I have drawn from 'Las ménades'. In both *Teoría del túnel* and 'Elogio del jazz', the former's apocryphal last chapter, and, indeed, in much of his subsequent fiction, in particular prior to his apparent 'descubrimiento del prójimo' (González Bermejo 1978: 120) [discovery of my fellow man], Cortázar envisages and discusses the desirability of a metaphysical and expressive revolution and freedom that largely pertains to the individual. But he also, as set out in my Introduction, discusses how these freedoms must be sacrificed in the move towards social revolution, which demands an insertion into history, into communication. As he states in *Teoría del túnel*:

> Si busca un fin *social*, la pura acción en nuestro siglo se adscribe forzosamente a un orden histórico, y eso paraliza y coarta su libertad. El paso de la soledad a la libertad realizada no puede darse si se renuncia previamente a estar solo. La acción con *fin social* comporta casi siempre esa renuncia. [...] Para estar libre — para buscar ser libre — se requiere el sacrificio previo de la 'libertad' dentro de una fórmula, partido, tendencia o fracción cualquiera. (2006c: 121)

> [If it has a *social* aim, pure action in our century necessarily assigns itself to an historical order, and that paralyses and restricts its freedom. The move from solitude to achieved freedom cannot happen if one has previously renounced being alone. Action with *a social aim* almost always entails such a renouncement. [...] To be free — to seek to be free — requires the previous sacrifice of 'freedom' within a particular formula, party, tendency or faction.]

In fact, as we saw, Cortázar ultimately aims to combine both forms of revolution, and certainly this was his stance in regard to, or as informed by, the Cuban Revolution, as intimated, albeit it in a somewhat implicit fashion, in the essay 'Algunos aspectos del cuento' in 1962, where he comments, for example, that 'se requiere hoy una fusión total de esas dos fuerzas, la del hombre plenamente comprometido con su realidad nacional y mundial, y la del escritor lúcidamente seguro de su oficio' (2006f: 383) [what is needed today is a total fusion of those two forces, that of a man fully engaged with his national and global reality, and that of a writer lucidly sure of his or her profession]. Importantly, he goes on to refer to the need for a storyteller's tales to emerge from 'una profunda vivencia' (383) [a deep experience], or else 'su obra no irá más allá del mero ejercicio estético' (383) [his work will not be anything more than a mere aesthetic exercise], before underlining that, at the same time, in order to communicate his or her message, the storyteller needs 'los instrumentos expresivos, estilísticos, que hacen posible esa comunicación' (383) [the stylistic, expressive instruments that make that communication possible]. In other words, in order for a more socio-political revolution to take place there is a need not just for poetism, but also, in effect, for what we have seen to be described by Cortázar as (a concern for) the aesthetic. In this there is a clear link with the practice of existentialist authors that Cortázar describes in *Teoría del túnel*, who, without reducing their praxis to such, nevertheless refuse to evade 'las dimensiones inteligibles' [intelligible dimensions], respecting 'las formas verbales' (2006c: 119) [verbal forms], essentially so as to be able to go beyond the singularity of the self and communicate, inform, and instruct.

What I am proposing, then, bearing in mind Cortázar's understanding of it as an aesthetic product, is that the seeds of his incorporation and use of *la música culta* in texts that deal with revolution based around or that includes the social were sown at an early stage, and that these seeds help explain why 'Reunión' and 'Alguien que anda por ahí', arguably his two most explicitly socio-political revolutionary short stories, are also two of his texts that invoke *la música culta* most strongly. In this regard, they also help us to see that the uneasy coming together of both revolution and communication (narration), freedom and ordered expression in 'Las ménades' constitutes an important, albeit tentative, first step towards the more overtly revolutionary ambitions of these later stories. Turning to these two stories, then, I shall consider how each of them seeks to co-opt *la música culta* into its revolutionary text and processes. Both, it is worth noting, concern the Cuban Revolution, though different stages of it, and can only properly be understood against the backdrop of Cortázar's previous literary aims and praxis and of his developing views and stance on revolution, both in Cuba and more generally.

'Reunión'

'Reunión' was published in *Todos los fuegos el fuego* in 1966.[22] It tells the story of the 1956 landing of the *Granma*, carrying eighty-two revolutionaries including Fidel Castro and Che Guevara, at Playa Las Coloradas in Cuba, and the subsequent perilous journey inland to meet up in the hills. It narrates, that is, one of the key moments of the revolutionary campaign in Cuba.[23] The story follows certain pages from Che Guevara's account of this campaign closely. Standish points out that 'Cortázar's plundering of Guevara's book is very evident: it is easy to identify passages from *Pasajes de la guerra revolucionaria* [*Episodes of the Cuban Revolutionary War*] that have been carefully rewritten and adapted by Cortázar' (2001: 123). That said, it is worth drawing attention to the work done by Soledad Pérez-Abadín Barro here, who, in a lengthy critical edition of the story, has demonstrated that it was probably written in February 1963 (2010: 43), meaning that Cortázar could not have had a copy of Che's book to operate from, since the latter was published a few months later. He would, however, have had access to a number of sources, including several articles published earlier, that went on to feed into *Pasajes de la guerra revolucionaria* (Guevara 1963), as well as to 'otros escritos del Che y [...] diversas fuentes documentales' (Pérez-Abadín Barro 2010: 44) [other writings by Che and [...] different documentary sources] to which details from Cortázar's story can be traced. I will say more about the range of literary sources that contribute to 'Reunión' that Pérez-Abadín Barro helps bring to light in due course. For now, what is important is to underline the clearly historical and revolutionary subject matter of the story.

Besides the literary models that inform and mould the story, 'Reunión' also engages with a musical model in the shape of Mozart's String Quartet No. 17 in

B♭ major, K.458 (Mozart 1941 [1784]), known as *The Hunt*. Again, Pérez-Abadín Barro has examined in some detail to what extent passages from the piece can be seen to match up with passages from the text, both in subject matter and form (2010: 87–101). The obvious parallel between the hunt motif and the situation in which the characters find themselves, hunted by Batista's forces whilst trying to reach the Sierra Maestra to meet up with Luis, gives us perhaps the most basic reason for Cortázar's choice of material here. In this respect, we might note that he thus ends up being complicit in the sort of practice that he roundly rejects in 'Soledad de la Música', some twenty-five years earlier, where he lambasts 'la llamada "música descriptiva" [...] ya descalificada por su propia invalidez estética [...] que, despreciando el valor absoluto de los fines musicales, intenta subordinarlos a una función imitativa' (Cortázar 1992: 291) [so-called 'descriptive music' [...] already disqualified on account of its own aesthetic invalidity [...] which, with scant regard for the absolute value of musical ends, tries to subordinate these to an imitative function]. Indeed, one of the examples he gives of these musical 'aberraciones' (291) [abominations] is precisely 'las "cacerías"' (291) ['hunts'].

However, the details surrounding the naming of this quartet can lead us down more positive avenues in terms of understanding how this piece of music fits into Cortázar's thought. The labelling of K.458 as *The Hunt* is not Mozart's doing, but is the name that was popularly associated with the piece on account of its first theme's recalling a hunting horn and, one suspects, because of the repeated imitative counterpoint of said theme during the first movement. John Irving, for example, states that:

> The name did not derive from Mozart — neither the autograph nor the Artaria first edition bears any trace of such a title, which can only be explained by association with the well-known eighteenth-century 'topic' of the 'chasse'. For Mozart's contemporaries, the first movement of K.458 evidently evoked the 'chasse' topic, the main components of which were the 6/8 tempo (sometimes featuring a strong upbeat) and triadic melodies based largely around the tonic and dominant chords (doubtless stemming from the physical limitations of the actual hunting horn to notes of the harmonic series). (1998: 69)

Key here is the importance of the topic. As Irving explains, '"Topics" [in Mozart's time] were recognisable "codes" according to which music was both composed and understood and thus provided a context for communication between the composer, the performer and the listener in the classical period — a kind of musical vernacular' (68). The terms used here point towards a way of understanding the association of *la música culta* with 'the social' that I have been examining in relation to Cortázar's early essays on music, and help offer another potential reason for the choice of this particular piece of music: it is not just that it operates (or operated) with this sense of communication between the various 'stakeholders' mentioned, but that it is an example of a musical work where the active involvement of the listeners has come to be written into the piece, in the form of its title. Indeed, in this sense, Mozart's *The Hunt* might be seen as a particularly clear example of a general principle of engagement found in this sort of classical music. As Danuta Mirka explains:

> In the late eighteenth century, the role of listeners as partners in a game proposed by a composer was particularly prominent in the string quartet. In this genre [...], at least part of the audience could have reasonably been expected to possess the theoretical knowledge necessary to participate in such a game with understanding and delight. (2009: xii)

Aside from the similarities with Cortázar's vision of (his) literature as a game in which author and reader participate,[24] this ties in with the call for communication and 'the social' that we saw in *Teoría del túnel* and reflects a general ethos of participation and partnership. It also both loosens the passive-audience/active-musician(-composer) binary of the *música culta* scenario set out in 'Las ménades' and undermines Cortázar's understanding of such a binary as constituting an accurate way of envisioning *música culta* performance in the first place.[25]

The 'game' to which Mirka refers is not one limited to matters of 'topic', however. Indeed, her focus is primarily on considerations of metre. This is significant, not least because Cortázar frequently made reference to the rhythm of Mozart's music in the course of his often eulogic descriptions of the latter's work. Certainly, one simple explanation for Cortázar's choosing a Mozart piece as one of the bases for 'Reunión' is that he was a huge admirer of the composer. In interview with Picon Garfield, for instance, he includes 'toda la música de cámara de Mozart' (1981: 128) [all of Mozart's chamber music] amongst the examples of classical music that he considers to be 'la mejor música que hay' (128) [the best music there is], resonating with Lucas's declarations of his musical deathbed preferences in *Un tal Lucas*, to which I alluded earlier. As mentioned above, however, and as I touched upon briefly in chapter 1, what is particularly notable is the extent to which Cortázar's affirmative comments on Mozart centre around the rhythm of his work. In interview with González Bermejo, for example, he talks of how 'usted no puede imaginar que en un cuarteto de Mozart, por ejemplo, en un determinado momento el ritmo se quiebre de golpe y sea sustituido por un silencio; se va todo al demonio' (1978: 103) [you cannot imagine that in a Mozart quartet, for example, at a given moment the rhythm should suddenly break down and be replaced by silence; the whole thing falls apart]. Moreover, on a number of occasions this is linked specifically to the way in which Cortázar aimed to write his prose. When talking about the 'ritmo final' [final rhythm] of his stories, for example, he explains that 'ahí no puede haber ni una palabra, ni un punto, ni una coma, ni una frase de más. El cuento tiene que llegar fatalmente a su fin como llega a su fin una gran improvisación de jazz o una gran sinfonía de Mozart' (Prego 1985: 170) [there cannot be there a single word, full-stop, comma, or sentence above what is called for. The story must reach its inevitable conclusion like a great jazz improvisation or a great Mozart symphony reaches its conclusion]. We are, in short, firmly in the realms of the musicalisation — or poeticisation — of language that Cortázar wrote about in *Teoría del túnel* and sought in his subsequent praxis:

> las frases que se me quedaban en la imaginación y que adquirían para mí un sentido profundísimo y un valor enorme eran siempre las frases que tenían un gran ritmo que, voluntaria o involuntariamente, eran casi como un verso metido en la prosa.

> Frases que tenían un encuentro de palabras, de aliteraciones, de choques de vocales y consonantes que les daban un valor rítmico y, por consiguiente, un elemento musical puesto que el ritmo es una de las bases, uno de los componentes esenciales de la música. (González Bermejo 1978: 102)
>
> [The sentences that stuck in my imagination and acquired for me a profound meaning and an enormous value were always those sentences that had a great rhythm that, voluntarily or involuntarily, were almost like a poetic verse slotted into the prose.
>
> Sentences that had a coming together of words, alliteration, clashes of vowels and consonants that gave them a rhythmical value and, as a result, a musical element since rhythm is one of the bases, one of the essential components of music.]

The mentions of jazz in this context are helpful for drawing attention to the fact that when Cortázar talks here about the rhythm of classical music and, specifically, that of Mozart, he has in mind to a substantial degree the notion of 'swing'. Indeed, both of the above quotations come after an extended discussion of this particular rhythmic characteristic of jazz, and I shall look in some detail at how Cortázar engages with swing in a more specifically jazzistic sense in subsequent chapters. For now, however, it is instructive to focus on understanding the role of rhythm generally in music as a key structuring element. Cortázar himself intimates this when he refers to how, in his early stories, 'la ubicación de las comas, el encuentro de un sustantivo con un adjetivo, un tiempo de verbo, la caída de una frase hacia el punto final, se dan como, mutatis mutandi, se diría [sic] una partitura musical' (González Bermejo 1978: 102) [the placing of the commas, the coming together of a noun with an adjective, a verb tense, the cadence of a sentence falling down towards the final full-stop, occur, *mutatis mutandi*, as a musical score would occur]. The analogy of the musical score recalls and brings to bear all that we have seen to be associated with this form of notation: it speaks of composition, of organisation, of structure, of aesthetics. And it is through just such terms that musicologists often describe the place and nature of rhythm: Thaut, Trimarchi, and Parsons, for example, state that 'rhythm is music's central organizing structure' (2014: 429); Levitin, Chordia, and Menon argue that 'musical rhythms [...] could contribute in a fundamental way to our aesthetic experience of music' (2012: 3716); whilst Roger Scruton, in his seminal work *The Aesthetics of Music* (1997), includes rhythm as one of the central elements that he submits to analysis.[26]

We have already seen how the aesthetic is tied in with the necessity of communication that accompanies the move into the social and, with it, the possibility of a more communitarian form of revolution and liberation. And the importance given to rhythm both in Mozart and in the way in which Cortázar felt stories should be written can be seen in this light. Put simply, rhythm provides the necessary structure or language which grounds musical expression, the invocation of language here being neither casual nor limited to Cortázar's allusion to and views on the musical score. As Mirka notes, taking Mozart as her object of study, 'Musical meter had its counterpart in poetic meter but was related to grammar in the sense that strong beats, as strong syllables, were called "grammatical" accents' (2009: xii).

In essence, that is, the very element (musicality) that Cortázar envisages as needing to be called upon to burrow into and undermine the structures and strictures of language in *Teoría del túnel* is also open to being recast as the structuring, aesthetic, and linguistic element that needs to be present alongside the pulsations and irrationality of what, with our examination of 'Las ménades' in mind, we might term the Dionysiac. We are back, that is, at the shifting and often contradictory way in which musical and linguistic elements are presented by Cortázar that I noted in the Introduction.

One suspects, of course, that it is this very (con)fusion that is key in understanding how the different elements Cortázar evokes might lead to the sort of liberationary and revolutionary expression and being (individual and social) that the author seeks. And in this sense it is significant that we are not allowed to rest in the notion that rhythm and metre constitute the purely aesthetic — or grammatical, in Mirka's terminology — grounding (or grounding aesthetic) of music and thus, in its incorporation into language, of text, at least in a way that understands this as a rigid and predictable structuring principle. Addressing the context of Mozart's era, Mirka points out that 'within the conceptual horizon defined by the metaphor of music as language, eighteenth-century playing with meter was a dimension of play with musical form and its topical decorum' (2009: xii): metrical play is about effecting alterations in the expected metre and rhythm. The analogy with the ludic alteration of language promoted by Cortázar is highly tempting, not least because this play depends, as does the linguistic equivalent, on the presence of the expected, a shared understanding of the rules of expression (the 'aesthetic rules' (Smoira Cohn 2010: 61)), in order for the unexpected to be possible. (As Dizzy Gillespie once said, 'sometimes, when you know the laws you can break them' (1979: 210).) Specifically, Mozart made frequent and often complex use of counterpoint and syncopation,[27] two elements that are bound up with exactly the sort of rupturing and playing with metrical and rhythmic expectations that concern us here.[28] Significantly, both counterpoint and syncopation have strong ties with jazz swing, and are often described in terms that suggest the sort of opening up of gaps, of tensions in the 'normal' fabric of expectation that we saw to be so important in 'Las ménades'.[29] David W. Stowe, for example, cites a music critic writing in 1940, who stated that '"there's conflict *inside* music. [...] In classical music you call it counterpoint. In American music you call it swing"' (1994: 46), whilst syncopation, insofar as it involves not underplaying 'so-called weak beats' (Schuller 1986: 8), has been described as a '"democratization" of rhythmic values' (8) and as being, 'in its broadest sense, [...] [a] juxtaposition of irregularity against regularity' (Belfiglio 2008: 210), again inviting a 'revolutionary' analogy of challenging bourgeois dominance and political hegemony.[30]

Turning back to Cortázar's statements over the course of a number of interviews, Mozart's music, as we have seen, is frequently mentioned both in relation to (its) rhythm and in the same breath as jazz, suggesting that, whether consciously or unconsciously on Cortázar's part, it is this combination of regularity and irregularity, 'predictability and surprise' (Levitin, Chordia, and Menon 2012: 3716) that, at least in part, underlies the Argentine author's interest in this composer in particular.[31] Certainly, there can be little doubt that the creation of tension is precisely what Cortázar sees as crucial in the rhythmic construction of his texts. In regard to his approach to the short story, as we saw in chapter 1, he is explicit in his reference to the creation of tensions in Mozart as a model for this genre of writing, talking of how:

> Quand on écoute les quintettes de Mozart, on perçoit très nettement la façon dont il prépare au fur et à mesure une tension qui attrape l'auditeur. Rien n'est plat, rien n'est linéaire. Il y a une concentration de forces qui ne se résolvent qu'à la fin. Et mes nouvelles cherchent la même chose. Elles finissent toujours par une phrase qui est une condensation dans laquelle chaque mot et chaque virgule sont fonction du rythme. (Olivares 1981: 56)

> [When one listens to Mozart's quintets, one perceives very clearly the way in which it gradually sets up a tension which traps the listener. Nothing is flat, nothing is linear. There is a concentration of forces which are only resolved at the end. And my short stories seek the same thing. They always end with a sentence which is a condensation in which each word and each comma are a function of the rhythm.]

Elsewhere, Cortázar describes the rhythm he achieves in the ending of his short story 'Continuidad de los parques' [Continuity of Parks] from *Final del juego* (1970a [1956]) as one where 'no hay interrupción de la tensión' (González Bermejo 1978: 104) [the tension is never interrupted]. And it is useful here, in the light of the discussion above, to revisit Cortázar's assertion of the need for a story to reach its conclusion like a jazz improvisation or 'una gran sinfonía de Mozart' (Prego 1985: 170) [a great Mozart symphony]. Mozart's symphonies make substantial use of syncopation, and one of the greatest of all, Symphony No. 41 in C major, is noted, amongst other things, for its repeated use of fugal sections and in particular the remarkable five-voice *fugato* of the coda of the final movement. Bearing in mind the importance of tension in the example of 'Continuidad de los parques', one suspects that the extent and impact both of Mozart's syncopation and of his contrapuntal technique in his symphonies may be a significant factor in Cortázar's specific choice of these works as metric examples of what he sought in his writing.[32] Along similar lines, it is perhaps unsurprising, then, that the musical centrepiece of 'Reunión' is also rich in both counterpoint and syncopation,[33] and we must consider the possibility that this is as important as the topic of the piece in understanding why it is being co-opted by Cortázar in this most overtly revolutionary text.

Finally, we can return to the story itself. With reference to a number of the elements of Mozart's music that I have been discussing, specifically in their emergence in *The Hunt* quartet, I will first examine some of the textual details of 'Reunión', in order to explore how this particular Mozart piece is worked into Cortázar's text. I will then look at the ways in which, I shall argue, the story fails in its revolutionary aims.

The Hunt constitutes a central thread that weaves its way through 'Reunión', returning in the consciousness of the protagonist at two key points in the story, as he recalls and muses upon the first, third, and fourth movements of the piece, the

Allegro vivace assai, the Adagio, and the Allegro assai. Appropriately enough, given what we have noted above, the first mention of this piece of classical music hints at the move into the social, coming, as it does, at the expense of the personal, or at least the focus on the intensely personal:

> Pienso en mi hijo pero está lejos, a miles de kilómetros, en un país donde todavía se duerme en la cama, y su imagen me parece irreal, se me adelgaza y pierde entre las hojas del árbol, y en cambio me hace tanto bien recordar un tema de Mozart. (Cortázar 1970f: 74)
>
> [I think of my son but he's far away, thousands of miles away, in a country where they still sleep in bed, and his image seems unreal to me, it tapers, and disappears among the leaves of the tree, and instead it does me so much good to remember a Mozart theme.] (1979a: 54)

In the two passages in question, the piece is used as a metaphor for both the struggle to get to the Sierra and the broader revolutionary aims at stake. In the first, continuing on from the quotation above, we are located within the opening movement of the quartet, with the third and fourth movements seen as a cipher for the hoped-for future revolution, if the current episode is a success:

> el movimiento inicial del cuarteto *La caza*, la evocación del halalí en la mansa voz de los violines, esa trasposición de una ceremonia salvaje a un claro goce pensativo. [...] [U]na victoria que sea como la restitución de una melodía después de tantos años de roncos cuernos de caza, que sea ese allegro final que sucede al adagio como un encuentro con la luz. [...] [A]lcanzaré a preguntarme si algún día sabremos pasar del movimiento donde todavía suena el halalí del cazador, a la conquistada plenitud del adagio y de ahí al allegro final. (1970f: 74–75)
>
> [the first movement of *The Hunt* quartet, the evocation of the *hallali*, the death flourish, in the gentle voice of the violins, that transposing of a savage rite into a clear introspective joy. [...] [A] victory that might be like the restoration of a melody after so many years of raucous hunting horns, it might be that final allegro which follows the adagio like an encounter with light. [...] I shall manage to wonder if some day we will know how to pass from the movement where the hunter's *hallali* still sounds, to the conquered fullness of the adagio and from there to the final allegro.] (1979a: 54–55)

In the second passage, which appears at the end of the story, we are now entering the third movement, with the fourth, symbolising 'la reconciliación con todo lo que haya quedado vivo frente a nosotros' (1970f: 75) ('the reconciliation with all that has remained alive in front of us', 1979a: 55–56), still in the future:

> sentía que estábamos entrando en el adagio del cuarteto, en una precaria plenitud de pocas horas [...] el dibujo del adagio que alguna vez ingresaría en el allegro final, accedería a una realidad digna de ese nombre. (1970f: 86)
>
> [I felt that we were passing into the adagio of the quartet, into a precarious plenitude a few hours old [...] the sketch of the adagio that would some day pass into the final allegro and accede to a reality worthy of that name.] (1979a: 64)

The music, that is, acts as a metaphor or a mould into which the revolutionary struggle in Cuba is to be imagined and fitted. Indeed, in this sense, Cortázar's choice of musical text could not be better: the first movement, with its focus on the propelling, hunting-horn topic and the inclusion of a variety of themes or melodies, speaks of the multiple actors caught up in the Cuban fight, both in general and in the specific circumstances in which the characters find themselves; the third movement, slow, 'sunny, jocular' (Irving 1998: 40), 'dramatically "static," lacking the sort of transitional and developmental material that would otherwise imbue it with dramatic momentum. [...] [M]usic that seems to float above the tensions, conflicts, and stresses of ordinary existence, conjuring up a sort of "dreamscape"' (Greenberg 2004: 21; 22) reflects aptly the calm, pregnant pause, laced with a light-hearted joviality when the characters meet up in the Sierra (Cortázar 1970f: 85); and the final movement — as a cipher for the utopic goal towards which the revolutionary struggle works — is, in the words of Irving, 'a triumph of organisation' (1998: 42), and, as Robert Greenberg puts it, 'a triumph of formal clarity and brilliance' (2004: 22), where the two main themes from the first movement (a metaphor for the struggle itself) are synthesised in 'a masterpiece of motivic integration' (22).

Beyond thematic metaphor, the Mozart piece is arguably also a mould into which the matter of the text itself is poured. Pérez-Abadín Barro posits numerous ways in which, for example, 'el decurso narrativo ha imitado la ágil andadura del primer movimiento del cuarteto, para transmitir esa sensación de desorden selvático y júbilo primitivo del *Allegro vivace assai* que [...] ha encauzado el relato desde el comienzo' (2010: 96) [the course of the narrative has imitated the agile path of the first movement of the quartet, to transmit a sense of the disorder of the jungle and the primitive joy of the Allegro vivace assai, which [...] has guided the story from the beginning]. Whilst it might be rather generous to see some of the traits and elements highlighted by Pérez-Abadín Barro as a textual rendering of the Mozart piece, there are similarities. On the level of the story as a whole, the repeated mention of trees, about which I will talk shortly, certainly appears as a 'topic', reiterated with variations throughout the text. Pushing the case for this being aligned with the main hunting theme which begins *The Hunt* quartet (Mozart 1941: bars 1–8) is the fact that these repetitions are grouped, broadly, in the first and final parts of the story, with a significant middle section devoid of any mention of them, thus mirroring the sonata form of the first movement of Mozart's piece, in which the main theme is worked in different ways in the exposition (bars 1–90) and in the recapitulation (bars 137–231) and coda (bars 232–end), but where the development section (bars 91–136), unusually, does not build on existing themes.[34] Meanwhile, within the first passage that deals with the Mozart piece directly, lines such as 'lo pienso, lo repito, lo canturreo en la memoria' (Cortázar 1970f: 74) ('I think it, I repeat it, I hum it in my memory', 1979a: 54–55) offer the same sort of 'bouncing outline' (Greenberg 2004: 12) as the main theme, as well as representing, both in form and meaning, a textual equivalent of the musical (imitative) counterpoint found throughout *The Hunt*.

However, for all that the themes and musical form of Mozart's piece are co-opted into the story by Cortázar, there is a further way in which *The Hunt* is present in 'Reunión'. Bound up with, but moving beyond, the level of metaphor, the musical work in the story is significant primarily in that it forms part of the *figura* [figure] that is developed and discussed in the two main passages where it is brought into the text. The notion of the *figura* in Cortázar's work is both complex and complicated, not least because it serves different functions and operates in different ways in the course of his literary production. Broadly speaking, *figuras* in Cortázar's texts are patterns or a sort of patterning found in the world by which the world might be apprehended and experienced 'as it is', in its plenitude, 'sudden confluences of apparently heterogeneous elements which supposedly produce a single "visión aniquilante" [annihilating vision]' (Moran 2000: 65), as Moran puts it, citing *Rayuela*, what Cortázar also describes in 'Cristal con una rosa adentro' (1973c: 127–29) [Glass With a Rose Inside] as a 'cristalización fulgurante' (129) [flashing crystalisation]. They are, then, bound up in Cortázar's fiction with the search for the sort of ontological (and expressive) liberation that he seeks. In *Los premios*, for example, Persio tries to see a hidden unity in and between the stars in the sky, the rigging of the ship he is on, a Picasso painting of a guitar, and an Apollinaire poem, which would give him 'una cifra, un módulo. [Y] [a]sí empezaré a abrazar la creación desde su verdadera base analógica, romperé el tiempo-espacio que es un invento plagado de defectos' (Cortázar 1981a: 90) [a cipher, a unit. [And] thus will I start to embrace creation from its true analogical base, I will break space-time, which is an invention riddled with defects]. In the successful bringing together of the *figura*, it is imagined, the characters would 'reach a personal "centre"' (Boldy 1980: 23), an ontological plenitude, whilst, in collapsing time and space as the different elements come together, the author would achieve 'a metaphysical centre [...] [which] in turn ratifies, metaphysically, the quest of the characters' (23).[35] The *figura*, then, can be usefully brought into the ways in which Cortázar's work presents and engages with music, not just in that it participates in the same ontological and expressive quest, but, more specifically, in the sense that, in putatively 'produc[ing] a single "visión aniquilante" [annihilating vision]' (Moran 2000: 65), the *figura* does away with the idea of different elements in the world as merely versions or performances of previous elements: to appeal to the terms and questions of my discussion in chapter 1, the *figura*, applied to the world of *la música culta*, might be seen to posit the (ideal) necessity of seeing musical performances of a piece of music not as attempts at achieving a perfect rendering of some putative original, but where the key would be to perceive and apprehend a oneness of (different) performances. That oneness, or unity, would absolutely not be locatable in a prior location or time, but would only exist as apparently different performance-events are envisioned as bringing forth and constituting a single (originary) entity, beyond the play of difference (and *différance*).

In the case of 'Reunión', the *figura* in question is made up principally of Mozart's *The Hunt* and the patterns of the high branches of the tree under which the narrator is sitting:

> siento [...] cómo la melodía y el dibujo de la copa del árbol contra el cielo se van acercando, traban amistad, se tantean una y otra vez hasta que el dibujo se ordena de pronto en la presencia visible de la melodía, un ritmo que sale de una rama baja, casi a la altura de mi cabeza, remonta hasta cierta altura y se abre como un abanico de tallos, mientras el segundo violín es esa rama más delgada

que se yuxtapone para confundir sus hojas en un punto situado a la derecha, hacia el final de la frase, y dejarla terminar para que el ojo descienda por el tronco y pueda, si quiere, repetir la melodía. (Cortázar 1970f: 74)

[I [...] feel how the melody and the sketch of the treetop against the sky draw near, become friends, feel each other out a few times until the sketch is suddenly organized into the visible presence of the melody, a rhythm coming from a lower branch, almost at the level of my head, rises to a certain height and then opens like a fan of stems, while the second violin is that thinner branch placing itself next to the other, to fuse its leaves into a point situated to the right, toward the end of the phrase, letting it end so that the eye moves down the trunk and can, if it wishes, repeat the melody.] (1979a: 54–55)

The visual images of the trees and the sound of the music are imagined as fusing, bringing with it a sense of order and meaning, of unity and oneness. Pérez-Abadín Barro suggests that 'el árbol con sus movimientos permite leer unas notas y reconstruir una melodía' (2010: 89) [the tree with its movements allows one to read some notes and reconstruct a melody], as if the forms of the branches constituted the score in which the Mozart piece might be read. Tempting though such an equating of score and branches may be, the text itself refuses such a reading: the music is at no point described as emerging from or being made possible by the *dibujo* being read. If anything, the music is primary here. Pérez-Abadín Barro intimates such a conclusion, when she states that 'el tema inicial del cuarteto *La caza* imbuye de ritmo [...] el dibujo' (86) [the initial theme of *The Hunt* quartet infuses the sketch with rhythm]. That is not to say, however, that the branches and leaves of the tree do not enjoy an innate rhythm of their own: prior to the Mozart piece coming into his thoughts, we read of the narrator 'siguiendo con ojos entornados ese dibujo casual de las ramas y las hojas, esos ritmos que se encuentran, se cabalgan y se separan, y a veces cambian suavemente cuando una bocanada de aire hirviendo pasa por encima de las copas' (Cortázar 1970f: 73–74) ('following with half-closed eyes that casual design of the branches and leaves, those rhythms that meet, ride upon each other, and separate, and sometimes gently change when a whiff of boiling air passes over the treetops', 1979a: 54).

What both the latter quotations point to is the importance of rhythm in the *figura* that the text and the narrator try to bring about into unity: this is the oneness across the elements that is sought. It is a oneness, moreover, that is based not on an attempt to return to an original performance, but on the idea of a foundational metre, a rhythmic grounding around which the tree and the music coalesce.[36] Significantly for the goal of bringing the elements here together, the description of the tree's rhythms shows them to be highly suggestive of the rhythm of *The Hunt*'s main hunting theme ('se cabalgan' ('[they] ride upon each other')), the (imitative) counterpoint of the piece ('se separan' ('[they] separate')), and the variation and modulation of the main themes ('y a veces cambian suavemente' ('and [they] sometimes gently change')) that Mozart effects in the course of the work.[37] We can imagine, then, that the coming together of all the elements in the *figura* would include the oneness not just between tree and music, but also between the different examples of imitative counterpoint in the latter, with this oneness or unity implying an end to temporal succession and difference, as we have noted. Against this, however, in underscoring the centrality of rhythm to this oneness, Cortázar's text draws attention to the persistent contradiction and (logical) impossibility of the 'authenticity' he is seeking here, in that rhythm is dependent upon and can only exist as a temporal phenomenon: rhythm and metre, that is, represent both the central tenet of the *figura* at stake at the same time as they also constitute the insistence of temporality that undermines the *figura*'s dissolution of temporal discreteness. Yet, as is ever the case with Cortázar, both are necessary.

The third element brought into the passage that describes this *figura* (leaving aside, for now, the addition of the star in this schema at the end of the story) is the revolution under whose banner the characters are fighting, in that, we are told, 'y todo eso es también nuestra rebelión' (1970f: 74) ('and all that is also our rebellion', 1979a: 55). The revolution, symbolised by Luis (Fidel Castro), would be both the result of the *figura* and, the text intimates, also part of the *figura* that comes together (at the moment of visionary unity, of course, there would be no difference between these two):

> también nosotros a nuestra manera hemos querido trasponer una torpe guerra a un orden que le dé sentido, la justifique y en último término la lleve a una victoria que sea como la restitución de una melodía. (1970f: 74–75)
>
> [we, too, in our way, have wanted to transpose a clumsy war into an order that gives it meaning, justifies it, and finally carries it to a victory that might be like the restoration of a melody.] (1979a: 55)

Indeed, reinforcing the image employed by the story here, it is worth recalling Cortázar's description of the *Casa de las Américas* in Cuba in 1980 as a great tree that '"*multiplica sus ramas*"' (cited in Montanaro 2001: 30) ['*multiplies its branches*']. Moreover, in using the *figura* in relation to the Cuban Revolution in this way in the story, Cortázar thus conveys the sense not just that the successful working through and vision of the *figura* would lead to a social revolution but, given the way he uses the *figura* in his work, that that revolution is also one that operates on an ontological, individual, and expressive level. This, of course, marries up with the way in which Cortázar, as I have commented, would go on to define the different levels on which the Revolution (and revolutions generally) should operate, crystallised in the idea they should work, as he put it in 1983, '"*también de adentro hacia fuera*"' (cited in Montanaro 2001: 48) ['*from the inside outwards too*'].

And yet, 'Reunión' fails to convince; it simply does not work particularly well, either as a story or as a scene of revolution. And it fails, at least in part, because the story engages with the Mozart piece in a way that falls prey to a number of the problems of *la música culta* that we have seen in previous texts; that is, the potentially revolutionary aspects of the music are either silenced or overwhelmed by issues that work against the ideas and aims into whose service Cortázar tries to marshal the quartet.

First, in presenting the classical piece as such a heavy-handed metaphor for the Revolution, Cortázar effectively sets up the stages of the revolution he both describes and foretells as a performance of the quartet: the latter constitutes the score that

Cortázar's narrative follows and that the characters are called to play out. Indeed, in this respect, 'Reunión''s relationship with *The Hunt* mirrors the relationship between the story and the numerous written texts with which it engages. As alluded to earlier, Pérez-Abadín Barro has mapped the intricate web of textual sources and allusions in the story in considerable detail (2010: 37–83), revealing the extent to which it uses prior texts as moulds. There are certainly variations on themes from earlier works (46), as some details are altered, but, contrary to Pérez-Abadín Barro's own conclusion, one is left with the overwhelming sense that this is a story that essentially brings together and re-enacts earlier texts. The pre-emptive echoes of 'Clone' are clear, not least in that the textual models with which Cortázar engages are literary (the stories of Jack London, as indicated in the story's epigraph),[38] historical, and suggestive of chains of texts that stretch back into the past, with passages that ended up in *Pasajes de la guerra revolucionaria* that Cortázar appears to have used among his base sources being themselves based on 'un diario personal' (Pérez-Abadín Barro 2010: 43) [a personal diary] of Che Guevara, for example. Moreover, in being used as the basis for the story's details, all of these texts come to operate intertextually. In other words, 'Reunión' is a text that, on every level, is bound by and as performance, as the reading and attempted re-enactment of previous written and classical music texts. The 'revolutionary' writing, like the story of social revolution found within that writing, is straitjacketed by these templates. And whilst, as I alluded to at the start of this chapter in relation to 'Clone', there is scope for a more positive interpretation, seeing here the production of a new text precisely through playing with and producing new, intertextual versions of existing texts, finally the historical determinism of the narrative ensures that the sense of a script (or score) being followed is dominant.

Similarly, returning to my musical discussion of rhythm and metre, we might say that the depiction and understanding of these elements as an 'organizing structure' (Thaut, Trimarchi, and Parsons 2014: 429), specifically aligned by Cortázar with the writing and operation of 'una partitura musical' (González Bermejo 1978: 102) [a musical score], ultimately prevails in 'Reunión'. Indeed, the early essay 'Elogio del jazz' provides us with a model for conceptualising what is going on here. In this essay, Cortázar draws attention to the lack of freedom in the Big Band jazz era, in the sense of its being dependent upon an arranger who 'trabaj[a] sobre un tema de cualquier autor' (2006d: 211) [work[s] on the song of some composer]. This trait of, or dependence on, musical arrangement is evidently focused on the idea of scored composition/arrangement and is identified by Cortázar specifically as the 'aesthetic' aspect of this particular type of jazz (212). His one caveat is found in the possibility of the 'inspiración del arreglo' (211) [inspiration of the arrangement], a notion that might correlate to the implementation, albeit scored, of the unexpected and rupturing rhythmic play to which I alluded earlier.[39] However, the 'arrangement' (of *The Hunt*) that is 'Reunión' fails to lodge itself into this latter category.

Before discussing this point, though, it is worth drawing attention to one of the most important consequences of this overwhelming sense of scripting and history in the story, which is that, given the ease of identification of the story's characters with revolutionary figures from the historical episode, we at no point doubt what the eventual outcome will be: we know that Luis is not dead and that they will meet up in the Sierra (and, beyond the limits of the text we are reading, that the Revolution will bear fruit). The effect of this is to empty the story of precisely the tensions and gaps that, I have argued, are fundamental to the way in which Cortázar aims to bring about a revolution in being, expression, and understanding, and which serve as the narrative basis for the resistance to the hegemonic forces of civilisation in 'Las ménades'.

In fact, both of these elements — the (lack of) inspiration of the arrangement in 'Reunión' and the writing out of tensions in the story — call to be understood as part of the same basic issue. A closer look at the way in which Cortázar's protagonist describes the *figura* and the revolutionary aim bound up with it is telling in this regard. Perhaps most immediately striking is the reiterated notion of bringing order, clarity, and resolution where there has been chaos, disorder, and uncertainty. And the classical music piece is at the heart of this. Thus, the quartet is introduced, as we have seen, with the protagonist talking of 'el movimiento inicial del cuarteto *La caza*, la evocación del halalí en la mansa voz de los violines, esa trasposición de una ceremonia salvaje a un claro goce pensativo' (1970f: 74) ('the first movement of *The Hunt* quartet, the evocation of the *hallali*, the death flourish, in the gentle voice of the violins, that transposing of a savage rite into a clear introspective joy', 1979a: 54). These lines are reminiscent of 'Las ménades' and repeat the move from the Dionysiac ritual to a more cerebral appreciation that we saw the narrator foster at the end of (and through) the earlier story. Moreover, in 'Reunión' they prepare the way for much of the subsequent *figura* section. We are told how, for example, in the *figura* that the narrator is imagining, '*el dibujo se ordena* de pronto en la presencia visible de la melodía' (1970f: 74, italics mine) ('*the sketch is suddenly organized* into the visible presence of the melody', 1979a: 55, italics mine). Similar comments are then made regarding how the revolutionaries have wanted to:

> *trasponer una torpe guerra a un orden que le dé sentido, la justifique* y en último término la lleve a una victoria que sea como *la restitución de una melodía después de tantos años de roncos cuernos de caza*. (1970f: 74–75, italics mine)

> [*transpose a clumsy war into an order that gives it meaning, justifies it*, and finally carries it to a victory that might be like *the restoration of a melody after so many years of raucous hunting horns*.] (1979a: 55, italics mine)

Revolution, tree branches, and Mozart's music are all depicted in the same manner, as bringing in order, explanation, and, in this last quotation, a clarity of (musical) expression. Finally, such terms are invoked again in relation specifically to the two central 'authors' that are found within the elements of this *figura*, as the narrator muses:

> Lo que se divertiría Luis si supiera que en este momento lo estoy comparando con Mozart, viéndolo *ordenar poco a poco esta insensatez, alzarla hasta su razón primordial* que aniquila con su evidencia y su desmesura todas las prudentes razones temporales' (1970f: 75, italics mine).

[What a kick Luis would get out of knowing that in this moment I am comparing him to Mozart, seeing him *put this recklessness to order little by little, raising it to its primal reason* which annihilates with its evidence and its excess all prudent temporal reasons.] (1979a: 55, italics mine)

The *figura*, then, the very symbol and potentiality of (genuine) revolution is seen as such not because it opens itself (and its viewer) up to a way of perceiving the world and the self that takes on board and welcomes in the tensions, drives, and pulsations of that self (and being generally), undoing the stultifying norms and structures of Western civilisation, but, quite contrastingly, because it orders and makes graspable, understandable, that which has resisted explanation, comforting clarity, and structure. And the reference to the 'razón primordial' [primal reason], overcoming the 'prudentes razones temporales' [prudent temporal reasons], rather than representing the undermining of human structures of understanding, in fact, even with its overflowing, boundary-negating 'desmesura' ('excess'), constitutes a recoiling into the most hackneyed teleological discourse. This is reinforced by a key characteristic of the story's *figura*. Moran, writing on Cortázar's late work *Prosa del observatorio* (1972), argues that that text 'points to a shift from arborescence to rhizomatics' (2000: 207). Drawing upon Deleuze and Guattari's seminal *A Thousand Plateaus: Capitalism and Schizophrenia* (1987 [1980]), he discusses the ways in which this work posits the need to replace the arborescent structures by which Western epistemology has understood and 'fitted' the world, structures based on 'binary choices and discrete bifurcations, designed to magnetize incommensurable events, forces, cultures, sexualities and so forth to unitary axes or centres' (Moran 2000: 206), with the rhizome, which, in Deleuze and Guattari's words, is 'not amenable to any structural or generative model' (1987: 12) and is 'opposed to all planes of principle and finality' (507). Whilst *Prosa del observatorio* points in this direction, Moran contends that it also still harks after a vision of Man that falls into the same teleological traps that Cortázar is trying to avoid. The arborescence of the *figura* in 'Reunión' signals similar problems, though more pronounced than those found in *Prosa del observatorio*. As we have noted, the *figura* and the revolution of which it is to be the herald are built around images of order that appear to contradict the professed aims of Cortázar elsewhere. Likewise, both the arborescent *figura* and the revolutionary episode being recounted in the story are structured on the basis of the sort of linear progression towards enlightenment that smacks of the very Western epistemology that Cortázar critiques: the *figura* repeatedly focuses on the 'copa del árbol' (1970f: 74) ('treetop', 1979a: 55), indicating the upward trajectory one is invited to take in attempting to coalesce its elements; and the struggle to reach the Sierra similarly represents a moving towards a privileged and enlightened vantage point. The 'arreglo' [arrangement] of the *figura* appears less inspired and innovative, than marshalled towards somewhat familiar ends, reflecting perhaps how the different (inter)texts of the story are also arranged in such a way as to produce such a story. And it is in these terms and as part of these textual procedures that we need finally to understand how Mozart's *The Hunt* contributes to the failure of 'Reunión', rather than marking out its revolutionary 'success' as a short story.

Having looked at the attention Cortázar gives in his essays and interviews —

and, indeed, in this text — to the importance of rhythm in music, including, specifically, that of Mozart, it is telling, and surprising, that, despite the (implicit) allusions in 'Reunión' to the rhythms of *The Hunt* and, more overtly, to rhythm(s) as a central aspect of the story's *figura*, both the *figura* and the text generally do not focus primarily on this aspect of *The Hunt*, but on its progression to its concluding movement and on the Revolution as a performance of such. More significantly still, in this respect, is the omission of the second movement, the Menuetto and Trio. Moderato from Cortázar's story, something critics have noted but not, to my knowledge, commented on in detail. This movement is, arguably, the most interesting in terms of its use of syncopation and rhythmic novelties. Greenberg comments on the syncopation found in the movement, for example (2004: 20), as well as on its 'rhythmic twists and turns' (21) which, amongst other things, 'mark it as truly original' (21). The omission of this movement, then, can be taken as a symbol of an erasure of precisely those rhythmic disturbances that enable the production of tension, the rupturing of the basic metre and pulse around which the work is built. Additionally, the selective choice of movements to be incorporated into the narrative also points towards what is increasingly evident as one reads the story more closely, namely that the *figura* in question, like the text we are reading, is a(n attempted) construction of reason, logic, and (human) planning. Rather than a poetism where the *figura* would be intuited, sensed, allowed to form in and of itself for the individual hopefully to glimpse and grasp, the *figura* in 'Reunión' is very much about the conscious pulling together of the different elements, where the unified vision would be the product of those elements bending to the will of the narrator (and, by implication, Cortázar). This is most clearly seen at the end of the text, where the protagonist informs us that 'yo veía cómo las hojas y las ramas se plegaban poco a poco a mi deseo, eran mi melodía, la melodía de Luis' (1970f: 86) ('I saw how the leaves and branches were bending little by little to my desire, they were my melody, Luis' melody', 1979a: 64). This is a long way from the ludic, aleatory, and rhizomatic approach to the world that Cortázar champions elsewhere in his texts. Indeed, one might say it is, rather, an approach which has more in common with the aesthetics of *música culta* construction and performance, the focus being on a sense of order, control, and the successful expression of the intent of the composer. It is not, of course, that the aesthetic is a sign of failure, but that the necessary balance in 'Reunión' between the aesthetic and the poetic (poetism), between the 'regular' rhythm and metre ('grammatical' structure) and the disturbance of that metre, is not present: the rupturing rhythmic element — arguably most clearly present in the Mozart piece in the one movement missing from 'Reunión' — is lost, as everywhere we look we see assured direction, determinism, and tight control. It is, thus, no coincidence, perhaps, that the story ends with an image that will be repeated in 'Clone', some fourteen years later. In that story we are told that 'ese centro era la música y en torno a ella las luces de ocho vidas, de ocho juegos, los pequeños ocho planetas del sol Monteverdi, del sol Josquin des Prés, del sol Gesualdo' (Cortázar: 1980: 95) ('that center was the music and around it the lights of eight lives, eight sets, the eight small planets of the Monteverdi sun, the Josquin des Prés sun, the Gesualdo sun', 1984: 46). It is an image that at once speaks of the centrality of the 'original' work and discloses to what extent the processes that seek to (re)produce that centre are essentially linguistic, the sun being presented, I argued in chapter 1, as the Word around which words circulated. In 'Reunión', the final image is remarkably similar:

> vi inscribirse una estrella en el centro del dibujo, y era una estrella pequeña y muy azul, y aunque no sé nada de astronomía y no hubiera podido decir si era una estrella o un planeta, en cambio me sentí seguro de que no era Marte ni Mercurio, brillaba demasiado en el centro del adagio, demasiado en el centro de las palabras de Luis como para que alguien pudiera confundirla con Marte o con Mercurio. (1970f: 86)

> [I saw a star inscribed in the center of the sketch, and it was a little star and very blue, and though I don't know anything about astronomy and wouldn't be able to say whether it was a star or a planet, I did feel sure that it was neither Mars nor Mercury, it shined too much in the center of the adagio, too much in the center of Luis' words to be mistaken for Mars or Mercury.] (1979a: 64)

At the heart of the *figura*, the music, language, and the Revolution in 'Reunión' is the same cosmic — and prelapsarian — centre. Moreover, that these fundamental elements of the story are underlined as not being that centre is clear in that we are told specifically that Roman gods (planets) associated with war (Mars), music, and language (Mercury) are not confusable with it. But, more than that, the centre here, it is suggested, *is itself* a planet. In other words, the centre is always, it turns out, bound up in and as the play of language, it is just another word, similarly to what we saw in respect of the human centre (Gesualdo) in 'Clone'. As Derrida argues, the centre is 'a sort of nonlocus in which an infinite number of sign-substitutions c[ome] into play' (2001 [1967]: 353–54). The *figura* in 'Reunión', with all its musical and revolutionary elements, ultimately emerges, then, as a map of and metaphor for the teleology of (frustrated) logocentric desire.

'Alguien que anda por ahí'

'Alguien que anda por ahí', written in 1976 and published the following year, shares many similarities with what might justifiably be called its earlier sister story: it concerns the arrival in Cuba by boat, 'updated' to a 'lancha eléctrica' (Cortázar 1977: 201) ('electric launch', 1984: 327), of a subversive character and is laced with references to *la música culta*, in this case various works by Chopin, as well as a number of other pieces of music. Once again, socio-political revolution and *la música culta* are brought together. One of the most obvious differences, however, is the context in which this story was written. 'Reunión' was written in early 1963, a time when the Revolution was flourishing and enjoying the whole-hearted support of numerous Latin American writers and intellectuals, including Cortázar. In contrast, by the time of writing of 'Alguien que anda por ahí' Castro had been in power for some seventeen years and the Padilla affair had had a drastic effect on the support commanded by the Revolution amongst those same figures.[40] There are two broad elements in relation to Cortázar here that we might dwell upon for the purposes of the current analysis. First, although not nearly to the extent of others, in the sense that he did not ultimately turn against the Revolution, Cortázar's faith and belief in the Revolution had taken a hit. Even if he subsequently reaffirmed his support for it, the fact that the (ethical) waters had been muddied is significant. Secondly, upon reaffirming his faith in the Revolution in 'Policrítica en la hora de los chacales' (Cortázar 1971) [Policriticism in the Hour of the Jackals], Cortázar reasserted his right and need to be able to criticise aspects of it, in effect adding to his defence against criticism from around this time (Cortázar 2006g; Cortázar 2006h) that his high-brow, distanced literary games, often involving the fantastic, did little to help the cause and were, in fact, decidedly bourgeois. For Cortázar, as we have already examined, 'proper' revolution and liberation had to take place on the level of the individual, of language, of logic, of writing, of one's concept of reality, as well as in the social sphere, something his work prior to this point should have made evident in any case, 'Algunos aspectos del cuento' (Cortázar 2006f), which I discussed briefly earlier, being a particularly salient example in this regard. Specifically, and building upon those earlier statements and stances, he was critical, post-Padilla, of a socialist revolution which ended up becoming as rigid and stultifying — as lacking in true freedom — as the hegemony it had sought to replace:

> simplemente porque cuatro o cinco o seis dirigentes no han hecho su autocrítica, se instala en el poder, por ejemplo, un puritanismo de las costumbres, digamos desde el punto de vista sexual, casi victoriano. Eso no lo acepto porque me parece una revolución fracasada. El hombre va a seguir siendo prisionero de sus tabúes, sus inhibiciones, sus imposibilidades. ¿Para qué diablos le sirve el socialismo? Para nada. (Poniatowska 1975: 33)

> [just because four or five or six leaders haven't done any self-criticism, a puritanism of traditions, let's say from a sexual perspective almost Victorian, for example, installs itself in power. I do not accept that because it seems to me to be a failed revolution. Man will continue to be prisoner of his taboos, his inhibitions, his impossibilities. What the hell use is socialism to him? None.]

Thus it was that the motive behind 'Alguien que anda por ahí' was described by Cortázar as 'una tentativa de mostrarles que se puede escribir un cuento fantástico [...] que tenga, a la vez, un contenido revolucionario' (González Bermejo 1978: 143) [an attempt at showing them that you can write a story in the fantastic genre [...] that, at the same time, has a revolutionary content].[41]

The story tells of the foiled attempt by the protagonist, a Cuban exile and apparent counter-revolutionary named Jiménez, working with contacts both within Cuba and in the US, from where he has journeyed to the island, to detonate a bomb in a factory in Cuba. Arriving at the hotel from where the following morning he is to carry out the plan, Jiménez, frequently displaying wistfulness and nostalgia for the Cuba of his past, spends time in the hotel's bar and restaurant, where, together with a stranger who is also in the bar, he listens to the pianist as she plays, amongst other things, several Chopin compositions interspersed with the tune 'Smoke Gets in Your Eyes' (1933). Eventually, Jiménez retires to his room, checking the door is locked before having a nap prior to the execution of the counter-revolutionary plan. He is awoken to find the stranger in his room sitting on his bed. The man reveals himself to be Chopin and, making allusion to the Polish composer's

Revolutionary Étude (Op. 10 No. 12), states that 'esta noche me hubiera gustado que tocara ese estudio que llaman revolucionario [...]. Pero ella no puede, pobrecita, no tiene dedos para eso. Para eso hacen falta dedos así' (Cortázar 1977: 210) ('tonight I would have liked for her to have played that étude they call the Revolutionary [...]. But she can't, poor thing, she hasn't got the fingers for it. For that you need fingers like these', 1984: 334), before proceeding to use his own fingers to strangle Jiménez.

As will be clear from this potted plot summary, 'Alguien que anda por ahí' is replete with references to music, in particular that of Chopin. To begin to appreciate the role played by music in the story, both as part of the narrative and as part of Cortázar's textual fabric, we thus need first to look in more detailed fashion at the different pieces and genres of music alluded to within the text.

Leaving aside for now the reiterative presence of the birdsong, to which I shall return later on, the musical references begin when Jiménez, having settled into his room and, important detail, checked for the first time 'que la puerta cerraba bien' (1977: 204) ('that the door locked well', 1984: 329), moves onto the hotel bar, initially to meet briefly with his contact, Alfonso. As the two men chat we are told that:

> el piano llegaba como de lejos [...] la pianista estaba [...] tocando muy suave una habanera y después algo de Chopin, pasando a un danzón y a una vieja balada de película, algo que en los buenos tiempos había cantado Irene Dunne. (1977: 204)

> [the piano reached them as if from far away [...] the piano player was [...] playing something very softly, a habanera and then something by Chopin, going on to a danzón and an old song from the movies, something that in the good old days [...] Irene Dunne [had sung].] (1984: 329)

The multiple and varied nature of the music being played is immediately apparent, with Chopin being singled out even at this early stage as the most important musical figure here. Carmen Vázquez notes this, remarking that 'el autor describe las piezas por su género — habanera, danzón, balada — y [...] sólo omite esta catalogación tan pertinente cuando se refiere a Chopin' (1986: 127) [the author describes the pieces by their genre — *habanera, danzón, balada* — and omits this highly pertinent categorisation only when he refers to Chopin]. As well as genre, the types of music mentioned stand out for their distinctive rhythms, in particular in the case of the *habanera* and the *danzón*, where there is much in the way of syncopation. The presence of these different types and rhythms of music will be an important factor in understanding of how music *per se* operates in the story.

The next musical reference is to another Chopin piece, this time, with more specificity, a prelude, as we are told that 'todo ahí era plácido y cordial y calmo y Chopin, que ahora volvía desde ese preludio que la pianista tocaba muy lento' (Cortázar's 1977: 204) ('everything there was placid and cordial and calm and Chopin, who was returning now with that prelude that the pianist was playing very slowly', 1984: 330). Although Cortázar does not tell us which prelude, if we take the reference to the piece being played slowly as an indication that the prelude in question is a slow one, rather than meaning that the work is simply being played too slowly (a reading further suggested by the description of the scene as 'plácido y cordial y calmo' ('placid and cordial and calm')), the range of possibilities is reduced, as noted by Pérez-Abadín Barro (2010: 102), to Op. 28 Nos. 2, 4, 6, 9, 13, 15, 20, and 21. However, given the significant technical difficulty of No. 21, the moderate difficulty of No. 9, and the fact that we are told at the end of the story that the pianist here only plays 'las cosas fáciles' (Cortázar 1977: 210) ('the easy things', 1984: 334), I would suggest that the list of possible preludes be pared down by one or two here. In any case, what is revealing is to consider the descriptions of these pieces by the great Chopin pianist Alfred Cortot as, respectively: 'Méditation douloureuse; la mer déserte, au loin…'; 'Sur une tombe'; 'Le mal du pays'; 'Voix prophétiques'; 'Sur le sol étranger, par une nuit étoilée, et en pensant à la bien-aimée lointaine'; 'Mais la Mort est là, dans l'ombre…'; 'Funérailles'; and 'Retour solitaire à l'endroit des aveux' (Cellier 1926: n.p.) ('Sad meditations; in the distance a deserted sea'; 'Beside a tomb'; 'Longing for one's country'; 'The end of Poland. (lit. prophetic voices)'; 'In a strange land, under a starry sky, thinking of the beloved one far away'; 'A young mother rocking her child' [though my own literal translation would be 'But death is there, in the shadows…']; 'A funeral procession'; and 'Returning solitary to the place where vows were made', Meier 1993: 65–66). Each in its own way prefigures or echoes one or more aspects of the story, be it the homesickness of both Jiménez and (the) Chopin (figure), or the former's demise at the end of the story.[42]

Following this, the pianist repeats the Irene Dunne song, which Jiménez now recognises as 'Smoke Gets in Your Eyes',[43] before:

> el piano volvía a Chopin, uno de los estudios que también Jiménez había tocado cuando estudiaba piano de muchacho antes del gran pánico, un estudio lento y melancólico que le recordó la sala de la casa, la abuela muerta, y casi a contrapelo la imagen de su hermano que se había quedado a pesar de la maldición paterna. (Cortázar 1977: 205)

> [the piano went back to Chopin, one of the études Jiménez had also played when before the big panic, as a boy, he had taken piano lessons, a slow and melancholy étude that brought back the living room of his house, his dead grandmother, and almost against his will the image of his brother who'd stayed behind in spite of the paternal curse.] (1984: 330)

Chopin wrote only two slow études: Op. 10 No. 3 and Op. 25 No. 7. Pérez-Abadín Barro considers that the étude in question here is 'sin duda […] el estudio *Op. 25, no. 7*' (2010: 102) [without doubt […] the étude Op. 25 No. 7]. However, with this being a difficult piece, given what we noted above regarding the technical skills of the pianist, it would seem more likely that the étude referenced here is the former, popularly nicknamed *Tristesse*. Furthermore, Fred Yu describes this piece in terms which underscore its relevance both to the memories triggered by the music in Jiménez's mind and, more broadly, to the general presence of the themes of nostalgia and lost homeland (both for Chopin and for Jiménez) in the story, focusing on 'the nostalgia, the wistfulness, and the emotion that flow through the music' (2009), and going on to describe how:

> it is […] reported that while Chopin was playing this for a student, he suddenly

began weeping and cried 'Oh, my homeland!' This etude is one of the best expressions of Chopin's nationalism and the love he felt for his Poland. (2009)

The next mention of the music being played in the bar is in the form of another Chopin piece, 'uno de los valses, la simple melodía donde Chopin había puesto algo como una lluvia lenta, como talco o flores secas en un álbum' (Cortázar 1977: 206) ('one of the waltzes, the simple melody into which Chopin had put something like slow rain, like talcum powder or pressed flowers in an album', 1984: 331). Suggesting once more the themes of nostalgia and memory of times past, it is hard, from this description, to say with any degree of certainty which of Chopin's waltzes is at stake here, although one can dismiss the most technically challenging, for the reasons already mentioned, and it could be that Op. Posth. 69 No. 2 in B minor is one of the more likely candidates. Rounding off the scene in the bar, as Jiménez leaves to return to his room, we are told that 'la pianista seguía tocando una melodía cubana' (1977: 206) ('the pianist went on playing a Cuban melody', 1984: 331).

Once back in his room, we find that Jiménez cannot get out of his mind either the waltz, which he hums to himself, or the prelude, despite his attempts at changing the tune in his head to 'Smoke Gets in Your Eyes'. As the music persists in his head, its role in making present moments from his past is a notable feature ('mezclándole el pasado y el presente' (1977: 207) ('mixing up past and present for him', 1984: 332)), underlining the reiterative melancholy and nostalgia found in the text and its music. Once asleep, we are informed that he dreams of his partner, Phyllis, in the United States and 'el festival de música pop' (1977: 207) ('the pop music festival', 1984: 332), using music in this instance as a cipher for a different sociocultural space. Finally, as the story approaches its denouement, as noted above, Chopin's *Revolutionary Étude* is invoked. Significantly, this étude, written at around the time of the failed November Uprising in Poland (1830–1831), after the composer had left the country, is the one Chopin piece that is identified directly in the story.[44] And it is primarily on this piece of music and the way in which it operates in Cortázar's text that I shall now focus, in addition to offering some consideration of the other pieces that I have enumerated.

Perhaps the most notable aspect of 'Alguien que anda por ahí' with respect to its musical engagement is that, in contrast to 'Reunión', it does not fall into the trap of offering up the music with which it engages as an easy metaphor, and much less as a script or score to be followed via a textual mapping either in terms of the narrative or its construction on Cortázar's part. This works in tandem with the fact that this is a fictional story, albeit set against an historical backdrop, a further way in which this later story avoids the straitjacketing of 'Reunión'. Contributing to this rejection of music (or, indeed, history) as a scripting device are both the lack of specificity of the pieces mentioned in the course of the narrative and the fact that they are so numerous: we are simply not allowed to plot the story against any of the pieces played by the pianist, at the same time as the continually changing musical background disavows the idea of a single performance of a musical work. There are, to be sure, elements that we can draw from several of the pieces mentioned in the story that tie in with and contribute to the themes, tones, and denouement of the narrative — the presence of Cuban music, the overwhelming sense of nostalgia, melancholy, and foreboding —, but this is not a story that poses as a musical performance or copying. Nevertheless, the issue of performance would appear to be introduced into the story at the end: the Chopin figure, having lamented the fact that the pianist did not play, and would not have been capable of playing, the *Revolutionary Étude*, proceeds to strangle Jiménez in what we infer to be a playing out of that étude, this figure, in contrast to the pianist, having the fingers for such a task. But this is not a performance in the usual sense; it is not a musical playing out of the notes on the score, an imitation of the 'original'. This is, rather, an enactment, a new 'take' on the étude that, unlike the singers in 'Clone' and unlike the orchestra in 'Las ménades', does not seek to reproduce a putatively perfect 'original' rendition. In short, the enactment of the *música culta* piece does not operate along the norms of *música culta* performance.[45]

Bound up with this move away from such norms, there is also a shift in the way certain dialectics are handled in the story, when taken in contrast to the presentation found in other musical texts by Cortázar that I have been examining. The significant presence of the nostalgic, for example, both in the musings of Jiménez and in the allusions to (and music of) Chopin,[46] as well as the way in which this is brought into and (con)fused with the present in Jiménez's return to the place of his nostalgia and in the presence of the dead Chopin in this story, motion towards the breaking down of temporal categories and binary terms that we have seen to be a central element of Cortázar's attempt at transgressing the norms and problems of language and thought in his fiction. Similarly, as in 'Las ménades', there is a blurring of the active/passive identification of the characters involved: the principal actor and agitator, Jiménez, ends up passively accepting his fate, each potential action written out as a possibility ('lo único posible era la sorpresa pero también en eso iba a pura pérdida, roto por adelantado; no le iban a responder los músculos, le faltaría la palanca de las piernas para el envión desesperado' (Cortázar 1977: 208) ('the only thing possible was surprise, but even in that he would be completely lost, broken ahead of time; his muscles weren't going to respond for him, he wouldn't have the leverage in his legs for the desperate [push]', 1984: 333)); meanwhile the most passive of characters in the bar ('bebía sin mirar su vaso, los ojos perdidos en la pianista' (1977: 205) ('was drinking without looking at his glass, his eyes lost on the piano player', 1984: 330)) ends up undertaking the most active of roles in dominating and killing Jiménez in his room. But one of the ways in which this story moves beyond 'Las ménades' is in casting aside precisely the element, or divide, that Cortázar identified in 'Soledad de la música' as being the most problematic: that of the interpreter, the mediator of the work, through whom alone can we know the composer's work. By the end of 'Alguien que anda por ahí', and this is one of the reasons why it is important to see the stranger as being Chopin, there is no mediator; the pianist in the bar is left behind, and the composer is now also the enacter, where what is being enacted is, as I argued before, not a performance of what he originally intended or composed, but a new enactment of it. It is not insignificant, then, that, when Jímenez opens his eyes at the moment when the stranger is in his room, we are told that 'fue como caer en un puro espacio sin barreras' (1977: 207) ('[it] was like falling into pure space without barriers', 1984: 332), recalling Cortázar's statement in 'Soledad de la música' that 'la barrera que distancia del poema al lector — lenguaje — existe bajo otra forma para desgajar la música de su oyente; esa barrera inevitable es la *interpretación*' (1992: 292) [the barrier that distances the reader from the poem — language — exists in another form to split the music off from its listener; that unavoidable barrier is *interpretation*].

This move away from (the problematic nature of) an interpreter and interpretation, in conjunction with the story's (attendant) refusal to allow itself to be seen as a textual performance (of a prior original), indicates that the key to understanding in what way music participates in and is fundamental to the revolutionary narrative we are presented with in 'Alguien que anda por ahí' is found elsewhere. Evidently enough, the presence of the *Revolutionary Étude* is significant: its very name, although not one given to it by Chopin, who did not name his works, implies such. Rather than a score to be performed, though, it is in some of the rhythmic and compositional details that we can locate the elements of the piece which are co-opted and harnessed by Cortázar, not just in the story's narrative of the Revolution, but in the text itself *as* revolution. Primarily, we should note that the *Revolutionary Étude*, aside from being an exceedingly difficult piece to play, is also notable for its polyrhythms and cross-rhythms, which, as Yu puts it, 'are used more and more to convey a sense of conflict and struggle towards the end of the piece' (2009).[47] It also contains syncopation and accentuated off-beats. In short, it is a piece of music that is imbued with the sort of (rupturing) rhythmic effects, built around and conveying conflict and tension, that we have seen Cortázar to promote. This is in addition to the fact that Chopin was a composer who, in general, made prolific use of counterpoint.[48] Looking more closely at the construction of the text before us, there is evidence of similar practices in the criss-crossing textual motifs and patterns that Cortázar writes into the fabric of his story. The different pieces of music can be seen as different themes or melodic lines, coming in and out of the story at different times. In particular, the fact that we have reiterated musical 'types' returning — the Romantic music of Chopin, Cuban rhythms, the show tune ballad 'Smoke Gets in Your Eyes' — lends itself to the idea that, as well as forming (part of) the narrative's contrapuntal operation, these constitute the textual polyrhythms and cross-rhythms of the story, not least in that the Cuban genres referred to are themselves hybrid musical forms.[49] Moreover, the *habanera* and *danzón* are both characterised by syncopation and cross-rhythms, leaving us with a story that creates cross-rhythms out of cross-rhythms. In addition to this, the text sets up its own motifs, in particular on the basis of 'Smoke Gets in Your Eyes', with both *humo/cigarros/fumar* [smoke/cigarettes/smoking] and references to eyes/variations of the verb *mirar* [to look at] appearing repeatedly throughout the narrative as reiterated riffs, which, taken together, might, likewise, be seen to form (contrapuntal) melodic lines. Indeed, we could add *manos* [hands] to the list of such riffs, as well as the 'ave nocturna' (Cortázar 1977: 202) ('night bird', 1984: 328), which is heard three times in the story. In relation to this last example, Vázquez notes that this bird 'es sin duda el sonido espontáneo de la naturaleza y de la realidad cubana' (1986: 126) [is without doubt the spontaneous sound of nature and Cuban reality], as well as being a classic augur of death, both of which constitute meanings and implications that fit into the narrative well. But, to engage in a more detailed analysis in this instance, we might also look at the varying representation of this riff as pointing to its role as a particularly striking example of the presence of polyrhythms, counterpoint, echoes, and variations within the text's weave. The three occurrences of this riff talk, respectively, of 'la sola inconfundible llamada del ave nocturna' (Cortázar 1977: 201–02) ('the single unmistakable call of the night bird', 1984: 328); 'la queja del pájaro' (1977: 203) ('the complaint of the bird', 1984: 328); and of how 'el ave nocturna cantaba' (1977: 207) ('the night bird sang', 1984: 332). There are at least three discernible content-patterns here: the description of sound is different each time ('llamada' ('call'), 'queja' ('complaint'), 'cantaba' ('sang'): A B C); the first two descriptions are nouns, the third a verb (A A B); and the word used for the bird itself alternates ('ave', 'pájaro', 'ave': A B A). To this we might add the syllable count of this last example (two, three, two). Each iteration of this theme, that is, participates, both within itself and between each other, in several patternings that further contribute to and enhance — or, at least, are highly suggestive of — the musical cross-rhythms and patterns into which this very thread is itself inserted. Moreover, if we focus on taking all three iterations together as, as I suggested above, one single strand, we can appreciate how the four patterns I have identified come to constitute a set of textual cross-rhythms or metric patterns that subtend the entirety of this melodic line, further enriched by other patterns including those formed through (assonantal) rhyme ('llamada'/'cantaba') and word order (noting the position of 'ave nocturna' ('night bird'), for example, in the two iterations in which it appears).

All of these elements of 'Alguien que anda por ahí' — the motifs, the complex rhythmic play, the musical allusions — also come together in the service of a further, potentially revolutionary, aspect of the story, in that they appear to coalesce into what I would contend is the *figura* of the text. This is not the same sort of *figura* as found in 'Reunión' or *Los premios*, in that it is neither explicitly announced nor subject to the desires and will of the protagonist (or Cortázar?). And therein lies part of the reason why it is more successful than either of those examples: it avoids a sense of being planned, calculated, and 'forced', in short, of being overly determined and, we might say, composed. Rather, there is simply the growing sense of the numerous elements of the story cohering somehow. The different pieces of music and the different rhythms both between and amongst those pieces constitute a part of this. Likewise, the frequent, brief allusions to cigarettes and to the glances between and made by the characters, bound up with 'Smoke Gets in Your Eyes', and the references to fingers and hands that trail their way through the story, create their own suggestive and often inscrutable patterns. What is more, all of these elements are in some way intertwined with other elements. So, aside from the link between the smoke/eyes patterning and the aforementioned song, we might consider the way the rhythmic play is tied in with the thematic toing and froing between the past and the present, nostalgia and current action, or the fact that there is a (musically) suggested connection between the two men, in that, we are told, the étude played by the pianist, that I have identified as possibly being *Tristesse* (Op. 10 No. 3), is one Jiménez used to play as a child and, of course, one composed and played by Chopin. In effect, there is the persistent suggestion in the way the story is written that the multiple patterns and rhythms of all these elements, both musical and textual, are cohering into a unified pattern, that singular vision where the different elements might map onto each other.

And yet, what is key to this story is not just that the *figura* never finally does coalesce (the same can be said of the *figura* in 'Reunión', although in that case it is, significantly, envisaged that it will), but that the patterns suggested simply do not meaningfully fit together, and neither does there appear any (textual) desire for them to do so. The ties and links I have outlined are fleeting, suggestive, but never fully explain or contain the constituent parts in question, which always suggest more; the patterns (smoke/eyes/hands) resist easy definition or description; there are no simple repetitions. In all these ways, then, the move from 'Reunión' to 'Alguien que anda por ahí' can be seen as a further example of the 'shift from arborescence to rhizomatics' (Moran 2000: 207) that Moran identifies in Cortázar's *Prosa del observatorio*: the explicit and purposely constructed aborescence that we saw in the earlier story has been replaced by the boundless, ever-moving *figura* of 'Alguien que anda por ahí', which resists any totalisation and displays the ateleology and 'overflowing [of] boundaries' (Moran 2000: 206) characteristic of the rhizome. Such features of the text are noted by Bernard Terramorsi, who comments on the fact that the presence of the fantastic in the story, escaping a rigid realism when addressing questions political, results in 'un texte polysémique, transgressif, qui excède tout système herméneutique si sophistiqué soit-il; un récit qui se situe comme *dehors* des modèles de pensée qu'il réinterroge obliquement' (1997: 157) [a polysemous, transgressive text, which exceeds every hermeneutic system, however sophisticated it may be; a story that situates itself *outside* of the models of thought that it re-examines obliquely]. But what I would add is that this is fundamentally tied up with the text's *figura*, a *figura* which co-opts the *Revolutionary Étude* in one final way. One of the most notable features of Chopin's piece is its lack of resolution. Again, Yu's analysis is useful, not least for the terms he invokes in describing the end of the piece, as he affirms that 'after a hard struggle, the piece ends quite as chaotically and dramatically as it began, yet in C major, leaving us with a sense of ambiguity — we are not sure if our hero prevailed or perished' (2009). Such an ending contrasts strongly with the sense of purpose, direction, and goals, both met and envisaged, of 'Reunión' and of Mozart's *The Hunt*. It also fits in more convincingly both with Cortázar's ideas of the complex *vaivén* [back-and-forth] of music, language, and freedom/revolution in his early essays and with his continued sense of revolution (and the Revolution) as an ongoing struggle, perhaps summed up most aphoristically in his observation in interview with González Bermejo that 'la perfección [en términos de los logros revolucionarios] no es de este mundo' (1978: 131) [perfection [in terms of revolutionary successes] is not of this world]. And, crucially, it is an unresolved ending that is transposed into Cortázar's narrative, made text in the refusal of the *figura* in 'Alguien que anda por ahí' to come together.

The point is surely that both music and text were composed with that very lack of finality in mind.

This, then, is how 'Alguien que anda por ahí' constitutes a revolutionary text. It employs *la música culta* in the form of Chopin's Romantic music in a way that discards the problematic traits of performance, of interpretation, of divides between those who are active and those who are passive; and it inserts the music into — makes it a fundamental element of — a *figura* that at all times resists identification and fixity of meaning, and which, following the lead of Chopin's *Revolutionary Étude*, refuses any neat resolution. It thus contributes to a *figura* that is 'revolutionary' in its resistance to simple patterning, to order, to the easy assignment of meaning, just as the story itself, in its fantastic elements (here, once again, the importance of seeing the Chopin figure *as* Chopin), works against logic, order, and a trite realism.[50]

We might, finally, ask, then, in what ways this textual construction and its suggestive engagement with multiple rhythms and rhythmic and 'melodic' patterns brings itself to bear on its own narrative *of* revolution and counter-revolution. We have seen how the *figura* in 'Alguien que anda por ahí' marks an advance on that of 'Reunión'. But a comparison with 'Las ménades' is also revealing in this respect. Whereas in that story *la música culta*, in both general terms and in the form of the narrator as a cipher for (the norms of) the world of *la música culta*, works against and resists the (con)fusion of apparent binary oppositions and divides, including those that are given to us in the story, 'Alguien anda por ahí', a text likewise built around *la música culta*, is a text where not only are we constantly made aware of the problematisation of easy divides and identifications, but where *la música culta* and the *figura* associated with it offer no challenge to that problematisation. The undermining of easy identification is evident in the story's title, of course, which could refer both to Jiménez, as a shadowy counter-revolutionary, and to the Chopin figure, who uses that line to describe himself. But there are many examples beyond this. Thus, Jiménez, the supposed counter-revolutionary, a Cuban, has a healthy contempt for elements of the US and US attitudes to Cuba ('York tenía su idea sobre el carácter de los cubanos y Jiménez la conocía y lo puteaba desde tan adentro' (Cortázar 1977: 203) ('York had his ideas about Cuban character and Jiménez knew [them] and cursed him from deep inside', 1984: 329)), with Julio Rodríguez-Luis, in an early review article on *Alguien que anda por ahí*, commenting that 'Jiménez no parece un contrarrevolucionario convencido, sino alguien indiferente en realidad tanto a la revolución como a la contrarrevolución' (1983: 16) [Jiménez does not seem like a convinced counterrevolutionary, but someone who in reality is indifferent as much to the revolution as to the counterrevolution]. Similarly, a question mark is raised over the possible complicity of York, the US accomplice of Jiménez, with the Chopin figure: as Jiménez, helpless to defend himself against the stranger, laments, 'La pistola, el primer pensamiento inútil; si por lo menos la pistola' (Cortázar 1977: 208) ('The pistol, the first useless thought; if at least the pistol', 1984: 333), we remember that it was at York's insistence that Jiménez did not take a gun with him. In this way, when, towards the end of the story, we read of how Jiménez 'se oyó preguntar ["¿quién eres?" al extranjero] absurdamente desde eso que no podía ser el sueño ni la vigilia' (1977: 209) ('heard ["Who are you?"] being asked absurdly [of the foreign man] from what couldn't be dream or wakefulness', 1984: 333), we are alerted yet again to the lack of clear identification (of apparently binary elements) in the text, the implication being that he had asked the question from somewhere in the liminal space between the two, or, indeed, in an indeterminate shifting between them. From 'Las ménades', then, we have come full circle: *la música culta* is now engaged with in a way that allows it to play a very different role; it now operates as a complicit part of a narrative that is solely concerned with challenging divisions, classifications, and facile signification.

Accordingly, then, we need to re-visit the superficial assignation of meaning to which the story as a whole is subjected, that is, that it concerns the defence of the Cuban Revolution (Rodríguez-Luis 1983: 16–17; Terramorsi 1997: 155–56; Mora Valcárcel 1979: 177). What if the bomb is the shaking up of a Revolution that had, as Cortázar on occasion intimated, become (in certain aspects at least) stultified or 'problematic'? What if the act of strangulation is not an act in support of a genuine revolution, but, rather, one which signifies the failure of the revolutionary act that Jiménez's bombing would thus have been, just as the November Uprising also failed? Certainly, several critics have noted the presence of a counter-narrative of critique of the Revolution in the story: Terramorsi draws attention to the 'coloration inquiétante' (1997: 157) [worrying tinge] as leading some people, erroneously in his opinion, to read the story through, and as, an anti-Cuban Revolution ideological lens; whilst Pérez-Abadín Barro observes astutely that there is a 'crítica [...] solapada' (2010: 103) [sly [...] criticism] of the Revolution here.

Two aspects of the story support the raising of such questions. First, one recalls the recurrent presence in the text of the song 'Smoke Gets in Your Eyes'. It is a song which tells of the burning fire of love producing smoke that hides the infidelity of the loved one. But does this refer to Jiménez, blinded to the achievements of the Revolution by a supposed desire to rebel against it? Or is it rather a reference to the Chopin figure, and Cuban revolutionaries more widely, blinded to the failures of the Revolution by their love for it? Secondly, and relatedly, we come back to the *Revolutionary Étude* itself. Despite its ambiguous ending, history proved it to be a piece that marked the failure of the November Uprising. Is this re-enactment of the étude, then, one which rewrites this as a success, as the counterrevolution fails? Or is a 'failure' still recorded, in that the music ciphers the idea that, with this strangulation, a revolution within the Revolution is killed off? What I am suggesting, then, is that, in 'Alguien que anda por ahí', based on and infused by Chopin's Romantic music and, in particular, his *Revolutionary Étude*, Cortázar discloses that the truly revolutionary move may be to question the very idea that a profound revolution can ever even be defined.

Notes to Chapter 2

1. 'Las ménades' is from *Final del juego* (1970a [1956]); 'Reunión' is from *Todos los fuegos el fuego* (1970f [1966]); 'Alguien que anda por ahí' is from *Alguien que anda por ahí* (1977). My analyses of these stories in this chapter do not seek or pretend to be comprehensive, and several aspects of them (for example, the nostalgic elements of 'Alguien que anda por ahí', in particular in relation to Cuba) deserve more detailed attention in their own right than I have space to give them here. My approach to the texts is focused in each case on the engagement with *la música culta* in relation to concepts of revolution.
2. Ana Luengo and Klaus Meyer-Minneman (2004: 21–27) set out a political reading of the story, where el *Maestro* is seen as representing Juan Domingo Perón, with the enthused public the popular masses whom he 'creates' and yet who turn against him, preferring instead the woman in red, whom Luengo and Meyer-Minneman identify with Eva Perón.
3. There are a number of articles dedicated to 'Las ménades', all of which reference its mythical engagement to a greater or lesser extent. See, for example: Planells (1975); Coulson (1985); Aliau (1997); Goyalde Palacios (2001); Luengo and Meyer-Minneman (2004); Huici (2009); Cantarero de Salazar (2014); and García Pérez (2015). The most sustained and insightful discussion of the mythical elements of the story is the Patricio Goyalde Palacios article, although the contribution of David García Pérez in this area is also worth highlighting. Standish also discusses the story briefly in his book *Understanding Julio Cortázar* (2001: 71).
4. In their analysis of the story, Luengo and Meyer-Minneman see the division of the characters into the different parts of the theatre as an allegory of the different sectors of Argentine society, the stalls and boxes being for the bourgeoisie and the cheap seats in the gods being the place of the lower classes (2004: 22–23).
5. The four pieces played at the concert, in order, are: *A Midsummer Night's Dream*, Op. 21, by Mendelssohn; *Don Juan*, Op. 20, by Strauss; *La mer*, L. 109, by Debussy; and Beethoven's Symphony No. 5 in C minor, Op. 67.
6. I shall look in more detail at 'El perseguidor' and the references in the story to these holes in chapter 5.
7. *A Fantasy of Doctor Ox* (2003) is a short story by Jules Verne, originally published in 1874. In it, the eponymous doctor runs an experiment to ascertain the effects of a certain gas on the plant, animal, and human life of the small town of Quiquendone. One of the results of the experiment is to produce high levels of aggression in the population.
8. The playing instructions for the third movement of *La mer*, 'Dialogue du vent et de la mer', are 'Animé et tumultueux' (Debussy 1983 [1909]: 223) [Animated and tumultuous].
9. García Pérez (2015) also talks illuminatingly on the oscillation between the Apolline and the Dionysiac in 'Las ménades', though not in the context of the myth of Orpheus.
10. Other critical works that focus on the alignment of el *Maestro* and Orpheus include: Coulson (1985); Salzman and Tola (1996); and Huici (2009). Coulson in particular makes a number of perceptive observations regarding the implied identification of the conductor with and as the god-poet.
11. Standish likewise notes that 'Orpheus seems also to be implied' (2001: 71).
12. The alignment of the blind man in 'Las ménades' with Teiresias is suggested by Coulson (1985: 108), Cantarero de Salazar (2014: 300), and García Pérez (2015: 281).
13. See Coulson (1985: 107–08) and Goyalde Palacios (2001: 37).
14. See Segal (1997: 295–97)
15. See Segal (2001: 14–15)
16. Teiresias appears as a high priest of Apollo in Sophocles' *Oedipus Rex* (2006).
17. See Gantz (1993: 529–30).
18. I will look at these stories in detail in chapters 5 and 3, respectively.
19. It is also worth commenting on the fact that, just before these lines, Cortázar makes clear both the extent to which he sees Buñuel as offering the sort of holes in reality mentioned in 'El perseguidor' and that this is tied in with an essential poetism: 'en el cine que usted hace hay siempre ese agujero vertiginoso en la realidad, ese asomo a otra cosa que en último término es

la única cosa que cuenta para los poetas' (2012b: 324) [in the films that you make there is always that vertiginous hole in reality, that glimpse of something else that is ultimately the only thing that counts for poets].
20. See, for example, Goyalde Palacios (2001: 40).
21. Both García Pérez (2015: 276) and Huici (2009: 289–90) present the fervour of the crowd as being produced by the music, but do not necessarily see this as the intention of *el Maestro*.
22. Earlier versions of 'Reunión' were published in the journals *Revista. Universidad de México* (Cortázar 1964) and *El escarabajo de oro* (Cortázar 1965).
23. The characters do not have the names of these figures, but it is soon evident that the narrator is Che and the Luis character with whom they finally manage to *rendez-vous* in the Sierra Maestra is Fidel.
24. Cortázar, through the figure of Morelli, sets out his concept of the *lector cómplice* [engaged reader] in *Rayuela* (2007: 560–61; 607–08). He also frequently underscored that literature for him was 'una actividad lúdica' (González Bermejo 1978: 148) [a ludic activity].
25. Aside from the scene as set out in the opening pages of 'Las ménades', other texts by Cortázar point to this binary understanding of the *música culta* concert. 'Soledad de la música' draws attention to this early on in the way it lays out the contrast between the active musicians who play and the passive audience that listens, for example (1992: 292–93). Beyond this, we might point to the Berthe Trépat concert scene from *Rayuela* (2007: 241–50), which is predicated on a similar setting, and the description of the classical music concert and concert-goers in 'Louis, enormísimo cronopio' from *La vuelta al día en ochenta mundos*, where the latter constitute 'un público tan bien educado' (1970c: 16) [an audience that was so well-mannered], not jumping onto the stage, but sitting where they are told.
26. An earlier and influential work related to this point is Cooper and Meyer's *The Rhythmic Structure of Music* (1960).
27. Syncopation is a rupturing of the regular rhythm of a piece of music, often by stressing the weak beats.
28. For an early study of counterpoint in Mozart, see King (1945). Mirka also writes in some detail on Mozart's use of syncopation (see 2009: 122–31, in particular).
29. In interview with González Bermejo, Cortázar also brings together Mozart and jazz to suggest that they both have a similar effect on him as a writer: 'la música me ayuda a entrar en un "ètat [sic] second", como dicen los franceses [...], y muy frecuentemente escuchando los discos de jazz o de Mozart, detengo el pick-up para ir a la máquina de escribir a causa de un pasaje que me lanza sobre la escritura' (1978: 108) [music helps me to enter into an 'état second' [trance], as the French say [...], and very often, listening to jazz or Mozart records, I pause the pickup to go to the typewriter on account of a passage that urges me to write].
30. To be sure, a full study of the relationship between (the terms) jazz swing, (classical) counterpoint, and syncopation is not my aim here. Rather, I am interested in how these different rhythmic elements as found in both jazz and, here, classical music are co-opted by Cortázar into his theory and praxis.
31. The importance of this combination, where a regular rhythmic base is ruptured or played on, is in evidence in the essay 'Del cuento breve y sus alrededores' (1973b: 59–82) [On the Short Story and its Surroundings], where Cortázar describes the sense of a short story being found, as it is in a poem or in jazz, in 'la tensión, el ritmo, la pulsación interna, lo imprevisto dentro de parámetros pre-vistos' (78) [the tension, the rhythm, the internal pulsation, the unforeseen within fore-seen parameters].
32. In this regard, it is worth clarifying the difference between the case of Mozart here and that of Bach's *The Musical Offering*, as dealt with in chapter 1 in relation to 'Clone', and which, as noted, is also founded on a series of fugues and canons. In this latter instance, where the focus of the story was on performance, versions, and re-enactments, and the idea of the attainment of the 'original', the central presence of reiterative musical patterns asks to be seen in a negative light, as repetition and imitation. With regard to the present discussion, however, the focus is on the rhythms generated by such patterns. As such, and given that the subject matter of the story ('Reunión') is revolution and the possibility of seeing the revolutionary potential in *la música culta*, the fugal (in this Mozart piece) emerges here as an affirmative element.

33. See Greenberg (2004: 11–25) and Irving (1998: 37–44) for a thorough technical analysis of *The Hunt* quartet.
34. The Sonata form consists of: the introduction (optional); the exposition; the development; the recapitulation; and the coda (optional).
35. See Boldy (1980: 21–25) for a fuller discussion of the *figura* in Cortázar's work.
36. This understanding of rhythm is supported by and found in chapter 82 of *Rayuela*, where Morelli talks about 'ese balanceo, ese *swing* en el que se va informando la materia confusa' (2007: 564) ('this swaying, this *swing* in which confused material goes about taking shape', 1966: 402).
37. See Greenberg (2004: 11–25) for how Mozart's piece can be seen in this way.
38. The epigraph, from Che Guevara, refers to 'un viejo cuento de Jack London, donde el protagonista, apoyado en un tronco de árbol, se dispone a acabar con dignidad su vida' (Cortázar 1970f: 67) ('a Jack London story in which the hero [...] leans calmly against a tree and prepares to die in a dignified manner', 1979a: 49).
39. I shall return in chapter 4 to the way in which Cortázar presents the music of the Big Band or Swing Era here.
40. For a brief synopsis, see King (2005: 76–78). For a short account of Cortázar's approach to the Cuban Revolution generally and the Padilla affair specifically, see Boldy (1980: 161–65).
41. Critics have responded differently to this marrying up of the fantastic and the political in this story (and generally in Cortázar's work). Carmen de Mora Valcárcel, in an early review of 'Alguien que anda por ahí', expresses her doubts as to whether this is advisable, seeing the fantastic as contrived when applied to concrete, political circumstances (1979: 182). Enrique Ajuria Ibarra, on the other hand, argues that in Cortázar's exploring any and all themes through the fantastic, '[se] confirma su compromiso literario con la realidad en todos los aspectos' (2005: 123) [his literary engagement with reality in all its aspects is confirmed]. Bernard Terramorsi, in a considered article on the story, says that it is remarkable that Cortázar has put a politically engaged story in a literary genre which produces 'des récits fondés sur l'impossibilité de leur propre réalisation, des récits de l'irreprésentable et de l'indicible' (1997: 164) [stories based on the impossibility of their own realisation, stories of the unrepresentable and the unsayable]. As I shall make clear in the course of my analysis, and in support of Cortázar's own stance, rather than being remarkable, it is in fact entirely fitting that a text that purports to be properly revolutionary should seek to bring these two elements together.
42. Chopin left Warsaw in November 1830 for Vienna, where he spent eight months. Via Munich and Stuttgart, he then moved to Paris, which he was to make his home. It was while he was in Stuttgart that he learnt of the failure of the November Uprising in Poland, which had begun shortly after he had left for Vienna, as the Russians took Warsaw. He would never return to Poland, and his time in both Paris and Vienna is marked by homesickness and nostalgia. Jim Samson, for example, refers to Chopin's 'nostalgia and despair, and the sincerity of his patriotism' (1985: 13). For an account of Chopin's life in these regards, see Jordan (1978: 91–119) and Samson (1985: 8–24). In relation to the theme of death in these preludes, and in the story itself, we might note that, as Irena Poniatowska puts it, 'death [...] was ever present in Chopin's thoughts' (2009: 147).
43. This piece was composed for the 1933 musical *Roberta*. The Irene Dunne rendition is from the 1935 cinema version.
44. Regarding the date of composition of the *Revolutionary Étude*, Ruth Jordan, referencing Brown (1972) notes: 'Tradition has it that during those demented night hours in Stuttgart [when Chopin learnt of the failure of the November Uprising as Warsaw fell to the Russians] Chopin composed his famous study in C minor (Op. 10, No. 12) popularly known as the March of the Revolution, although Maurice Brown maintains that "there is no particle of evidence for this most firmly entrenched legend in the Chopin literature"' (1978: 105).
45. In arguing that Cortázar is engaging with Chopin's music here in a way that eschews the idea of performing a reading of a score, it may be worth noting Jeffrey Kallberg's contention, referencing Eugène Delacroix's comments on the pianist, that 'Chopin's improvisations [in the form of sketches that he played as a pianist], we may deduce from Delacroix's remarks, provided listeners with even more profound insight into his powers of imagination than did his finished

works' (2001: 409). This assertion of the power and privileged potential of improvisation starts to move us towards elements that I will discuss further on in the chapters on jazz.
46. The nostalgia that marked Chopin as a person, following his departure from Poland, is also found in his music. Thus, his compositional return to the Polonaise shortly after moving to Paris was charged with sense that 'the dance form [had become] for the nostalgic exile a potent symbol of Poland, and specifically a Poland oppressed' (Samson 1985: 103). Likewise, the 1836 song *Leci liście z drzewa* is, as Samson notes, a nostalgic and 'passionate lament for Poland' (103).
47. A cross-rhythm is a polyrhythm that is a systemic feature of a piece of music, rather than a momentary occurrence within it.
48. It is not without reason that Chopin is often recognised as having introduced a 'revolutionary' technique in his works and playing (see, for example, Hinson (1993: 65)).
49. The hybrid nature of Cuban musical genres, including the *habanera* and *danzón*, is charted in Carpentier (1984 [1946]). For more detail, including on the nature and importance of the *habanera* and *danzón* form, see Manuel (2009: 1–112).
50. Terramorsi makes the case for other ways in which 'Alguien que anda por ahí' is a subversive text. He argues that, by giving the ghost the positive role, Cortázar subverts 'le scénario mythique du spectre persécuteur' (1997: 160) [the mythical scenario of the harassing spectre]. For Terramorsi, this 'anticonformisme' [anticonformism] on Cortázar's part 'est en soi un "contenu révolutionnaire"' (160) [is itself a 'revolutionary content'], simultaneously subverting 'un genre littéraire [...] et une vision du monde' (160) [a literary genre [...] and a vision of the world].

CHAPTER 3

Tango:
Nostalgia and Creativity

Tango's place in Cortázar's thought and work differs notably from that of both *la música culta* and jazz: it is not mentioned in any explicit form in the early essays to which I have referred thus far in this study, most strikingly 'Soledad de la música', and yet it is a reiterative presence in his writing, including in his fiction and poetry. One way of reading this state of affairs would be to conclude that tango was a musical form whose presence in Cortázar's *œuvre* was due to its Argentine, and more specifically *porteño*, character, bound up inescapably both with Cortázar himself as such and with his broader interest in describing and reflecting upon innately Argentine characters, places, and themes in his work. Its absence in his more theoretical music-related musings would, according to this line of thought, indicate that it is not a musical genre to which Cortázar appeals as he seeks to examine how music might, variously, respond to, repeat, and possibly escape from the metaphysical and expressive ties with which he wrestles. Indeed, that tango represents the only musical form in which Cortázar participated to the level of being involved in a discographic release merely reinforces the impression that tango is a music that spoke to and was entrenched in the author more in its practice than in its theoretical significance and possibilities.¹ There is, moreover, more than a grain of truth in such a reading, and I will examine several of the facets just mentioned in due course. But there is also much that can be gleaned from Cortázar's engagement with tango that feeds directly into the debates that I have addressed in the preceding chapters. There are numerous statements across a variety of interviews, for example, that chime both with the terms and questions that we have seen to arise in the course of Cortázar's discussions of music and language generally, and with the specific issues of scripting and revolution that I have argued undergird some of the key Cortazarian texts built around *la música culta*. I shall examine these in the following pages, as well as exploring the way in which these statements operate in tandem with Cortázar's repeated practice of alluding to and citing tango lyrics in his fiction and tango-poetry. In this respect, this chapter will build upon groundwork that has been laid by several critics who have focused in some detail on such texts (and in particular the poems from the 'Con tangos' and other sections of *Salvo el crepúsculo*, several of which, as noted, were also set to music and released as the album *Trottoirs de Buenos Aires*), albeit in this case through the thematics and theoretical terms of my first two chapters.² Where I depart most keenly from previous studies of Cortázar's tango, however, is in the importance I give to two of his most overtly tango-related short stories, 'Las puertas del cielo' from *Bestiario* (1993a [1951]) and 'Tango de vuelta' [Return Trip Tango] from *Queremos tanto a Glenda* (1980), and in particular the relationship that is constructed between them. I shall, then, end this chapter by analysing to what extent these stories enable us both to crystallise and to advance our understanding of the role that tango plays in Cortázar's work, resonating with the conflicting terms and pulls of his engagement with *la música culta*, and adumbrating some of the debates surrounding jazz and jazz improvisation that will underpin the remaining chapters of this study.

Tango for Cortázar: An Appraisal

If 'Soledad de la música' fails to mention tango by name, there is nevertheless a strong case to be made for the applicability of the lines of this essay that are more readily identifiable as relating to the world of *la música culta* to this fundamentally Argentine musical genre as well. Exhibit A in such a case would be the fact that the only type of music that Cortázar explicitly signals as an exception to the problems of '*la interpretación*' (1992: 292) [*interpretation*] is jazz, as I shall discuss in subsequent chapters. Moreover, several decades later, in interview with Prego, Cortázar states baldly that 'el tango se toca como la música llamada clásica' (1985: 163) [tango is played like so-called classical music], thus confirming the alignment of the problems that we have observed Cortázar to locate in *la música culta* — problems that are signalled initially in 'Soledad de la música' — with tango too. Indeed, both in this interview and in his interview with González Bermejo he goes into some detail as he explains the drawbacks and sticking points of tango, all of which take up the concerns he outlines in relation to *la música culta* both in that early essay and elsewhere. Thus, prior to his conclusion regarding the similarity of tango and 'so-called' classical music, he states that 'el tango [...] permite únicamente una ejecución basada en la partitura y sólo algunos instrumentistas muy buenos [...] se permiten variaciones o improvisaciones mientras todos los demás de la orquesta están sujetos a una escritura' (Prego 1985: 163) [tango [...] only permits a performance based on the score and only a few very good instrumentalists [...] allow themselves variations or improvisations whilst the rest of the orchestra is subject to a writing]. The same guilty parties are present: the score, on the basis of which each interpretation or performance is produced, and the attendant lack of freedom and improvisation. And these complaints are reiterated in conversation with González Bermejo, as Cortázar talks of how:

> el tango [...] no da libertad de improvisación, de búsqueda de nuevas cosas a los intérpretes sino de manera muy estrecha [...] es muy monótono en el sentido de que a partir de una fórmula orquestal dada sólo permite raras diferencias de interpretación, salvo en el bandoneón con el que algunos ejecutantes [...] se permiten variaciones o improvisaciones muy hermosas aunque siempre limitadas por el esquema rígido de la forma. (1978: 109–10)

[tango [...] allows its performers no freedom to improvise, to seek out new things except in the narrowest ways [...] it is very monotonous in the sense that starting from a given orchestral formula it only allows very occasional differences in interpretation, except in the case of the *bandoneón* with which some performers [...] allow themselves very beautiful variations or improvisations, although always limited by the rigid schema of the form.]

He also adds that 'en definitiva, el tango es rutinario' (109) [definitively, tango is routine], thus connecting this musical form to the broader notions of custom, habit, and order that, as we have seen, represent markers of exactly what Cortázar tries to break free from in his work.[3] Indeed, beyond the problematic characteristics it apparently shares with other forms of music, tango, for Cortázar, has issues of its own. Specifically in relation to its origins and nature, for example, Cortázar alludes to its restrictive and restricted identification, affirming that 'con todo el tango sigue siendo un mundo pequeño y limitado, como Buenos Aires es una ciudad pequeña y limitada con relación al mundo entero' (109) [with all that, tango is still a small and limited world, just as Buenos Aires is a small and limited city in relation to the whole world].

Bringing these comments together, it is scarcely surprising that we should find some starkly negative statements by Cortázar about tango as a whole, most obviously in the repeated description of tango as being 'musicalmente [...] pobre' (109) [musically [...] poor]. In interview in 1984 with Jason Weiss, for example, he states that 'I think that the tango on the whole, especially next to jazz, is very poor music' (1991: 53), whilst, talking to Prego, he decides hyperbole is the path to take in making the same point, affirming that 'el tango es muy pobre con relación al jazz, el tango es pobrísimo, paupérrimo' (1985: 163) [tango is very poor in comparison to jazz, tango is extremely poor, exceedingly poor].

Given these statements and the apparent problems Cortázar identifies in tango, it might seem odd that this music should feature so prominently in his work. But feature it does, across a wide range of texts and eras, Peiró commenting that tango is a more prominent presence in Cortázar's work than one might think (2006: 73). It is not my intention to give an exhaustive list of all the places where tango appears or plays a role in Cortázar's writing, but a broad overview of the range and type of tango engagement is apposite, not least to get a sense of its pervasiveness in his corpus.[4] In Cortázar's novels, most notably *Los premios* and *Rayuela*, tango is, amongst other things, bound up with the (Argentine) characterisation and identity of key figures;[5] in his short stories it appears, variously, as the source of the underlying theme or story being narrated ('Torito', from *Final del juego* (1970a [1956]), 'Tango de vuelta'),[6] a concrete presence in the form of the tango world generally ('Las puertas del cielo'),[7] as an element which 'crea ambiente' (Fralasco 2005: 132) [creates an atmosphere], as in the case of 'La noche de Mantequilla' [Butterball's Night] from *Alguien que anda por ahí* (1977), or as a more general constant backdrop (*Diario de Andrés Fava*).[8] Beyond these selected examples from his fiction, Cortázar also wrote about aspects of tango in his non-fiction writing, perhaps most notably the short piece 'Gardel' (1970b: 136–41),[9] as well as incorporating and transforming tango lyrics in his poetry, as is most strikingly the case, as I have indicated, in poems from

Salvo el crepúsculo, where he also glosses this use of tango in short prose segments, not forgetting that several of these poems were used as actual tango lyrics on the *Trottoirs de Buenos Aires* album. And then there are less easily classifiable texts like 'Un gotán para Lautrec' [A Tango for Lautrec], a part historical, part fictional prose piece that accompanies the drawings of Uruguayan artist Hermenegildo Sábat in the work *Monsieur Lautrec* (Cortázar and Sábat 1980), in which Cortázar references sixteen sets of tango lyrics as he uses the music to effect a bridge between Toulouse-Lautrec and the world of Buenos Aires.[10]

In almost all of the examples mentioned above, as well as more generally across a number of other texts, the engagement with tango also includes tango lyrics being placed, or woven, either overtly or covertly, into the textual fabric. This in itself highlights a fundamental difference between Cortázar's use of tango and his use of other musical genres, in that, even taking into account his allusion to certain jazz and blues lyrics, notably in *Rayuela*, it is the lyrical nature (the lyrics and their subject matter) of the *tango-canción* [tango-song], the tango to which Cortázar was most drawn, that constitutes the principal element of his deployment of tango.[11] That said, as is implied by the case of 'Las puertas del cielo' and its primary setting of the world of the *milonga* [tango club] and tango performance, it is not only the lyrics of tango that surface in Cortázar's work: other elements, including dance, music, and, indirectly, art, specifically in joint art-literature projects with Sábat and Pat Andrea, are also brought to bear on his 'tango texts'.[12] It is clear, then, that the negative appraisal of tango that we find in some of Cortázar's most clear-cut statements on the musical genre are only part of the story, and, indeed, as the persistence and multivalency of tango in his work suggest, alongside such commentary we also find a counterbalancing strand of appreciation for the music. Cortázar himself was at pains to point out such. When asked by González Bermejo if he considered himself to be 'un desertor del tango' (1978: 108) [a deserter of tango], Cortázar replies simply, 'En absoluto' (108) [Absolutely not]. Even more starkly, shortly after his declaration in interview with Prego that tango is 'pobrísimo, paupérrimo' (1985: 163) [extremely poor, exceedingly poor], he states that 'no me gustaría que esto que he dicho acerca del tango y su pobreza sea considerado como una idea negativa, que yo no manejo en absoluto' (165) [I wouldn't want what I have said about tango and its poverty to be considered as a negative idea, which I absolutely do not hold to]. If this clarification fails entirely to convince, it is its rather insistent denial of his negative appraisal of tango that falls flat rather than the idea that he holds a more affirmative view of the music *as well*.

Particularly revealing for understanding the nature and basis of Cortázar's positivity regarding tango is the interview with Eduardo Olivares, published in *Le Monde de la Musique* in 1981. Already, in conversation with González Bermejo, Cortázar had described the 'especie de solución de belleza' (1978: 109) [kind of beautiful solution] in tango music, and here it is the first music he mentions when listing genres that he values (Olivares 1981: 56). Contrary to the impression given from his elevation of jazz and general discussion of music in 'Soledad de la música', he denies, in this late interview, that it is possible to 'parler de genres majeurs et mineurs' (58) [speak of major and minor genres], and dwells upon the particular qualities of Carlos Gardel, without question one of the mainstays of Cortázar's evident fondness for and praise of the merits of tango throughout his life and work.[13] Gardel will come up at several points during my discussion of specific instances of Cortázar's engagement with tango. For now, however, it is enough to draw attention to some of the central reasons why Cortázar was such a fan of the singer, with one of the principal of these being that Gardel was particularly capable of doing justice to tango's ability to express 'les valeurs et les fausses valeurs du peuple argentin' (58) [the values and the false values of the Argentine people]. The importance of tango in Cortázar's praxis thus points to the importance of 'local' identity, not only in his engagement with music, but also in terms of his broader metaphysical concerns regarding identity, being, and language. And, as with so many other areas of Cortázar's work and thought, any consideration of the local must look to embrace and take in all its constituent elements, 'good' and 'bad'. For Cortázar, tango does precisely this, being above all an expression of every aspect of the Argentine, transmitting 'le sentiment de cafard, de nostalgie, d'effondrement qui habite les Argentins' (58) [the feeling of depression, of nostalgia, of collapse that inhabits Argentines]. And it is within this context that he refers to how Gardel, at the forefront of the tango world for so long, 'a exprimé la sensibilité de tout un pays pendant plus de trente ans et [...] l'exprime encore' (58) [expressed the sensibility of an entire country for more than thirty years and [...] still does].[14] Indeed, Cortázar's declarations to Olivares echo those made earlier to González Bermejo, when he underlines the extent to which tango does not shy away from the negative aspects of Argentine identity:

> Puede imaginarse lo que representa para mí el tango como expresión de Buenos Aires, de lo bueno y lo malo de los argentinos. Pero si usted mira críticamente al tango como expresión de un pueblo sobre todo de una ciudad, el resultado dista de ser positivo. Allí están muchas de nuestras frustraciones, nuestros tabúes, nuestros complejos; no hay prácticamente nada bueno, todo es malo o en todo caso todo es triste, desesperanzado. (1978: 109)
>
> [You can imagine what tango represents for me as an expression of Buenos Aires, the good and the bad of Argentines. But if you look critically at tango as an expression of a country and above all of a city, the result is far from positive. You will find many of our frustrations, our taboos, our complexes; there is practically nothing good, everything is bad or in any case everything is sad, despairing.]

Importantly, as Cortázar points out in the 'Con tangos' section of *Salvo el crepúsculo*, the role and effect of tangos in this regard is not reserved for some putative overarching set of timeless traits, but is (also) tied in with the ongoing process of traumatic sociohistorical change and events in Argentina, which the songs ('máquinas mnemónicas' (2009: 74) [mnemonic machines]) take in and, subsequently, trigger in the listener.[15] Moreover, both this openness to fundamental and historically-inflected characteristics and traits of identity and being in Argentina and of the individual Argentine, together with the expressive richness of tango, exemplified and epitomised in the voice of Gardel, point towards the underlying value and sway of tango for Cortázar as being found not just in its appeal to the local, but also —

and not unrelatedly — in its profound identification as a music of human emotions and feelings, this being located in elements that stretch beyond the genre's lyrics and their singing, in that, for example, 'il y a par ailleurs quelque chose dans le rythme du tango, dans la façon dont on le danse, un érotisme nocturne, qui est peut-être très négatif et cafardeux. Mais ce sont des sentiments humains' (Olivares 1981: 58) [there is, in addition, something in the rhythm of tango, in the way it is danced, a nocturnal eroticism, which is perhaps very negative and downbeat. But these are human feelings].[16]

At this point we are evidently some way from the theoretical concerns and revolutionary wranglings with which we have noted Cortázar to engage as he brings music into both his essays and stories. That is not to say, as observed, that the inclusion of *la música culta* in his work does not owe something to his fondness for such music and the emotions, at least of awe and wonder, that certain pieces inspire within him. But tango's hold on Cortázar appears to come very much in spite of supposed musical failings that he does not shirk from mentioning at several junctures. Moreover, whereas *la música culta* is, despite its problematically linguistic operations, explicitly marshalled to revolutionary ends by Cortázar, in the case of tango, rather than posit some way in which this music might offer a viable route towards the attainment of his broader ontolinguistic goals, Cortázar instead appears to indulge tastes and pulls that seem, at first sight at least, to run counter to those goals, not least in that it is a personal, local music that revels in and is inextricably intermeshed with nostalgia. Robert Farris Thompson, for example, talks of how 'if nostalgia is a country, tango is its capital' (2005: 25), and Cortázar is unapologetic on several occasions in underscoring the extent to which tango goes hand in hand for him with a wallowing in nostalgia and the nostalgic. Music, for Cortázar, 'está muy ligad[a] a tu vida personal, es imposible separar una serie de nostalgias y vivencias de otro tiempo' (Prego 1985: 165) [is very tied in with your personal life, it's impossible to separate [from it] a series of nostalgic memories and experiences from another time], something we have seen in the case of the protagonist (and the Chopin figure) of 'Alguien que anda por ahí' in relation to other musical forms, and which I will go on to note in regard to Cortázar's relationship with jazz too in chapter 6. And, in the case of tango, more than with any of these other genres, Cortázar positively yields to and delights in its nostalgic pulls, adding, 'Cuando pongo un disco de Gardel estoy viendo el patio de mi casa, toda mi familia; ese disco hace pasar imágenes, figuras' (Prego 1985: 165–66) [when I put on a Gardel record I am seeing the patio of my house, all my family; that record makes images, figures pass before me]. Similarly, towards the end of his life, he had no qualms in admitting to passing time in nostalgic reverie, during which he would write his tango-poems, stating in 1981 that 'depuis deux o trois ans, dans mes heures de nostalgie, j'écrivais des poèmes pour moi. Au fond, c'étaient des paroles de tango' (Olivares 1981: 58) [for two or three years, in my hours of nostalgia, I would write poems for myself. Essentially, they were tango lyrics], as well as commenting on his involvement in the *Trottoirs de Buenos Aires* project in a letter in March 1980, 'No me pegues, pero hice un disco de tangos aquí en París, mirá lo que son las nostalgias' (2012c: 240) [don't hit me, but I've done a tango record here in Paris, that's nostalgia for you]. What is evident is that, for all his desire radically to alter and disturb accepted linguistic and ontological forms and operations, as he goes on to say in this letter, 'es que yo siempre fui un sentimental, un tierno y un cursi, y lo mejor es que no lo lamento' (240) [the thing is I always was a sentimental chap, a softie, corny, and the best thing is I'm not sorry about it].

It appears, then, that tango discloses, or allows Cortázar to disclose, a pull that is contrary to the one that we have seen to guide his general theoretical engagement with music and the role played by *la música culta* in some of his key fictions: rather than looking forward, seeking the new or to renew existing structures and epistemologies, it shows a man drawn to the past, to home, to the comforting, and to what he himself described as the 'rutinario' (González Bermejo 1978: 109) [routine]. Hints of an awareness of this contradiction appear to be found when, for example, he congratulates himself upon noticing that he has written the tango-poem 'Rechiflao en mi tristeza' (Cortázar 2009: 69) [Crazy in My Sadness], having refused to 'hundirme en la nostalgia de la tierra lejana' (70) [sink into nostalgia for the distant homeland]. And yet several aspects of this survey of Cortázar's engagement with tango contain disjunctures and aporia that destabilise such a conclusion, suggesting that the opposition between Cortázar's linguistic, ontological, and revolutionary aims on the one hand and, on the other, the draw to the personal, the local, to home and the past is an opposition which cannot be sustained, perhaps most fundamentally in the sense that any 'authentic' expression and communication of the human must retain what it is that makes one human, and these latter elements are an essential part of that; they are an essential part of any individual. This is why Cortázar underscores these aspects of tango so forcefully. It is not, then, that all that Cortázar associates with tango should be seen as a drag on his wider aims and musical directions, but that it must be part of what is expressed in an 'authentic' manner, despite the supposed musical failings of the genre itself: tango as home, as origins must be bound up with a 'revolutionary' — in the sense of forward-looking and defamiliarising — expressive form, whilst retaining its familiarity. We are back, it would seem, at the need to bring together apparently contradictory drives and entities. But an understanding of how tango — both itself and in its emergence in and use by Cortázar — might already contain the germ of how these putatively opposing pulls can be drawn together and, thus, of how tango can be seen both to affirm and yet also to work against the 'poverty' Cortázar identifies in it, is found in the fault line that courses through perhaps its central characteristic, to which I have already been referring: nostalgia.

Nostalgia

The starting point for examining the relationship between nostalgia and tango in Cortázar's work must be the recognition that there are two distinct planes on which this relationship operates. I have alluded to both in passing above, but it is important to set them out more clearly at this stage. For one, there is the nostalgia of the images and contexts that are conjured up by and through the act of listening to tangos. The nostalgia at stake here is one which becomes, then, in many respects a fundamentally personal question of what tango recalls and revives, sending the individual listener back both temporally and spatially to what we might term the (original) listening context. The reference alluded to above where Cortázar describes putting on a Gardel record as being a return to 'el patio de mi casa, toda mi familia' (Prego 1985: 165–66) [the patio of my house, all my family] is an indication of this, and these lines reflect a discourse that is given more room to expand in the 'Con tangos' section of *Salvo el crepúsculo*, where he talks of '[las] magdalenas de Gardel o de Laurenz tirando a la cara'los olores y las luces del barrio (el mío, Banfield, con calles de tierra en mi infancia, con paredones que de noche escondían los motivos posibles del miedo)' (2009: 74) [Gardel's or Laurenz's sobbing throwing into my face the smells and lights of the neighbourhood (mine, Banfield, with earth streets in my childhood, with walls that at night would hide the possible reasons to be afraid)].[17] Likewise, in the earlier 'Gardel', Cortázar comments that:

> a Gardel hay que escucharlo en la victrola, con toda la distorsión y la pérdida imaginables; su voz sale de ella como la conoció el pueblo que no podía escucharlo en persona, como salía de zaguanes y de salas en el año veinticuatro o veinticinco. (1970b: 136)
>
> [you must listen to Gardel on a gramophone, with all the distortion and loss imaginable; his voice emerges from it just as the people encountered it, people who weren't able to hear him in person, just as it would emerge from hallways and living rooms in '24 or '25].

In this sense, however, these lines go further: it is not just that the (subsequent) act of listening to tango ineluctably evokes the time and place in which one used to listen to it in one's formative years; there is also a clear element here of the willed recreation of a condition of listening that furthers such nostalgic evocation. Little surprise, then, that Cortázar should reiterate the ability of tango to bring back past times, not just when listening to a physical disc, but when 'el ronroneo de un tango en la memoria me trae más imágenes que toda la historia de Gibbons' (2009: 70) [the purring of a tango in my memory brings me more images than the whole of Gibbons's history].

But if the fact that, as Héctor Fralasco puts it, Cortázar 'creció en un hogar en que se hablaba y se escuchaba [*sic*] tangos por la radio y en el piano que tocaba su hermana' (2005: 167) [grew up in a home in which tangos were talked about and listened to on the radio and on the piano that his sister played] is undoubtedly key in understanding this evocative power of tango for the author, tango's identification with Argentina and, more specifically, Buenos Aires, also feeds into the particularly personal nostalgia of his relationship with the music, a result of the coming together of tango's inherently *porteño* character and Cortázar's (and many of his characters') (quasi-)exilic condition of being in Paris.[18] Tango, that is, becomes a marker of a nostalgia not just for the times and places of childhood, but also, more generally, for the place of Buenos Aires and Argentina as a whole: as Cortázar states in interview with Weiss, tango is 'the music that sends me back to my youth again *and* to Buenos

Aires' (1991: 53, italics mine). In this sense, where Svetlana Boym in her work on nostalgia underscores that 'the music of home, whether a rustic cantilena or a pop song, is the permanent accompaniment of nostalgia' (2001: 4), we might add that, in this case of tango, this is redoubled by the music's being perhaps the ultimate symbol and identifier *of* that home. Notably, it is an aspect of tango's meaning for Cortázar and his texts whose full presence and charge are foreshadowed in writings dating from before the author's definitive move to Paris, with Peiró (2006: 74) noting that tango is evoked from afar as a marker of (the nostalgia for) the distant homeland in the poems of 'Razones de la cólera' [Reasons for Anger], dating from 1949, before Cortázar settled in Paris in 1951.[19] Nevertheless, as might be expected, one of the clearest statements of this aspect of the nostalgic meaning of tango for Cortázar is found in one of his later texts, 'Un gotán para Lautrec', where he declares wistfully that 'silbar viejos tangos centrados en melancólicos destinos de ida o de venida es una de mis muchas maneras de seguir estando en Buenos Aires, sobre todo ahora que ya no puedo volver' (1993b: 238) [whistling old tangos focused on melancholic destinations of a journey or a return is one of my many ways of still being in Buenos Aires, especially now that I cannot go back]. Tango here, then, is not just a 'memorative sign' (Rousseau 1779: 267) of the *porteño*'s home, it *is* (an innate signifier of) that home.

It is worth noting that both of these elements that combine to form the particularities of tango's nostalgia for Cortázar are also found in his fiction, perhaps most unsurprisingly in the character of Oliveira in *Rayuela*, who, we are told, for example, in a scene in the chapters set in Paris (chapter 20) in which, significantly, given the context of the present discussion, he is sharing *mate* with la Maga, 'canturreaba el tango ["Flor de fango", de Gardel]' (2007: 219) [was softly singing Gardel's tango ['Flor de fango']]. When taken together with his citing of tango lyrics on other occasions in these Paris chapters, it is clear that, as Peiró comments, *Rayuela* underlines 'la fuerte vinculación de un argentino con la cultura del tango, incluso (o sobre todo) si se encuentra desplazado o en el exilio' (2006: 85) [the strong link of an Argentine with tango culture, including (or above all) if he/she is displaced or in exile], with tango culture and Argentina (Buenos Aires) here being rendered synonymous.[20] Similarly, back in the Argentine capital, the idea of the restoration of the original listening context of tango that we have seen to characterise Cortázar's relationship with the music is also in evidence in the case of Oliveira when he states that 'no puedo oír ciertos tangos sin acordarme cómo los tocaba mi tía, che' (Cortázar 2007: 745) ('I can't listen to certain tangos without remembering how my aunt used to play them', 1966: 562).

As alluded to above, there is, however, a further plane on which the nostalgia of and related to tango is to be understood, and one which must be taken equally into account in an examination of the way in which tango and nostalgia play themselves out in Cortázar's thought and work. The continuation of a quotation by Thompson that I referred to earlier provides as useful a way as any into this aspect of tango, as the notion of tango as the capital of an imagined country called nostalgia is supplemented by the explanation that 'tango writes of time, loss, and love' (2005:

25). Put simply, it points to the nature of tango lyrics, concerns, themes, and emotions as essentially nostalgic, to the point where Thompson even describes the renowned tango lyricist Homero Manzi (1907–1951) as having invented 'a grammar of nostalgia' (41).

Several critics have linked this characteristic of tango to its history. Tango originated at the end of the nineteenth century in the *arrabales* or *barrios* [slums/suburbs] of Buenos Aires, being born, musically and socioculturally, from the coming together at that time of European immigrants, 'young men of the elite class' (Nielson and Mariotto 2006: 13), internal migrants from the provinces, and blacks. As Jorgelina Corbatta puts it, it was the 'resultado de un proceso en el que se aúnan al menos tres vertientes principales: la criolla, la africana y la europea manifiestas en especies musicales afines. O sea: la milonga, el candombe y la habanera, y el tango andaluz [respectivamente]' (1994: 63) [result of a process in which at least three main strands combined: the creole, the African, and the European, manifested in the related musical types. That is, the *milonga*, the *candombe* and the *habanera*, and the Andalucian tango [respectively]].[21] The role of the European immigrants in the creation of tango has often been particularly strongly emphasised, and, the importance of the other elements notwithstanding, it is, to a large — though not exclusive — extent in this key strand in the early history of tango that we find the origins of the nostalgia that pervades tango's 'content'. Taylor, for example, refers to the 'intensity of the nostalgia of the Argentine immigrant and his painful lack of a sense of belonging and permanence in his new country' (1976: 284), whilst, on a different tack, Corbatta alludes to, and implicitly agrees with, Ernesto Sábato's (1968) contention that the hybridisation caused by mass immigration at the end of the nineteenth century into Buenos Aires led to the 'nostalgia de otro tiempo y lugar' (Corbatta 1994: 63) [nostalgia for another time and place] that characterises tango. When adding in the further contribution to these sentiments found in the form of the 'desperate lack of roots and [...] introspective fatalistic pessimism' (Taylor 1976: 274) that were brought to the *arrabales* by the migrants from the pampas, one starts to grasp the inherent longing for a sense of home that grounds the conditions of tango's origins. Indeed, in this light, it is no surprise that, as Christine S. Nielsen and Juan Gabriel Mariotto, amongst others, observe, melancholy is one of the characteristic emotions of tango, and one which is 'expressed in terms of nostalgia' (2006: 22).

Alongside the identification of nostalgia as a characteristic emotion of the genre is its prevalence as an essential theme of tango lyrics. Focusing on the 'return to the *barrio*' (Taylor 1976: 281) motif, Taylor, for example, comments on the repeated nostalgia in tangos, following the characters' departure from the *barrios*, for 'familiar faces, for traditional houses and their patios converted into slum dwellings or *conventillos*, and for gardens and their grape arbors' (281). Perhaps the most significant aspect here is that, whilst there are elements that are reminiscent of or evoke the provinces, the nostalgia that one finds in tango lyrics, and certainly those of the New Guard — the period of tango to which Cortázar himself was drawn —, is centred around the urban space of Buenos Aires and its *arrabales*.[22] The nostalgia of the immigrants and the internal migrants from the pampas, that is, was transposed into and given form as a *porteña* nostalgia of and for the *barrios* of the Argentine capital, the suburbs that 'una vez abandonado[s] se torna[n] el paraíso perdido' (Corbatta 1994: 66) [once abandoned turn into the lost paradise], and which in the music's lyrics thus came to represent, in a manner that recalls and reconnects us with Cortázar's own nostalgic experiencing of tango, 'la infancia y el pasado perdidos en donde todo era — al menos en la memoria evocativa — apacible y seguro' (66) [lost childhood and the lost paradise where everything was — at least in evocative memory — pleasant and safe].[23]

A useful lens for unpacking the nature of the nostalgia at stake in Cortázar's engagement with tango, in relation to both the strands I have identified, is found in the work of Svetlana Boym, to which I have already alluded. Boym identifies two nostalgic tendencies.[24] The first of these she calls restorative nostalgia, a nostalgia which 'stresses *nostos* and attempts a transhistorical reconstruction of the lost home [...;] the return to origins' (2001: xviii). Several aspects of this form of nostalgia resonate with the characteristic tango emotions and themes to which I have been referring. The motif of the return to the *barrio* certainly chimes with the notion of the return home, and its potential connection with the *nostos* of modern (restorative) nostalgia identified by Boym is strengthened when one considers the terms with which she describes this locale: it is 'a home that is both physical and spiritual, the edenic unity of time and space before entry into history' (8), a 'yearning for a different time — the time of our childhood' (2007: 8), as she points up that restoration 'signifies a return to [this] original stasis, to the prelapsarian moment' (2001: 49). The characterisation of the Buenos Aires *barrios* as the lost paradise of 'la infancia' (Corbatta 1994: 66) [childhood] would seem to fit this template well. Indeed, such an alignment is further reinforced by the nature of the restorative operation in this nostalgic tendency, which, leaning upon Eric Hobsbawm's influential work 'Inventing Traditions' (1983), Boym sees not so much as a (necessarily) faithful restoration of what once was, as a move that 'builds on the sense of loss of community and cohesion and offers a comforting collective script for individual longing' (2001: 42). It does not take much imagination to see this as a mould into which the migrant communities that were central to the birth of tango fit. And, similarly, neither does it require much effort to appreciate how Cortázar's own personal relationship to tango might be conceived as an example of a restorative nostalgic tendency, not least because the distinctly personal resonances and pining for the lost home — one, we might recall, that is firmly tied in with 'mi infancia' (Cortázar 2009: 74) [my childhood] — are framed within an understanding of the inherently collective nature of the tango script, made up of a common repository of tango songs and references, and particularly starkly felt by the Argentine in exile, or distanced from the homeland. As Cortázar comments, 'a nosotros los tangos nos vuelven en una recurrencia sardónica cada vez que escribimos tristeza, que estamos llovizna, que se nos atasca la bombilla en la mitad del mate' (69) [tangos come back to us with a sardonic recurrence every time that we write sadness, that we are drizzle, that the metal straw gets blocked halfway through our *mate*]. Perhaps the clearest way in which Cortázar's own engagement with tango dovetails with the restorative nostalgic tendency, though, is found in what I have identified as the author's self-confessed focus on the importance of recreating the original listening context of tangos ('a Gardel *hay* que escucharlo en la victrola [...] como salía de zaguanes y de salas en el año veinticuatro o veinticinco' (1970b: 136, italics mine) [you *must* listen to Gardel on a gramophone [...] just as it would emerge from hallways and living rooms in '24 or '25], a move that relates to Boym's description of how 'restorative nostalgia ends up reconstructing emblems and rituals of home and homeland' (2001: 49), in this case both in terms of content and form of consumption.

The concept of restorative nostalgia also serves to bring form and content, Cortázar and tango (generally) together in broader ways. In her exploration of the term, Boym points to Hobsbawm's idea that restored traditions 'ref[er] to a "set of practices, normally governed by overtly or tacitly accepted rules and of a ritual of symbolic nature which seeks to inculcate certain values and norms of behavior by repetition which automatically implies continuity with the past"' (Boym 2001: 42). Within the context of tango, this resonates with the genre's (quasi-)'ritualised' focus on conformity with and return to a traditional value system and the socioeconomic limitations of the *barrios*, which Cortázar himself signals in conversation with Prego, where we also see a further association of the *arrabales* with an earthly paradise:

> OP: Otra *constante* [...] es la del viaje en busca de un destino que de alguna manera misteriosa le está señalado [a la mujer], al que sigue el regreso tras la derrota. Como si el viaje fuera una especie de transgresión a *unas reglas* del juego no escritas.
> JC: Claro. [...] 'No salgas de tu barrio, sé buena muchachita/casate con un hombre que sea como vos'. Es decir, el consejo de *la conformidad total*.
> OP: Eso es, *'conformidad'*, la *aceptación*. En la mayoría de los tangos la felicidad proviene de la *aceptación* de *una situación pre-edénica*. Si transgredís el *código*, sos expulsado y sólo podés venir en busca del perdón. (Prego 1985: 168, italics mine)
>
> [OP: Another *constant* [...] is the journey in search of a destiny that in some mysterious way is signalled [to the woman], followed by the return after the defeat. As if the journey were a sort of transgression of *certain* unwritten *rules* of the game.
> JC: Exactly. 'Don't leave your suburb, be a good little girl/marry a man who is like you'. That is, the advice of *total conformity*.
> OP: Yes, *'conformity'*, *acceptance*. In most tangos, happiness comes from the *acceptance* of *a pre-Edenic situation*. If you transgress the *code*, you are expelled and can only come back asking for forgiveness.]

As Aldo Mazzucchelli further notes, 'El letrista de tango [...] aconseja al que es distinto que [...] reconozca cual [sic] es su lugar — que resultará siempre el lugar tradicional, aquel que lo mostraría fiel a su nacimiento' (2006: 25) [The tango lyricist [...] advises the person who stands out [...] to recognise what his/her place is — which will always be the traditional place, the place that would show he/she was being faithful to his/her birth].

Moreover, in the emphasis placed by Boym on this idea of strict rules and rituals 'characterized by a higher degree of symbolic formalization and ritualization than the [...] customs and conventions after which they were patterned' (2001: 42), we can also, moving from tango lyrics to tango's production and consumption, glimpse Cortázar's own emphasis and insistence on the scripted and formulaic nature of tango which we examined earlier, with this being, hence, likewise, bound up with a wider sense of the idea of restorative nostalgia. In other words, the ritualisation of the consumption of tango that Cortázar advocates is matched by (what he sees, negatively, as) the ritualisation of its production. That is, he simultaneously apparently bemoans the fact that tango is 'rutinario' (González Bermejo 1978: 109) [routine] and emerges from 'una fórmula orquestal dada' (110) [a given orchestral formula], just as he decries its *porteño* parochialism, but also exhibits a personal relationship with tango that is built precisely around fetishising a re-performance of the original listening context, which includes a willed return to — or restoration of — that same parochial locale.

What is perhaps most notable about Cortázar's reiterated stressing of tango's limitations for escaping from its scripted musical form is that he does nevertheless mention exceptions to such, even as he insists on his primary appraisal of tango's possibilities. In particular, in interview with both Picon Garfield and González Bermejo he makes reference to the Argentine saxophonist Gato Barbieri (1936–2016), who, with the significant caveat that he was essentially a jazz musician, engaged with tango in a way that broke it out of its moulds and strictures, as Cortázar talks of 'algunos — como Gato Barbieri — que han hecho experiencias para ir sacándolo [el tango] de los moldes, para intentar cosas nuevas' (González Bermejo 1978: 109) [some — like Gato Barbieri — who have created experiments to take [tango] out of its moulds, to try new things]. But Cortázar immediately returns thereafter to his assertion that 'el tango es muy monótono' (110) [tango is very monotonous], and there is a sense that the Barbieri 'exception' is seen primarily as jazz rather than tango *per se*, with Cortázar stating significantly that 'con un tango [Barbieri] crea una canción de "free jazz"' (Picon Garfield 1981: 131) [with a tango Barbieri creates a 'free jazz' song].[25] And yet this this aside does two things, both of which are related to each other. Firstly, it draws attention to the fact that Cortázar's depiction of tango as being musically rigid and unopen to improvisation and invention needs to be, at the very least, as we shall see, properly caveated; and, secondly, it, significantly, points to a different concept of tango and one which can be understood through the second of Boym's nostalgic tendencies: reflective nostalgia.

If restorative nostalgia focuses on the *nostos*, the home to which a return is desired or whose restoration is sought, reflective nostalgia 'dwells in *algia*, in longing and loss' (Boym 2001: 41). That is, the reflective nostalgic revels in the gap between him or herself and the home, ruminating on and breathing in the separation and the 'patina of time and history' (41) that have worked upon and altered the object of the remembrance; he or she — citing Susan Stewart — 'is "enamored of distance, not of the referent itself"' (50), with the result that homecoming is 'perpetually defer[red]' (49). Several elements emerge from this basic set of notions that are of significance when mapping this form of nostalgia onto tango both generally and in the form of Cortázar's particular engagement with it. Firstly, the renouncing of the restorative nostalgic idea of 'total reconstructions of monuments of the past' (41) where 'memory gaps' are 'patch[ed] up' (41) in favour of a vision that accepts and embraces the 'inconclusive and fragmentary' (50) leads to different possibilities for how that past (home) is dealt with and utilised: as Boym suggests, '*Re-flection* suggests new flexibility, not the reestablishment of stasis' (49). The result of this is a nostalgia where 'the past opens up a multitude of potentialities, nonteleological possibilities of historic development' (50), a nostalgia, that is, which has a 'utopian dimension' (342), understood — importantly, following Boym — nonteleologically, a 'form of deep mourning that performs a labor of grief both through pondering pain and through play that points to the future' (55). This shift in direction towards a forward-looking, nonteleological nostalgic operation is, as this last quotation implies, built around the crucial element of play. Put simply, 'instead of recreation of the lost home, reflective nostalgia can foster a creative self' (354). What is particularly significant for our present purposes is what Boym has to say here about the relationship between the collective and the individual in this respect, with collective memory and shared memorial signs (of home) becoming the field of play of that individual creativity. Thus, when Boym affirms that 'culture has the potential of becoming a space for individual play and creativity, and not merely an oppressive homogenizing force' (53), we can start to see how this might be overlaid onto (Cortázar's) tango: the putatively homogenising, scripted nature of the music to which Cortázar so often referred is present, yet there is also an affirmation of something that moves beyond this.

Returning, first of all, to tango in general, there are a number of ways in which we can see the genre to fit into Boym's statement. Certainly, as we have seen, it has elements that emphasise ideas of conformity and homogeneity. Indeed, beyond those examples I have already outlined — and beyond the not entirely unproblematic idea of musical scripting that Cortázar frequently reminds us of —, we might also consider the extent to which tango is often described and defined via a series of set expectations, motifs, and stock characters. The *compadrito*, for example, 'emulador del donjuanismo, presuntuoso, bailador y hablador; y [que] tiene aficiones de "señorito" por su inclinación por el tango' (Hwangpo 2009: 258) [Casanova imitator, conceited, dancer, gift of the gab; and [who] wants to be a refined gentleman with his predilection for tango], was both a figure key to the creation of the tango and a recurrent character in tango lyrics and their stories, alongside the *milonguita*, 'the dance hall girl become prostitute [...] [who] had often been deceived by promise of a better life in the world of the tango' (Taylor 1976: 279). (I shall say more about both of these figures in due course.) Taylor goes on to outline several other characteristics, personae, and themes that came to be associated with tango, in particular in the New Guard/Golden Age to which Cortázar was drawn, including *el pueblo gris* [the grey nation], *el mufarse* [moping], *el hombre gil* [the naïve and foolish man], the cuckold, and the aspiration of social betterment (1976: 276–81). Corbatta underlines this reiterative or even prescriptive nature of tango themes in her reference to the idea that, with the tango 'Mi noche triste', 'se introducen una serie de temas (en su mayoría variantes del tema del amor) de larga descendencia y que, por décadas se identificarán con el tango' (1994: 65) [is introduced a series of themes (most of which are variations on the theme of love) of long descent and which for decades will be identified with tango]. Similarly, in regard to the choreography of the tango, as Nielsen and Mariotto observe, there are 'strict rules about torso positioning and arm and hand placement' (2006: 21) when it comes to the tango embrace, and, as regards the dance movements, 'there is a cylindrical space within which the tango dancers must operate, referred to as the *sphere of contention*, out of which it is not proper to move' (19). And yet, as Nielsen and Mariotto point out repeatedly, tango is also characterised by a creative breaking free from such strictures: skilful dancers have 'far more freedom to determine directions and movements' (19), whilst, in being 'biological and organic in design', tango is 'limitless in its conception as a dance' (20); and by elements of rebellion: 'Tango lyrics not only justified certain types of behavior termed "criminal" by the ruling party, but also challenged the concept of the rule of law' (25), with the authors drawing attention amongst other things to the transgressive nature of the *milonguita* (about which I shall say more shortly in relation to 'Las puertas del cielo'), even if the tango stories portrayed the results of such transgression as being negative. As Savigliano observes, it may be that these female figures are 'just making fools of themselves [...] according to the tango authors' morals, but who believes that their morals are the actual end of the story?' (1995: 71).[26]

These traits of tango, in addition to what Gloria Dinzel and Rodolfo Dinzel refer to as the tango dancer's 'playing with space and time' (2000: 15) and to the more risk-taking innovation of later (post-1950s) tangos in particular, pointed to both by Cortázar's example of Gato Barbieri and, more importantly in the history of tango, by the key figure of Astor Piazzolla, a composer and *bandoneón* player who altered the genre irrevocably with the introduction of 'complexity, chromatic melodies, dissonance, new instruments, and changes in rhythm' (Nielsen and Mariotto 2006: 18),[27] all signal the viability of understanding tango — this most nostalgic of musical genres — as engaging with and being steeped in a reflective nostalgic tendency. It is, then, in such creative and, we might add, nonteleological terms that we can read Mazzucchelli's observation that in tango there is 'hasta cierta nostalgia utópica' (2006: 33) [even a certain utopic nostalgia].

Such a recognition of tango's challenging and creative characteristics is also to be found amongst a number of scholars working on tango in relation to Cortázar. Fralasco, for example, begins his study precisely by rejecting an understanding of tango as being simply about rigidity, and underlines the creativity involved in the genre (2005: 9–11). His allusion to the essentially oral nature of early tango and examples of less strict adherence to a fixed interpretation of tango scores are well-noted, and could be extended to a more detailed discussion of the presence of innovation and even improvisation in tango well before Piazzolla, including in both the Old and New Guard.[28] Meanwhile, Rosa Serra Salvat sums up what is the key point in connecting these observations back to the case of Cortázar, when she affirms that tango is not just ('not merely' (Boym 2001: 53)) a marker of home in his work (within what we have identified as a restorative nostalgic tendency), but also 'una fuente constante de tensiones y por tanto de creatividad a través de toda su obra' (2002: 307) [a constant source of tensions and attendantly of creativity across his entire work]. It may be, that is, that Cortázar's statements in interviews and pieces such as 'Gardel' show an author keen to push the rigidity of tango and its place as a marker of a Buenos Aires which he seeks to restore or return to, not least in his recreation of the original listening context, but, Serra Salvat intimates, his actual use of tango in his fictions and poetry speaks of a very different approach to the genre, to this essential symbol of the nation(al past), one that resonates with the creativity and play associated with Boym's reflective nostalgia.

The examples of such reflective nostalgic creativity and play in Cortázar's use of tango in his work are, in fact, numerous, and include what Fralasco puts down to memory lapses on Cortázar's part. In the case of the author's apparent reference to the tango 'Muñeca brava' in *Los premios*, for instance, Fralasco sees the presence of lyrics from another tango, 'Mano a Mano' (1920), as well, indicating that 'es posible que la memoria le haya jugado una mala pasada' (2005: 117) [it's possible that his memory has played a trick on him]. Rather than unfortunate memory lapse, however, these lines are open to being seen more affirmatively as an example of the acceptance of the 'patina of time' (Boym 2001: 41) and 'the imperfect process of remembrance' (41) characteristic of the reflective nostalgic, as well as constituting, along similar lines, a conscious act of ludic invention, with tangos and their lyrics as the building blocks of such. Indeed, this seems a more plausible reading when one considers the extent to which this sort of lyrical blurring, adaptation, and recasting occurs in Cortázar's writing. Cortázar, that is, does not generally return us to past lyrics in his 'tango texts'; rather, past lyrics and tango themes are rendered new and/or put to new purposes. This can take the form of tango lyrics, commonplaces, and themes being inserted into stories for the purpose of characterisation and plot advancement (we might consider the story 'Torito' or the novel *Los premios* here),[29] to semi-hidden tango lyrics there for the knowing reader to spot, such as the citation of the tango 'Mano a mano', Cortázar's favourite tango sung by Gardel, in 'Lugar llamado Kindberg', again, as shown here, not rendered verbatim, but moulded to the syntactic and narrative requirements of Cortázar's text:

> nunca tuve tanta suerte, *fuiste bueno. Bueno y consecuente*, entona Marcelo revancha bandoneón, pero la pelota sale de la cancha, es otra generación, es una osita Shepp, ya no tango, che. (1974: 99)
>
> [I never had such good luck, *you were good. Good and [principled]*, Marcelo intones his concertina Gardel revenge, but the ball goes out of bounds, it's a different generation, it's a little Shepp bear, no more tango, eh?] (1984: 187, italics mine)
>
> *fuiste buena, consecuente*, y yo sé que me has querido ('Mano a mano' (Romano 1991: 39, italics mine))
>
> [*you were good, principled*, and I know that you have loved me]

This tango, in fact, plays a particularly important role in Cortázar's engagement with the genre, and provides an example of one of the clearest forms of ludic creativity to be found in his work: the malleable use of tango lyrics and titles in the service of new *literary* inventions. Thus, for instance, in the 'Con tangos' section of *Salvo el crepúsculo*, the first lines of 'Mano a mano' ('Rechiflao en mi tristeza, hoy te evoco y veo que has sido | en mi pobre vida paria sólo una buena mujer' (Romano 1991: 39) [Crazy in my sadness, today I evoke you and I see that you have been | in my poor, outcast life just one good woman]) are taken as the title and opening lines of an entirely new poetic composition:

> 'Rechiflao en mi tristeza'
> Te evoco y veo que has sido
> en mi pobre vida paria
> una buena biblioteca.
> (Cortázar 2009: 69)
>
> [Crazy in My Sadness
> I evoke you and I see that you have been
> in my poor, outcast life
> a good library.]

It is a technique also on display in the much earlier poem '1950 Año del Libertador, etc.' from the 'Razones de la cólera' section of *Salvo el crepúsculo*, whose epigraph and opening line ('Y si el llanto te viene a buscar' (2009: 322) [And if weeping comes looking for you]) is also a line from 'Muñeca brava'. Guillermo Anad (2004) has commented on these examples as part of a wider study of the ways in which Cortázar utilises and manipulates old tangos in a number of poems from *Salvo el crepúsculo*, and it is evident from this critical work, together with further examinations of similar procedures in operation in, for example, Cortázar's creative use of sixteen tangos in his writing of the essay to accompany Sábat's drawings in *Monsieur Lautrec*,[30] that this sort of inventiveness and creativity is a fundamental characteristic of Cortázar's incorporation of tango. In this respect, the fact that, as Anad points out, Cortázar infuses his texts from 'Con tangos' with lyrics devoid of quotation marks might not simply be, as the critic contends, an example of the author showing his proposal 'de integrar el lenguaje del tango al discurso poético' (Anad 2004: 113) [to integrate the language of tango into the poetic discourse], but, more significantly, a way of indicating that these lyrics are loosened — freed even — from their location in the past tango and are now to be identified as a part of this new narrative born from the reflective nostalgic freedom 'to choose the narratives of the past and remake them' (Boym 2001: 354). Certainly, in redeploying these tango quotations, Cortázar's texts resonate with the dwelling on the 'inconclusive and fragmentary' (Boym 2001: 50) that is characteristic of this nostalgic tendency, a tendency reinforced by a recurrent rejection or deferral of the return home in his tango engagements. Thus, for example, within the lyrics of the piningly nostalgic tango 'La Cruz del Sur' from the *Trottoirs de Buenos Aires* record, Cortázar writes of how, 'Me duele un tiempo amargo | lleno de perros y desgracia | la agazapada convicción de que volver es vano' (Cortázar, Cantón, and Cédron 1980) [A bitter time | full of dogs and misfortune hurts me | the crouching conviction that it is futile to go back].[31]

The extent to which such creative play underpins Cortázar's recourse to tango is, as Walter Bruno Berg points out, not limited to the realm of tango lyrics.

Framed within the idea of the '*tango nuevo*' (2000: 239) [new tango] — suggestive of Piazzolla's *nuevo tango* — Berg offers a short analysis of the tangos of *Trottoirs de Buenos Aires* that draws attention to instances where Cortázar refashions and breaks free from the codified norms of tango in thematic, discursive, linguistic, and poetic terms.[32] Whilst insightful, the examples given by Berg are not always convincing or sufficiently detailed, but the thematic departure signalled by the adapting of tango themes to fit Cortázar's exilic condition is significant, as 'la identificación con el terruño, pues, *a distancia* [...] está lo suficientemente marcado como para producir un matiz temático que significa, frente al repertorio codificado del género, *ruptura*' (2000: 243) [the identification with the homeland *at a distance* [...] is marked enough to produce a thematic nuance which means, faced with the codified repertory of the genre, *rupture*]. Indeed, along similar lines, Marilyn G. Miller further comments on these tangos that:

> in language and tone, [Cortázar's] original lyrics for the songs on the record bend the tango to accommodate the experiences and lexicon he has acquired in Paris and other cities far from Buenos Aires, without erasing the themes and phrasings of the master *letristas* of yesteryear. (2016: 16)

The central element that Miller picks up on here from Berg is this notion of *código* and *ruptura*, code and rupture: the rules, moulds, and norms of tango versus the (dis)rupturing of these tango 'staples'. For Berg, Cortázar's tangos can only be called 'new' to a degree, and the instances of rupture do not come at the cost of 'el *reconocimiento* de estructuras conocidas' (2000: 239–40) [the *recognition* of known structures] on the part of the listener. It is a critical take that Miller interprets as an argument that 'Cortázar doesn't look so much for originality as for a productive tension between *código* and rupture, between expected and novel features' (2016: 16), thus aligning the author's tango praxis with the 'tango renovation' (16) of figures such as Piazolla. Moving beyond the case of Cortázar's tangos in the *Trottoirs de Buenos Aires* project, such an understanding of Cortázar's practice can, in line with the examples and analysis given above, be judged to hold equally for his (literary) use of tango more generally, and it is not hard to see how it also dovetails with the terrain on which Cortázar's engagement with *la música culta* plays out: code and rupture are essentially script/score and invention/departure — concepts which we have seen to be key to an understanding of both 'Clone' and 'Reunión', for example — under different names. (I shall say more on this resonance later.) And, similarly, following the argument I have been advancing, it is far from an unwieldy stretch to map these terms onto those of restorative and reflective nostalgia, respectively.

This is not, however, a game of synonym-identification, and neither is it a question of flattening out these terms in, or as a result of, an attempt at conflating and confusing them; there is a reason why I have been suggesting that Cortázar's engagement with tango be seen specifically in these nostalgic terms. Boym stresses early on in her study that restorative and reflective nostalgia 'are not absolute types, but rather tendencies' (2001: 41), and this gives an indication of their value as a lens through which to understand Cortázar's tango, in that they help us move away from seeing it as *either* script/code *or* invention/rupture, or as concerning the 'tension' between the two, towards an understanding of the author's engagement with this genre that is more slippery and less clearly defined, one which takes into account that the discourse of national narrative and return to or restoration of home in Cortázar's 'tango texts' is bound up with and often segues into that more creative, individual play. This in itself raises questions regarding the way in which tango (in Cortázar) operates at a textual and ontological level, but, within the ambit of the questions on which this study seeks to focus, it also provides a potentially more useful starting point from which specifically to address the issue of how tango and Cortázar's engagement with tango might offer a series of possibilities and vistas for expression that tap into, but are not bound within, the terms and stage through and on which we have seen *la música culta* to be played out in Cortázar's work. Understood through these two nostalgic *tendencies*, that is, tango appears in Cortázar's texts as a far more promising form of expression, including as a potential model for the author's writing practice, than his statements in interview might suggest. Tango, in the reading I am positing, brings together the importance of creation and play, personal home and emotions, whilst underscoring that the code, the '"accepted rules [...] [,] values and norms of behavior"' (Hobsbawm, cited in Boym 2001: 42) are also an essential component. It thus suggests the possibility of a form of expression that is both inherently nostalgic, in the lay sense of pining after the past and the home(ly), and yet simultaneously newly creative and forward-looking. The question of how this reading of tango is worked through by Cortázar's texts and, relatedly, of how this might impact the author's own writing practice, is one that is answered by turning to two of Cortázar's most overtly tango short stories, 'Las puertas del cielo' and 'Tango de vuelta', two stories which, as I shall show, constitute a narrative couple embraced in their own tango dance.[33]

'Las puertas del cielo'

Published in 1951 in the collection *Bestiario*, 'Las puertas del cielo' tells the story of three principal *porteño* characters: Doctor Marcelo Hardoy, a well-to-do lawyer; Mauro, a working-class man; and Celina, a *milonguera*, or cabaret dancer/worker, in a seedy tango club (*milonga*). Mauro and Celina are both, then, of a different social class to Hardoy, although Mauro in many ways straddles the divide between (the worlds of) the other two: he had rescued Celina from her *milonga* life and installed her in his conformist world of 'el patio, las horas de charla con vecinos y el mate' (Cortázar 1993a: 113) ('the courtyard in his own house, long hours of bull session with the neighbors, and *mate*', 2013: 103), although in reality she had never wanted to leave the tango-world of the *milonga*. Ex-clients of his, the relationship between Mauro and Celina and Doctor Hardoy is one that revolves around the latter's voyeuristic desire to observe the lower classes in their *milonga* milieu: 'Íbamos juntos a los bailes, y yo los miraba vivir' (1993a: 111) ('We went to the dances together and I watched them live', 2013: 101), thus acting, as mentioned in chapter 2, as a possible precursor of the onlooking narrator of 'Las ménades'.[34] Against this backdrop the story tells, via Hardoy as narrator, of the death of Celina and the response of the two male characters to this event, with the main narrative focusing on Hardoy's taking Mauro to a *milonga*. Here they both appear to see Celina, returned to her 'paraíso al fin logrado' (1993a: 124) ('paradise finally gained', 2013: 112), but finally fail to acknowledge this to each other, preferring to fall back on the idea that it was merely a woman who looked like her, and thus missing the chance for the sort of reconciliation or coming together — in this case between men from different social backgrounds — that Cortázar's texts so frequently set up, only to frustrate.

This basic outline already reveals that tango is an important element of 'Las puertas del cielo', but the extent to which the story is steeped in this musical genre, the dance, and the tango world generally is significant. The centrality of the main *milonga* setting is clearly key here, *milongas* in this context being clubs, cabarets, 'tango joints — a space and a time when and where tango bodies get together to produce *tanguidad* (tanguity, tango-ness)' (Savigliano 1997: 30), an underworld, at least in the context of this story, separated from the respectability of middle-class society. And the narrative, in a manner that draws upon the self-confessed, underclass-porn voyeurism of the narrator, describes in some detail the different musical genres and delights at the *milonga* in question (the Santa Fe Palace), those who participate in the dancing encounters (the *milongueros* and *milongueras*), and the mature tango singer Anita Lozano, who 'conservaba toda la voz para los tangos' (Cortázar 1993a: 119) ('still had voice enough to do a tango', 2013: 108). There is also the dominant presence of the *milonguita* and the *compadrito*, the archetypal or 'main characters of the passional tango plots' (Savigliano 1995: 47) to whom I alluded earlier, with Celina and Mauro being explicitly presented as examples of these two figures, respectively. The *milonguita* was:

> usually described as a young, sensual and self-confident woman, born into a lower-class family, who escaped from the *barrio* and from a future as a housewife, in exchange for a life of excitement, luxury and pleasure in the cabarets [*milongas*] of Buenos Aires. (Tossounian 2016: 34)

Savigliano, more succinctly, calls her a 'rebellious broad' (1995: 47). It is a mould from which Celina appears cast, to the extent that her very being is portrayed as a literal embodiment of this tango-world: her hips and mouth evidence that 'estaba armada para el tango' (1993a: 120) ('she was built for the tango', 2013: 108), and, even in death, Hardoy observes that she had 'una frente baja que brillaba como nácar de guitarra' (1993a: 109) ('the low forehead, which was bright as the mother-of-pearl on a guitar', 2013: 99). The *compadre*, or — in his pale imitation — the *compadrito*, is 'el plebeyo de las ciudades y del indefinido arrabal, como el gaucho lo fue de la llanura o de las cuchillas' (Borges and Bullrich 1968: 11) [the lout of the cities and the endless *arrabal*, as the *gaucho* was of the plains and knives], 'emulador del donjuanismo, presuntuoso, bailador y hablador' (Hwangpo 2009: 258) [Casanova imitator, conceited, dancer, gift of the gab].[35] Originally a figure often involved in knife fights over a woman, the *compadrito* ended up as a character who was more typically a romantic hero, what Savigliano refers to as the 'whiny ruffian' (1995: 61), lamenting the loss of his lover (a *milonguita*) to a richer, more well-to-do man, the *bacán* or *niño bien* [sugar daddy/playboy].[36] An identification apparently less central to the story, though, if anything, more explicit, Mauro is described as being just such a figure as Hardoy details the way in which Mauro dresses for the *milonga* in typical *compadre* or *compadrito* fashion, alongside a more covert set of allusions to the character's postures and possibly his role in tango dance:

> Se puso un traje azul y pañuelo bordado, lo vi echarse perfume de un frasco que había sido de Celina. Me gustaba su forma de requintarse el sombrero, con el ala levantada, y su paso liviano y silencioso, bien compadre. (Cortázar 1993a: 114)[37]
>
> [He put on a blue suit, stuck an embroidered handkerchief in the upper pocket, and I saw him put on some perfume from a bottle that had been Celina's. I liked the tilt of his hat with the brim snapped up, and his silent walk, loose and bouncy[, quite the *compadre*].] (2013: 104)

Moreover, although putatively from outside of the tango/*milonga* world, Mauro's depiction as a *compadrito* also brings with it a possible tango-identification for Hardoy himself as a representation of the aforementioned *niño bien*. Certainly, given that, as Savigliano comments, one of the principal aspects of the *milonga* world for such men was that in the 'cabarets [...] at the center of the ruffianesque tango stories [...] the *niño bien* escaped the restrictions of his class' (1995: 63), there would seem to be scope for conceiving of this character in such a way. And even if we opt not to follow this alignment, Hardoy's role as observer and narrator dovetails remarkably well, for example, with Alberto Vaccarezza's *sainete* entitled *La comparsa se despide* (1932) [The Comparsa Bids Farewell], in which the ideal nature of a popular tango plot is set out from 'the perspective of an outsider, a voyeur of a tangoesque dramatic ambiance' (Savigliano 1995: 48). Indeed, following this line further, we might also note that the overall conceit of 'Las puertas del cielo' of the nostalgic pining for a lost *milonguita* lover on the part of the *compadrito* provides a further way in which this short story is imbued with and characterised as tango, this being a common theme of tango lyrics of the New Guard period.

This last observation also moves us onto the more general role of nostalgia and an emphasis on the past in the story. Whilst the plot signals Mauro as the figure caught up in sad and wistful reveries for his now-dead lover, it is in fact the proclivity of the narrator Hardoy to look back on and remember Celina that underpins 'Las puertas del cielo', to the extent that, aside from dominating large parts of the story, it acts as a structuring narrative motif in its references to thinking about and/or remembering the *milonguita* character: 'yo pensaba en Celina' (Cortázar 1993a: 108) [I was thinking about Celina]; 'yo estaba otra vez con Celina y Mauro' (109) [I was back with Celina and Mauro again]; 'estuve todo el tiempo pensando en Celina' (112) [I was thinking all the time about Celina]; 'toda esa mañana había estado pensando en Celina' (112) [all that morning I had been thinking about Celina]; 'cuando vi a las muchachas [del Moulin Rouge] pensé en la carrera de Celina' (113) [when I saw the girls [from the Moulin Rouge] I thought about Celina's career]; 'me acordé de repente de Celina' (119) [I suddenly remembered Celina]; 'yo pensaba en Celina' (119) [I was thinking about Celina]. Beyond Celina herself, Hardoy's narrative is also notable for the general inclusion of numerous flashbacks and recountings of memories, largely concentrated around the tango-world of the *milonga*. Indeed, a number of the examples above involve reminiscences on the part of Hardoy of his time with Celina and Mauro in these places. The first mention and description of a *milonga*, for instance, comes precisely in this flashback form, as Hardoy recalls the time when 'estaba otra vez con Celina y Mauro en el Luna Park, bailando en el Carnaval del cuarenta y dos' (109) ('I was [back] with Celina and Mauro again, the carnival, Luna Park, 1942, dancing', 2013: 99). What is more, these episodes often focus on the different and specific elements that make up tango *per se*, from dance to music to the sense-markers of the *milongas*: 'Otra vez la vi girando entusiasta en brazos de Mauro, la orquesta de Canaro ahí arriba y un olor a polvo barato. Despues bailó conmigo una machicha, la pista era un horror de gente y calina' (1993a: 111) ('Again I saw her whirling enthusiastically in Mauro's arms, Canaro's Orchestra on the platform and the smell of cheap powder. She danced a *machicha* with me afterward, the floor was a hell of thick smoke and bodies', 2013: 100). In effect, then, the representation of the tango world in the text is inseparable from a nostalgic process of remembrance, a fact underlined by Hardoy's comment towards the end of the story that the *milonga* is 'un sitio donde el recuerdo crecía de cada cosa como pelos en un brazo' (1993a: 120) ('a joint where memories sprouted from everything like the hair on your arms', 2013: 109).

The most significant coupling of tango and nostalgia in the text, however, is, as we shall see, that played out against this narrative background by and through the tangos that actually appear within the text. The first of these can be identified as 'A la luz del candil' (1927), sung by Carlos Gardel, a tango written from a first-person perspective in which one Alberto Arenas hands himself over to the police to arrest him for — and here we might consider a certain further form of intertextuality with(in) the Gesualdo story found in 'Clone' — murdering his beloved and her lover (his friend), whose remains, in the form of her braids and his heart, he carries in his suitcase. Fralasco comments that this is not a nostalgic tango (2005: 38), but this is to focus too exclusively on the central narrative of the lyrics. The importance of nostalgia in relation to this tango is shown by Hardoy's description of the way in which the singer 'insistía en la nostalgia' (Cortázar 1993a: 117) ('was very heavy on the nostalgia', 2013: 106). The nostalgia, then, emerges from the manner in which the song is sung, leading to the sense that the singer is channelling the protagonist's wistful remembrance of the love and friendship he once enjoyed. Hardoy's additional comment on the appropriateness when singing tangos of the microphone's being in the form of 'el bastón cromado con la pequeña calavera brillante en lo alto, la sonrisa tetánica de la rejilla' (1993a: 117) ('the chrome [pole] with the little skull glittering on top, and the frozen spasmodic smile of the gridwork', 2013: 106) further underlines that this particular song fits in with a more generic association of tango with the (now-lost) past. Moving on, for now, from 'A la luz del candil', the second, and central, tango to figure in 'Las puertas del cielo' is the one announced by the aforementioned Anita, who proceeds to sing it, as 'un tango viejo' (1993a: 121) ('an old tango', 2013: 109). In this instance, it is worth noting not just that, yet again, it is a tango that draws us to the past but, importantly, that its immediate effect is to act as a memory trigger for both Mauro and Hardoy of a past *milonga* evening with Celina:

> cuando la orquesta se abrió paso con un culebreo de los bandoneones [Mauro] me miró de golpe, tenso y rígido, como acordándose. Yo me vi también en el Rácing, Mauro y Celina prendidos fuerte en ese tango que ella canturreó después toda la noche y en el taxi de vuelta. (1993a: 121)

> [when the piece opened with a gut-twisting few bars from the accordions [Mauro] shot me a look like a punch, he was remembering. I also, I saw myself at the thing for the Giants, Mauro and Celina holding one another tight, this same tango, she hummed it all night long, even in the [return trip] taxi.] (2013: 110)

Having established the extent to which this story brings together and is imbued with tango, memory, and nostalgia, we are left with the question of how to understand this thematic blend and its significance. One initial approach (one that will end up exceeding its own terms) is to consider how (far) we can identify the pulls that are evident in the narrative with either restorative or reflective nostalgic tendencies. There certainly appear to be hints towards the former, not least when Hardoy comments, 'curiosa la crepitación que le daba el parlante a la voz de Anita' (1993a: 123) ('weird how Anita's voice [crackled] over the speakers', 2013: 111). This line, to which our attention is drawn by the adjective 'curiosa' ('weird'), recalls Cortázar's insistence in the essay 'Gardel', contemporary with 'Las puertas del cielo', that 'a Gardel hay que escucharlo en la victrola, con toda la distorsión y la pérdida imaginables' (1970b: 136) [you must listen to Gardel on a gramophone, with all the distortion and loss imaginable], as he strives to recreate, or restore, the original listening context. Moreover, such a restorative reading is supported by the fact that this line in 'Las puertas del cielo' is also the textual cue for Celina to come into view for the first time, that is, the moment when she appears to have been restored to her *milonga*, the home from which she was wrenched by Mauro. Indeed, in more general terms, the underlying constant in the story of Celina's desired return to, or restoration of, 'su cielo de milonga' (Cortázar 1993a: 120) ('her [...] [milonga] heaven', 2013: 109) resonates with the restorative nostalgic desire to 'return to the [...] prelapsarian moment' (Boym 2001: 49), and Hardoy's assertion as he contemplates her in the Santa Fe Palace that this represents her 'duro cielo conquistado' (Cortázar 1993a: 124) ('hard-won heaven', 2013: 112) further chimes with the aim of the restorative nostalgic to 'reconstr[uct] emblems and rituals of home and homeland in an attempt to conquer and spatialize time' (Boym 2001: 49). Similarly, the trip by Hardoy and Mauro to a *milonga* constitutes not just a conscious return to a past haunt of both men, but, specifically, the restoration of a pre-Celina past for Mauro ('Nunca la llevé a ese *Palace* [...]. Yo estuve antes de conocerla' (Cortázar 1993a: 115) ('I never took her to this Palace [...] I [came] here before I met her', 2013: 104)) in order to 'olvidar' (1993a: 115) [forget], a move decidedly opposed to the deliberate dwelling in 'longing and loss' (Boym 2001: 41) of the reflective nostalgic.

Yet there are also important aspects of just such a reflective nostalgic tendency on display here, not least in the distinctly personal nature of the longing and the memories that are triggered by and through the collective cultural terrain of diverse aspects of the tango world. Perhaps the most significant element in this regard is the *milonga* setting itself, which proves to be inherently problematic for a restorative nostalgic reading, and, indeed, for a straightforward 'tango reading' of the text, pushing instead a reading that suggests a far greater focus on challenge and transgression than on a 'comforting' retreat to the 'codified' home. Tango is, as Cecilia Tossounian sets out, a genre that stages the very disruptive societal issue that it also seeks to resolve: in the years that coincide with the New Guard, 'women began experiencing a more open romantic and sexual life' (2016: 31), an occurrence tied in with the 'rapid economic growth [...] [which] mobilized many sectors of society' (31) and the attendant ability of more economically-independent women in particular to 'socialize with men without the supervision of the family' (31). Tangos, in the return to the *barrio* of the *milonguita*, thus — and as Cortázar himself implicitly recognises in the excerpt from the interview with Prego to which I referred earlier (Prego 1985: 168) — both depict this supposedly problematic 'gender disruption' (Tossounian 2016: 31) and offer a rejection of it. 'Las puertas del cielo', however, effectively reverses the classic tango narrative. Here, it is not the *barrio* that appears as the 'lost paradise' (Tossounian 2016: 34) or home to which the *milonguita* would return to rediscover the desirability of conformity to traditional roles, mores, and codes, leaving the 'decadent life of the cabaret' (34) and the potential material and sexual freedom it offered behind. Instead, it casts the *milonga* as that returned-to locale. In short, in rewriting the basic narrative in this way, 'Las puertas del cielo' not only discloses tango's fundamental paradox of giving a stage to that which it seeks to reject, but subverts its attempts to counter the transgression of which it warns, in the process profoundly destabilising a (tango-based) restorative nostalgic reading of the story.[38]

This reading of the *milonga* setting is further enhanced when one examines the nature of these sites of tango performance, and hence the nature of the transgression they represent, in more depth. Savigliano, within the context of a novel and entertaining piece on the ethnography of 'Las puertas del cielo', brings out a number of crucial aspects of the *milonga* location in this regard. On the one hand, as Savigliano notes, 'milongas emerge as a rough, shady world, highly competitive and *hierarchical, codified* in terms of selfish interests, *male dominance*, and even moral corruption' (1997: 32, italics mine), and she is aware of their status as 'cultural bastions of an endangered *national identity*' (50, italics mine). And yet they are also sites of 'democratic, even revolutionary experiments that allow for age and class differences to blur, male and female differences to explode' (32). Focusing on the way in which, alongside the machista dominance, the *milongas* offer 'a female sensuality that is beyond everyday life parameters' (40), allowing female pleasure that, moreover, 'defies otherwise accepted age parameters of old and young' (40), and bringing out the disruption of social and class barriers in making available to men women who would 'be absolutely unavailable to them in other contexts because of their class and or age difference' (42), Savigliano's text insists on the revolutionary and, crucially, transgressive nature of *milongas*, pushing well beyond an understanding of this as being solely on the level of gender roles. She talks, for example, of the idea that 'invitations and acceptances to dance in the milonga can also mean a transgression of everyday life social barriers, a matching of (socially) odd parts. The milongas and their danced tangos are, from this point of view, a revolutionary experience' (43),[39] with the most potentially destabilising disruption in the specific case of 'Las puertas del cielo' being that of the boundary of life and death that appears with the emergence of Celina at the end of the story. As Savigliano notes, in 'Las puertas del cielo' we have the dramatic assertion of 'the power that tango exerts over certain bodies, enough to transport the dead and the living into a common ground of nocturnal collapse' (1997: 48). Such a transgressive, revolutionary collapsing of boundaries corresponds, of course, to exactly the kind of overcoming of (binary) divides that Cortázar pursues and advances in his work, and this alignment is reinforced further by Hardoy's lament — despite going on to describe the club in some detail — that 'nada [...] [del Santa Fe Palace] pueda ser realmente descrito' (Cortázar 1993a: 115) [nothing [...] [of the Santa Fe] can really be described], thus figuring the *milonga* in question as being in some sense beyond linguistic expression and structure. This, we must remember, is, in the tango that is 'Las puertas del cielo', the identity of the home to which there is a return.[40, 41]

If the *milonga* setting opens a window onto the identification of this nostalgia-drenched story as being one that carries with it an essential challenge to the ideas of 'safety' and conformity that tango putatively conveys, it is, however, in the tangos of the story themselves that we find some of the most explicit and significant markers of the reflective nostalgic tendencies that contribute and relate to these more challenging and disruptive possibilities, as well as an attendant sign that 'Las puertas del cielo' is, above all, a story that posits the potential ability of tango to effect such a challenge via its own (nostalgic) means. Principally, these markers consist of the sort of creativity and invention in the use of existing tango lyrics and narratives that we have observed across other texts. In the case of the first tango, identified as 'A la luz del candil', we are given two citations, both of which, as Fralasco notes, are not as they appear in the original tango itself.[42] Thus, the original tango reads:

> Las pruebas de la infamia
> las traigo en la maleta
> las trenzas de mi china
> y el corazón de él.
>   (Romano 1991: 118)
>
> [The proof of the infamy
> I have it in the suitcase
> My darling's braids
> And his heart.]

In Cortázar's story, however, this becomes simply, '*Las trenzas de mi china las traigo en la maleta*' (1993a: 117) [My darling's braids I have them in the suitcase]. This alteration, which Fralasco opines 'no es significativa' (2005: 43) [is not significant], thus reverses the order of the two lines in question and, notably, though more subtly, changes the referent corresponding to the direct object '*las*' [them] of the verb form '*traigo*' [I have], which now refer only to the '*trenzas de mi china*' [my darling's braids] rather than '*las pruebas de la infamia*' [the proof of the infamy], which comprised the lover's hair *and* the friend's heart. These changes could be seen to pre-empt by almost thirty years the shift that we observed in the story of Gesualdo in 'Clone', where the original murder of his wife and her lover was rendered in the story as the murder only of the former, as well as hinting obliquely, in the reversal of the line order, at the reversal of the *barrio/milonga* polarity that I have identified in 'Las puertas del cielo'. In any case, what we see is precisely the sort of creative play and invention of new narratives associated with reflective nostalgia. In the case of the second citation from 'A la luz del candil', the original 'yo soy gaucho honrado' (Romano 1991: 118) [I'm a respectable *gaucho*] appears instead as '"yo soy un hombre honrado"' (Cortázar 1993a: 117) ('I'm a respectable man', 2013: 106).[43] What might once again be seen, as Álvarez-Schüller (2008: 19) comments, as nothing more than a memory slip on Cortázar's part could also be construed as a deliberate inventiveness that refashions the original lyric in such a way as to leave behind the ultimate marker of Argentine national identity, and one whose generic nature is bolstered by the lack of article, to be replaced by an affirmation of individuality. It is a move, then, that, in its focus on the individual rather than the national, offers a further resonance with the reflective nostalgic tendency.[44]

The sources that lie behind the second tango sung at the *milonga* are harder to discern. The lyric we are given is, '*tanto, tanto como fuiste mío, y hoy te busco y no te encuentro*' (Cortázar 1993a: 122) [so much, so much were you mine, and today I look for you and I do not find you], with the words '*Tanto como fuiste mío*' (123) [so much were you mine] repeated once more a little further on in the text. The first part ('*tanto, tanto como fuiste mío*' [so much, so much were you mine]) seems to be taken from the tango 'Tanto' by Carlos Bahr and Elías Randal, a tango that tells of a lost lover whose love turned cold, though with the gender of the lost beloved changed ('Tanto, | tanto como fuiste mía').[45] This is most obviously to reflect the fact that the singer of this tango in 'Las puertas del cielo' is a woman. However, the swapping of the roles of singer and lover could also be seen to marry up with the *milonga*'s challenging of gender roles and possibilities. Turning to the second part of the lyric ('*y hoy te busco y no te encuentro*' [and today I look for you and I do not find you]), this appears likely to come from the 1941 tango 'Mariposita' by Francisco García Jiménez and Anselmo Aieta, in which the narrator, drowning his sorrows, describes how he has lost his 'muchacha de mi barrio' [girl from the suburbs] to the bright (*milonga?*) lights of the 'centro' [centre]. Here, we read 'te busco y no te encuentro' [I look for you and I do not find you],[46] the lyric in Cortázar's story adding '*y hoy*' [and today], again an indication of a shift towards the new circumstances of the present performance rather than a harking back to the past of the tango.[47] In effect, then, 'Las puertas del cielo' gives us here a tango that amalgamates (at least) two different tangos, itself a creative act, and where each lyrical borrowing is subjected to its own creative rewriting. In each case, the original tango narrative resonates with the situation in which Mauro (and possibly Hardoy) finds himself, in speaking nostalgically of a lost love, yet in each case a simple restoration of the tango invoked is denied, in preference to a creativity built around an insistence on updating and/or renewing: the pining — the *algia* — is unquestionably present, but, rather than a 'return to the original stasis' (Boym 2001: 49), the focus is on present 'play that points to the future' (55), perhaps underscored by the fact that 'Tanto' dates from 1948, some six years after the 'Las puertas del cielo' is set.

What emerges from both these tangos, then, is that they ultimately combine an engagement with and harking back to the past with a determined willingness to play with that past in an inventive fashion that is both present-ing and forward-looking: the version of 'A la luz del candil' that we are given in the story takes us back to an old tango now infused with greater nostalgic purchase, yet shifts it creatively in a more individualised direction; the second 'amalgamated' tango, meanwhile, is even more creative in its lyrical play, whilst also insisting more trenchantly on its ties with a lost past in being referred to specifically as a 'tango viejo' (Cortázar 1993a: 121) ('old tango', 2013: 109), and in acting explicitly as a memory trigger for Mauro and Hardoy. In essence, the blurring of boundaries that we have seen to be associated with the tango-world of the *milonga* and to be stressed by the story's challenge to the boundary between life/death, is found in these tango songs, transposed to the question of their relationship to time, their identification as markers both of a restorative nostalgic desired return to a lost past and of a reflective nostalgic 'pondering [of] pain and [...] play that points to the future' (Boym 2001: 55), and, relatedly, the extent to which they *both* repeat the code, rules, and scripts of tango *and* rupture these elements. Furthermore, the insistence found in Savigliano's depiction of the *milonga* on blurring and transgression rather than on co-habitation of putatively opposed or conflictive terms reiterates the significance implied by this frame of restorative and reflective nostalgic *tendencies*. Tango and the tango world in 'Las puertas del cielo', in other words, are a space of the other, of alterity, not so much understood as a term in opposition to the (civilised) self, despite the repeated explicit references to the *milongueros* and *milongueras* on Hardoy's part as monsters ('yo iba a esa milonga por los monstruos' (Cortázar 1993a: 117) [I used to go to that *milonga* for the monsters]),[48] but, rather, as a locus of otherness in the sense of one in which boundaries between self and other, male and female, restorative and reflective nostalgia, and so on are broken down, thus leading to a space and time that would be radically 'other' to that of the self, predicated on divisions, categorisations, and limits. (In this sense, the tango world presented to us in 'Las puertas del cielo' pre-empts the breaking down of such barriers in the concert scene in 'Las ménades'.) Tango, that is, is shown by this story indeed to operate at this blurred, or erased locus where the difference between terms and distinctions generally collapse. Thus, whilst we necessarily find ourselves identifying examples of the code or script maintained, and of the creative rupture and play of such, 'Las puertas del cielo' shows us that an analysis of Cortázar's engagement with tango must move past this to consider how they are combined and (con)fused in his texts.

And it is against this backdrop that we need to read the story's denouement, where the possibility is raised of creating, as Boldy puts it, 'a possible union between the intellectual Hardoy and the "natural" Mauro' (1980: 86). What is required for such a reconciliation, which, again, constitutes an example of the coming together of 'opposing' sides or doubles that Cortázar seeks throughout his work, is the mutual recognition of both men that they have actually seen Celina: Hardoy's narration informs us that both have seen her, but they need to admit this to each other, thus acknowledging a collapse of their existing conception of the possible, of the limits of reason, and of the ultimate division between life and death, and entailing the attendant collapsing of the boundaries that separate them from each other. Key here, then, is Celina's identification *as* tango ('ella es el tango en su esencia' (Peiró 2006: 76) [she is the essence of tango]) and, as noted above, the fact that this vision is located in the tango-world of the *milonga*, the story's end thus reinforcing the locus, role, and nature of tango as, as I have been contending, a site of boundary collapse and blurring. But what is most important is how we characterise and understand the two terms — Hardoy and Mauro — in question at this point in the text. On the one hand, both characters to an extent resist easy categorisation: Mauro is of the underclasses, yet also sanitises Celina; Hardoy is an aloof, bourgeois observer seeking to tame the 'monsters' he observes by making notes about them ('las notas que llenan poco a poco mi fichero' (Cortázar 1993a: 110) ('notes that fill my files a bit at a time', 2013: 100)),[49] who, nevertheless, can be aligned with the *niño bien* tango figure.[50] This itself speaks of the artificiality of the very barriers and categories that (this) tango (text) works to collapse here and in general. But, leaving that aside, the putative categories that present themselves in this Hardoy/Mauro comparison are based around some of the principal themes and terrains we have seen Cortázar to engage with in his recourse to music: Hardoy is a man who writes (the narrative we are reading and 'virtually' in the form of his files within that narrative), Mauro is a tango *compadrito*; Hardoy is primarily an observer of the *milonga*, Mauro is generally a participator in it. We have, that is, is an anticipation of both the observer/performer divide of 'Las ménades' and the writing/music duality of 'Clone', stories which, I have argued, are both to an extent pre-empted in this earlier story's *milonga* setting and tango allusions. Significantly, however much these two later stories may bring these respective elements together, both, in their own way, work to maintain a difference between the two terms at stake, either on the level of the narrative ('Las ménades') or formally in the separation of the music-narrative and a description of how that narrative was written ('Clone' and its epilogue). In contrast to these stories, 'Las puertas del cielo' presents tango and the tango world as a potential conduit for such boundaries between writing (Hardoy) and music (Mauro) finally to be collapsed and the terms blurred or fused.

Whatever the promise, however, the story records a failure, as the mutual acknowledgement fails to materialise. Significantly, the instant when the opportunity is missed can be pinpointed to a moment characterised by linguistic addition, as Mauro recasts his initial enquiry '¿Vos te fijaste?' (Cortázar 1993a: 124) [Did you see?] as '¿Vos te fijaste cómo se parecía?' (124) [Did you see how much she looked like her?], the extra words cementing in meaning and in their insistence on language a move back into the comfort of what is within logic and reason. Yet it is notable that the character who triggers this failure is not Hardoy, the man of writing, but Mauro. And in describing Hardoy as feeling, yes, relief at this retreat, but also 'lástima' (124) ('pity', 2013: 113), what 'Las puertas del cielo' finally points to is the image of the writer who on some level wants to engage, to align and confuse himself and his writing practice with tango and its simultaneously restorative and reflective world of nostalgia and creativity.[51] And it is this germ that is grasped and allowed to develop almost three decades later in 'Tango de vuelta'.

'Tango de vuelta'

The story 'Tango de vuelta', both in its appearance in *Queremos tanto a Glenda* (1980) and its subsequent inclusion as 'El tango de la vuelta' in the Pat Andrea project (Andrea and Cortázar 2002 [1984]), occupies an important place in Cortázar's tango writing. In particular, as part of the more determined 'tango turn' of Cortázar's latter years, when his engagement with the genre extended to 'Un gotán para Lautrec', the *Trottoirs de Buenos Aires* album and various sections of the posthumous *Salvo el crepúsculo*, 'Tango de vuelta' constitutes Cortázar's most sustained fictional and narrative work related to this musical genre.[52]

The text tells the story of Matilde and her first husband Emilio, an Argentine couple who had been living as political exiles in Mexico. Matilde, tired of a life of 'miseria y espera' (Cortázar 1980: 75) ('misery and waiting', 1984: 65) had, five years prior to the story's setting, returned to Argentina, fabricated Emilio's death (by heart attack), thanks to false documents prepared by an old friend, and married the rich businessman Germán, thus opting for a life of comfort and material wealth. Emilio, however, has somehow discovered what Matilde has done and the details of her new life, and has returned from Mexico to find her. After striking up a relationship with Flora, Matilde's maid and the nanny to her young son, Carlitos, Emilio — whom Flora knows as Simón — gains access to Matilde and Germán's house (Germán is away on business throughout the time of the story) and aims to take revenge on Matilde. Matilde, however, having realised that Emilio has returned in this way, is prepared for this, and kills him in the ensuing fight. She then commits suicide by overdosing on pills.

The title of the story is significant in underlying the connections between this narrative and the world and stories of tango and its lyrics, connections that I shall tease out and explore in the course of this analysis. But the title's significance in this regard is not just in the description it gives of this story of love, betrayal, and revenge as being a tango. More particularly, the formulation 'Tango de vuelta' sends us back very specifically to the text and world of 'Las puertas del cielo'. The central tango in that earlier story is the one which I have identified as a remodelled blend of 'Tanto' and 'Mariposita'. It is, we recall, 'un tango viejo' (Cortázar 1993a: 121) ('an old tango', 2013: 109) from a past *milonga* night shared by Mauro, Celina, and Hardoy which *returns* to be performed in the present narrative of the story. Moreover, it is identified by Hardoy as the tango that, on that occasion in the past, Celina hummed all night, including in the 'taxi de vuelta' (1993a: 121) [return trip taxi]. It is, then, in at least two senses, a *tango de vuelta*, leading to the possibility that the story 'Tango de vuelta' represents a return of or is in some way tied to that central tango from 'Las puertas del cielo'. And, indeed, when we consider that that tango is one that speaks of the (re)engagement with and recasting of old(er) tangos, we begin to glimpse the idea that, in turn, Cortázar's story of that name is to be seen not just as a (conscious or unconscious) return of that earlier tango, but also as replicating its procedures, in terms of (re)engaging with and recasting its own (tango-narrative) precursor (itself signalled by the titular reference): 'Las puertas del cielo' and its myriad tango elements, including, of course, a particular focus on its diegetic *tango de vuelta*. In effect, then, if Cortázar's tango-poems and lyrics of this later period take up and refashion earlier tangos and tango-poems, 'Tango de vuelta' represents the transferral of this process to his narrative prose, with (the world of) 'Las puertas del cielo' as its base-model. I shall examine in more detail the nature of these connections and reworkings in due course, but even a cursory appreciation of the basic plot of the later story points to the sense that it constitutes a revisiting of the lost female lover narrative found in both 'Tanto' and 'Mariposita', as well as of the rediscovery of such a lover by the male figure that forms the structural bones of 'Las puertas del cielo'.

The link between 'Tango de vuelta' and 'Las puertas del cielo' does not, however, solely signal the centrality of tango and the wider tango world to the former text. In pointing back to the importance of a previous (fictional) narrative in understanding the issues which it takes up and to which it responds, 'Tango de vuelta' also discloses that *writing itself* is at the heart of its concerns and an axial element of its nature. Indeed, in this respect, it is worth noting that this is not, in fact, the story of Matilde and Emilio. The text begins with a long preamble in which the narrator, Flora's new partner, gives a detailed account of his *modus operandi* in constructing the story we are about to read. Strictly speaking, and in distinctly Borgesian fashion, that is, this is the story of the writing — or, more usefully, given the tango nature of the narrative, the composition — of a story.[53]

This opening gambit of 'Tango de vuelta', then, demands closer scrutiny. In a move that further reinforces my contention that this story constitutes a recasting (or at least builds upon the fundamental elements) of 'Las puertas del cielo', the narrator is presented primarily not in terms of his ambulance day job, but, taking up the story-writing and (virtual) note-taking mould of Hardoy, as a writer. In this instance, he is a writer who comes across as utterly dedicated to this calling, but also uninterested in actually publishing his work, thus repeating the private nature of Hardoy's *fichas* (as well as possibly hinting at and expanding the sense that these notes were in fact mental, rather than physically written):

> A mí me gusta escribir para mí, tengo cuadernos y cuadernos, versos y hasta una novela, pero lo que me gusta es escribir [...] no me interesa que lean lo que escribo, [...] me gusta cuando se me acaba un cuaderno porque es como si hubiera publicado todo eso, pero no se me ocurre publicarlo. (Cortázar 1980: 71–72)
>
> [I like to write for myself, I've got notebooks and notebooks, poetry, and even a novel, but what I like to do is write [...] I'm not interested in people reading what I write, [...] I like it when I finish a notebook, because it's as if I'd already published it, but I haven't thought about publishing it.] (1984: 61)

The narrator begins his explanation of the way in which this narrative has been put together by referring to the process of recounting a story as one of constructing a 'perfecta telaraña' (1980: 71) ('perfect [spider's] web', 1984: 60). Although the word is not explicitly used at this point, this description inevitably invokes the idea of *tejer* [weave/knit], with this verb finally emerging later on in the text as we are told of how Flora 'se encerraba en su pieza para escuchar la radio o tejer' (1980: 81) ('she would [...] shut herself up in her room to listen to the radio or knit', 1984: 73), a description which, once more, takes up an element of 'Las puertas del cielo', in this case the image of Celina in her suburban life and her 'largos entresueños al lado de *la radio*, con un remiendo o *un tejido* en las manos' (1993a: 113, italics mine) ('her long daydreams beside *the radio* with some [darning] or *knitting* in her hands', 2013: 102–03, italics mine). Picking up on the invocation of this term in the text's opening salvo, Serra Salvat (2002: 311) notes the relevance here of Cortázar's tango-poem 'Las tejedoras' [The Weavers] from the 'Con tangos' section of *Salvo el crepúsculo*, a piece that brims with cognates of the verb *tejer*. The *tejedoras* in question appear as figures (essentially, Argentine Parcae) weaving together the basic aspects, experiences, and memories of life itself, and the poem ends with the image of their knitting or weaving 'en un silencio insoportable | de tangos y discursos' (Cortázar 2009: 67) [in an unbearable silence | of tangos and speeches].[54] This final line encapsulates the two foundational strands of 'Tango de vuelta' that I have identified, and, mapped onto the story, discloses the nature of the weave around which its opening is built as being precisely a question of writing (language) and tango (music).[55]

Bearing in mind the context of the language/music debate against which Cortázar's engagement with music is played out, such a mapping also draws attention to the sense that 'Tango de vuelta' is a story constructed on the basis and through the operation of putatively divergent pulls, both in regard to the language/music dialectic and more generally. In this, the story might simply be seen to tap into the apparent contradictions that we have seen to lie at the heart of (Cortázar's presentation of and engagement with) tango (throughout his work). But, in fact, 'Tango de vuelta' represents a particularly sharp commentary on this aspect of (Cortázar's) tango, as well as offering a potential move beyond it. Once again, the title of the story is significant: as alluded to above, the central *tango de vuelta* of 'Las puertas del cielo', based around the tangos 'Tanto' and 'Mariposita', plays explicitly with both the restorative nostalgic look-back and (desired) return to the past and the reflective nostalgic creative and inventive playing with that past, now cast anew and renewed. And this procedure appears, in broad terms, to underlie the principal method for the composition of 'Tango de vuelta' too, as the narrator informs us that it is woven together from a combination of Flora's reminiscences and memories and — primarily his own — creative imagination, in that 'Flora me contó tantas cosas de su vida sin imaginarse que después yo las revisaba despacio entre dos sueños y algunas las pasaba a un cuaderno' (Cortázar 1980: 72) ('Flora told me so many things about her life without imagining that later on I would go over them slowly, between dreams, and would put some into a notebook', 1984: 61). Importantly, however, the narrator goes on to reveal that, in the case of the story we are about to read, it ended up becoming impossible to tell these two strands apart, as 'llegó el día en que me hubiera sido imposible distinguir entre lo que me contaba Flora y lo que ella y yo mismo habíamos ido agregando' (1980: 72) ('the day came when it would have been impossible for me to distinguish between what Flora was telling me and what she and I myself had been [adding]', 1984: 62). What is more, a closer look at the compositional details of the narrative of 'Tango de vuelta' discloses that this (con)fusion of the two putatively distinct elements/nostalgic tendencies is also written into each one. The description we are given of Flora's memories, for example, shows them to be characterised by being both numerous and varied: the narrator, who uses Flora in a way that recalls Hardoy's use of Mauro and Celina, states that:

> la dejaba tranquila algunos días, le alentaba otros recuerdos y en una de ésas le sacaba de nuevo aquello y Flora se precipitaba como si ya se hubiera olvidado de todo lo que me llevaba dicho, empezaba de nuevo y yo la dejaba porque más de una vez la memoria le iba trayendo cosas todavía no dichas. (1980: 72)

> [I would leave her alone for a few days, encourage other memories from her and then at one point would bring up the subject and Flora would launch into it as if she had already forgotten everything she'd told me up till then, she would start again and I would let her because more than once her memory would throw up things that hadn't yet been said.]

The hints here at 'individual reminiscences that could suggest multiple narratives' (Boym 2001: 53) and the cherishing of 'shattered fragments of memory' (49) of reflective nostalgia are clear. In contrast to this, the apparently inventive or creative element, in the form of the narrator's contributions to the (re)fashioning of these memories, is shot through with an underlying rejection of the reflective nostalgic tendency: the memory fragments or 'pedacitos' are seen as 'ajustables a los otros pedacitos' (Cortázar 1980: 72) ('[capable of being] fitted into other little bits', 1984: 61), a line which recalls Hardoy's description in 'Las puertas del cielo' of how he made sure to 'reunir y ordenar mis fichas' (1993a: 112 ('coll[ect] and reord[er] my [files]', 2013: 101). Indeed, the imagination and creativity employed as these memories are threaded together is directed entirely towards the sort of understanding of the verb *tejer* that, far from the (affirmative) focus on this as an act of 'crear' (Serra Salvat 2002: 311) [creating], reveals it to be an act designed to shore up a mental *telaraña* whose distinctly Borgesian purpose is to block out any idea that life and reality might escape our narrative constructs and control:

> cómo no decirse que a lo mejor, alguna que otra vez, la telaraña mental se ajusta hilo por hilo a la de la vida, aunque decirlo venga de un puro miedo, porque si no se creyera un poco en eso ya no se podría seguir haciendo frente a las telarañas de afuera. (Cortázar 1980: 71).

> [how can we not say that perhaps, at some time or another, the mental [spider's] web adjusts itself, thread by thread, to that of life, even though we might be saying so purely out of fear, because if we didn't believe in it a little, we couldn't keep [...] [facing the] outside [spider's] webs.] (1984: 60)

Thus, the narrator's role is one where he looks for 'los puntos de sutura, la unión de tanta cosa suelta' (1980: 72) ('the stitches of the suture [...], the coming together of so many scattered [...] things', 1984: 61) in order to sew together the different memory fragments, as he presents the composition of the tango-story as above all an attempt to create exactly the sort of linguistic wall that we have seen Cortázar repeatedly to invoke and lament, shutting out anything that might challenge the veracity of its narrative:

> [Flora y yo] necesitábamos como todo el mundo que aquello se completara, que el último agujero recibiera al fin la pieza, el color, el final de una línea viniendo de una pierna o de una palabra o de una escalera. (1980: 72)
>
> [[Flora and I] needed, like everybody, to have that [...] [completed], for the last hole finally to receive the piece, the color, the end of a line coming from a leg or a word or a staircase.] (1984: 62)

The *tejer* of the story in front of us, that is, turns out to return us in more than one way to that image in 'Las puertas del cielo' of Celina 'con *un remiendo* o un tejido en las manos' (1993a: 113, italics mine) ('with *some* [*darning*] or knitting in her hands', 2013: 102–03, italics mine), and, in the process, resonates starkly with Boym's description of the restorative nostalgic emphasis on 'patch[ing] up the memory gaps' (2001: 41).

This (con)fusion of the two 'pulls' in operation in the composition of Matilde and Emilio's story continues within the narrative itself, where it is played out in terms that engage more overtly with the grounding threads of tango and writing. Indicative of this is the recurrent narrative motif of the 'novela' (Cortázar 1980: 77) [the novel], which is mentioned (explicitly) on four occasions. This novel essentially pairs up with the tango of the title to reiterate the tango/literature, composition/writing dialectic, and shifts attention from memories/creation (and, broadly, restorative/reflective nostalgia) towards (the related) script/invention as a way to frame the story's (con)fusion of elements. One effect of foregrounding such terms, it might be noted, is to point up the extent to which Cortázar's engagement with tango here is treading on the same ground and grappling with the same questions as his texts on *la música culta*, not least 'Clone', which, as mentioned, follows 'Tango de vuelta' in *Queremos tanto a Glenda*. Indeed, redolent of my discussion of 'Clone' and the notion of the (chain-like) performance of pre-written scripts or scores, the role of the novel in 'Tango de vuelta' is largely to draw attention to and highlight the idea that Matilde and Emilio's story is a script that they can do nothing to change. Thus, the first time the novel is mentioned we read of 'esa novela abandonada boca abajo en el sofá, algo ya escrito y que ni siquiera era necesario leer porque ya estaba cumplido antes de la lectura, ya había ocurrido antes de que ocurriera en la lectura' (Cortázar 1980: 77–78) ('that novel left face down on [the] sofá, something already written and which it wasn't even necessary to read because it had already happened before being read, had already happened before happening in the reading', 1984: 68). Similarly, a page later, after looking up 'bigamy' in the dictionary and wondering why she has done so, given that 'sabía que era imposible cambiar nada' (1980: 79) ('she knew it was impossible to change anything', 1984: 69), Matilde goes on to refer to knowing 'que la novela tirada en el sofá estaba escrita hasta la palabra fin, que no podía alterar nada' (1980: 79) ('that the novel thrown onto the sofa was written down to the words The End, that she couldn't change anything', 1984: 69). The most significant lines regarding the novel, however, occur towards the end of the story. Having been placed, Matilde assumes, by Flora on an empty bookshelf, the volume's implied identity as the very story we are reading is reinforced, as the literary motif is combined with a stereotypical marker of tango tales (the knife) and a further allusion to (then) future events being already written (the crystal ball):

> la veía muy bien boca abajo en el único estante vacío donde Flora la había puesto sin cerrarla, veía el cuchillo malayo que el Cholo le había regalado a Germán, la bola de cristal sobre su zócalo de terciopelo rojo. (1980: 83)
>
> [she could see it very clearly, open and face down on the one empty shelf where Flora had put it, she saw the Malayan knife that Cholo had given Germán, the crystal ball on the base of red velvet.] (1984: 74)

The fact that the book is placed on the only empty shelf can also be seen to act as a reference back to the beginning of the text: this novel, like (as?) the text we are reading, represents the completed filling of 'el ultimo agujero' (1980: 72) ('the last hole', 1984: 62).[56]

But if this insistence on scripting threads its way through Matilde and Emilio's narrative, it is countered by the nature of that narrative. Put simply, the scripted nature of the story is constantly both reiterated and yet at the same time subverted, undermined, and blurred, often in a *mise en abyme* of the scripted and the invented, and, yes, of restorative and reflective nostalgic tendencies, where each ends up folding fluidly into and becoming indistinguishable from the other. This happens in the story on three fundamental levels and in relation to three distinct, though interrelated, musico-textual 'scripts' with which, as I have intimated, the narrative at the heart of 'Tango de vuelta' engages: the central *tango de vuelta* of 'Las puertas del cielo'; 'Las puertas del cielo' itself; and (the) tango (world) generally.

On a basic level, the story of 'Tango de vuelta' is replete with details that cast it as a traditional tango story, a reconstruction of and a harking back to this most Argentine set of 'emblems and rituals' (Boym 2001: 49). Emilio, for example, is portrayed as the classic *compadrito*, his dress and posture being referred to on several occasions in the course of the narrative, which — reminiscent of the description in 'Las puertas del cielo' of Mauro's attire — draws specific attention to the fact that 'se vestía con una campera negra y pantalones terrosos, [...] el pañuelo blanco en el cuello' (Cortázar 1980: 73) [he wore a black jacket and earthy-brown trousers, [...] the white handkerchief round his neck].[57] As Álvarez-Schüller notes, the stereotypical image of the *compadrito* is also as a man 'der sich gegen eine Laterne lehnt und raucht' (2008: 41) [who leans against a lamppost and smokes], and Emilio's first appearance, repeated a number of times after this, is characterised by his smoking as he leans against a tree. Additionally, both Emilio and Matilde are, at several stages in the story, described in ways that appear to portray them as executing moves and postures found in tango dance. Serra Salvat in particular draws attention to this, noting how we are told of Emilio's having 'los ojos rápidos para el quite y el despegue' (Cortázar 1980: 73) ('his eyes quick for the get-up-and-go', 1984: 62), a term belonging to tango choreography (Serra Salvat 2002: 312), and commenting that the reference to how 'Matilde se echó atrás, golpeándose la espalda en un sillón, ahogando un alarido' (Cortázar 1980: 73) ('Matilde drew back, bumping into an easy chair, muffling a shriek', 1984: 63) can be understood likewise. Beyond this, as in tango dance, where 'the lack of verbal exchange is considered a tango trademark' (Savigliano 1997: 43), so do the couple here at no point exchange words, whilst, as Álvarez-Schüller remarks, the blurred fusing of the two bodies as they fight at the end is redolent of 'der Tanz eines Tangopaares' (2008: 42) [the dance of a tango couple].[58] At the same time, however, as Álvarez-Schüller further notes, these most traditional of details are also subjected to a certain subtle adaptation and updating: the lamppost is, here, a tree; the traditional suit worn by the *compadrito* has been replaced in Emilio's case by a jacket (*campera*).

If these examples point more to identifiable instances of scripted tradition and (modernised) departure, turning to the plotline itself we see a more marked melding of the stereotypical tango narrative and its creative subversion. The sense that the couple have been living in an endless (traditional) tango is conveyed by the allusion to how, even from before their departure to Mexico, they had been in 'una guerra de silencios y de engaños y de estúpidas reconciliaciones que no servían de nada, los telones para el nuevo acto, para una nueva noche de cuchillos largos' (Cortázar 1980: 75) ('a war of silences and deceptions and stupid reconciliations that weren't worth anything, the curtain ready for the new act, for a new night of long knives', 1984: 65), but the specifics of the tale related here are more problematic in this respect. On the one hand, 'Tango de vuelta' gives us the return home to Buenos Aires of the female character, Matilde thus repeating the role of the *milonguita* who returns to the *barrio* after pursuing in vain her social, romantic, and materialistic dreams: the past is restored in the return home. But, recalling the problematisation of this tango trope in 'Las puertas del cielo', in this case, the return home is not *to* the *compadrito* after failing to find true love and happiness with a wealthy man, but *from* the *compadrito* to a life of elevated social standing and material comfort.[59] Thus, the story also posits Mexico — the locus that is distant from the *barrio* — as being the 'rightful' home abandoned by the woman. In other words, both locations are identifiable as *both* the home *and* the 'other space', and we can no longer tell with any certainty which is the 'real' home-to-be-restored. The tango script of the return home, and the attendant restorative nostalgic move that it conjures up, is thus shot through with subversive invention which, in reflective nostalgic style, 'perpetually defer[s] [any definitive narrative or teleological] homecoming' (Boym 2001: 49). Moreover, we might additionally note here that the putative 'return home' that we are given in 'Tango de vuelta', in being a return to a 'civilised' space, is also a reversal of the return home found in 'Las puertas del cielo', where Celina returned to her underground *milonga* home, which was itself a reversal of the more traditional tango return to the *barrio*. As we can see, though, in the case of 'Tango de vuelta', a reversal of a reversal does not mean a stable return to from where you started!

Moving on from the expansive umbrella of tango narratives generally, we also find elements of 'Tango de vuelta' that engage specifically with the plotlines in the tangos from 'Las puertas del cielo'. 'Mariposita' tells, in a traditional story, of a man lamenting his lover's preferring a rich man to him; 'Tanto', not dissimilarly, is a tale of a man who has lost or been abandoned by his lover. Emilio and Matilde's story repeats these tropes, only here, rather than tears ('Tanto') or trying to find the lover in order to get her back ('Mariposita'), Emilio decides to take the path of vengeance, thus suggesting a creative playing with the scripts it initially appears to be repeating. Beyond 'Tanto' and 'Mariposita', however, there are, in fact, a number of precedents for such a revenge narrative, which was a common element of Old Guard tangos before the 'masculine revengeful character [...] was progressively substituted by the tango's whiny male who surrendered himself to cigarettes and alcohol to ease his pain' (Viladrich 2006: 275). Significantly, one such precedent is found in the 1927 tango 'A la luz del candil', which features, of course, in 'Las puertas del cielo'. In other words, the invention that enables the narrative of 'Tango de vuelta' to prise itself away from the script offered by 'Tanto' and 'Mariposita' (the *tango de vuelta* of 'Las puertas del cielo') is in fact a recreation of the revenge narrative of the earlier story's other tango. That said, we should also recall that the tango 'A la luz del candil' has the *compadrito* kill his loved one and her lover, whilst the version found in 'Las puertas del cielo' has only the loved one being killed. 'Tango de vuelta', then, in giving us a story where the woman and the *compadrito* are killed — and killed by the woman –, restores the double murder of the original tango, thus undoing the invention of 'Las puertas del cielo', at the same time as it alters the identity of the murdered male and shifts the agency from the *compadrito* to the *milonguita*. Indeed, similarly, it is notable that the drinking that characterises the male character in 'Mariposita' has been transferred in 'Tango de vuelta' to the female figure, with references to Matilde's drinking her 'segundo whisky' (Cortázar 1980: 82) [second whisky] — in a scene that takes place by 'la luz de la lámpara' (82) [the light of the lamp] — and being 'borracha' (83) [drunk]. Once again, there is script and there is invention, but each element appears to be both simultaneously.

The question of female agency — and taking one's own life can be read here as an act of the utmost assertion of self-determination — also plays a significant part in a further, and arguably the most immediately notable, aspect of the story in which we see a conflation of supposedly divergent pulls: the narrative perspective. The importance of this element of 'Tango de vuelta' is heightened by the fact that it was ultimately the failure to reconcile and (con)fuse narrator (Hardoy) and actor (Mauro) that led to the slipping away of a genuine escape from the normative, binary, and logical structures of society (and language) in 'Las puertas del cielo'. And an early indication that this later story will be concerned precisely with 'correcting' this through the manner in which it shows the narrator and the narrative to operate is found immediately following the compositional preamble. Here, the dual insistence on the part of the (here clearly male) narrator in relation to the appearance of Emilio in Buenos Aires that 'lo veo realmente, lo estoy viendo' (72) [I can really see it/him, I am seeing it/him] and then, a little further on, that this figure 'no tenía nada de fantasma [...] no era un fantasma' (73) ('there was nothing of the ghost about him [...] he wasn't a ghost', 1984: 62) responds directly to and dismisses the two 'ways out' of the potential recognition of Celina's immanent corporeality in the earlier story, that is, that Hardoy and Mauro were only seeing someone who looked like Celina, or that it was a ghost. This 'corrective line' is maintained and developed from this point on. As the tale continues, the narrative perspective undergoes a shift, as it becomes increasingly difficult not to read the text as being written from Matilde's perspective. This is not entirely consistent, but, generally speaking, the narrative comes across principally as emanating from and revealing the inner thoughts, fears, and doubts of the female protagonist as she works through the nature and implications of Emilio's apparent return; the following passage is a typical example of this:

> pero entonces cómo Milo había podido, imposible imaginar que la madre de los Recanati se quedara callada tanto tiempo si sabía, ni siquiera por el gusto de esperarlo a Germán y decírselo en nombre de Cristo o algo así, te engañó para que la llevaras al altar, exactamente así diría esa bruja y Germán cayéndose de las nubes, no puede ser, no puede ser. (1980: 77)
>
> [but then how had Milo been able, impossible to imagine that the Recanatis' mother would have been silent so long if she knew, not even for the pleasure of waiting for Germán and telling him for the sake of the Lord Jesus or something like that, she tricked you so you'd lead her down the aisle, that's exactly what the old witch would say and Germán falling down out of the clouds, it can't be, it can't be.] (1984: 67)

It is thus possible to read this as the appropriation of the narrative perspective by the female figure, mirroring the assertion of agency within that narrative itself, and breaking with tango tradition and moulds: as Savigliano notes, 'fewer than 2 percent of all tangos have been written by women and [...] fewer than 4 percent (including those written by men) put tango lyrics between female lips' (1995: 55).[60] And yet, in keeping with the reading I have been advancing here, it is also possible to comprehend this not as a subversive move, but as the silencing of the female voice: this *is* a text written by a male internal (and external) author and the apparently intimate anxieties and emotions of Matilde are nothing but a male voice pretending to speak for and as the most personal thoughts of this female figure.

The complexity of the narrative perspective comes to a head in the final pages of the text, as Serra Salvat has noted (2002: 312–13), where it becomes even more difficult to pin down. As we read of the erotic encounter between Flora and Emilio (Simón), it is still initially plausible to understand this as Matilde's assumptions or imagination as regards how Flora was perceiving the act. But this soon gives way to a sense that it is more likely to be from Flora's or from the extra- and homodiegetic (male) narrator's perspective. At the point at which Emilio exits Flora's bedroom to search for Matilde, however, the line 'Buena madera, buena casa la de Germán Morales' (Cortázar 1980: 84) ('Good wood, a good house Germán Morales has', 1984: 76), as he tests out the first step on the staircase, throws us into Emilio's perspective. And the shifts continue at pace. Shortly afterwards, for example, we read that:

> El golpe contra la cómoda le llegó a Carlitos desde un sueño intranquilo, se enderezó en la cama y gritó, muchas veces gritaba de noche y Flora se levantaba para calmarlo, para darle agua antes de que Germán se despertara protestando. (1980: 84)

[The blow against the dresser reached Carlitos in his restless sleep, he sat up in bed and cried out, he cried out a lot at night and Flora would get up to calm him, give him some water before Germán [...] [woke up] angry.] (1984: 76)

Here, then, we are back at either the extra- and homodiegetic narrator's or, conceivably, Matilde's viewpoint, whilst, the very next line, 'Sabía que era necesario hacer callar a Carlitos porque Simón no había vuelto todavía' (1980: 84) ('She knew she had to quiet Carlitos because Simón hadn't come back yet', 1984: 76) reintroduces the persuasive sense that we have Flora's perspective (since she is the only one who knows him as Simón), without completely discarding that this could also still be the main narrator's (and internal author's) voice. It is only at the end of the text, as we are reintroduced to the first person, that we are returned definitively to the (internal) authorial figure with which the text began. And yet, at the same time, stretching over all of these twists and turns is what we were told in that preamble: the entire narrative is, supposedly, from an impenetrable fusion of Flora and the author-narrator's perspectives. In other words, according to this later reading, whether the perspective is that of a male or a female character, or of the principal narrator (author), what we, in fact, have before us is a voice that precisely refuses gender definition ('imposible distinguir entre lo que me contaba Flora y lo que ella y yo mismo habíamos ido agregando' (1980: 72) ('impossible [...] to distinguish between what Flora was telling me and what she and I myself had been [adding]', 1984: 62)).

Bringing these myriad possibilities together, we thus see how the reference at the end of the story to the fighting Matilde and Emilio as 'cuerpos desnudos vueltos una sola masa [...] en *una maraña confusa*' (1980: 85, italics mine) ('naked bodies wrapped in a single mass [...] in *a confused tangle*', 1984: 76, italics mine) is, by this point, reflected in vertiginous fashion in the text's destabilising construction of narrative perspective. On one level, we can understand the story to be giving us different — and often blurred, multiple, or hard to identify — claims to agency on the part of both male and female diegetic characters, as they seem to assume control of the narrative, usurping the author-narrator's authority somehow; on another level, if we attempt to move beyond this and convince ourselves of the ultimate primacy and control of that author-narrator, we find here too an hermetic amalgam of male and female perspectives, where, moreover, as I have argued, each of those strands is identifiable as having what we might broadly see as restorative and reflective nostalgic tendencies, or elements, in a manner that, once more, refuses any delimitation between the two.[61] In this way, then, 'Tango de vuelta' marks a contrast with what we saw in chapter 2 in relation to *la música culta* to be the largely either/or destabilisation of identification in 'Alguien que anda por ahí' or the gender — and general — (con)fusion of elements in 'Las ménades', where 'appropriate' delimitations are finally redrawn. 'Tango de vuelta', that is, persistently refuses our attempts to reach any definitive answer to the question of its narrative perspective and control, effectively enacting textually the boundary-collapsing, label-defying nature of the *milonga* signalled by Savigliano. Returning to the ending of 'Las puertas del cielo', then, we might conclude that 'Tango de vuelta''s response to that earlier story's retained separation of author/narrator and (tango) character is to operate at every turn to (con)fuse its own particular version of those figures and their respective narrative levels, weaving together the *maraña* [tangle] of Emilio and Matilde's dancing, tango bodies with the *telaraña* [(spider's) web] of Flora's and the diegetic author's narrative, into one impenetrable, pulsing *masa confusa* [confused mass].[62] In so doing, the *tejer* [weave] of this later text is thus one which ends by rendering the boundary between tango (dance, plot, music) and writing (language, narrative) impossible to trace.

To end this examination of Cortázar's engagement with tango on the motif of *tejer* is, in many ways, highly apt. It is an engagement in which the divergent pulls of restorative and reflective nostalgia, script, or moulds, and creativity, evident both in Cortázar's writing and in his interviews on tango, are woven together in, ultimately, highly complex ways. But, as should already be clear, this motif is also significant for what it tells us about some of the differences between how Cortázar deals with and uses tango and how he tends to approach *la música culta*. On several occasions in the preceding analysis we have seen how the play of the aforementioned tendencies and pulls resonates with the terms and issues addressed in relation to the latter genre. The notion of performing pre-written or pre-composed scripts or scores is, after all, not just present in Cortázar's lament in interviews regarding the strictures of both musical types, but is also found across texts such as 'Tango de vuelta' and 'Clone'. However, whereas, for example, the latter's performative chains come in a narrative characterised by an insistence on the attempt at a perfect or accurate rendering of such scripts both musically and textually, even if the result is an inevitably and, importantly, identifiably imperfect version of such, the *tejer* of tango, as developed most profoundly in 'Tango de vuelta', shows tango — in Cortázar's use of it — to be predicated on a deliberate weave of the restorative, the (national) script, the home(ly) on the one hand and the creative, the forward-looking, the subversive on the other, where the unravelling of that weave is resisted, just as 'Tango de vuelta' ends with the image of the *maraña*, in both form and content.[63] Cortázar's own shifting presentation of tango throughout his work and words, then, is also a part of this, as is the way in which he aims in his writing to incorporate the putatively negative (restorative nostalgic) aspects of tango that he himself signals into a (musical) writing practice that positively makes a (reflective nostalgic) virtue of them. In this, Cortázar's tango is like tango itself: a music of home, of the nation, of reaffirmed social values, codes, and customs that is shot through with a defiant insistence on the shifting subversion of the transgressive.

Notes to Chapter 3

1. The album *Trottoirs de Buenos Aires* (Cortázar, Cantón, and Cédron 1980) [*Pavements of Buenos Aires*] is an album of ten tracks, six of which have lyrics written by Cortázar. These are: 'Medianoche aquí', 'Tu piel bajo la luna', 'Veredas de Buenos Aires', 'Java', 'La camarada', and 'La Cruz del Sur'. Of these, 'Java' and 'La camarada' are poems that also appear in the section 'El agua entre los dedos...' [Water Through One's Fingers...] of *Salvo el crepúsculo* (2009 [1984]) [*Save Twilight*]. The poem 'La camarada' is a carbon copy of the album track, whilst the album version of 'Java' differs in having an additional line in both the third stanza and the chorus, and

with one line of the fifth stanza being different in the two versions. 'Veredas de Buenos Aires' and 'La Cruz del Sur' are related to the 'Con tangos' [With Tangos] section of *Salvo el crepúsculo*. In the case of these poems, the album version of 'Veredas de Buenos Aires' has two additional lines, and 'La Cruz del Sur' is an amalgam of what are two separate poems in 'Con tangos', 'La mufa' and 'Milonga', followed by four additional stanzas and a final refrain, which are not in the literary versions. Mesa Gancedo (2002: 421–25) offers a useful account of the (varied) dating and history of these tango-poems, as well as that of other tango-poems in Cortázar's corpus.

2. Whilst tango has not received as much critical attention as jazz in Cortazarian scholarship, there are, nonetheless, several notable studies of different lengths and nature, in particular since the turn of the century. The largest work on tango in Cortázar is Fralasco (2005), a somewhat sprawling account of numerous texts in which Cortázar engages with the musical form. Despite its lack of clear structure or focus, it is a useful text in detailing some of the precise ways in which tango lyrics and themes are taken up by Cortázar in his writing. The other long-form study to have been published is Álvarez-Schüller (2008), which probably does not receive the attention it merits on account of being in German. Among the more notable scholarly pieces of a narrower focus are: Serra Salvat (2002), which looks specifically at the engagement with tango in the 'Con tangos' section of *Salvo el crepúsculo*; Savigliano (1997), which addresses 'Las puertas del cielo' in an engagingly novel manner, adopting an ethnomusicological approach both redolent and critical of elements of the character Dr Hardoy's *modus operandi*; Peiró (2006: 68–86) offers a general take on tango in Cortázar as part of his broader study of music in the author's work; Anad (2004) analyses Cortázar's tango-poems, focusing, like Serra Salvat, primarily on 'Con tangos'; Berg (2000) takes *Rayuela* and, in particular, the tango-poems that Cortázar wrote for the *Trottoirs de Buenos Aires* project as he sketches out, albeit in frustratingly underdeveloped terms, an approach to Cortázar's tango engagement to which I shall refer in more depth further on in this chapter; Mesa Gancedo (2002) picks up on some of Berg's ideas and talks with greater bibliographical detail of the different tango-poems that Cortázar wrote; and Miller (2016) takes up some of the directions indicated by Berg and Anad to examine the tango-nostalgia relationship in Cortázar's work. Again, I shall say more on this in due course.

3. Relatedly, Cortázar and Prego discuss the underlying general advocacy of conformity to class and gender norms in the narrative of tango lyrics themselves. Cortázar, for example, sums up the advice given to women in tangos as 'el consejo de la conformidad total' (1985: 168) [the advice of total conformity], before giving the examples of 'Flor de fango' (1917) and 'Muñeca brava' (1928), as tangos that show the fall that awaits women who attempt to move socially upwards out of the *barrio*, in search of their own decadent pleasure. I shall return to the notion of conformity in the course of this chapter.

4. Most of the aforementioned scholarship that addresses tango in Cortázar's work includes some form of enumeration of at least the principal texts and ways in which Cortázar engages with this musical genre, but the most comprehensive in this regard are Peiró (2006: 68–86) and, in particular, Fralasco (2005: 127–61).

5. Specifically on some of the more notable tango elements of *Los premios*, see Serra Salvat (2002: 308–09) and Peiró (2006: 77–78). On *Rayuela* there is, of course, a great deal of scholarship. Some works that look at the engagement with tango in the novel include MacAdam (2001: 50), Berg (2000: 233–39), and Álvarez-Schüller (2008: 47–61).

6. On 'Torito', see Fralasco (2005: 53–62). I shall examine 'Tango de vuelta' in more detail in due course; existing scholarship on this story is in relatively short supply, but see Serra Salvat (2002: 311–13) and Álvarez-Schüller (2008: 40–43).

7. Much has been written on 'Las puertas del cielo', but one of the most in-depth works from a tango perspective is from tango scholar Marta E. Savigliano (1997). I shall examine this story in more depth further on in this chapter. Viviana Álvarez-Schüller also examines the story from this angle (2008: 15–22).

8. Peiró refers to the presence of 'el tango de fondo en innumerables escenas de la obra [*Diario de Andrés Fava*]' (2006: 74) [tango as a backdrop in numerous scenes in the work [*Diary of Andrés Fava*]].

9. This piece was originally published in *Sur* in 1953 (Cortázar 1953).

10. For an overview of the use of tango in 'Un gotán para Lautrec', see Miller (2016: 18–20).
11. In interview with Picon Garfield (1981: 131), Cortázar describes the influence of tango in his work in its presence as a theme and as lyrics that he inserts, knowing that Argentine readers will pick up on these. I will say more about these aspects in due course.
12. The Sábat Project, *Monsieur Lautrec*, has already been detailed above; the Pat Andrea project is entitled *La puñalada/El tango de la vuelta* (Andrea and Cortázar 1982a; 1982b; 2002 [1984]) [*The Stabbing/The Return Trip Tango*]. The story behind this project is long and complicated, but essentially it concerns a series of thirty-four drawings by the Dutch artist Pat Andrea from 1979 which show frenetic and violent scenes of stabbings, where the poses and movements of the characters often appear highly stylised (thus lending themselves to an alignment with dance). Cortázar was initially asked to provide a prologue to accompany a book edition of these drawings, but instead sent a story, 'Tango de vuelta', which he had recently published in *Queremos tanto a Glenda* (1980), changing its title to 'El tango de la vuelta'. In 1982 the book was published, with Cortázar's story translated into Dutch and French. The Spanish edition was produced in 1984 but never distributed, following health issues suffered by the publisher Elizabeth Franck. The books were only discovered, lying in boxes in a storage facility in Miami, in 2000.
13. Carlos Gardel (1890–1935) was a French-Argentine tango singer, actor, and composer. He is the most significant and well-known figure in the history of tango. As Julie M. Taylor puts it, Gardel is 'possibly the single most important element of tango lore' (1976: 285), going on to state that 'Gardel has remained, as its aesthetic and technical acme, the artistic embodiment of the tango for enthusiasts of any stratum of society' (285).
14. In the short essay 'Gardel', Cortázar writes similarly, 'Cuando Gardel canta un tango, su estilo expresa el del pueblo que lo amó' (1970b: 137) [when Gardel sings a tango, his style expresses that of the people who loved him].
15. For a useful guide to the history of tango and its place as a marker of and cultural metaphor for Argentine and, particularly, *porteño* identity, see Collier (1995) and Nielsen and Mariotto (2006). On the African roots of tango, as part of a broader history of the music, see Thompson (2005).
16. The importance of genuine emotion is evident when Cortázar describes Gardel in his essay named after the singer, stating at one point that 'la pena o la cólera ante el abandono de la mujer son pena y cólera concretas, apuntando a Juana o a Pepa, y no ese pretexto agresivo total que es fácil descubrir en la voz del cantante histérico de este tiempo' (1970b: 137) [the sorrow and anger at being left by his woman are concrete sorrow and anger, aimed at Juana or Pepa, and not that totally aggressive pretext which is easy to discover in the voice of the hysterical singer these days].
17. Pedro Laurenz (1902–1972) was a tango composer and *bandoneón* player.
18. In interview with Weiss, Cortázar emphasises the extent to which tango was present in his childhood home: 'I grew up in an atmosphere of tangos. We listened to them on the radio, because the radio started when I was little, and right away it was tangos and tangos. There were people in my family, my mother and an aunt, who played tangos on the piano and sang them. Through the radio, we began to listen to Carlos Gardel and the great singers of the time' (1991: 53).
19. 'Razones de la cólera' was not published until 1984, as part of *Salvo el crepúsculo*.
20. Two of the most obvious instances of Oliveira quoting tango lyrics in the Paris chapters are found in chapters 21 and 29, where he cites the 1928 tango 'Eche veinte centavos en la ranura' (Cortázar 2007: 232) and Gardel's 1917 tango 'Mi noche triste' (Cortázar 2007: 323), with some lyrics apparently seeping in from another Gardel track, 'Cuando tú no estás' (1933). There are also other, less explicit, references to tangos and tango lyrics in these chapters, the most important of which, in terms of its link with idea of being in Paris, distant from Buenos Aires, is in the reference in chapter 36 to Gardel's 'Anclao en París' (1931) in the lines, 'pobrecito Horacio anclado en París, cómo habrá cambiado tu calle Corrientes, Suipacha, Esmeralda, y el viejo arrabal' (Cortázar 2007: 363) ('poor little Horacio *anclado en París*, set down in Paris, as the tango says, *cómo habrá cambiado tu calle Corrientes, Suipacha, Esmeralda, y el viejo arrabal*', 1966: 211). In interview with Prego, Cortázar underlines the inherent connection between Oliveira,

as a *porteño*, and tango: 'Oliveira es profundamente porteño y eso significa haber crecido un poco dentro del clima del tango y de las letras de tangos, evidentemente. [...] Oliveira [...] es un hombre de tango y ha asimilado eso' (1985: 160–61) [Oliveira is profoundly *porteño* and that means having grown up within the climate of tango and tango lyrics, evidently. [...] Oliveira [...] is a tango man and has assimilated that].

21. The term *milonga* here is being used to refer not to the location and dance event that forms the backdrop to 'Las puertas del cielo', but to a genre of music and its accompanying dance that arose in the 1870s in Argentina. Thompson comments that 'milonga furthered a tradition of aesthetic dueling: pugnacity as poetry, battling as dance' (2005: 121), adding that 'early milongas [...] vaunt potent songs of nostalgia' (121). The *milonga* itself emerged from the *payada*, a genre consisting of 'dueling guitarists improvising verses on the pampas' (122). For more detailed discussion of the *milonga* see Thompson (2005: 121–49); on the *candombe* see Carámbula (2005); on the *habanera*, see Thompson (2005: 111–20). For a good overview of tango's origins and early years, see Collier (1995) and Archetti (1999: 136–40).

22. In interview with Prego, Cortázar identifies his tango tastes as lying 'en la época de los años veinte a cuarenta' (1985: 165) [in the era of the twenties to the forties]. This period coincides with what is generally considered to be that of the New Guard (*Guardia Nueva*), although scholars identify the different eras in tango history as corresponding to slightly different periods. In broad terms, the Old Guard (*Guardia Vieja*), which consisted of smaller groups of musicians and focused more on dance than lyric, constitutes the earliest tangos up until roughly 1920, although the Gardel tango, 'Mi noche triste' (1917), which appears in Cortázar's work on several occasions, is often seen as a 'game-changer', marking this important shift in tango. The New Guard, which brought with it a move towards a greater and more sophisticated lyrical focus, concentrating on nostalgia and romance, and a reduction in the aggressiveness and richness of the dance form (Archetti 1999: 138), is generally seen as running from this time until approximately 1935–1940, although some critics place the end of this era a little earlier. Some scholars view the New Guard as being another term for the so-called Golden Age of tango; others class this as a separate era following on from the New Guard in around 1935–1940 and lasting until 1950–1955; there are also those who view the Golden Age as spanning this entire period from 1920 to 1955. For different guides to this classification of the periods of tango's history, see, for example: Collier (1995); Azzi (1995); Archetti (1999: 136–40); Nielsen and Mariotto (2006: 13–17); and Baim (2007: 112–13).

23. Corbatta, writing in the early 1990s, alludes to a continuing — and evolving — relationship between tango and nostalgia in the idea of a (contemporary) tango revival, where tango is both vehicle for and object of an Argentine nostalgia (1994: 71).

24. My initial mapping of Boym's two categories of nostalgia, restorative and reflective, onto Cortázar's tango took the form of conference papers given at the Latin American Studies Association Congress in 2012 (San Francisco) and the Conference of the Association of Hispanists of Great Britain and Ireland in 2013 (Oxford). My thanks to those who were at these events for their contributions to the debates that followed the presentations, which have helped guide my thinking on these matters.

25. Cortázar goes on to add here that Barbieri 'sabe improvisar maravillosamente *a base de un tango*' (Picon Garfield 1981: 131, italics mine) [can improvise marvellously *on the basis of a tango*], implying that, for Cortázar, what Barbieri is playing is somehow not 'really' tango.

26. Savigliano highlights both of the elements mentioned here as she concludes that 'tango, both in its lyrics and choreographies, has recorded women's abilities to subvert and negotiate' (1995: 69). She makes particular reference to the different choreographic strategies that the female dancer could employ to subvert and challenge their male partners and the established (gender/choreographic) order, whilst essentially remaining with the overall codes of the dance (60; 69–70). For further analysis along these lines, bringing in broader social subversions and challenges found within tango, see Archetti (1999: 136–60).

27. Piazzolla revolutionised tango in the 1950s. Heralding 'a paradigmatic change in the tango' (Azzi 2002: 37), Piazzolla kept 'tango's essential spirit' (35), but brought in elements of jazz and classical music to transform the genre and establish what was termed *nuevo tango* [new tango]. Thompson (2005: 209–10) underlines in particular the extent of the improvisation and

improvisational techniques found in Piazzolla's music composition and practice. For brief details on Piazzolla's life and music, see Azzi (1995: 156–59).
28. Thompson (2005: 168–218) gives a detailed analysis of the role of creative innovations in the music, rhythm, and instrumentation of tango throughout its history, in particular in the earlier periods, focusing on the role of black culture and musicians. In relation to the period of the 1920s, to which Cortázar was so drawn, he comments that 'tango was in a state of creative ferment' (Thompson 2005: 175), and other scholars have also pointed to the musical richness and development of the New Guard era, María Susana Azzi, for example, describing the 1920s as seeing 'an aesthetic and technical evolution both in the composition and performance of tango music' (1995: 119). But if the New Guard or Golden Age was musically more complex and sophisticated, this also brought with it an important shift in the nature of tango. The earliest tangos, the tangos of the early part of the Old Guard, were 'entirely improvised' (Collier 1995: 47), and even as the compositions started to acquire 'definitive shape and form after 1910' (51), improvisation remained an important part of the music. The tango of the New Guard, however, 'drastically reduc[ed] the degree of improvisation [...] [as] conductors became more concerned with details and nuances in the orchestration than with the performances of improvised solos' (Archetti 1999: 137). This is clearly in line with the criticisms Cortázar levels at tango, but we might reflect on the fact that these criticisms appear to be based on Cortázar's own choice of preferred tango period, and where this happens to be the one that, arguably, involves the least improvisation and freedom from/most focus on the score of all.
29. Fralasco examines this aspect of 'Torito' in detail (2005: 53–62).
30. See Miller (2016: 18–20).
31. A further example of the idea that the nostalgia on display in Cortázar's (tango) texts is not one that takes the form of an actual desired return home is found in *Rayuela*. Oliveira may cite and hum tangos whilst in Paris, but his first reaction to a tango upon returning to Buenos Aires is decidedly cool, and certainly not one that speaks of the joyful recovery of the previous experience of tango at and as home. As Oliveira recalls the lyrics '*Mi diagnóstico es sencillo: / Sé que no tengo remedio*' (2007: 382) [*My diagnosis is simple: | I know there is no cure*], we are told that 'la idea de la palabra diagnóstico metida en un vals le había parecido irresistible a Oliveira, pero ahora se repetía los versos con un aire sentencioso' (382) ('the idea that a word like "diagnosis" should turn up in a waltz was irresistible to Oliveira, but now he was repeating the lines in a sentention sort of way', 1966: 226–27). As Peiró points out, it is as if tango here 'significara su abandono de las costumbres europeas y el reencuentro con la América profunda a la que no desea retornar' (2006: 86) [signified the leaving behind of European customs and the re-encounter with a deep America to which he does not want to return].
32. Daniel Mesa Gancedo (2002) picks up on some of Berg's insights, further exploring the thematic shifts from classic tango in Cortázar's tango-poems, whilst also drawing attention to the 'aparente "anarquía métrica"' (426) [apparent 'metrical anarchy'] that some of these display. For Mesa Gancedo, this is an indication of Cortázar's attempt to 'forzar la melodía para no componer "tangos clásicos"' (426) [force the melody so as not to compose 'classical tangos'].
33. These two stories date from 1951, coincidentally the year in which Cortázar moved to Paris, and 1980, respectively. Whilst not denying that, as Miller notes (2016: 5), Cortázar's engagement with tango shifted and mutated over the course of his career, not least in the meaning it gained for the author from precisely this move to the French capital, the way in which my subsequent analysis shows these stories to operate together underlines the extent to which Cortázar's recourse to tango over the course of his life can be conceived of and understood as an evolving narrative 'whole', thus mirroring the narrative arc in relation to *la música culta* that emerged from my analysis of 'Las ménades', 'Reunión', and 'Alguien que anda por ahí' in chapter 2.
34. Picon Garfield (1981: 96) draws attention to the similar roles played by the narrators of these two stories, as well as by the narrator in 'El perseguidor'.
35. The terms *compadre* and *compadrito* are often used interchangeably, and, in practical terms, this is not necessarily inaccurate. Strictly speaking, the *compadre* was 'usually well-respected [...], a semi-urban type [...] [with] fierce independence, masculine pride and a strong inclination to settle affairs of honour with knives' (Collier 1995: 37). The *compadritos* were 'young men,

mostly native-born and poor, who sought to imitate the manners and attitudes of the *compadres* [...], sometimes in rather exaggerated fashion' (38). Importantly, the *compadritos* were a vital component in tango's birth and early development (43–47), as well as being a stock character of tango lyrics, from the aggressive, knife-wielding (anti)hero of the Old Guard lyrics to which Jorge Luis Borges was drawn (1955; Borges and Bullrich 1968: 11–12) to the narrator of tearful confessions of love, longing, and alcohol (Savigliano 1995: 63–65) of the *tango-canción* [tango-song] preferred by Cortázar.

36. See Savigliano (1995: 47–48; 61–69) for a detailed exposition of the shift from what she defines as the ruffianesque tango style to the romantic style that 'took shape from approximately the 1880s to the 1930s' (47). To an extent this maps onto the move from the more aggressive, violent tango of the Old Guard towards the more nostalgic tango lyrics of the New Guard, centred around the bemoaning of the lost loved one, but, as Savigliano points out, the ruffianesque and romantic styles 'mostly [...] overlapped, making them styles, not stages. [...] [T]he ruffianesque tango underwent a process of romanticization, but this process was not altogether unidirectional' (47).

37. Simon Collier describes the typical *compadrito* fashion as a 'slouch hat, loosely tied neckerchief, high-heeled boots' (1995: 38), whilst Taylor talks of the *compadrito*'s 'façade of stylized clothes and movements [...] with his rings and perfumes, his tight black suit and long hair, his high-heeled shoes and carefully studied postures' (1976: 276). In reference to Mauro's suit, blue was a common early *compadrito* colour for this garment, as visualised, for example, in the *compadrito* dancer in Teresa Pereyra's painting *Tango canyengue* (1998) (see Thompson (2005: 150–51)).

38. Similarly, though less significantly, if we follow the identification of Mauro and Hardoy with the *compadrito* and the *niño bien* respectively, then the narrative of 'Las puertas de cielo' plays with the traditional role of and relationship between these characters: Hardoy does not putatively appear as a rival suitor, and the standard 'fleeting and conflictive' (Savigliano 1995: 63) encounter between the two fails to materialise.

39. Savigliano develops these lines of analysis in much more detail in this article, drawing attention, amongst other things, to the *milonga* as an anti-capitalist site of challenge to the 'hectic pace of productivity' (1997: 37).

40. Álvarez-Schüller, referencing Savigliano, takes up a mainly socio-political reading of this story, though, rather than transgression, argues that the characters observed by Hardoy in the *milonga* setting are part of the social classes drawn to Peronism. Bearing in mind Cortázar's negative stance at the time of writing the story with respect to this political system, Álvarez-Schüller thus sees the combination of the draw of the *milonga* for these characters and Hardoy's condescending presentation of them to indicate the story's suggesting that 'die Anziehungskraft des herrschenden Systems scheint so stark zu sein, dass diese Leute, genauso wie Celina, nicht in der Lage sind, sich ihm zu widersetzen' (2008: 18) [the appeal of the ruling system seems to be so strong that these people, like Celina, are unable to resist it]. Jean Franco (1998: 40–44) also looks briefly at the socio-political commentary of 'Las puertas del cielo', and rightly questions Cortázar's later alignment of Hardoy with himself and his own contemporary views of the Peronist masses (Picon Garfield 1981: 97), drawing attention to the 'irony [in the depiction of Hardoy, which] seems to intervene to prevent such an identification' (Franco 1998: 41).

41. Boldy (2005: 379) underscores that the nature of the *milonga* heaven to which Celina is restored is one that is sanitised by the gaze of Hardoy, where she no longer has to work as a prostitute. Whilst the reading I am offering focuses on a broader understanding of the *milonga* setting, the romanticisation of the *milonga* that Boldy correctly identifies nevertheless acts as a further marker of how it is taking the place of the similarly romanticised *barrio* home of tango narratives.

42. Álvarez-Schüller notes and comments on this source in more detail (2008: 18).

43. Observing the apparent lack of connection between the tale told in 'A la luz del candil' and the story of 'Las puertas del cielo', Álvarez-Schüller (2008: 19) posits the intriguing suggestion that this line could be a reference to the line 'Yo soy un hombre decente' (Romano 1991: 115) [I am a decent man] from the tango 'Un tropezón' (1927). As Álvarez-Schüller explains, this tango has a narrative that is remarkably similar to that found in the Cortázar story.

44. As Boym puts it, 'Restorative nostalgia evokes national past and future; reflective nostalgia is more about individual and cultural memory' (2001: 49).

45. Lyrics to this song are from <http://www.todotango.com/english/music/song/774/Tanto/>.
46. Lyrics to this song are from <http://www.todotango.com/musica/tema/484/Mariposita/>.
47. Álvarez-Schüller (2008: 20) alludes to two further tangos to which these lines may point, 'Margo' (1945) and 'Te aconsejo que me olvides' (1926), though I do not find the case to be compelling.
48. Boldy, for example, draws attention to this presentation in the story (1980: 41; 43).
49. There are several references to Hardoy's *fichas*, which suggest that these are to be taken at face value as literal notes and note-taking. Nevertheless, at one point Hardoy comments on 'mis fichas sobre Celina, no escritas nunca pero bien a mano' (1993a: 112) [my files on Celina, never written down but very much to hand]. The hesitancy and uncertainty thus introduced are perhaps appropriate given the aspects of the story that my analysis has brought out. Boldy emphasises this reference as indicating that these are 'virtual index cards' (2005: 378).
50. Álvarez-Schüller argues that Hardoy does indeed belong to the tango world, his frequent visits leading to his being, in effect, a *milonguero* himself (2008: 22).
51. Along not dissimilar lines, Franco describes Hardoy at the end of the story in more positive terms than Mauro, noting that, in contrast to the latter, he 'experiences the "sublime" through the impossible and visionary resurrection of the dehumanized original [Celina]' (1998: 44).
52. As Mesa Gancedo (2002: 421–25) notes, a number of the tango-poems found across several sections of *Salvo el crepúsculo* date from much earlier periods, whilst some are indeed later texts. The fact that these were drawn together — a number being previously unpublished — in this late text is nevertheless significant, given the other tango publications of this period.
53. Moreover, and along these lines, it is not hard to see a certain inverted mirroring here of the epilogue to 'Clone' in which the author/extradiegetic narrator (Cortázar) discloses the process by which that story, which follows 'Tango de vuelta' in *Queremos tanto a Glenda*, came to be constructed, although, in an initial marker of the differences between the worlds of *la música culta* and tango and their respective composition, it is notable both that the compositional discussion in 'Tango de vuelta' is formally fused with the narrative and that the narrator is also a character in that narrative, albeit in the minor role of the ambulance driver who attends the scene at the end of the story. In both respects, this 'tango text' is thus less insistent on separating composition and performance than its *música clásica* counterpart.
54. Anad (2004: 115–16) also discusses 'Las tejedoras', though not in terms of identifying a link with 'Tango de vuelta'.
55. The motif of weaving or knitting is found in numerous texts across Cortázar's writing. Moran argues that 'the textile metaphor [...] threads its way through all of Cortázar's work in a manner which defies thematization' (2000: 83), and goes on to give several examples of the motif's presence in different Cortázar texts. In relation to texts already discussed in this study, and beyond the more general sense in which 'Alguien que anda por ahí' and 'Reunión', for example, weave different rhythmic, textual, and musical strands into their narrative constructions, we might draw attention to the reference in 'Clone' to Gesualdo locking himself away in castles 'donde habrían de tejerse a lo largo de los años las refinadas telarañas de los madrigales' (Cortázar 1980: 95) ('where over the years the delicate [spider's] webs of the madrigals could be woven', 1984: 46), which also repeats the *telaraña* motif found here in 'Tango de vuelta'.
56. There are several elements in the story that are strongly suggestive of a deliberate 'scripting'. For example, we are told that Matilde 'nunca había comprendido demasiado que Germán insistiera en poner el dormitorio de Carlitos al lado del salón' (Cortázar 1980: 80) ('[had] never understood too well why Germán had insisted on putting Carlitos's bedroom next door to the living room', 1984: 71), leading to the implication that the only reason for this was so that, years later, the events we are reading about could take place in this particular manner, with Flora, for instance, hearing Carlitos's cries on the fateful night, having to attend to him downstairs and remain with him there, watching the murderous scene unfold.
57. It should be noted, however, that, whereas Mauro plays the role of the (later) whiny ruffian 'version' of the *compadrito*, more aligned with the New Guard, Emilio here, both in his physical depiction and in his more violent, revenge-seeking plotline, is more reminiscent of the older *compadrito* figure more commonly — though not exclusively — found in the tangos of the Old Guard.

58. Álvarez-Schüller also sees in the figures of Flora and Carlitos watching the fight/dance of Emilio and Matilde a representation of the tango audience (2008: 42).
59. The shift from the traditional tango identifications in terms of the correlation between the different male figures and the 'return home' opens up the possibility, hinted at by the political undertones of Matilde and Emilio's move to Mexico in the first place, that such a change is bound up precisely with the effects of 'history and [the] passage of time' (Boym 2001: 49) on the past home, and resonates with Cortázar's focus on tango as absorbing and representing the sociohistorical changes and traumas of Argentine history (2009: 74). It is also a further indication, following my analysis of the revolutionary narratives of 'Reunión' and 'Alguien que anda por ahí' in chapter 2, of how the political brings itself to bear on Cortázar's engagement with different musical forms. Indeed, along those lines, it is worth signalling certain connections between 'Alguien que anda por ahí' and 'Tango de vuelta', not least the fact that, for Matilde in the latter story, 'cerrar todas las puertas con doble llave era igual' (Cortázar 1980: 76) ('double-locking the doors didn't matter', 1984: 66): Emilio, like the stranger in 'Alguien que anda por ahí', was inevitably going to find a way in anyway, as is stated explicitly further on in the narrative: 'era absolutamente seguro que la puerta de entrada se estaba abriendo o iba a abrirse y no se podía hacer nada' (1980: 82) ('it was absolutely clear that the main door was being opened or was going to be opened and nothing could be done', 1984: 73).
60. Contemporary with 'Tango de vuelta', 'Clone' provides evidence that Cortázar was aware of the issue of the lack of female agency in tango composition, and, moreover, that the increase in female composers was a question of shifting and changing the traditional bases and nature of such, when, in lines I noted in chapter 1, the character Paolo makes reference to how 'ahora hay mujeres que también componen tangos y ya no se canta siempre la misma cosa' (1980: 89) [there are also women composing tangos now and it's not always the same thing being sung anymore].
61. As a further nod to this reading, it is worth noting the allusion made early on in the narrative to how Flora 'canturreaba bagualas' (Cortázar 1980: 74) ('was humming *bagualas*', 1984: 64). The *baguala* is a folkloric music from north eastern Argentina. It is built upon 'une structure mélodique de 2 à 4 notes, mais le plus souvent 3' (Plisson 1987: 221) [a melodic structure of 2 to 4 notes, but most often 3], and yet, far from being 'pauvre musicalement' (221) [musically poor], it is, for example, characterised by a singer who uses 'falsetto and a rich ornamentation called *kenko* to declaim his verses, which are often improvised' (219). The coming together of the unchanging structuring elements and the creative reinforces the merged cohabitation of the two pulls found throughout 'Tango de vuelta'. Meanwhile, Michel Plisson's refutation of the apparent musical poverty of the *baguala* offers a satisfying parallel to the way in which Cortázar's negative appraisal of tango in some of his interviews — couched in exactly the same terms — is likewise revealed by his own work to be somewhat hastily simplistic.
62. Serra Salvat draws attention to the thread constituted by the terms *telaraña*, *araña*, and *maraña* in the text (2002: 313).
63. Similarly, whilst 'Reunión', as we saw in chapter 2, can be perceived as offering a complex weave of different musical and literary texts, ultimately the sense of a narrative that follows and is bound by those texts as 'scripts' is dominant.

CHAPTER 4

Jazz:
The Theoretical Framework

As with all the main musical genres that figure significantly in his work, at the heart of Cortázar's engagement with jazz lies a profound love of the music. And whilst it is unquestionable that he was an inveterate admirer of both *la música culta* and tango,[1] it is, in matters musical, as a jazz fan that Cortázar is perhaps best known. Reflecting this, jazz is a constant presence in his writing, not only as the subject of what we might term theoretical essays such as 'Elogio del jazz' and 'Soledad de la música', both of which I shall examine in more detail shortly in relation to jazz, but also in his novels, short stories, and other miscellaneous prose (and poetic) pieces. To be sure, jazz is not the central or persistent subject of more pieces of his prose fiction than, for example, *la música culta*, its starring roles being generally limited to 'El perseguidor', chapters 10–18 of *Rayuela*, the unfinished short story 'Bix Beiderbecke', and, to a lesser degree, 'Lugar llamado Kindberg'.[2] But as a recurrent motif, its pervasiveness in comparison to other musical genres is unrivalled,[3] a pervasiveness reflected in the critical attention it has received down the years.[4]

In numerous interviews, Cortázar explained the origins of what would be a lifelong relationship with this musical genre, and whilst the details are occasionally a little at variance, the essence remains the same. In interview with González Bermejo, for example, he states:

> cuando era muy joven, tendría 15 años, el jazz llegó a la Argentina en aquellos discos de 78 revoluciones que pasaban por las radios y fue así que, en medio de nuestra música folklórica y sobre todo el tango, se deslizó un cierto Jelly Roll Morton, después Louis Armstrong y la gran revelación que fue Duke Ellington. (1978: 104)
>
> [when I was very young, about 15 years old, jazz arrived in Argentina in those 78s they used to play on the radio and thus it was that, in the middle of our folk music and especially tango, a certain Jelly Roll Morton slid into my consciousness, then Louis Armstrong and the great revelation that was Duke Ellington.]

These three figures — Jelly Roll Morton, Louis Armstrong, and Duke Ellington — are repeatedly described by Cortázar as being 'mis predilectos' (Picon Garfield 1981: 127) [my favourites],[5] and I will explore in due course the significance of the particularities of Cortázar's tastes in jazz, since they are instructive both as to his claims with regard to the power and possibilities of the musical genre and as to some of the internal problems and pitfalls of his arguments and stance.[6] Indeed, these are the two central areas on which I will focus my attention over the following three chapters, for Cortázar's engagement with jazz, whilst overwhelmingly affirmative, is also riven with problematics not dissimilar to those set out in regard to language, music, and the poetic in my Introduction, a similarity which, as we shall see, is ultimately unsurprising given the extent to which jazz is slotted into the terms and debates found in Cortázar's early essays. In this respect, it must also be noted at the outset that, as I have intimated here, Cortázar's interest in jazz is that of an aficionado, a jazz fan who played a little trumpet; it is not that of a musicologist nor of someone who was overly cognisant of — or at least concerned with — the intricacies of jazz history and jazz technique. As he states in 'Elogio del jazz':

> ¿Qué sé yo de las sucesiones de séptima dominante o de los acordes de novena [...]? Diatonismo, por ejemplo, me ha sonado siempre como un sistema métrico para cristales de anteojos; en fin, que estoy frente al jazz en la misma inopia que muchos de sus creadores, lo que en alguna medida me asegura una aprehensión inmediata de su esencia. (2006d: 205)
>
> [What do I know about series of dominant sevenths, or ninth chords [...]? Diatonism, for example, has always sounded to me like a metric system for spectacle lenses; basically, I approach jazz just as cluelessly as many of its creators, which to an extent ensures that I have an immediate grasp of its essence.]

His writings on jazz, that is, are generally couched in terms of, and brought to bear on, the wider issues I have been discussing over the course of the preceding chapters, often with varying levels of disregard for musical accuracy or internal coherence.

Given that Cortázar was not writing as an expert on music, it would, to this reader's mind, be inappropriate and unhelpful to submit his writing and thought on jazz to a detailed, musicological dissection that would ultimately fail to take into adequate consideration the broader ontolinguistic purposes and ideas with which his engagement is intimately bound up. Nevertheless, it is also often the case that, in pointing up some of the issues of coherence and accuracy found in his work with regard to jazz, we can gain a more satisfying picture of his recourse to this musical genre, satisfying in the sense that we can uncover both the complex ways in which Cortázar marshals jazz to his own ends and the tensions that emerge as he does so. My aim over these three chapters on jazz is to walk this, admittedly fine, hermeneutic line and, above all, to avoid lapsing into the sort of unquestioning acceptance of Cortázar's presentation of and claims for jazz that has plagued too many of the scholarly pages dedicated to this aspect of his work.[7] The present chapter will focus on the bulk of Cortázar's claims, drawing primarily, in the first instance, on his essays and interviews, and seeking critically to set out the theoretical framework that Cortázar constructs for jazz. After establishing Cortázar's broad claims for jazz, in particular in relation to *la música culta* and language, I will explore the three key areas that underpin these assertions: race, improvisation, and swing. Chapters 5 and 6 will then draw upon these areas as they examine in a more in-depth fashion some of Cortázar's main 'jazz' fictions and question a number of the tenets on which Cortázar's claims for jazz appear to be based.

Jazz: A Theoretical Overview

One of the most important texts for understanding the position of jazz in Cortázar's thought is 'Elogio del jazz'. A response to an article entitled 'El jazz y la música moderna' [Jazz and Modern Music] by Daniel Devoto (1950 [1948]), a musicologist-critic, the essay's importance is revealed when Cortázar announces that this could 'constituir el capítulo final de *Teoría del túnel*' (2006d: 204) [constitute the final chapter of *Tunnel Theory*], before adding, 'mientras lo escribía en 1947 [...] advertí frecuentemente la presencia del jazz como fenómeno revelador' (204) [while I was writing it in 1947 [...] I often noticed the presence of jazz as a revelatory phenomenon]. Given these statements, one immediately suspects that Cortázar is about to link jazz with the sort of poetic language, or the poeticisation of language, that he discusses and advocates in the earlier text, and this is confirmed when he states that 'la música culta se mueve dentro de una estética, mientras el jazz lo hace dentro de una poética. La música es un producto musical, y el jazz es un producto poético' (207) [*la música culta* moves within an aesthetic, whereas jazz does so within a poetics. Music is a musical product, and jazz is a poetic product]. In advancing this take, Cortázar is, then, retaining *both* the suspicion of 'music' found in his assertion in *Teoría del túnel* that 'la música [es una] form[a] analógic[a], simbólic[a]' (2006c: 65) [music [is a] symbolic, analogical form] *and* the alignment of music and the poetic evident in his declaration there that '*la poesía es, como la música, su forma*' (89) [*poetry is, like music, its form*]. Turning to another key early essay, 'Soledad de la música', whilst the statement in 'Elogio del jazz' emphasises the primacy of the poetic rather than the musical in its presentation of jazz, in contrast to the terms invoked in that earlier essay, we can nevertheless see the common thread that links these two texts to be, once again, the distinction Cortázar draws between *la música culta* and jazz. In both cases, jazz is different, jazz is privileged. Whether it be defined (negatively) as 'musical', as in 'Elogio del jazz', or aligned with (the problems of) poetry (with a small 'p'), as in 'Soledad de la música', the essential message regarding *la música culta*, together with other forms of scored music, or what ends up being denominated simply as 'la música' by Cortázar at times, as we have seen,[8] is that this is 'aesthetic' music and is, relatedly, bound up with (the problems of) language, literary language, and processes of reading and writing. This much we saw in detail in chapter 1. In contrast, jazz is 'musical' not in an aesthetic sense, but in the sense that it is, in the terms employed in 'Soledad de la música', the musical essence (beyond (the problems of) language) and, to use the formulation preferred in 'Elogio del jazz', poetic (as opposed to poetry). It is, then, in these two texts — 'Soledad de la música' and 'Elogio del jazz' — that Cortázar lays out the case for jazz as a privileged form of expression (and being), and it is, resultantly, to a large extent to these texts that I shall turn in order to explore the nature of that case.

In the introductory chapter of this study I detailed the initial way in which

Cortázar differentiates music from poetry in 'Soledad de la música'. Taking as his starting point Paul Valéry's bemoaning of the 'desdichada condición del poeta, obligado a construir su Obra con palabras, elementos impuros y sujetos a los peores malentendidos' (Cortázar 1992: 290) [unhappy condition of the poet, obliged to construct his Work with words, impure elements subject to the worst misunderstandings], Cortázar contrasts the poet's unfortunate need to use language with musical expression, emphasising that 'mientras lo poético en sí guarda sólo una relación de analogía con el vehículo que intenta expresarlo, la música es *una* con su expresión sonora' (290) [whilst the poetic in itself has only a relationship of analogy with the vehicle that tries to express it, music is *one* with its sonorous expression]: music collapses the divide between Idea and expression, a divide that is written into its linguistic counterpart. Of course, Cortázar soon steps back from this simple affirmation of the musical, in pointing out that music generally erects this barrier once more in the form of interpretation (of a score, actual or implied), although, as I argued, the barrier set up by the process of musical interpretation is, in fact, double, as the separation between composer (or ('originary') Work) and musician is supplemented by that between musician and listener. However, Cortázar exempts one type of music from the *impasse* implied by the introduction of the intermediary performer: jazz, in that, he argues, 'Entre ellos [los *jazzmen*] no hay *autores* y *ejecutantes*, músicos e intérpretes. [...] No tratan de ejecutar creaciones ajenas; apoyan su orquesta sobre una melodía y un ritmo conocidos, y *crean, libremente, su música*' (294) [Amongst them [the jazzmen] there are no *authors* and *performers*, musicians and interpreters. [...] They don't try to perform others' creations; they set their orchestras up on a known melody and rhythm, and *create their music freely*]. A similar point is also made in interview with González Bermejo, where Cortázar declares that:

> a diferencia de la música llamada clásica [...] donde hay una partitura y un ejecutante que la interpreta con más o menos talento, en el jazz, sobre un bosquejo, un tema o algunos acordes fundamentales, cada músico crea su obra, es decir, que no hay un intermediario, no existe la mediación de un intérprete. (1978: 105)
>
> [unlike so-called classical music [...] where there is a score and a musician who interprets it with more or less talent, in jazz, on the basis of a sketch, a theme or some basic chords, each musician creates his/her work, that is, there is no intermediary, there exists no mediation by an interpreter.]

And in 'Elogio del jazz' he is at pains to emphasise that 'el jazz merecedor de recuerdo es siempre creación y jamás — JAMÁS — interpretación' (2006d: 205) [jazz deserving of being remembered is always creation and never — NEVER — interpretation]. Gone, then, is the divide between composer and performer, a work and its representation, ideation and expression. And for Cortázar it is this characteristic of jazz which makes it essentially different from other musical forms, and, thus, which renders it a form of musical expression that adheres to his opening description in 'Soledad de la música' of how music avoids language's problematics. In addition, this bringing together of idea and expression, composition and performance mirrors what Cortázar envisages as a different relationship between performer (jazzman) and audience/listener. In chapter 2, we saw how the story 'Las ménades' insists with some detail on the performer/audience divide in the classical music scenario, thus underscoring the revolutionary significance of the way in which it is spectacularly broken down within that story, as the crowd invades the stage and kills and devours the musicians. But whereas in this narrative the collapsing of that divide and breaking of that barrier run counter to the characteristics and prevailing sensibilities of *la música culta*, in the later text 'Louis, enormísimo cronopio', Cortázar underscores that such a reconfiguration of the performative space is a *characteristic* of the jazz man/jazz aficionado relationship at jazz concerts, as he writes of how 'esta noche el teatro está copiosamente invadido por cronopios que no contentos con desbordarse por la sala y trepar hasta las lámparas, *invaden el escenario* y se tiran por el suelo' (1970c: 14, italics mine) [tonight the theatre is copiously taken over by *cronopios* who, not content with spilling out over the auditorium and climbing up even on the lights, *invade the stage* and throw themselves on the floor].

This breaking down of the divide between audience and performer can be seen to reflect the initial assertion in 'Soledad de la música' that, in contrast to words which are 'sujetos a los peores malentendidos' (Cortázar 1992: 290) [subject to the worst misunderstandings], music does not, apparently, have to be interpreted by its public: that separating gap is closed, as the lack of discursive structure in musical communication allows the Work to be 'directly' reproduced in the listener:

> *Decir el Mensaje*: tal la agonía del poeta, porque la Poesía y el Mensaje son *indecibles* y sólo arriban al espíritu por obra de una intuición ajena a todo mecanismo lógico, a toda estructura discursiva...
> En tanto, el músico sonríe. (292)
>
> [*To say the Message*: that is the agony of the poet, because Poetry and the Message are unsayable and only reach one's spirit by a work of intuition that is foreign to all logical mechanisms and all discursive structures...
> Meanwhile, the musician smiles.]

In this sense, jazz appears somehow to lend itself to the sort of experiencing of music towards which Cortázar points at the end of this essay, when he refers to how 'la Música debe surgir, pura porque *nuestra*, desde el centro mismo de cada hombre' (295) [the Music must surge up, pure because it is *ours*, from the very centre of each man]. It may be that communication of the originary Idea is, as detailed in the rest of this essay, written out, but as evidenced by his words several decades later in interview with González Bermejo, Cortázar consistently posits, following Sartre, that jazz, whilst not communicating information 'de tipo inteligible o de tipo discursivo' (1978: 107) [of an intelligible or discursive type], is instead capable of communicating 'cosas que ningún lenguaje, ninguna escritura pueden comunicar. Y [Sartre] se refiere a sentidos — no solamente a la comunicación de placer o de estados de ánimo —; a la comunicación de ciertas dimensiones de la realidad' (107) [things that no language, no writing can communicate. And [Sartre] refers to senses — not just the communication of pleasure or states of mind —, but to the communication of certain dimensions of reality]. As Peiró, citing *Historia de cronopios y famas* (Cortázar 1962), sums up, for Cortázar jazz is a 'puente entre el hombre y su propia realidad [...] gracias a su capacidad no sólo de transmitir, sino de hacer "sentir al oyente las sensaciones, sentimientos o reflexiones del ejecutante sin intermediarios"' (2006: 58–59) [bridge between man and his own reality [...] thanks to its capacity not just to transmit, but also to make 'the listener feel the sensations, feelings or reflections of the performer with no intermediary'].

Two elements from this discussion, however, require further comment. The first is that it leaves unanswered the question of why jazz is able to catalyse such feelings and sensations within the listener when, one assumes, other forms of music cannot. The pertinence of this question is signalled not least by the fact that the thoughts expressed by Cortázar in the later interview take up Sartre's musings on music generally, and are ambiguously framed within the interview context, in terms of the extent to which Cortázar is referring specifically and only to jazz. It is a question to which I shall return further on in this study. The second element is the use by Peiró of the image of the bridge, an image repeated by Hernán Loyola (1994: 72), amongst others, when writing on jazz in the work of Cortázar. The problem with this metaphor is that it undermines the collapsing of divides and closing up of separations that Cortázar claims for jazz, in that it cements the existence of two sides between which a bridge is necessary, whilst simultaneously signalling the difficulty of moving away from a model for collapsing said divides which does not invoke the logic of communicative transfer *from* one element *to* another.

What is clear from this initial examination of the claims for jazz that Cortázar sketches out in these early essays is that they owe little to a musicological perspective on this musical genre. From the start, Cortázar's engagement with jazz is bound up with the question of how (artistic) expression and practice can come to represent, or work to effect, a fundamental shift in the way in which we express and experience being. Indeed, this, for Cortázar, is where jazz's value resides. As he argues in 'Elogio del jazz', jazz is 'uno de los caminos ciertos para ir a buscarse, acaso a encontrarse' (2006d: 213) [one of the sure paths for going to seek oneself, maybe to find oneself]; it is 'una lección de contenido metafísico, donde la música cesa de ser un arte para convertirse en una prueba, la prueba del hombre' (216) [a lesson of metaphysical content, where music ceases to be an art to become a test/proof, the test/proof of man].

A further circumstance that points towards this conclusion is the repeated and significant similarity of Cortázar's theorising on the nature and possibilities of jazz and certain aspects of Antonin Artaud's concept of the theatre of cruelty. Cortázar's knowledge of and admiration for Artaud are well documented. Perhaps most notably, Cortázar's first work for *Sur* magazine in 1948 was a note entitled 'Muerte de Antonin Artaud' (Cortázar 1948) and the French playwright and thinker also featured in several of Cortázar's subsequent interviews and essays.[9] Several critics have drawn attention to the influence of Artaud on Cortázar's surrealist tendencies,[10] and some attempts have been made at studying Cortázar's texts through a more sustained appeal to the ideas found in Artaud's development of the theatre of cruelty.[11] But, whilst these are both areas of Cortázar's writing where an engagement with Artaud's work is fruitful, the importance of the latter in an examination of Cortázar's writings on and ideas about jazz has, perhaps surprisingly, not been properly taken into account.[12] This importance, however, is particularly striking in relation to the notion of the collapsing of divides between different actors in the jazz process on which I have been commenting.

In his work *The Theatre and its Double* (Artaud 1993),[13] Artaud sets out a lengthy and not wholly coherent set of discussions on and prescriptions for this radically new type of theatre, the 'Theatre of Cruelty' (1993: 68). Amongst the precepts he describes in the first manifesto for this kind of theatre are that 'we will not act written plays' (76) and, with regard to the *mise-en-scène*, that 'the old duality between author and producer will disappear, to be replaced by a kind of single Creator [...] responsible for both the play and the action' (72). These citations underscore that the key points of a removal of performance as a reading or interpretation of a text and the closing of the divide between composition and performance are common elements to both Artaud's theatre and the ideal elements of jazz for Cortázar.

Other elements from Artaud's work strengthen this sense of a common purpose. Leading on from the collapsing of the separation between composer and performer, idea and expression, for example, we have the reconfiguration of the usual divide between performers and audience. Artaud comments that, in the theatre of cruelty, 'we intend to do away with stage and auditorium, replacing them by a kind of single, undivided locale without any partitions [*barrière*] of any kind' (74). The resonance with both the central 'revolutionary' scene in 'Las ménades' and, more pertinently, the description of the Satchmo concert in 'Louis, enormísimo cronopio', where the 'barrier' of the stage is also rendered meaningless, is evident. In both Cortázar's presentation of jazz and Artaud's envisaged theatre of cruelty, that is, one finds a profound concern for the systematic dismantling of the sort of divides Cortázar identifies within both linguistic expression and musical composition and performance.

Beyond this collapsing of apparently binary divides, a further element linking Artaud's theatre and Cortázar's jazz is found in the idea of risk or danger, of standing against a safe and conventional approach to the respective artistic genre, a reflection of an attendant rejection of the unthinking acceptance of existing and, hence, comforting routines, customs, and structures of Western being, against which Cortázar so often sets his ideas. For Artaud, the rejection of such an approach is key to his theatre of cruelty, and his first manifesto (1993: 68–78) details a call to eschew Western theatrical conventions on every level, from language used to musical instruments employed, from costume to props. Significantly, it is a rejection based on his conception of contemporary theatre as being 'in decline [...] [b]ecause it has broken away [...] from Danger' (31). A (re)insertion of just such a sense of danger pervades much of his description of the envisaged theatre of cruelty:

> Now it seems to me the best way of producing this concept of danger on stage is by the objective unforeseen, [...] the sudden inopportune passing from a mental image to a true image. (32)

> Everything that acts is cruelty. Theatre must rebuild itself on a concept of this drastic action pushed to the limit. (65)

> If theatre wants to find itself needed once more, it must present everything in love, crime, war and madness. (65)

Moving onto Cortázar, jazz and jazz musicians are often described in similar terms, in many ways a correlate of the fact that the jazz of which Cortázar speaks is generally a jazz that is not concerned with reading and rendering a pre-existing score. Thus Oliveira in *Rayuela*, for example, describes 'los juegos de Dizzy Gillespie sin red en el trapecio más alto' (Cortázar 2007: 177) ('Dizzy Gillespie's tricks as he swung on the high trapeze without benefit of net', 1966: 47), and the basis for the character Johnny Carter in 'El perseguidor', the saxophonist Charlie Parker,[14] was one of the leading proponents of bebop, a form of jazz which was predicated on breaking away from conventional jazz moulds and taking melodic and rhythmic risks, as I shall examine in more detail further on.[15] Key here is that this notion of danger or risk translates into a sense of fear and threat, not just in terms of musical conventions and expression, but also, more widely, with regard to the securities and being of both musician and listener. Cortázar is not the only one to see such a threat in experimental jazz music and its proponents. John Litweiler, for example, describes the jazz composer Bob Graettinger's music as 'a threat to our very sanity' (1985: 18), a statement which recalls Johnny's apparent loss of (conventional) sanity and his envisaged effect on others in 'El perseguidor' ('a Johnny no se le puede seguir así la corriente porque vamos a acabar todos locos' (Cortázar 1970d: 145) [you can't keep going along with Johnny's ideas or we'll all end up mad]). Indeed, the fear thus provoked by these jazzmen in the threat they are perceived as representing is referred to numerous times by Cortázar. Bruno at one point admits that 'a lo mejor le tengo un poco de miedo a Johnny' (117) ('maybe I'm a little afraid of Johnny', 2013: 196),[16] and in 'Clifford' we are told of the trumpeter Clifford Brown's music's being 'como un aletazo que desgarra lo continuo' (Cortázar 1970b: 109) [like a wing-swipe that rips the continuous order of things], a line which resonates with Marcos's reference in *Libro de Manuel* to 'los órdenes estatuidos, manera elegante de esconder el miedo al gran aletazo' (1973a: 254) [the established orders, elegant way of hiding the fear of the great wing-swipe]. Moreover, the conjunction of these two quotations confirms that the breaking of conventional musical moulds and the willingness to create music which is dangerous and a threat is tied up with a more general threat to the conventions of human society and being, not just generally but politically. Again, the centrality of the challenge to existing, and divisive, structures comes to the fore in an understanding of Cortázar's presentation of jazz.

Significantly, this is also what is found in Artaud's theatre of cruelty. Here too examples of the envisaged injection of danger into the theatre are bound up with the instilling of general fear and unsettlement:

> Another example would be to have a fabricated being appear, made of wood and cloth, completely invented, resembling nothing, yet disturbing in nature, able to reintroduce on stage the slightest intimation of the great metaphysical fear underlying all ancient theatre. (1993: 32)

What is at stake here is foregrounded in Artaud's preface, not found in the English translation, where he declares that:

Ceci amène à rejeter les limitations habituelles de l'homme et des pouvoirs de l'homme, et à rendre infinies les frontières de ce qu'on appelle la réalité.
Il faut croire à un sens de la vie renouvelé par le théâtre. (1964: 18)

[This leads to the rejection of the usual limitations of man and of his powers, and renders infinite the frontiers of what we call reality.
One must believe in a sense of life that is renewed by the theatre.]

The parallel with Cortázar's own notion of a return to an originary humankind beyond its current discursive, societal, and binary structures is marked, and underscores the similarity of both the goal and the way in which such a goal can potentially be achieved as the two authors go about describing the art form in question.

Jazz and Race

Cortázar's treatment of jazz, however, is not simply a question of the transposition of any one set of preceding ideas onto this form of music. Several other elements are at play here, and one of the most significant is in relation to race. In effect, this constitutes the first way in which Cortázar narrows down exactly what he is referring to when he discusses this genre of music, a narrowing down which, as we shall see, is crucial for appreciating both the claims Cortázar is making for jazz and the tense precariousness of those claims. 'Soledad de la música' contains one of the most clear-cut statements with regard to the importance of race in Cortázar's engagement with the genre, as he talks of 'el *jazz* — el creado por los negros, y único que merece tal nombre' (1992: 294) [jazz — the jazz created by black men, and the only one that deserves such a name]. The identification of the artists with which he is concerned as being specifically 'los *jazzmen* negros' (294) [the black jazzmen] continues into 'Elogio del jazz', where, once more, he underscores that 'authentic' jazz, the jazz that offers an escape from the structures and barriers of Western ontology and expression, must be understood as that of 'el *jazzman* negro' (2006d: 210) [the black jazzman]. Turning to Cortázar's fictional and other (non-essayistic) work, whilst we could note that the principal jazz figures to whom Cortázar refers are almost invariably black, what is perhaps more pertinent here is the way in which blackness or negritude comes to the fore as a whole, and particularly so in the earliest works.

Some of the first stories in which jazz — or at least the closely-related blues and spiritual music — figures are found in the posthumous collection *La otra orilla*.[17] In both the stories in which this music has a significant role, 'Llama el teléfono, Delia' [The Telephone's Ringing, Delia], written in 1938, and 'Retorno de la noche' [Return of the Night], written in 1941, the reiterated allusion to the blackness of the female singer is striking.[18] Thus, in the former, the blues track playing on the radio in the background is mentioned twice, with the first reference being to how it is a blues 'cantado por la misma muchacha de piel oscura que Delia admiraba en las revistas de radio' (Cortázar 2004: 36–37) [sung by the same dark-skinned girl that Delia admired in the radio magazines], and the second alluding to 'aquella voz morena' (38) [that black voice]. The blackness of the singer has become fixed to and an essential qualifier of the singing voice itself: the very music is identified as black. In 'Retorno de la noche', the protagonist, apparently a ghost looking at her dead body, finds music coming back to her from her memory at different points in the story. Four times we read the words 'la voz de una mujer negra' (71) [the voice of a black woman] or 'la voz de la mujer negra' (71; 73; 78) [the voice of the black woman], and the songs to which the text alludes are either traditional Negro spirituals ('I Know the Lord Laid His Hands on Me'; 'Deep River') or a spiritual song written by a black composer ('My Heart is Anchored in the Lord', by Virginia Davis). Both these stories concern phantasmal beings and the idea of the boundary between death and life being porous, if not unstable (and certainly questioned). In other words, even in these early, 'lesser' (for Cortázar) stories, music bound up with what we might broadly label jazz history, and very specifically and conspicuously black music, is linked to the destabilisation of the most stark of all binary divides and the undermining of realist modes of narrative dependent on this binary.[19]

The most obvious and important of the factors invoked and evoked by such a pronounced focusing on and engagement with the blackness of jazz, however, is the socio-political arena of the USA of the nineteenth and twentieth centuries, the context from which jazz, and certainly its precursors, emerged. The origins of jazz are complex, coming out of a series of different musical types and histories. In many cases, these musical types are the product of a syncretism of African rhythms and music and European-American music, for example in the case of the Congo Square (or public slave) dances that took place in New Orleans throughout much of the nineteenth century (and which are considered an important 'player' in the genesis and development of jazz).[20] And it is to this city and its musical traditions in this period that one looks when wanting to identify jazz's birthplace, noting in particular that the New Orleans of this time was characterised, amongst other things, by the presence of Spanish and French influences. These, together with the African and European-American traditions, combined to give hybrids including salsa, samba, and calypso, as Ted Gioia describes in his seminal work on jazz history (1997: 6). Indeed, as Gioia points out, this history perhaps sheds some factual light on one of early jazz's most important figures, Jelly Roll Morton's claim that 'if you can't manage to put tinges of Spanish in your tunes, you will never be able to get the right seasoning, I call it, for jazz' (Lomax 1973 [1950]: 62). Jazz did not finally emerge in its own right until the first two decades of the twentieth century, and, beyond the specifics of New Orleans,[21] also owes a considerable debt of influence to musical genres such as the cakewalk, blues, ragtime, and Negro spirituals.[22]

One of the fundamental elements that unite many of these different traditions is their origins and/or prevalence among the African slaves of the pre-abolition USA (the Congo Square dance, Negro spirituals, for instance), or, in the case of, for example, the blues and ragtime, the African-American population in the years following the Emancipation Proclamation of 1863, although even here these genres are seen to come, at least in part, from forms brought over to America by black slaves. The importance of these origins to Cortázar's presentation and conception of jazz is evidenced by the inclusion of two of these genres in the early stories I have just examined. In short, jazz is a music bound up with enslavement and, more particularly, with forms of expression that, in their very existence, grant a voice (literal or otherwise) to the voiceless and the oppressed. As Gioia notes, the blues, for example, is an 'idiom to articulate personal statements against oppression and injustice' (1997: 12), whilst spirituals such as 'Oh! Let My People Go', or, as it became known, 'Go Down, Moses', are explicit laments of slavery and demands for liberation. It is a song recorded amongst others by Louis Armstrong, arguably Cortázar's favourite jazz musician.[23] Likewise, Amiri Baraka, one of the most important writers on jazz of the twentieth century, talks of how 'Negroes played jazz as they had sung blues or, even earlier, as they had shouted and hollered in those anonymous fields, because it was one of the few areas of human expression available to them' (2010 [1963]: 16). Cortázar's jazz, that is, is a music concerned and inextricably intertwined with (the demand for) freedom, both expressive and ontic. And, while in 'Elogio del jazz' he comments on this 'liberación profunda' (2006d: 209) [profound liberation] offered by jazz in the context of its appearance in Europe at a time (c. 1915–1930) when 'una cantidad de europeos *coincidieron desde sus diferencias instrumentales* — verso, música, novela, pintura, conducta, ciencia — en una corriente común de liberación humana que yo he llamado en otra parte poetismo' (208) [many Europeans *coincided from their different fields* — verse, music, the novel, painting, conduct, science — in a common current of human liberation that I have called elsewhere *poetism*], it is jazz's social and racial origins that fundamentally underlie the genre's particular liberatory impulse.

That these connections are at the forefront of Cortázar's mind at the start of his writing career is nowhere more evident than in the poem 'Jazz' from *Presencia*, a poem which brings together the sociohistorical charge of the music with a number of allusions to the more ontological and metaphysical aspects of jazz's possibilities which will prove enduring in Cortázar's engagement with it. Indeed, this poem is significant in setting down a number of concerns and avenues that recur in Cortázar's later 'jazz texts', as I shall intimate here before developing further on in this and subsequent chapters.[24]

The first thing to note about the poem is its form: the strict sonnet structure might seem to be the antithesis of the notion of freedom, but it pre-empts the discussion in *Teoría del túnel*, 'Soledad de la música', 'Para una poética', and 'Elogio del jazz', in which the need for poetry *and* language, for music(alisation) *and* language, for an approach to expression that incorporates the characteristics of poetism *and* existentialism, emerges so strongly. I will take up this line of enquiry in relation to the poem's form in chapter 6. For now, we might, more generally, focus on the fact that the first quartet harnesses this idea of jazz as where both sides (of whatever binary) are brought together in tension, foreshadowing not only the discussion in the essays dealt with in my Introduction, but also the persistent idea in Cortázar's work of the necessary, if always frustrated, reconciliation of self and other:

> Es, incierta y sutil, tras de la tela
> donde un hilo de voz teje motivo,

> y no es, si en el oído sensitivo
> encuentra sombra impar, no encuentra vela.
>   (Denis 1938: 19)

[It is, uncertain and subtle, behind the fabric
where a thread of a voice weaves a motif,
and it is not, if in the sensitive ear
it finds an odd shadow, does not find a candle.]

It is also worth noting here the focus given to the bridging of musician (voice) and listener. As we have seen, the issue of communication and its possibilities or not is at the heart of much of Cortázar's dealing with jazz and music generally, and these first lines of 'Jazz' tie in with the awakening of sensibilities and understanding in the listener that we saw him describe jazz as being capable of several decades later in interview with González Bermejo, where this would be a communication not 'de tipo inteligible o de tipo discursivo' (1978: 107) [of an intelligible or discursive type], but, rather, intuitive and (properly) poetic. The relationship and connection between the two 'players' in the jazz scenario are, then, even at this early stage, signalled as being of paramount importance.[25]

At risk of labouring this analysis of the first quatrain of the poem, it is arguable that one of the most significant elements here is the apparently simple question of what the subject is. The title might seem to suggest jazz is to be taken as such, but the feminine adjectival form 'incierta' [uncertain] belies this. The most likely identity of the subject, then, is the 'noche negra de los cantos' (Denis 1938: 20) [black night of song] in the sonnet's first tercet, but this is referred to there in the second person, which undermines this identification. As a result — and tellingly —, there remains an element of doubt as to what lies at the centre of a poem about (and titled) 'Jazz'. That is to say, its resistance to definition, to language and naming, is foregrounded, set out at the start of Cortázar's writing on it, and thus we can say that the idea of liberation from both binary divides and linguistic operations and structures is embedded within the very first lines Cortázar dedicates to this musical genre.

Moving to the second quatrain, we find the sociohistorical support for this sense of freedom, as Cortázar specifically invokes jazz in the context of the breaking of the nineteenth-century chains of black slavery, combining this with a further statement of jazz as breaking moulds and structures of civilisation and rationality:

> Que está fuera del molde y de la escuela
> en un regocijarse de nativo
> —libertar de eslabones y cautivo
> sonido— que una selva hurtada anhela.
>   (Denis 1938: 19)

[For it is outside of the mould and school
in the rejoicing of a native
—set free from chains and captive
sound— who pines for a stolen jungle.]

The first tercet, following on from these lines, is interpreted by López-Lespada as revolving principally around the 'renuncia del propio ego' (1998: 113) [renunciation of the [poet's] ego]:

> Bébeme, noche negra de los cantos
> con tu boca de cobre y aluminio
> y hazme trizas en todos tus refranes.
> (Denis 1938: 20)

> [Drink me, black night of song
> with your mouth of copper and aluminium
> and make me shattered in all your refrains.]

But these lines are also rich with more complex allusions: the presence of negritude is felt once more in the colouring of the night, for example, and what one imagines is a trumpet or saxophone is personified in a way that foregrounds yet further the notion of voice, which, as chapter 6 will argue, proves to be possibly more important than has generally been realised in Cortázar's engagement with jazz. Besides this, the way in which the effect of the music on the poet is described is also significant, not least in the blurriness in identifying what it is that engages with the poetic I in the latter's expressed desire. If we take this entity to be jazz, then it is perhaps more appropriately defined as the setting and experiencing of jazz: the poetic I, after all, pleads to be drunk down by the somewhat abstract 'noche negra de los cantos' [black night of song], whose mouth is (also) the horn instrument being played. Importantly, this move might be understood as the coming together of self and other, music and listener, the unification that Cortázar desires throughout his work, but the immediate call to be shattered into pieces, as we imagine the poetic I re-emerging from the mouth of the instrument, exploding out with the musical notes, problematises such unification even as it affirms it. On the one hand, the oneness of the two terms — the music and the listener — is maintained, insisted upon even; but this shattering also represents the refusal or rejection of the silent, because non-vocalised, and formless, because non-imageable, totality that, it is implied, is the result of the ingesting of the listener in the previous lines. What this tercet does, then, is describe poetically the 'theoretical' issues from Cortázar's early essays: the unavoidable move from Word to words, from silent solitude to expression; the necessity of the music being produced, of the bell being rung. That it does so in an image that, both in its contained togetherness and its subsequent shattered outpouring, maintains a unity of music and listener speaks of Cortázar's belief in jazz: the problems and complexities bound up with expression and communication are there, and yet Cortázar allows a blanket-like sentiment to settle over them, a sentiment that somehow jazz simply can overcome.

The final tercet of the poem reiterates the sense of unity, broadening this out to a wider collective, whilst also introducing a sense of religiosity, which will prove to be a recurrent feature of Cortázar's jazz:

> yo quiero ser, contigo, uno de tantos
> entregado a una música de minio
> y a la liturgia ronca de tus manes.
> (Denis 1938: 20)

[I want to be, with you, one of so many
dedicated to a minium music
and the hoarse liturgy of your manes.]

López-Lespada's noting of the reference to the manes, 'las almas virtuosas de los familiares muertos en la costumbre de la antigua Roma' (1998: 115) [the virtuous souls of dead family members in the beliefs of Ancient Rome], further helps us to observe how the poem ends with an indication, or at least hint, of the bringing together of the ultimate binary terms of life and death, something we have also seen to be intimated in relation to tango at the end of 'Las puertas del cielo'.

'Jazz', the first of Cortázar's 'jazz texts', thus pre-empts many of the themes and ideas with which we have seen Cortázar to be deeply concerned in both his fiction and non-fiction writing. It foregrounds the notion of an escape from binary and linguistic structures and divides, and grounds this in jazz's innate historical ties to black enslavement and black liberation from enslavement. Blackness is, then, fundamental to Cortázar's engagement with and claims for jazz right from the earliest of texts.

Of course, the notion that jazz represents or offers some form of liberation or escape, some sort of authenticity, that is bound up with its (sociohistorical) 'colour' is not unique to Cortázar. Perhaps most pertinently, Cortázar has been shown by Jason Borge (2011) to be working within, or, as Borge suggests, as the culmination of, a very particular strand of Latin American and more specifically Argentinian writing on the subject of jazz. The picture Borge paints of the critical background against which Cortázar was writing at the time of 'Jazz', 'Soledad de la música', 'Elogio del jazz', and the stories that came to be brought together in *La otra orilla* highlights a number of elements that resonate with the precise terms in which Cortázar speaks with regard to jazz. For instance, when Borge refers to how 'like other Latin American avant-garde publications, the Argentine journal *Martín Fierro* greeted jazz with primitivist ecstasy tinged with fear' (2011: 63), citing an article by Ulises Petit de Murat in 1927 which talks of how 'the dynamics of jazz, with its syncopation and "sharp and nervous palette" of sound fills the listener with "almost physical sensations of trepidation"' (64), it is hard not to see a pre-echo of the sort of fear and danger that Cortázar alludes to in relation to jazz. Of course, in Cortázar's discourse, this fear or trepidation is very much affirmed as the way to shake up our sense of society, self, and the world, an affirmative element not obviously found in the early jazz criticism to which Borge refers.

The most significant current in the jazz writing prior to Cortázar, though, is related to the primitivist element mentioned here, which is itself bound up, or comes to be bound up, with the discourse of race. Indeed, Borge points out that 'Argentine writers were the first in Latin America to rigorously examine jazz not only as a technically sophisticated musical genre but also as a cultural practice inseparable from the African diaspora and postcolonial legacies of slavery' (2011: 64). Moreover, the terms with which this discussion is carried out by critics writing on jazz in the years prior to Cortázar's arrival on the scene are heavily redolent of the latter's assertions in 'Soledad de la música' and 'Elogio del jazz' in particular identifying black jazz as legitimate or 'true' jazz. Commenting on a further example of Petit de Murat, writing in 1934, for instance, Borge writes that the critic 'argu[es] that African descent is the *sine qua non* of "authentic" musical expression. [...] [O]nly black musicians are capable of summoning the "primitive" inspiration necessary to perform jazz' (2011: 66). Similarly, in the 1940s, critics such as Néstor Ortiz Oderigo, continued to fall back on such racial essentialism, with Borge citing his declaration in 1945 that '"the Afro-American songbook has exerted a singular influence on the aesthetic formation, structure and even the spirit of legitimate expressions of jazz of pure black roots"' (2011: 73). In effect, then, colour is being used as a way of creating what Borge terms a 'privileged space of otherness' (72), and it is difficult to see how Cortázar could be said not to be following in these critical footsteps. Indeed, Cortázar's writing on black jazz draws upon several of the tired racist notions of blackness that belong both to early Argentine jazz criticism and to (post) colonial discourse more generally, be it the idea of the 'noble savage', surely implied in Cortázar's reference to how black jazzmen already knew 'con ignorante sabiduría' (1992: 294) [with ignorant wisdom] the answer to the expressive conundrum that he is trying to answer in 'Soledad de la música', as well as in his description in 'Elogio del jazz' of black jazzmen as playing '*inocentemente*' [*innocently*], with little care for 'los hallazgos en profundidad' (2006d: 213) [profound discoveries], or the allusions to the hackneyed tropes of black sexuality in 'Louis, enormísimo cronopio', where Cortázar describes how:

> ahí está Trummy Young que toca el trombón como si sostuviera en los brazos una mujer desnuda y de miel, y Arvel Shaw que toca el contrabajo como si sostuviera en los brazos una mujer desnuda y de sombra, y Cozy Cole que se cierne sobre la batería como el marqués de Sade sobre los traseros de ocho mujeres desnudas y fustigadas. (1970c: 17)

> [there's Trummy Young playing the trombone as if he were holding a naked, honey-skinned woman in his arms, and Arvell Shaw playing the double bass as if he were holding a naked, dark-skinned woman in his arms, and Cozy Cole hovering over the drums like the Marquis de Sade over the backsides of eight naked and whipped women.]

In understanding the contemporary Argentine critical currents within which Cortázar is working, or, at least, on from which he follows, we are thus called to ask to what extent we can see Cortázar's claims for and use of specifically black jazz to be both an appropriation of the particularities of black historical discourse of freedom from slavery and a reinscription within a more general racial (and racist) essentialism built upon a primitivist and exoticist privileging of the 'black other'.[26]

A further fundamental issue emerges here. As Borge points out, one of the effects of the essentialist discourse on black jazz is what it implies about the white critic, namely that 'if jazz is the natural domain of black musicians, Petit de Murat and other white Argentine critics like him possess the unique capacity to interpret such "native" intelligence' (2011: 66). In support of this, Borge cites the approach found in *Swing* magazine in the 1930s, which operated on the basis that 'jazz criticism

[...] should be serious-minded and practiced only by "extremely cultured critics" since "[jazz is] complicated music, and even, if you will, an enigma to the majority of music critics"' (69). Cortázar's depiction of musicologists exhibits a somewhat schizophrenic relationship to this racialised schema of jazz understanding. On the one hand, in texts such as 'Elogio del jazz' he is highly critical, even disparaging, of white musicologists and critics, portraying them as 'estos [...] imbéciles (blancos, claro está [...])' (2006d: 206) [these [...] imbeciles (white, of course [...])] who fail to see that jazz cannot be judged and valued simply in relation to *la música culta* and *música culta* 'metrics'. Their failure to understand jazz, moreover, is seen by Cortázar to be unsurprising given that 'de oídos blancos se trata' (208) [we're talking about white ears]. And yet, whilst this may seem to show Cortázar rejecting the privileging of white critics that Borge describes, it is not accompanied by a similar repudiation of the idea that there *is* a select group (of writers) who do 'get' jazz. Quite the reverse, in fact, as Cortázar talks of certain critics, such as Hugues Panassié, Charles Delaunay, and André Hodeir who, unlike others, write 'sobre lo que el jazz *es* (sin aspirar a ser otra cosa) y no sobre lo que el jazz debería ser para alcanzar el respeto condescendiente de la musicología' (206) [on what jazz *is* (without aspiring to be something else) and not on what jazz should be in order to obtain the condescending respect of musicology]. Such a statement, of course, carries with it the assumption that Cortázar also possesses the ability to 'get' jazz 'as it is'. Moreover, the irony found in Cortázar's accusation of condescension on the part of the opposing band of musicologists is compounded, first, by the fact that Cortázar and the three critics he names happen to be white and, secondly, by the fact that their 'proper' understanding of jazz is, let us not forget, implicitly contrasted in Cortázar's essay with the 'innocent' playing of the black jazzmen in question who are not overly interested in 'los hallazgos de profundidad' (213) [profound discoveries], even if he intimates otherwise when asserting that he approaches jazz 'en la misma inopia que muchos de sus creadores, lo que en alguna medida me asegura una aprehensión inmediata de su esencia' (205) [just as cluelessly as many of its creators, which to an extent ensures that I have an immediate grasp of its essence].[27]

When surveying Cortázar's engagement with jazz, then, it is hard not to draw the conclusion that the problematic presentation of 'authentic', 'primitive' black jazz by a cultured white author found in early jazz criticism is still present in Cortázar's undeniably Crocean stance. Not only that: such a presentation is, if anything, rendered more awkward by Cortázar's dehistoricising appropriation of jazz's liberationist origins and nature. Thus, it is tempting to see Cortázar as falling foul of a number of issues addressed by Baraka. In 'Jazz and the White Critic' (2010), he explains how jazz is, for him, about the attitude and approach of each player, and that this attitude needs to be understood socially and culturally for the player in question (18–20). One might, then, reasonably ask whether Cortázar's focus, both explicit and implicit, on the idea of liberation and the giving of a voice is one which, to a large degree, ignores the ongoing and evolving sociocultural environment and factors to which different jazzmen were responding, arguably with the exception of the exploration in 'El perseguidor' of the case of Charlie Parker.[28]

And yet, it bears remembering that, in contrast to the critics mentioned above, Cortázar is, of course, not attempting to write jazz criticism. The difference may be moot, but it nevertheless causes us a certain hesitation. Charles Hartman, responding to some of Baraka's claims regarding the racial appropriation of jazz in his later essay 'The Great Music Robbery' (Baraka and Baraka 1987), focuses on the fact that 'jazz itself is the product of cultural dialogue, born of African and European musics' (Hartman 1991: 149). For Hartman, whilst it does not 'solve the problems of cultural imperialism' (149), the nature of jazz as a dialogic American music does 'overar[ch] them' (149). In short, Hartman here is drawing upon one of the characteristics of jazz that are most germane to Cortázar's own, non-musicological engagement with the genre: its potential as a music that collapses differences and brings down barriers (of language) erected between people. We are thereby reminded that jazz is, above all, to be understood within the terms of the broader questions and debates that inform and infuse Cortázar's *œuvre*. Nevertheless, Cortázar, unlike Hartman, does place the idea of liberation — 'la liberación profunda' (2006d: 209) [profound liberation] — at the heart of his engagement with jazz, linking this specifically with negritude and all that that entails in sociocultural and historical terms. In this sense, the ethical problems discussed by Baraka, and which Hartman emphasises he is not trying to wish away, still very much make their presence felt in the case of the Argentine author.

Improvisation

However we view Cortázar's invocation of and focus on the sociohistorical origins of jazz, the implicit importance he thus grants the idea of expressive freedom in relation to this musical form constitutes both the pivotal characteristic of jazz for Cortázar and the element of it with which he is most concerned. Earlier, I drew attention to the way in which Cortázar's early essays in particular evoke jazz as the clearest example of how language — or more generally expression — can be musicalised or poeticised. And in this respect we can once more see how jazz fits into Cortázar's broader concerns regarding language, concerns which, again, resonate with those of Antonin Artaud. In the preface to *The Theatre and its Double* Artaud discusses how he aims to 'briser le langage pour toucher la vie' (1964: 18) [break language so as to touch life]. Following the first manifesto, he clarifies his concept of the theatre of cruelty in correspondence, drawing attention to this linguistic aspect and expanding the initial declaration of intent:

> The word cruelty must be taken in its broadest sense, not in the physical, predatory sense usually ascribed to it. And in so doing, I demand the right to make a break with its usual verbal meaning, to break the bonds once and for all, to break asunder the yoke, finally to return to the etymological origins of language. (1993: 79)

The similarities between these statements and Cortázar's general aims and specific claims for jazz are striking: such a breaking of expressive norms and structures is precisely what Morelli calls for in *Rayuela*, where, as Etienne notes, 'el escritor tiene que incendiar el lenguaje, acabar con las formas coaguladas e ir todavía más allá' (Cortázar 2007: 620) ('the writer has to set language on fire, put an end to its coagulated forms and even go beyond it', 1966: 447). And it is, for Cortázar, just such a continual playing with and shaking up of (its) language that jazz works to effect. Indeed, the association of jazz with the manipulation and transformation of its language, and, by extension, with language *tout court*, is stark at times, perhaps most strikingly where we read that 'el jazz es como un pájaro que migra o emigra o inmigra o transmigra' (2007: 204) ('jazz is like a bird who migrates or emigrates or immigrates or transmigrates', 1966: 70).

There are several ways of understanding the nature of jazz along these lines, not least in terms of the broad sweep of jazz history and its underlying ethos. From its beginnings as a musical form that brought together a variety of genres and influences, jazz has been built upon a refusal to stand still. A potted history of jazz would inevitably involve tracing a line of constant development and evolution from trad, or hot, jazz to Big Band jazz to bebop to cool jazz to free jazz, which in itself brushes over a whole host of more nuanced evolutions, pathways, and geography-based bifurcations.[29] It is an aspect of the genre that is repeatedly noted by commentators, critics, and practitioners, early and recent: André Hodeir, for example, whom Doris Sommer (1998: 230–31) suggests could be the basis for the character of Bruno in 'El perseguidor', and whom Cortázar, as we have seen, mentions in 'Elogio del jazz' as an example of a jazz writer who actually knows what he is talking about (2006d: 205–06), refers to jazz's 'prodigious cadence of constant renewal' (Hodeir 1959: 40), while, to pick a more modern and non-academic example, the promotional prose for the 2008 album *Add to Friends* by the jazz quartet Fourscore talks in similar terms of how 'for nearly a hundred and twenty years, jazz has been the flexible quintessence of constant renewal. What is avantgarde today can turn into tradition tomorrow' ('FourScore — Add to Friends' 2008).[30] And what is true for the broad sweep of jazz history is also true for particular styles and movements within it: once again invoking the same terms, Louise McKinney, for instance, in her book on New Orleans culture makes reference to the 'constant renewal of New Orleans jazz' (2006: 144).

Along similar lines, we can see Cortázar himself, in interview with González Bermejo, referring to:

> la manera en que [el jazz] puede salirse de sí mismo, no dejando nunca de seguir siendo jazz. Como un árbol que abre sus ramas a derecha, a izquierda, hacia arriba, hacia abajo..., permitiendo todos los estilos, ofreciendo todas las posibilidades, cada uno buscando su vía. Desde ese punto de vista está probada la riqueza infinita del jazz; la riqueza de creación espontánea, total. (1978: 104–05)

> [the way in which [jazz] can come out of itself, without ever not still being jazz. Like a tree that opens its branches to the right, to the left, upwards, downwards..., allowing all styles, offering all possibilities, each person looking for his/her path. From that point of view the infinite richness of jazz is proven; the richness of total, spontaneous creation.]

But this quotation also points towards the most fundamental identification of jazz as being engaged in the renewal and mutation of its own language: not so much the processes of the broad shifts and transmogrifications of its dialects, but the way in which it operates at the level of its notes, the nuts and bolts of its musical idiom. And it is here that we reach the pivotal role played by improvisation in Cortázar's writing on and valorisation of jazz, for it is, for Cortázar, the improvisational qualities of jazz that enable it to escape from the internal structures of language, that is, from discursive logic and thought, as he sets out in a number of interviews, as well as, in particular, in 'Soledad de la música' and 'Elogio del jazz'. Thus, in 'Soledad de la música', when Cortázar talks of how 'los *jazzmen* negros [...] [n]o tratan de ejecutar creaciones ajenas; apoyan su orquesta sobre una melodía y un ritmo conocidos, y *crean, libremente, su música*. [...] [L]ate a cada instante una nueva música nacida de la jubilosa matriz del viejo tema' (1992: 294–95) [black jazzmen [...] don't try to perform others' creations; they set their orchestras up on a known melody and rhythm, and *create their music freely*. [...] Each moment there pulses a new music born from the jubilant womb of the old theme], it is the practice of improvisation that he has in mind: the creation of something new in the moment. Similarly, in 'Elogio del jazz' Cortázar refers to how improvisation 'no es sino el nacimiento continuo e inagotable de formas melódicas y rítmicas y armónicas' (2006d: 209) [is nothing less than the continuous and tireless birth of new melodic, rhythmic, and harmonic forms], whilst in 'Así se empieza' from *La vuelta al día en ochenta mundos*, watching Lester Young perform 'Three Little Words', he refers to how 'sentí más que nunca lo que hace a los grandes del jazz, esa invención que sigue siendo fiel al tema que combate y transforma e irisa' (1970b: 7) [I felt more than ever what makes the jazz greats, that invention that remains faithful to the theme that it fights and transforms and makes iridescent].

It is clear that improvisation is central to what Cortázar considers to be 'authentic' jazz. In interview with Prego, for instance, he states that 'El jazz [...] está basado [...] en el principio de la improvisación (1985: 163) [Jazz [...] is based [...] on the principle of improvisation], and in 'Elogio del jazz' he declares in no uncertain terms that 'la *improvisación* [...] constituye la razón misma del jazz[.] [...] [C]onstituye la esencia primera y última del jazz' (Cortázar 2006d: 209–10) [*improvisation* [...] constitutes the very reason for jazz. [...] It constitutes the first and last essence of jazz]. As Goialde Palacios states, in Cortázar's work 'la improvisación [...] se constituye como un componente fundamental sin el que no puede hablarse propiamente de música de jazz' (2010: 485) [improvisation [...] is a fundamental component without which one cannot properly talk of jazz music].[31] In particular, bound up with the idea of improvisation as being about inspiration and creative freedom is, as intimated above, the attendant sense for Cortázar that improvisation does not involve repetition, the repeating or rehashing of old forms or previous improvised pieces. This is stated baldly by Cortázar as he describes jazz solos as being 'de pura improvisación, que [los jazzmen] naturalmente no repiten nunca' (Prego 1985: 163) [of pure improvisation, which [jazzmen] naturally never repeat], where 'la riqueza imaginativa del *jazzman* le permite tomar cien veces un mismo coro sin *repetirlo* ni *repetirse*' (Cortázar 2006d: 211) [the imaginative richness of the jazzman allows him to take the same chorus a hundred times without *repeating it* or *repeating himself*]. And this principle carries on into the practice of jazz recording based around 'takes', about which Cortázar has much to say, that is, the series of recordings of the same song, with different solos and performances in each, with one being chosen as the definitive version (or take) to be used for release. In 'Take it or leave it', a sub-section of 'Melancolía de las maletas' from *La vuelta al día en ochenta mundos*, Cortázar sets out the key difference between jazz takes and rehearsals, the practice which one finds, for example, in *la música culta*:

> El ensayo va llevando paulatinamente a la perfección, no cuenta como producto, es presente en función de futuro. En el **take** la creación incluye su propia crítica y por eso se interrumpe muchas veces para recomenzar; la insuficiencia o el fracaso de un **take** vale como un ensayo para el siguiente, pero el siguiente no es nunca el anterior en mejor, sino que es siempre otra cosa si realmente es bueno. (1970c: 172, emphasis in original)

> [The rehearsal gradually takes you towards perfection, it doesn't count as a product, it's a present based on the future. In the **take** the creation includes its own critique and for that reason it is often interrupted to start again; the insufficiency or failure of a **take** has value as a rehearsal for the next one, but the next one is never the previous one only better, but is always something different if it really is good.]

This idea of the same piece, but completely different each time, is underscored in a later interview with Prego, where Cortázar refers to how, in jazz takes, 'siendo siempre la misma es también otra cosa' (1985: 163) [being always the same it is also something else], itself an echo of an earlier statement in 'Soledad de la música', albeit where he does not specifically mention takes, in which he talks of the 'melodías viejas' [old melodies] which spring from the jazzmen's instruments 'con la gracia proteiforme y ubicua de ser siempre las mismas y, sin embargo, cada vez nuevas músicas' (Cortázar 1992: 294–95) [with the proteiform and ubiquitous grace of being always the same and yet new music every time].

What is clear, then, is the importance of the (effective and putative) non-iterability of the 'authentic' jazz improvisation in Cortázar's presentation of it. Such a view of improvisation is, as Goialde Palacios intimates (2010: 485), somewhat problematic, and chapter 6 will address this in greater depth. But, regardless of these concerns, what is central for my present purposes is to understand why this appears as such an important characteristic of jazz in Cortázar's eyes. Turning to Artaud's theatre of cruelty and Jacques Derrida's writing on it proves useful in this respect. Once again, the similarities between Cortázar and Artaud are striking, with the dramatist declaring that 'once spoken, all speech is dead and is only active as it is spoken. Once a form is used it has no more use, bidding man find another form' (Artaud 1993: 56). For Derrida, this signals that:

> the 'grammar' of the theater of cruelty [...] will always remain the inaccessible limit of a representation which is not repetition, of a *re*-presentation which is full presence, [...] of a present which does not repeat itself, that is, of a present outside time, a nonpresent. (2001: 313)

What Derrida is indicating here in relation to Artaud also applies to Cortázar's insistence upon the non-repeatability of jazz improvisations, in that it suggests a desire to move beyond language, to remove the condition of language that is, in Derrida's thought, its iterability.[32] Of course, the point here is that this represents a *desire*, and, as we shall see, one undermined by a more exacting analysis of Cortázar's claims and of the relationships with jazz that emerge on the part of both his characters and Cortázar himself. Nevertheless, the repeated assertion that 'authentic' jazz improvisations are not and cannot be repeated underscores, and, ultimately, is what allows Cortázar to affirm, the potential of jazz as a form of expression not bound by the rules, structures, and strictures of discursive thought and language. This is outlined particularly clearly in interview with González Bermejo where Cortázar describes jazz (improvisation) as 'una creación que no está sometida a un discurso lógico y preestablecido sino que nace de las profundidades' (1978: 105) [a creation that is not subjected to a logical and preestablished discourse, but which is born from the depths]. Jazz is, as we saw earlier, thus capable for Cortázar not of communicating information 'de tipo inteligible o de tipo discursivo' (107) [of an intelligible or discursive type], but, instead, of communicating 'cosas que ningún lenguaje, ninguna escritura pueden comunicar [...] sentidos [...] la comunicación de ciertas dimensiones de la realidad' (107) [things that no language, no writing can communicate [...] senses [...] the communication of certain dimensions of reality]. This helps us understand why what separates Johnny Carter, the saxophonist in 'El perseguidor', from the rest of humanity 'no tiene explicación' (1970d: 146) [has no explanation], as well as indicating the link between jazz and the central claim made by Cortázar in his fiction, interviews, and essays, namely that jazz, and jazz improvisation in particular, can smash through the linguistic and civilised façade we live in, the 'explosión de la música' (121) [explosion of music] which Cortázar describes in 'El perseguidor' as the moment when 'la costra de la costumbre se rajó en millones de pedazos' (121) [the scab of habit was shattered into a million pieces], the *costra* being the conventions of society, the mask of language covering humankind and the world, and the dividing barriers erected by it. One could, once more, even use Artaud's statement as an accurate summary of what Cortázar is describing here: 'Briser le langage pour toucher la vie' (Artaud 1964: 18) [Break language so as to touch life].

Given the nature of improvisation that emerges from Cortázar's writing, it is unsurprising that, as many critics have noted,[33] it is linked so strongly and clearly by Cortázar with surrealism and, more particularly, the surrealist practice of automatic writing. In 'Elogio del jazz' he is clear that jazz improvisation is like 'los juegos de la escritura automática y el dibujo onírico que llenaron la primera y más alta etapa del surrealismo' (2006d: 209) [the games of automatic writing and dream drawing that filled the first and highest stage of surrealism], going as far as to claim that '"la inmaculada concepción" del poema automático no es sino el exacto mecanismo (o abolición del mecanismo) de la ejecución jazz' (210) ['the immaculate conception' of the automatic poem is nothing less than the exact mechanism (or abolition of mechanism) of the jazz performance]. And in interview with González Bermejo Cortázar states that:

> el jazz es la sola música entre todas las músicas — con la de la India — que corresponde a esa gran ambición del surrealismo en literatura, es decir, a la escritura automática, la inspiración total, que en el jazz corresponde a la improvisación. (1978: 105)
>
> [jazz is the only music among all types of music — along with that of India — that corresponds to that great surrealist ambition in the realm of literature, that is, automatic writing, total inspiration, that in jazz corresponds to improvisation.]

The caveat regarding Indian music is significant in that it points to the fissures in Cortázar's general claims for the uniqueness of jazz, but what stands out here is the bringing together of jazz, surrealism, automatic writing, inspiration, and improvisation, as reinforced in interview with Prego, where, discussing jazz takes and improvisation, Cortázar tells of there being 'una analogía muy tentadora de establecer con el surrealismo. [...] [E]ra la única música que coincidía con la noción de escritura automática, de improvisación total de la escritura. [...] [E]l jazz me daba a mí el equivalente surrealista en la música' (1985: 163) [a very tempting analogy to be drawn with surrealism. [...] It was the only music that coincided with the notion of automatic writing, of total improvisation in writing. [...] Jazz gave me the surrealist equivalent in music].

Remembering that Cortázar was a writer not a musician, what we see in all of these examples is the understandable step of exploring to what extent jazz, with all the potential Cortázar has identified in it, can be aligned with a similar linguistic or writing practice. That said, it is worth noting that the statements from the interview with Prego in particular present this analogy as one that occurred to Cortázar in the past, with a clear suggestion that he might, by the latter years of his life, have been less easily persuaded of its usefulness or accuracy. It is, rather, more in terms of the shared ideal of an escape from the rigid structures and norms of (linguistic) expression that the value of this analogy is found. Indeed, along these lines it is also worth noting that the alignment of jazz improvisation with automatic writing does not lead towards the latter appearing as a model for the way Cortázar feels he should, or does, write his texts. As Goialde Palacios writes, 'La obra de Cortázar no está realizada bajo los dictados de la inspiración absoluta y del libre fluir de la conciencia, como proponían los representantes del movimiento surrealista' (2010: 486) [Cortázar's work is not realised through dictation from absolute inspiration and the free flow of consciousness, as proposed by the proponents of the surrealist movement].[34] Rather, jazz retains its attractiveness as a model for writing *in its own right*, with jazz takes in particular being put forward as what Cortázar aims for in his writing, not least in that they carry with them the sense of risk and danger that we have seen to be an important characteristic of jazz for the author. In 'Take it or leave it', for example, Cortázar affirms that 'lo mejor de la literatura es siempre **take**, riesgo implícito en la ejecución, margen de peligro[.] [...] Yo no quisiera escribir más que **takes**' (1970c: 172, emphasis in original) [the best of literature is always **take**, the implicit risk in the performance, a margin of danger. [...] I wouldn't want to write anything but **takes**], an affirmation repeated in interview with Picon Garfield (1981: 130). At the same time, we should be wary of taking this statement at face value: an examination of the handwritten and annotated typed manuscripts of stories such as 'Clone', 'Anillo de Moebius', and, in particular, 'Historia con migalas' [Story with Spiders] from the Benson Latin American Collection (Cortázar 1982: 5) makes clear that Cortázar's stories were worked on, altered, and perfected to a considerable degree. Similarly, when critics such as Saúl Yurkievich describe Cortázar's writing as 'prosa *take*' [*take* prose] as opposed to 'prosa literaria' (2003: 32) [literary prose], referring to his 'portentoso don de la improvisación [donde] [l]a improvisación es el primer motor de la escritura de Cortázar' (14) [portentious gift for improvisation [where] improvisation is the primary driver of Cortázar's writing], to the extent that it is possible to say that 'de la improvisación nace la mayor parte de su prosa breve, la prosa abierta' (31) [most of his short prose, the open prose, is born from improvisation], we need to ask to what extent the claims of Cortázar regarding the jazzistic nature of his writing are being accepted as true, without an examination of whether they stand up to scrutiny. It is not, to be sure, a question of Yurkievich (and others) failing to analyse Cortázar's writing style, which he does remarkably well. Rather, it is a question of whether such affirmations are only made possible by a somewhat nebulous understanding of what the nature and reality of jazz improvisation actually is. These questions will be explored in chapter 6.

Rhythmic Challenge

Before engaging in that discussion, however, we must draw attention to a further element of jazz which figures frequently in Cortázar's writing on and engagement with this music: swing. The importance of swing, understood broadly as the defining rhythmic foundation and characteristic of jazz, lies not just in the fact that Cortázar identifies it as central to jazz's power and potential, but also in the way that it offers a different model for understanding how Cortázar sees jazz in relation to and as a model for his own literary practice. Already we have seen how rhythmic elements, including those found in, or associated with, swing, such as syncopation and polyrhythms, are mentioned by Cortázar in relation to *la música culta*, in particular Mozart, and how these contribute to his own approach to short story writing especially. And the sorts of issues and ideas which pertained to this earlier discussion are also relevant here. But in looking at swing in a more specifically (and multifaceted) jazz context, rather than simply as a byword for certain rhythmic characteristics, those issues and ideas can be opened up further. Again, I shall examine this in depth in the following chapter, but it is necessary first to build up a more detailed understanding of the nature of Cortázar's claims for (the potential and power of) swing, and to locate these claims historically and musicologically.

One of the confusions when dealing with swing in jazz is that the term itself refers to two distinct, though not unrelated, phenomena: the specific period in jazz history known as the Swing Era (roughly from the early 1930s to the early-mid 1940s) and what Matthew W. Butterfield has described as 'the central rhythmic quality native to jazz' (2011: 3).[35] The basis of this rhythmic quality is the propulsive and lilting effect of a particular way of playing quavers (eighth notes), where, to simplify greatly, the downbeats are given more emphasis and weight (length) than the upbeats. In contrast to his lauding of swing in this latter sense, about which I shall say more shortly, Cortázar's rejection of Big Band or Swing Era music is strident. As we saw in chapter 2, this rejection comes initially as part of a discussion in 'Elogio del jazz' in which the focus of Cortázar's attention is not the rhythms of Swing music, but its reliance upon composition and arrangement. This, for Cortázar, aligns this type of jazz with *la música culta* in that, for example:

> Beethoven, notando una sinfonía, operaba dentro de un proceso análogo — digo: análogo — al de un *arranger* notando un trozo de *swing*. Y la orquesta del Colón, tocando la *Séptima*, hace exactamente lo mismo que los muchachos de Glenn Miller tocando *Serenade in Blue*. (2006d: 211–12)[36]
>
> [Beethoven, writing down a symphony, worked within an analogous process — I say: analogous — to that of an *arranger* writing down a piece of Swing. And the Colón Theatre's orchestra, playing the Seventh, does exactly the same as Glenn Miller's boys playing 'Serenade in Blue'.]

Indeed, Cortázar goes as far as to state quite plainly that 'es en el *swing* donde cabe apreciar las influencias de la música culta sobre el jazz' (212) [it's in Swing where one can appreciate the influences of *la música culta* on jazz], this fact explaining, for Cortázar, the 'relativa comprensión del *swing* por parte de los musicólogos' (212) [relative understanding of Swing on the part of musicologists], further underscoring the short shrift he generally gives to this group of people. More precisely, Big Band jazz is a music characterised for Cortázar by a rigidity of structure and expectation ('para que luego este clarinete toque tal cosa mientras esas trompetas se despachan metódicamente tales otras' (211) [so that then this clarinet plays such and such while those trumpets methodically knock off this and that]). The result is that 'no hay allí sitio para la improvisación instantánea' (211) [there is no place there for instantaneous improvisation], although Cortázar recognises in a footnote tailor-made for a Derridean reading that this general rule has notable exceptions, in the form of the arrangements of Fletcher Henderson and, in particular, the 'profunda y hermosa [...] técnica de Duke Ellington' (211) [profound and beautiful [...] technique of Duke Ellington].[37] In a later interview with Picon Garfield he again singles out Ellington as an exception, but reiterates his overall stance *vis-à-vis* this type of jazz, stating that 'no me acostumbraba nunca al "swing" o a los "big bands"' (1981: 127) [I never got used to Swing, or the Big Bands].

It is worth underlining that Cortázar's views on Swing are not particular to the Argentine author, in the sense that there is a general consensus that this was an era of structured composition and arrangement where 'the swing bands emphasized the value and sound of the whole at the expense of the virtuosity and spontaneity of the soloist' (Rutkoff and Scott 1996: 98), with scholars such as Paul Lopes, for example, echoing Cortázar in talking of how Swing bands' 'initial orientation was to emulate symphonic orchestras in creating legitimate popular music performance' (1999: 32). But looking beyond Cortázar's texts is helpful in disclosing further ways in which Swing jazz is aligned — or came to be aligned — with the sorts of problems and traits that Cortázar looks to oppose in his work. As the period progressed, for example, the music turned ever more 'stagnant and formulaic' (Rutkoff and Scott 1996: 95), as well as being a distinctly commercialised product, of consumerist value above all.[38] Meanwhile, aside from the musical considerations, the 'rigid organization and structure of the swing bands [themselves] became suffocating' (98) for the new musicians involved in them.

All that being said, the broad rhythmic trait known as swing *is* one of the elements that characterise the music of the Swing Era, and it is notable that there are examples in the *discada* [record session] scene (chapters 10–18) in *Rayuela* of musicians and tracks from this period, such as Lionel Hampton, Duke Ellington, and 'Four O'Clock Drag' by the Kansas City Six.[39] But swing itself goes beyond the particular way in which music of the Swing Era swung (without this meaning that Swing Era music, in the hands of a Duke Ellington, for example, could not demonstrate this richness, in terms of what swing could be and transmit). Again, to quote Butterfield, 'swing designates a general rhythmic ethos — a mysterious quality purportedly transcending representation in musical notation' (2011: 3); along similar lines, Hodeir referred to swing as a 'vital drive', identified as 'a combination of undefined forces that creates a kind of "rhythmic fluidity" without which the music's swing is markedly attenuated' (1956: 207); and there have been numerous attempts at defining exactly what swing is, both from a broad, overarching perspective, as found in Charles Keil's notion of 'engendered feeling' (1966: 345), to more technical and restricted analyses such as that of Friberg and Sundström (2002), examining different swing ratios. But it remains a varied and elusive phenomenon: Count Basie, for example, 'said that beyond being music you can pat your foot by, he couldn't define it' (Broyles 2011: 298). The appeal to Cortázar of swing, resistant to definition and constantly eluding attempts to 'nail it down' or set out any strict limits to its nature, is, thus, self-evident. And the fact that some of the most well-known statements about swing come from (musicians tied in particular to) hot jazz, prior to the Swing Era, both signals its diffuseness as the defining characteristic of jazz from its earliest stages and gives a basis for understanding why this type of jazz was so highly regarded by Cortázar.[40] Louis Armstrong, for example, to whom Cortázar referred as the representative of 'el jazz en s[u] ápic[e]' (2006d: 208) [jazz at its zenith], famously said of jazz (and, by implication in context, its swing essence) '"Man, if you gotta ask [what it is], you'll never know"' (cited in Broyles 2011: 298).

Conversely, a further Louis Armstrong quotation on swing is instructive for its contrast with both Cortázar's texts and wider jazz writing. In one of his appearances on the Bing Crosby radio show, Armstrong remarked, '"Ah, swing, well we used to call it syncopation — then they called it Ragtime, then blues — then jazz. Now, it's swing"' (cited in Argyle 2009: 172). Whilst this statement underscores and helps explain why the syncopation of some of the classical pieces we looked at in chapter 2 offered Cortázar such fertile ground for exploring the potential of *la música culta* as a genre that could encode a challenge to the dominant discourse and orthodoxy generally, it underplays the extent to which swing within jazz was — or came to be — more than simply a specific rhythmic effect. That is to say, the specificity of the jazz context determines a number of salient points for understanding why jazz swing is 'different' and, attendantly, why it is so valorised by Cortázar.

The fact that jazz swing is not merely a question of rhythm is already implied in its resistance to definition, but is underlined in chapter 16 of *Rayuela*, where the description of the 1928 track 'Hot and Bothered' by Duke Ellington and his orchestra that the *Club de la Serpiente* is listening to ends, 'entre riffs tensos y libres a la vez, pequeño difícil milagro: *Swing, ergo soy*' (Cortázar 2007: 195) ('with riffs which were both tense and [free] at the same time, a difficult minor miracle: "I swing, therefore I am"', 1966: 64), connecting swing with a metaphysics of being. Indeed, this link is extended from individual ontology to a broader sense of what constitutes authentic reality as the text goes on to refer to a further Ellington composition stating that 'era casi sencillo pensar que quizá eso que llamaban la realidad merecía la frase despectiva del Duke, *It don't mean a thing if it ain't [got] that swing*' (2007: 195) ('it was almost easy to come to the conclusion that what was called reality deserved that disparaging phrase of the Duke's, "It don't mean a thing if it ain't got that swing"', 1966: 64).

Besides this, although its sense of breaking free from regularity, of a liberation from strict, orthodox, ordered metre is one it shares with syncopation, cross-rhythms, and polyrhythms generally, jazz swing is also tied specifically — and highly significantly — to the racial elements of the music. Gunther Schuller in his seminal work *Early Jazz: Its Roots and Musical Development* (1986: 10–16) sets out a strong analysis of the African roots of swing, as he argues persuasively for the overarching African origins of much of jazz more broadly. In the course of this discussion he draws attention, as Butterfield puts it, to the idea of 'the emergence of swing as an outcome of the superimposition of a European metrical framework upon African rhythmic impulses' (2011: 4),[41] whilst black musicians — such as Louis Armstrong and Jelly Roll Morton — were key in subsequently cementing swing's centrality and popularity in jazz, arguably, as I have intimated, most notably in the hot jazz period. More significant in the context of the present discussion, however, is the nature of the shift from hot jazz to Big Band jazz, and then from the Big Band Era to that of bebop. In his rather negative appraisal of Swing music in 'Elogio del jazz', Cortázar at one point comments, 'Sospecho a veces que los musicólogos estiman el jazz en términos de *swing*, tal vez porque éste fue llevado a la popularidad por *intérpretes* blancos' (2006d: 212) [I suspect that musicologists respect jazz in terms of Swing, perhaps because this type of jazz was made popular by white *interpreters* (musicians)]. This contrasts with his presentation of 'authentic' jazz in this essay, be it that of 'un ejecutante negro de la pura línea *hot*' (212) [a black musician from the pure hot jazz tradition], or more broadly 'los *jazzmen* negros' (215) [black jazzmen] in general, as being very specifically black, thus bringing us back to the 'colouring' of Cortázar's engagement with jazz. The effect of this is to point up the racial aspects of the Swing Era. The bands that Cortázar seems to have most in mind when criticising Swing music are the white Big Bands, such as those of Benny Goodman, Glenn Miller, and, a precursor to the main Big Band Era, Paul Whiteman, who comes in for particularly sardonic critique from both

Ronald in *Rayuela* (2007: 178) and Cortázar himself in 'Elogio del jazz', where his reaction to the white critics André Cœuroy's and André Schaeffner's description of the most complete jazz band as being that of Paul Whiteman is simply, '¡Oh, boy!' (Cortázar 2006d: 209). And, certainly, these bands constitute the most obviously commercial(ised) and popular examples from the era. Bringing together the commercial and racial factors outlined here, the picture thus emerges of the Swing Era as one characterised by its (white) exploitation of (essentially) black music and — we might add — of black musicians.[42]

This framework is essential for understanding, in turn, how and why bebop emerged and, most importantly, what it represented in societal, racial, and musical terms. As Peter Rutkoff and William Scott state, 'By asserting its artistic identity and drawing on African-American blues, bebop enabled jazz musicians to liberate themselves from white control' (1996: 95). This was appreciated by some early critics: Ross Russell, for example, commented that 'bebop is a music of revolt: revolt against big bands, arrangers, vertical harmonies, soggy rhythms, non-playing orchestra leaders, Tin Pan Alley — against commercialized music in general' (1959: 202). Central to this revolt, indeed, highlighted by many jazz writers as being *the* central terrain on which it was carried out, was the rhythmic shift effected by bebop musicians — the distinction of *their* brand of swing — as they emerged from the Swing Era. Thus, Rutkoff and Scott draw attention to how 'bebop's incendiary style, pulsing rhythm, and intensity contrasted with the melodic, linear, and commercial qualities of swing' (1996: 91) and Russell notes that 'bebop rhythm differs formally from swing rhythms, because it is more complex and places greater emphasis upon polyrhythmics. It differs emotionally from swing rhythm, creating greater tension, thereby reflecting more accurately the spirit and temper of contemporary emotions' (1959: 189). Rather than in improvisational terms, then, as Benjamin Givan puts it:

> [the] chief distinctions [of Swing and bebop] are [...] to be found either in musical domains [...] such as rhythm-section practices and surface-level rhythmic and melodic features, or outside the musical sphere altogether, in the realm of culture, politics, and history. (2010: 52)

Swing, then, as the rhythmic pulsion of jazz rather than as simple syncopation, is bound up with a mesh of different strands of freedom, renewal, revolt, and advance, in metaphysical, musical, and racial terms.

In the midst of this multivalent understanding of swing, however, it is worth highlighting the fact that, as is clear from the quotations just cited, one of the most notable characteristics of the move from Swing to bop is the higher level of complexity. As Thomas Owens puts it in his work on bebop, 'bebop rhythm sections produce a more complex, multilayered texture than their swing-era counterparts' (1996: 6). And this in turn draws out yet further the two fundamental aspects of swing that inform Cortázar's valorisation of and engagement with it: its constantly shifting indefinability and its relentless production of tension. I have already commented at some length on the attractiveness of the former to Cortázar's sensibilities and aims, but it is also striking how often he draws attention to the tension that results from swing. On the one hand, this reminds us of the use of syncopation and cross-rhythms in his '*música culta* texts' to produce tension. But it also underscores the way in which *jazz* swing renders the production and nature of that tension more complex and intense, with bebop being a particularly extreme example of this, as alluded to by Russell in the quotation above. This heightened sense of tension in jazz swing is, notably, also foregrounded by Hodeir, who, in his seminal *Jazz: Its Evolution and Essence* (1956), states, with specific reference both to hot jazz and to later hard bop figures such as Miles Davis, that 'jazz consists essentially of *an inseparable but extremely variable mixture of relaxation and tension*' (240). And a similar focus on this tension is found in Cortázar's own words and texts: describing Satchmo's hot jazz he refers to how his improvised playing 'asciende a una tensión extremada' (Picon Garfield 1981: 129) [ascends to an extreme tension]; his portrayal of Duke Ellington in the *discada* scene draws attention to his orchestra's 'riffs tensos' (Cortázar 2007: 195) [tense riffs]; and in relation to his own stories, as we saw in chapter 2, he underlines the importance of the tension he creates not being interrupted (González Bermejo 1978: 103), this creation of tension being linked specifically with the introduction of swing (Prego 1985: 170).

This characteristic of jazz, then, at least in part explains why, despite his predilection for the rhythms of Mozart as a basis for his writing, Cortázar ends up talking more frequently, both in interviews and in his own texts, of incorporating swing (a jazz term) into his praxis, rather than the broader and less jazz-specific terms of syncopation, polyrhythms, and cross-rhythms.[43] Jazz swing offers Cortázar a particularly privileged musical model for what he prizes and seeks, capturing the heightened tension to which he aspires and which he views as fundamental to a breaking free from the routine and norms of both literature and being. And the rejection of Swing Era jazz, certainly in its blandest and most commercial forms, in favour of hot jazz and, more strikingly, bebop, is a central part of this, going some way to making sense of why the musicians he refers to both in his fictions and his other writings are predominantly (though not exclusively) linked with these forms.[44]

Improvisation and swing, then, as Matías Barchino Pérez (2002: 499) notes, are key elements for understanding how Cortázar and his texts construct a theoretical basis for the claims of freedom he makes for jazz music. They are key not just for their basic rupture with and challenge to existing forms and structures, but, crucially, for their role and context within jazz history, understood musically, socioculturally, and racially. And yet each of the claims Cortázar makes for jazz, and the way he brings in improvisation, swing, and other elements that contribute to jazz's identity and power, are, as we have seen, scarcely simple and frequently plagued with caveats. To understand just how nuanced and problematic this engagement with and theorising of jazz is, we must look in more detail at Cortázar's fiction itself, examining how, far from resolving these issues, his own work insists on deepening them further. With this goal in mind, I shall turn in the following chapter to the most sustained pieces of fictional writing in Cortázar's *œuvre* that have to do with jazz and the issues I have been looking at: 'El perseguidor' and chapters 10–18 of

Rayuela. Each represents a very different approach to and take on jazz, and it is precisely the differences as well as the similarities between these two pieces of writing in this respect that make them so useful for revealing and understanding the often sinuously complex role played by jazz in Cortázar's work, which the present chapter has only started to explore.

Notes to Chapter 4

1. On *la música culta* see, for example, Picon Garfield (1981: 128); on tango see Prego (1985: 165) and Cortázar's short essay 'Gardel' (1970b: 136–41).
2. 'El perseguidor', published in *Las armas secretas* (1970d [1959]), is a lengthy short story based around the life and music of the bebop saxophonist Charlie Parker, in which the roles of and interplay between critic/biographer and jazz musician are examined; chapters 10–18 of *Rayuela* take in a 'session' of the *Club de la Serpiente* [Serpent Club], a group of bohemians and intellectuals, in the Parisian section of the novel, who meet to share drink, conversation, and a love of a wide range of jazz records which form the musical and atmospheric backdrop to these chapters; 'Bix Beiderbecke' is an unfinished early story based around the eponymous jazz cornettist which was only finally published in the first volume of Galaxia Gutenberg's *Obras completas* (Cortázar 2003: 1107–14); 'Lugar llamado Kindberg' is a short story that engages with the free jazz saxophonist Archie Shepp, published in 1974 in *Octaedro*.
3. I shall refer to a number of Cortazarian works in which jazz is mentioned or alluded to over the course of the following three chapters, but as a brief indication of the extent to which jazz pervades his work, we might note its presence in fictional works such as: *Diario de Andrés Fava*, *Libro de Manuel*, 'Mudanza' [Move] from *La otra orilla* (2004 [1945]) [*The Other Shore*], 'Carta a una señorita en París' [Letter to a Young Lady in Paris] from *Bestiario* (1993a [1951]), 'Silvia' from *Último round* (1973b [1969]) [*Last Round*], 'Vientos alisios' [Trade Winds] and 'Las caras de la medalla' from *Alguien que anda por ahí* (1977), 'Orientación de los gatos' [Orientation of Cats] from *Queremos tanto a Glenda* (1980), and a number of appearances in *Un tal Lucas*. Beyond his fiction, there are numerous references to jazz, notably in several pieces in *La vuelta al día en ochenta mundos*, including 'Así se empieza' (1970b: 6–13) [One Starts Thus], 'Clifford'(1970b: 109), 'Louis, enormísimo cronopio' (1970c: 13–22), 'La vuelta al piano de Thelonious Monk' (1970c: 23–28) [Around Thelonious Monk's Piano], 'No hay peor sordo que el que' (1970b: 142–59), and 'Melancolía de las maletas' (1970c: 166–72). This is not by any means a comprehensive list of the places where Cortázar's work engages with jazz, but should suffice to make clear that jazz is a constant and reiterated presence in his texts.
4. The scholarship on jazz in Cortázar's work is too extensive to list in any sort of detail here, but some of the more notable contributions include Gyurko (1988); Loyola (1994); Sommer (1995); Peyrats (1999); Goialde Palacios (2010); and Couture (2016).
5. Jelly Roll Morton (1890–1941) was a central figure in ragtime and early jazz, principally as a pianist and composer; Louis Armstrong (1901–1971) was one of the leading jazz figures of the hot jazz era, mainly as a trumpeter, though his career continued well into the 1960s, and he ended up at least as well known for his singing as for his playing; Duke Ellington (1899–1974) was a pianist, composer, and bandleader whose fame and greatest success came as part of the Big Band, or Swing, Era of the 1930s and 1940s. For a short introduction to Jelly Roll Morton, see Giddins (1998: 69–76); on Louis Armstrong, see Teachout (2009) for a useful biography and Schuller (1989: 158–97) for a more in-depth analysis of his role and importance in jazz; on Duke Ellington, see Schuller (1989: 46–157).
6. Further examples and details of Cortázar's jazz preferences are found in Chesnel (1977).
7. Whilst useful in other ways, this is the case, for example, in Gordon (1980), Tyler (1996), and Peyrats (1999).
8. See, for example, 'Elogio del jazz' (Cortázar 2006d: 207).
9. See, for example, Kerr and others (1974: 39) and Cortázar's essay 'Así se empieza' (1970b: 6–13).
10. Perhaps the most significant is Picon Garfield (1975: 46, 135, 159, 203).

11. See, for example, Troiano (1984).
12. Elements and (adapted) passages from my earlier work Roberts (2009) on Cortázar and Artaud are incorporated at several points in the following pages.
13. Artaud's collection of essays was first published (in French) in 1938.
14. Dizzy Gillespie (1917–1993) was one of the greatest trumpeters that jazz has seen. Although a highly successful and influential musician across a number of decades, he is best known as a major force in the bebop era. For an excellent introduction to Gillespie, see Shipton (1999). Charlie 'Bird' Parker (1920-1955) was one of the all-time great saxophonists, and, again, was one of the key musicians of the bebop era. There are numerous works on Parker that deserve attention, amongst which are Woideck (1996), Martin (2001), which focuses on his improvisational technique, and Priestly (2005). It is worth also noting Gillespie's autobiography *To Be or Not... To Bop: Memoirs of Dizzy Gillespie* (1979), which, aside from being revealing on Gillespie himself, also contains a number of useful insights into the Bird.
15. On these characteristics of bebop, see, for example, Gioia (1997: 202–04) and Collier (1978: 350–55).
16. Gyurko (1980: 223–25) addresses this point in relation to Bruno in 'El perseguidor'.
17. I am not wishing to suggest that spiritual music or blues can simply be conflated with jazz. They are, of course, very different forms of music. Isabel Gallego (2002), for example, has touched upon the contrast between blues and jazz in relation to *Rayuela*, whilst Peiró argues that the blues in *Rayuela* counteracts the novel's frequent intellectual references, given that it stands in counterdistinction to jazz, which is 'mucho más cerebral' (2006: 67) [much more cerebral]. However, in the present study I will not look to distinguish too readily between Negro spirituals/blues and jazz as they appear in the texts I am analysing, although that is not to say that such a study would not be fruitful. My reasons for not dealing with these forms of music as separate categories, aside from the fact that little attention is given to the blues or Negro spirituals *as* separate categories in Cortázar's essays and interviews, are threefold: firstly (and principally), because they are, as I shall go on to outline, a fundamental part of the history and development of jazz and, as such, are bound up with the same issues surrounding race and freedom on which I will be focusing (Gioia, succinctly, talks of how 'blues and jazz [...] have remained intimate bedfellows over the years, [...] an intimacy so close that, at times, it is hard to determine where the one ends and the other begins' (1997: 20); Berndt Ostendorf (1979: 596–97) underscores the connection between Negro spirituals/hymns, minstrelsy, and early jazz; whilst David Sager (2002) also talks about characteristics of Negro spirituals (use of the flattened seventh and 'elaborately subdivided rhythms' (275)) which were found in the New Orleans (and the South more generally) of the formative years of the jazz story, characteristics which clearly tie in with those that would go on to be associated with jazz); secondly, and in relation to blues as by far the most frequently mentioned of these musical forms in Cortázar's work, the basic twelve-bar blues structure was used as the basis for a vast number of jazz tunes, standards, and improvisations by many of the jazz figures most recurrent in *Rayuela* and Cortázar's texts more generally (Keith Waters, for example, comments that the '12-bar blues structure remains one of the most persevering and prevalent frameworks in the jazz tradition' (1996: 26)); thirdly, as will become apparent in the final chapter of this study, the vocal aspect of, in particular, the blues — in relation to female singers above all —, is a key element in understanding the primacy of jazz as a whole in Cortázar's thinking and work.
18. Jazz is also referred to specifically in 'Mudanza' from this collection, but it does not play a significant or reiterated role in the story.
19. The power of the black female voice is further evident in 'Lucas, sus errantes canciones' from *Un tal Lucas* (1979b: 149–51). Referring to the traditional song 'So You're Going to Leave the Old Home, Jim', Cortázar gives us a comparison between the version by the Scottish music hall singer Sir Harry Lauder that Lucas heard as a child and that by the black blues singer Ethel Waters that he hears twenty years later. In the hands of Sir Harry Lauder, Cortázar comments that 'la canción era mecánica y rutinaria, una madre despedía a su hijo que se marchaba lejos y Sir Harry era una madre poco sentimental' (149) [the song was mechanical and routine, a mother saying goodbye to her son who was going far away and Sir Harry was not a very sentimental mother].

When sung by Waters, in contrast, it is transformed into a moving, beautiful song of deep human value where 'sólo cuenta una voz murmurando las palabras de la tribu, la recurrencia de lo que somos, de lo que vamos a ser' (151) [the only thing that counts is a voice murmuring the words of the tribe, the recurrence of what we are, of what we are going to be]. And at the heart of this transformation is the fact that, in the voice of this black female blues singer, the song 'se llenaba de negritud desde las primeras palabras' (150) [was filled with blackness from the first words].

20. See Gioia (1997: 3–39) for an excellent account of the early years in the formation and origins of jazz.
21. The issue of whether New Orleans actually is the birthplace of jazz is one that has generated much debate in jazz scholarship. For an overview of this debate, see Sager (2002: 271–73). As Sager comments, Lewis Porter gives what is probably the most balanced appraisal of the matter when he states that 'it is undeniable that ragtime was being played and partially improvised elsewhere, and the blues was gradually spreading out of the South, and as a result something like jazz probably developed in other cities. Yet it seems equally undeniable that the music we think of today as jazz was initially a product of New Orleans and its environs' (Porter, Ullman, and Hazel 1993: 19–20).
22. See Baldwin (1981: 210–16), for example, on the characteristics of the cakewalk, which include improvisation, polyrhythms, and 'swing'. The cakewalk was one of the musical (and dance) genres that were prevalent during the decades which led to jazz, and while it is not generally seen as a *direct* antecedent of jazz, it is bound up with its rhythms and gestation, and is very much tied in with the later ragtime. The debate about the relationship between ragtime and jazz is complex, with different scholars adopting different positions on the matter, including the somewhat reductive — and largely rejected — stance of seeing them as essentially the same. For a brief overview of this debate, see Sager (2002: 272–73). For more on the relationship between the blues, Negro spirituals, and jazz, see above.
23. Whilst, as mentioned earlier, Armstrong is referred to on several occasions by Cortázar as being amongst his three favourite jazz musicians, the awe-struck manner in which he frequently refers to Satchmo, not least in 'Louis, enormísimo cronopio', suggests a particular affinity on Cortázar's part for the trumpeter.
24. Martha López-Lespada has written in detail on this poem (1998), and my reading here draws upon her insights, whilst also casting my own take on the ways in which the poem is to be understood in relation to the broader engagement with jazz on Cortázar's part.
25. Chapters 5 and 6 will examine the complexities of this dynamic in more detail, in particular in relation to *Rayuela* and 'El perseguidor'.
26. It is worth noting here that there is considerable internal deconstruction of the racial essentialism on display in Cortázar's writing on jazz. His insistence upon the exclusive claims of black jazz as authentic jazz is undercut by, for example, the presence of white jazz musicians amongst those he presents in the most favourable light. Perhaps the most significant example of these is Bix Beiderbecke, who is the subject of an (unfinished) short story (2003: 1107–14) and who is mentioned on several other occasions in Cortázar's work, not least in the *discada* scene in *Rayuela* (2007: 168–69; 170; 202).
27. The tendency to essentialise the black jazz figure is not limited to the Argentine context. Theodor Adorno's essay 'On Jazz' (1989 [1936]), for example, is considered by Catherine Gunther Kodat to be 'one of the very earliest attempts to think through modern, white fantasies of "primitive," "vital" black energies' (2003: 3), and Gioia (1988) has written usefully on the primitivist myth surrounding jazz that characterised early European jazz criticism, not least the work of Panassié. For Gioia, what is more, this has led directly to just the sort of misapprehension of jazz that we find to be ubiquitous in Cortázar's presentation of it: 'One result of this [glorification of primitivism] is a false opposition, posed repeatedly in the literature of jazz, between music of inspired creativity, on the one hand, and that of "cold" intellectualism, on the other. The implication here is that jazz musicians can or should aspire to states of inspiration that "transcend" or "stop short of" mental processes' (47). This provides further evidence of how such primitivist discourse can be seen to underpin Cortázar's entire approach to jazz.

28. The extent to which 'El perseguidor' is imbued with specific references and allusions to the life, character, and music of Charlie Parker has been examined by a number of critics. One of the most comprehensive studies in this regard is Borello (1980). Nevertheless, it is debateable whether this amounts to what Baraka is talking about here (see chapter 5).
29. One of best histories of jazz charting many of these paths and trajectories remains Gioia (1997).
30. Reflecting this need endlessly to change and evolve, Cortázar's texts provide a number of examples of the failure to do so. For instance, when talking of 'Hot and Bothered' by Duke Ellington, a piece that the *Club de la Serpiente* are listening to in *Rayuela*, we are told that the swing in this track, once cutting edge, 'empezaba a endurecerse después de treinta años' (2007: 195) ('was [...] getting to be a little stiff after thirty years', 1966: 64). Similarly, in *Libro de Manuel*, Andrés muses on how 'la primera vez que un pianista interrumpió su ejecución para pasar los dedos por las cuerdas como si fuera un arpa, o golpeó en la caja para marcar un ritmo o una cesura, volaron zapatos al escenario; ahora los jóvenes se asombrarían si los usos sonoros de un piano se limitaran a su teclado' (1973a: 27) [the first time a pianist interrupted his/her performance to strum the strings as if they were a harp, or banged on the piano frame to mark a beat or a caesura, shoes were thrown onto the stage; now, young people would be amazed if the sonorous uses of a piano were limited to its keyboard].
31. Although, as I shall discuss in chapter 6, Goialde Palacios is one of the few critics to pick Cortázar up for idealising improvisation, here he accepts without question the idea that improvisation is the central and determining characteristic of jazz. Yet, as Raymond F. Kennedy puts it, the 'importance of improvisation to jazz, though generally assumed, is by no means fully accepted' (1987: 37). Max Harrison, for example, talks of the tendency in jazz writing to indulge 'in a false primacy of certain aspects such as improvisation, which is neither unique nor essential to jazz (1980: 561), whilst Schuller refers to 'rhythm and inflection', not improvisation, as 'the elements that most obviously distinguish jazz from the rest of Western music' (1986: 6). Conversely, the jazz pianist Bill Evans declared, '"I believe it [improvisation] is necessary to jazz"' (Pleasants 1969: 57).
32. Derrida uses the term iterability to refer to the underlying condition and nature of all language, broadly understood, whereby every sign carries within it the possibility of being (re)iterated or cited in different contexts. These different contexts result in the sign having, in its iteration, both the same and yet also a different meaning. See Derrida's 'Signature Event Context' (1982 [1972]: 307–30).
33. Amongst more recent examples, see Goialde Palacios (2010) and Anderson (2013).
34. For a more general examination of Cortázar and surrealism, see Picon Garfield (1975).
35. For a comprehensive and generally excellent study of the Swing Era, see Schuller (1989).
36. The Glenn Miller Orchestra was one of the most popular and influential Big Bands of the Swing Era (see Schuller (1989: 661–77)). 'Serenade in Blue' was a hit for the Orchestra in 1942.
37. For an excellent appraisal of Fletcher Henderson's role and influence in the Swing Era, see Magee (2005).
38. On the commercial(ised) nature of Swing Era jazz, see DeVeaux (1997: 116–31).
39. It is worth noting here that the Kansas City Six was a small unit formed from the Count Basie Orchestra, which was already pushing beyond Swing's limits and definitions. As Douglas Henry Daniels comments, 'Basie's Kansas City Six, with [its] reliance on swinging riffs [...] provides clues as to how bop grew out of swing' (2006: 102).
40. In interview with Prego, for example, Cortázar states that 'el viejo jazz de New Orleans y el llamado jazz de Chicago en el fondo es mi jazz' (1985: 165) [the old jazz of New Orleans and so-called Chicago jazz is, deep down, my jazz]. New Orleans jazz and Chicago jazz are terms that, although indicating particular nuances and historical movements of hot jazz, are nevertheless used broadly interchangeably with the latter term.
41. See also Deveaux (1991) for a useful overview of the role and importance of African origins and elements in jazz historiography.
42. On various ways in which this exploitation manifested itself, see, for example, Rutkoff and Scott (1996: 96–98) and Borshuk (2004: 263–64).

43. See, for example, González Bermejo (1978: 102–03); Prego (1985: 169–70); Picon Garfield (1981: 130); and Olivares (1981: 56).
44. Amongst the most obvious examples are Louis Armstrong, Charlie Parker, Thelonious Monk, Lester Young, Clifford Brown, and Bix Beiderbecke.

CHAPTER 5

From Jazz Theory to Jazz Practice

In the examination of jazz in Cortázar's work that I have undertaken so far, my focus has largely been on establishing a sense of the author's claims for and vision of this musical genre, with this being constructed predominantly from his essays and interviews on the subject. This is, I believe, a necessary step, but one that should be understood essentially as the grounding for a more critical and far-reaching appraisal of Cortázar's engagement with jazz, based on the works of fiction in which jazz plays a central role. In shifting my attention to such works, then, principally in the form of 'El perseguidor' and the *discada* scene (chapters 10–18) from *Rayuela*, as set out at the end of the preceding chapter, this present chapter will take up several strands of my discussion thus far, showing how, in comparison to the basic theoretical frameworks found in his non-fictionalised statements on jazz, Cortázar's main ideas regarding this form of music are taken in more developed, nuanced, and often very different directions by these texts.[1] There will, then, be a certain amount of revisiting of the areas discussed in the previous chapter, but, perhaps appropriately, my aim will be to offer a fundamentally new take on these themes.

Pursual Not Attainment

'No es culpa tuya no haber podido escribir lo que yo tampoco soy capaz de tocar' (Cortázar 1970d: 171) ('It's not your fault that you couldn't write what I myself can't blow', 2013: 238), Johnny tells Bruno in 'El perseguidor'. It is in many ways one of the most important lines in the story, and immediately underscores the more complex and often more tentative image of jazz that emerges in the transferral of Cortázar's 'jazz theory' to his fictional world. Certainly, it is a recognition of the theoretical and metaphysical binds and contortions that I examined in the course of my Introduction, pertaining to the difficulties of both expressing and communicating what is beyond language, issues that are generally not allowed fully to encumber the essays and interviews in which we have seen Cortázar to talk most freely and at length on jazz; and it intimates that, despite claims otherwise, jazz, like writing, cannot be said to have attained the ontoexpressive panacea to which Cortázar aspires. Indeed, the story's title itself indicates such in its reference not just to Bruno in his pursuing (or not) of Johnny's 'essence', or, alternatively, of the commercial and critical success of his biography of the latter, but also to Johnny, pursuing a new vision and experiencing of the world and himself, both in words and, crucially, in his jazz saxophone playing. In other words, jazz may appear as a privileged medium in this story and in Cortázar's work more generally, as we have seen, but 'El perseguidor' is central to underscoring that its value and power lie in its ability to point to and suggest such a vision and 'understanding', to be a conduit to (enable access to) them, rather than presenting these as *faits accomplis* in the music itself.[2]

Turning to *Rayuela*, a similar inference can be drawn from the repeated references in chapter 12 to various jazz figures whose songs are being played by the *Club de la Serpiente* as 'intercesores' (Cortázar 2007: 178; 179) ('intercessors', 1966: 48; 49) and illusions, in the sense that what they are and represent is not tangibly real. Rather, it is a question of to what they enable access: something that, in itself, is implied, never fully graspable:

> Pero todo eso, el canto de Bessie [Smith], el arrullo de Coleman Hawkins, ¿no eran ilusiones, y no eran algo todavía peor, la ilusión de otras ilusiones, una cadena vertiginosa hacia atrás, hacia un mono mirándose en el agua el primer día del mundo? [...] Oliveira [...] sentía que la verdad estaba en eso, en que Bessie y Hawkins fueran ilusiones, porque solamente las ilusiones eran capaces de mover a sus fieles, las ilusiones y no las verdades. Y había más que eso, había la intercesión, el acceso por las ilusiones a un plano, a una zona inimaginable que hubiera sido inútil pensar porque todo pensamiento lo destruía apenas procuraba cercarlo. (2007: 179–80)

> [But all this, Bessie [Smith]'s singing, Coleman Hawkins's cooing, weren't they illusions, or something even worse, the illusion of other illusions, a dizzy chain going backwards, back to a monkey looking at himself in the water on that first day? [...] Oliveira [...] felt that the truth now lay in that Bessie and Hawkins were illusions, because only illusions were capable of moving their adherents, illusions and not truths. And there was more than this, there was intercession, the arrival through illusions to a plane, a zone impossible to imagine, useless to attempt conception of because all thought destroyed it as soon as it attempted to isolate it.] (1966: 49)

Indeed, the terms used here ('plano' ('plane'), 'zona' ('zone')) themselves speak of a vague identification that is beyond reach, an impression further conveyed by the (crossed-out) appearance of the further descriptor 'una región' [a region] in the manuscript version of the novel (1982: 2).[3] As Pilar Peyrats comments, 'En el Club de la Serpiente [...] esta música actúa como intercesor, flujo de conciencia, catalizador y ritual' (1999: 36) [In the Serpent Club [...] this music acts as an intercessor, a flow of consciousness, a catalyst and a ritual].

For all that, whilst both these texts reiterate that the vision and being to which jazz points remain ultimately unattainable or, more properly, that any declaration of their attainment remains premature, this problematic in and of itself does not preclude Cortázar, as we have seen, from presenting jazz — and, specifically, black jazz improvisation — as constituting a form of expression that nevertheless escapes, to a significant degree at least, the problems, strictures, and structures of language. And it is this which allows it to take up its place in Cortázar's thought and work as a liberating pathway by which the desired 'plane' *might* be reached. Both 'El perseguidor' and the *Club de la Serpiente* chapters from *Rayuela* offer ample examples of this characterisation of jazz, and thus reinforce some of the central tenets of the jazz theory framework that emerged from my earlier discussion.

On several occasions in the course of 'El perseguidor', for instance, reference is made to Johnny and the vision of the world of which he talks and that he attempts to reach through his jazz as being beyond (rational) explanation, in effect exemplifying Cortázar's musings on and claims for jazz in 'Soledad de la música': of his experiencing of the elasticity of the world when travelling on the metro, Johnny states that 'la verdadera explicación sencillamente no se puede explicar' (1970d: 112) [the true explanation simply cannot be explained]; further on, Bruno declares that 'la distancia que va de Johnny a nosotros no tiene explicación, no se funda en diferencias explicables' (146) [the distance between Johnny and us has no explanation, it is not based on differences that can be explained], before going on to describe Johnny's discourse in similar terms in alluding to his 'explicaciones inconcebibles' (151) [inconceivable explanations]. In a more oblique fashion, in *Rayuela*, when Ronald puts on a record by Coleman Hawkins as Gregorovius is explaining the meaning of the term 'Lutetian' to La Maga, we are told that 'esas explicaciones [...] le estropeaban la música' (2007: 175–76) [those explanations [...] were wrecking the music for her]. In each instance, the object in question is jazz or bound up with jazz, and is shown to be resistant — even anathema — to discursive, rational thought and explanation, as is more insistently implied in the long quotation above. Moreover, along these lines, a significant clue as to how jazz might operate in terms of being a communicable form of expression (both of itself and as a conduit towards the 'zona inimaginable' ('a zone impossible to imagine')), is found in a later part of the *discada* scene (chapter 18), where, in the context of an attempt to 'entender el Club, entender *Cold Wagon Blues*, entender el amor de la Maga [...] como una epifanía; entenderlos, no como símbolos de otra realidad quizá inalcanzable, pero sí como potenciadores' (2007: 206) ('understanding the Club, understanding the *Cold Wagon Blues*, understanding La Maga's love [...] like an epiphany; understanding them, not as symbols of some other unattainable reality perhaps, but as agents of potency', 1966: 72), Oliveira declares in his internal monologue, 'Damn the language. *Entender*. No inteligir: entender' (2007: 208) ('*Maldita lengua*. To understand. Not to make sense: to understand', 1966: 74). In rejecting the verb 'inteligir' ('to make sense [of]'), Oliveira is rejecting understanding based on intellect, thought, inference, and, following the etymology of the word, reading (*legere*). By contrast, understanding in the sense of the verb *entender* is, again to refer to the etymology, about stretching or tending (*tendere*) inwards (*in*).[4] I will return in my Conclusion to the question of how this process of understanding might work in more concrete terms, but it is nevertheless notable that this passage pre-empts Cortázar's description in interview with González Bermejo of how jazz does not communicate information 'de tipo *inteligible* o de tipo discursivo' [of an *intelligible* or discursive type], but 'cosas que ningún lenguaje, ninguna escritura pueden comunicar' (1978: 107, italics mine) [things that no language, no writing can communicate], and thus starts to clarify how we are to visualise such an alternative form of communication.

Bound up both with this idea of a new or radically different expressive and communicative form and with the sense of a constant leading towards, rather than an attaining of, the envisaged ontolinguistic promised land, Cortázar's 'jazz fiction', in particular 'El perseguidor', draws attention to two areas of importance that require further exploration. The first of these is the relationship of jazz to time. In my discussion of 'Soledad de la música' I examined the way in which the unfurling of a piece of music, or its Idea, in time was wont to be seen in a negative light as the inescapable *expression* of that originary Idea.⁵ In this sense, time is tied up with the broad notion of language, an expressive system that operates by stringing ideas and concepts together sequentially, and in which past, present, and future are determining terrains, encoded into its (grammatical and verbal) structures. Such a concept of time as being divisible into discrete, sequential moments measured by the clock is also, and attendantly, often presented by Cortázar as part and parcel of the ordered and categorised structure of Western civilised being and society. To take the example of two stories to which I have already referred in this study: Marini in 'La isla a mediodía', a character belonging to a world of flight timetables and modern-life expectations, is described with several references to his 'reloj pulsera' (1970f: 125) [wristwatch], an artefact that he starts to try to prise himself away from upon making the move to the supposedly more 'authentic' and timeless locale of Xiros; Alina in 'Lejana. Diario de Alina Reyes', a marker of civilised decorum and life choices, and a concert pianist, writes a diary, a form, that is, that insists on the rigid delineation and division of sequential time, and which disappears from the narrative at the moment when the character moves towards what appears initially to be a reconciliation and fusion with her vagabond 'other' in Budapest. In both of these cases, then, a locus outside of the Western concept of and dependence on linear, sequential time is associated with the sort of being at which Cortázar and his stories aim. It is thus not surprising that a similar schematic is to be found in 'El perseguidor', with several critics drawing attention to the fact that the story sets out and opposes two types of time, broadly aligned with Johnny and his searching jazz and Bruno and his writerly, strait-laced worldview, respectively. Robert Y. Valentine, for example, in an early article on the story, lays out the contrast between Bruno who 'shackles himself with sequential time' (1974: 176) and Johnny 'in search of the total, timeless freedom' (177), an opposition that can be overlaid onto what Jaume Peris Blanes describes as the 'concepción inmediata, visible y unidimensional de la realidad que encarnaba Bruno [...] y la experiencia multiforme y pluridimensional de Johnny' (2011: 84) [immediate, visible, and one-dimensional conception of reality embodied by Bruno [...] and the multiform and multi-dimensional experience of Johnny]. Certainly Johnny talks at length in the story about the sort of concept of time that he seeks and the general preoccupation he has with this topic, which 'me agarra por todos lados' (Cortázar 1970d: 110) [grabs me from all sides]. Thus, in a reference to 'normal' time, he speaks of wishing that 'me pudiera olvidar del tiempo' (103) [I could forget about time], conceiving it instead through the idea of a container pertaining to a certain quantity of time but in which different quantities of things can be fitted. Repeatedly, he refers to a different relationship with time that he envisions or has experienced when playing his saxophone, conveyed by his allusion to the idea of an 'ascensor de tiempo' (109) [time lift] or his attainment of a state where 'por un rato no hubo más que siempre' (176) ('for a while there wasn't anything but always', 2013: 241), both of which emerge as ways of describing a sort of temporal hiatus or timelessness, in which 'todo es elástico' (1970d: 111) [everything's elastic]. It is also notable that, once again, this desired state or moment is aligned with a lack of understanding, with Johnny commenting, for example, that:

> cada vez me doy mejor cuenta de que el tiempo... Yo creo que la música ayuda siempre a comprender un poco este asunto. Bueno, no a comprender porque la verdad es que no comprendo nada. [...] Yo creo que la música ayuda, sabes. No a entender, porque en realidad no entiendo nada. (105–06)
>
> [I keep realising better that time... I think the music always helps me understand all this a bit. Well, not understand because the truth is I don't understand anything [...] I think the music helps, you know. Not to understand, because the fact is I don't understand anything.]

And the implied corollary of such an affirmation, namely that this temporal locus is outside of or a challenge to (the time of) language and reason, is underscored in the grammatical and logical violence of Johnny's declarations that 'esto lo estoy tocando mañana[.] [...] Esto ya lo toqué mañana' (104) ('I'm playing this tomorrow[.] [...] I already played this tomorrow', 2013: 186).[6]

Unsurprisingly, it is made abundantly clear that Johnny's vision and concept of time stands in stark opposition to that of Bruno, with Johnny criticising the numerical, ordered nature of the latter's understanding of time, as he complains of how 'tú no haces más que contar el tiempo [...]. A todo le pones un número' (1970d: 100–01) [all you do is keep time [...]. You put a number on everything]. Jaime Brenes Reyes identifies Bruno's time as that of 'our contemporary capitalist economy, [which] serves as foundation for productivity and efficiency. The capitalist individual moves according to the clock and due dates, as in the case of Bruno' (2010: 1), and, certainly, this is evident from even a cursory reading of the story. Tellingly, on several occasions Bruno turns to and invokes precisely this 'standard' concept of time as a way of seeking refuge from the implications of Johnny's thoughts and words, most notably when he mentions how 'me he puesto a pensar en pasado mañana y era como una tranquilidad' (Cortázar 1970d: 120–21) ('I began to think of the day after tomorrow and it was like tranquillity descending', 2013: 199). Indeed, this line is echoed towards the end of the story, when we are told how, in an effort at tackling Johnny's increasingly troubled mind and ideas of abandoning everything, Tica 'hacía lo possible por tranquilizarlo y obligarlo a pensar en el futuro' (1970d: 181) [did everything possible to calm him down and make him think about the future].

The role of music, and specifically Johnny's bebop jazz, in all this is summed up when Johnny affirms its ability to remove him from Bruno's time and insert him into the alternative conception of time, with the concomitant move outside of linguistic expression intimated by and embedded in his prose at this point:

> La música me sacaba del tiempo, aunque no es más que una manera de decirlo. Si quieres saber lo que realmente siento, yo creo que la música me metía en el tiempo. Pero entonces hay que creer que este tiempo no tiene nada que ver con... bueno, con nosotros, por decirlo así. (107)
>
> [Music took me out of time, but that's just a way of saying it. If you want to know what I really feel, I believe that music put me into time. But, then, you'd have to believe that this time has nothing to do with... well, with us, so to speak.]

Certainly, such ideas are reflected in descriptions of and writing on both jazz improvisation and jazz swing, notably in reference to musicians from the bebop and avant-garde/free jazz periods. In an article on transcriptions of a Sonny Rollins solo on 'All the Thing You Are' from his 1963 album *Sonny Meets Hawk!*, where the saxophonist plays with Coleman Hawkins and Paul Bley, for example, we read of 'attempts to visually capture the way in which Rollins's melodic lines sound as though they are outside of time' (Rusch, Salley, and Stover 2016: 6), while double-bassist Red Mitchell once commented that in swing '"it isn't really rigid metronomic time that counts"' (cited in Prögler 1995: 47). Turning to the work of jazz writer and philosopher Jacques Réda we find a similar, if more developed, line of thought in relation to swing. Réda argues that the emphasising of the weak beats, which lies at the heart of swing, has a radical temporal effect:

> En s'établissant sur le renversement des temps faibles de la mesure en temps forts, le rythme du jazz a opéré une figuration musicale de ce que serait l'inversion de l'*avant* et de l'*après*, <u>proprement non pensable</u>, mais susceptible d'effets psycho-physiologiques générateurs d'une impression de suspens et de progrès simultanés ou comme réciproques: le progrès se suspend parce que le suspens progresse. Voilà le *swing*. [...] Dans ce renversement des causes et des effets [...] résid[e] [...] le sens du *swing*. (2010 [1990]: 17–18; 20, underscore mine)
>
> [In being based on changing the weak beats in the bar into strong beats, jazz rhythm has put into effect a musical figuration of what would be the inversion of *before* and *after*, <u>strictly speaking unthinkable</u>, but susceptible to psycho-physiological effects that generate an impression of suspense and progress, either simultaneous or as if reciprocal: the progress is suspended because the suspense progresses. That is swing! [...] In this reversal of causes and effects [...] lies [...] the sense of swing.]

Drawing a connection with Cortázar's thought, it is notable that Réda's argument here should invoke terms that likewise suggest a beyond of thought and logic.

Returning to 'El perseguidor', several critics appear to have the lines from the story cited above, as well as others previously mentioned, in mind when addressing the powers of Johnny's jazz playing. Peris Blanes, for example, with specific reference to the latter, declares that 'esa vivencia de la realidad en quiebra sólo podía expresarse a través de un discurso también en quiebra, refractario a las formas tradicionales del relato' (2011: 84) [that experience of ruptured reality could only be expressed through a discourse that is also ruptured, rejecting traditional narrative forms], whilst Valentine claims, more succinctly, that 'Johnny's art (his jazz) takes him outside of time. [...] His music transcends time' (1974: 176). Such affirmations are, however, somewhat precipitous. It is undoubtedly the case that Johnny alludes to his music's having such power, not least when describing the 'ascensor de tiempo' (Cortázar 1970d: 109) [time lift] and the timeless, infinite moment he attains through his jazz. Yet, there is also a sense of a pulling back from such certainty: his music 'ayuda' (105; 106) [helps], in addition to the fact that it is hard simply to cast aside the fundamental problem Cortázar associates with the very act of playing itself: the unfurling of 'the Music' as, at its core, a move into temporal expression, into the 'linguistic'. As Djelal Kadir suggests, 'El perseguidor' does not so much present Johnny's (temporal) goal achieved as 'Johnny's *quest* [...] for [...] a magical moment outside of time and beyond temporality' (1973: 73, italics mine), as we return to the quotation from Johnny with which I began this analysis.

The second area of importance to emerge from 'El perseguidor' in relation to the current analysis is the extent to which Cortázar draws attention in the narrative to the characteristic of jazz as open-ended and endlessly shifting, a trait which dovetails with my analysis of the role of time in the story:

> Johnny ha abandonado el lenguaje *hot* más o menos corriente hasta hace diez años, porque ese lenguaje violentamente erótico era demasiado pasivo para él. En su caso el deseo se antepone al placer y lo frustra, porque el deseo le exige avanzar, buscar, negando por adelantado los encuentros fáciles del jazz tradicional. [...] Veo ahí la alta paradoja de su estilo, su agresiva eficacia. Incapaz de satisfacerse, vale como un acicate continuo, una construcción infinita cuyo placer no está en el remate sino en la reiteración exploradora, [...] en la creación continua de su música. (1970d: 132-33)

> [Johnny abandoned the language of [hot jazz] more or less current ten years ago, because that violently erotic language was too passive for him. In his case he preferred desire rather than pleasure and it hung him up, because desire necessitated his advancing, [searching], denying in advance the easy [encounters] of traditional jazz. [...] I see here the ultimate paradox of his style, his aggressive vigor. Incapable of satisfying itself, useful as a continual spur, an infinite construction, the pleasure of which is not in its [end point] but in the exploratory [reiteration] [...] in the continuous creation of his music.] (2013: 208-09)

Such a passage speaks to the understanding of jazz *per se* as a never-ending process of renewal and change that I touched upon in the previous chapter: hot, or trad, jazz must be replaced by a new 'lenguaje' ('language'), in this case the bebop of Charlie Parker or Dizzy Gillespie, such a trajectory of 'avanzar, buscar' ('advancing, [searching]') being an inherent trait of jazz, as we have seen, in terms of the history of the (sub-)genres that constitute this musical form. With regard to the present discussion, jazz, that is, is a path of constant renewal and reformulation rather than the reaching of a destination. In a similar vein, these lines also refer to the praxis of the improvised jazz solo, specifically of Charlie Parker, via the figure of Johnny, but also more generally. Jason C. Bivins notes that 'the centrality of improvisation to jazz complicates the use of teleology' (2015: 110), and this can be seen in part as an allusion to improvisation as constituting a microcosmic parallel to the endless propulsion of jazz history, as I suggested in chapter 4: as in the case of the latter, that is, jazz improvisation is based around the notion of an endless search, as we have seen Kadir to imply, rather than an attained goal, offering ephemeral glimpses of the sort of expressive and ontological plenitude the soloist seeks, rather than any firm or stable footing in such terrain. (The connection here with my discussion of the concept of time and the putative eternal moment in 'El perseguidor' thus starts to become more readily apparent.) Indeed, such is strongly implied by Cortázar's 'jazz texts'. As early as 'Soledad de la música', Cortázar talks of the 'goce de cada músico [de jazz] con su propia obra *inmediatamente olvidada*' (Cortázar 1992: 297) [ecstasy of each [jazz] musician with his own *immediately-forgotten* work], whilst in 'Elogio del jazz', he refers to jazz improvisation as 'el nacimiento continuo e inagotable de formas melódicas y rítmicas y armónicas, instantáneas y perecederas' (2006d: 209) [the continuous and tireless birth of instantaneous and perishable melodic, rhythmic, and harmonic forms], before going on in this text to describe the playing of Louis Armstrong as a 'fluir inacabable' (210) [endless flowing] and the music of a jam session as 'naciendo y muriendo instantáneamente' (213) [being born and dying instantaneously]. These references and formulations are then taken up further on in his corpus, not least when he speaks of Louis Armstrong's music as 'esa música que crea y que se deshace en el instante' (1970c: 17–20) [that music which he creates and which is undone in the moment], a description played out in the *discada* scene in *Rayuela*, where, in reference to Satchmo's 'Don't Play Me Cheap', Cortázar alludes to 'una perfecta pausa donde todo el swing del mundo palpitaba en un instante intolerable' (2007: 182) ('a perfect pause where all the swing of the world was beating in an intolerable instant', 1966: 52). The notion of such momentary glimpses is also a commonplace of much jazz criticism: commenting on Thelonious Monk, for example, in a statement that brings together three of the most significant jazz players in Cortázar's œuvre, Hodeir contends that 'there are moments, fleeting though no doubt they are, when Monk rises to summits which neither Armstrong nor Parker, in their records at any rate, ever managed to reach' (2001 [1959]: 133).

Beyond their reference to the fleeting nature of these moments of jazzistic epiphany, Hodeir's words also bring into focus the importance of the record in an analysis of the nature of improvisation, in particular as it emerges in Cortázar's texts. As I have argued, the claims Cortázar makes for jazz improvisation are bound up in quite explicit terms with the notion of non-iterability, which itself contributes to jazz, or, more properly, Cortázar's jazz, being opened up as a form of expression not constricted by the properties and nature of language, at least as conceived in Derridean terms. For Cortázar, as we have seen, the value of jazz improvisation appears to lie in the fact that 'no [se] repit[e] nunca' (Prego 1985: 163) [it is never repeated]. Yet this, of course, is exactly what happens when an improvised solo is recorded: it is rendered infinitely repeatable, or iterable (repeatable in different contexts). Hodeir's comment, then, albeit inadvertently, points towards the deleterious effect of the imprinting of the inspired jazz solo on shellac (or, by extension, any modern recording media),[7] in that it literally 'writes out' the ephemeral glimpse of an ontological plenitude supposedly found in it, precisely because such a momentary opening-up to a beyond is *necessarily* outwith the bounds of the inherent linguistic condition of iterability. In this sense, it is worth noting the repeated references in the *discada* scene in *Rayuela* to the condition of the Club's records (the 'writing'/inscription of the music) and the effect of the record player's stylus (the 'reader' of such writing) on them, specifically in relation to the impact of these two factors on the music to which the Club's members are listening. The very first paragraph of chapter 10 mentions 'un disco viejo con un áspero fondo de púa, un raspar crujir crepitar incesantes' (Cortázar 2007: 168) ('an old record with a deep needle-scratch, an incessant scratch rasp scrape', 1966: 40), and similar descriptions abound thereafter: there is 'un adagio de Mozart que ya casi no se podía escuchar de puro arruinado que estaba el disco' (2007: 176) ('an adagio from Mozart that could barely be heard because the record was in such bad shape', 1966: 46), 'la crepitación de la púa' (2007: 182) ('the scratching of the needle', 1966: 52) after Satchmo's 'Don't Play Me Cheap' has finished playing, and mention of Bessie Smith's recording of 'Baby Doll' where 'la púa crepitaba horriblemente' (2007: 178) ('the needle made a terrible scratch', 1966: 48) (and the B-side 'Empty Bed Blues' is similarly affected by the fact that 'se oía chirriar la púa en el viejo disco' (2007: 179) ('the needle scratched on the old record', 1966: 48)). Moving on, Champion Jack Dupree's 'Junker's Blues' is a listening experience hindered by 'la púa [que] hacía un ruido horrible' (2007: 191) ('and the needle [that] was making a horrible noise', 1966: 59), and when Ronald puts on a record by Waring's Pennsylvanians, we are told that 'desde un chirriar terrible llegaba el tema que encantaba a Oliveira, [...] todo entre un humo de fonógrafo viejo y pésima grabación' (2007: 202) ('after a terrible scratching they reached the theme that fascinated Oliveira, [...] all wrapped up in the smoke of an old phonograph and a bad recording', 1966: 69). The result, then, is the creation, in effect, of a barrier that obstructs any clear or entirely faithful access to the 'original' and, by extension, loses any (originary, epiphanic) moment of plenitude, as is conveyed when, of Bessie Smith's 'Baby Doll' recording we are told that:

> algo empezó a moverse en lo hondo como capas y capas de algodones entre la voz y los oídos, Bessie cantando con la cara vendada, metida en un canasto de ropa sucia, y la voz salía cada vez más ahogada. (2007: 178)[8]
>
> [something began to move down deeper as if there were layers and layers of cotton between voice and ears, Bessie singing with a bandaged face, stuck in a hamper of soiled clothes, and her voice got more and more muffled.] (1966: 48)

And it is through such an understanding that we can approach the most significant of Cortázar's textual engagements with recording and records, in 'El perseguidor'. During one of the sessions in Paris, we are told that Johnny produced a performance of the piece 'Amorous', commonly taken as a reference to Charlie Parker's 'Lover Man',[9] that attained the sort of heights with which we are concerned. Art Boucaya, a member of the Johnny's quintet, describes Johnny having played in a way that 'no había oído jamás' (1970d: 136) ('I'd never heard before or since', 2013: 211), ending in 'un soplido capaz de arruinar la misma armonía celestial' (1970d: 136) ('a blast [capable of] split[ting] the fuckin' celestial harmonies', 2013: 211), a line which conveys the notion of a rending apart of the sense of an ordered and readily-understandable world. Johnny vehemently opposes the existence of the recording of his performance of 'Amorous' and demands the disc be destroyed. In Bruno's narration this appears to be because Johnny considered the piece to be of poor quality ('lo primero que dijo Johnny fue que todo había salido como el diablo, y que esa grabación no contaba para nada' (1970d: 136) [the first thing Johnny said was that it had been terrible, that that recording counted for nothing]). Yet it is notable that what counts for nothing is, Johnny says, not the solo, not the performance, but, very specifically, the recording, that is, that which inscribes what was glimpsed in the playing within a system of *différance*, of repeated representation, and thus entailing its negation. Indeed, in this sense it is highly significant that Bruno should inform us that the recording of 'Amorous' was released 'justo cuando la segunda edición de mi libro entraba en prensa' (179) ('just as the second edition of my book went to press', 2013: 244). We are invited to see disc and book (a second edition, we might note, which is an exact repetition of the first, left 'tal cual' (1970d: 179) ('as was', 2013: 244)) as essentially synonymous in form and consequence.

And yet this alignment of record and written text also points to a more fundamental implication here: one of Derrida's principal arguments, as set out, for example, in 'Signature Event Context' (1982 [1972]: 307–30) is that iterability is not reserved just for writing; it is a condition of language *per se*, written and oral. In other words, the insistence on the problematic iterability of records in Cortázar's texts points to an underlying problematic of musical expression *tout court*. Bringing this present discussion together with my analysis of the temporal concerns found in the story, we can thus nuance the argument that I discerned in 'Soledad de la música' regarding the unfurling of jazz (improvisation) in time as an entry into essentially linguistic operations and processes. Put simply, this move is, in fact, on the one hand, an essential part of jazz's potential power: it allows jazz to work towards ecstatic, timeless moments; but it also carries with it the inevitable 'failure' of the music to achieve its temporal dislocation in any *sustainable* form, since a putative sustaining of such a dislocation — for example by recording it — would disclose that the music was (always already) bound by iterability, an inherent characteristic on whose disavowal jazz is (for Cortázar) predicated. Jazz, that is, must constantly flee that which it pursues.

Collapsing Boundaries

What is clear from the discussion above is the extent to which the endless forward-momentum of jazz is intimately entwined with Johnny's extra-linguistic and necessarily frustratingly fleeting glimpses of something other. And it is within these terms that we can understand Bruno's more general presentation of Johnny's jazz as standing in opposition to tired form(ulation)s of apparent satisfaction and attainment: Johnny's is a 'jazz [que] desecha todo erotismo fácil, todo wagnerianismo por decirlo así, [...] una música que no facilita los orgasmos ni las nostalgias' (Cortázar 1970d: 133) [jazz [that] casts aside all facile eroticism, all Wagnerism, so to speak, [...] a music that does not provoke orgasms or nostalgia]. The two central examples offered here of nostalgia and facile eroticism are not aleatory, and each serves both to problematise and to lead beyond the superficially simple point being made regarding (Johnny's) jazz's supposed constant advance and refusal to double back on itself. I shall return to the issue of nostalgia within the context of Cortázar's jazz in chapter 6.

Turning to chapters 10–18 of *Rayuela*, we see that eroticism and sexual contact generally are present on a number of occasions. Here, however, in contrast to the lines cited from 'El perseguidor' above, far from eschewing 'todo erotismo fácil' [all facile eroticism], the jazz played at the *discada* is often portrayed in terms which render it highly erotic. Most notable in this regard are the description of Louis Armstrong's recording of 'Don't Play Me Cheap' in chapter 13 and the depiction of the effect of the Duke Ellington track 'The Blues with a Feeling' on the couples dancing to it in chapter 17:

> la llamarada de la trompeta, el falo amarillo rompiendo el aire y gozando con avances y retrocesos y [...] entonces la eyaculación de un sobreagudo resbalando y cayendo como un cohete en la noche sexual. (Cortázar 2007: 182)

> [the trumpet's flaming up, the yellow phallus breaking the air and having fun, coming forward and drawing back and [...] then the supersharp ejaculation slipping and falling like a rocket in the sexual night.] (1966: 51–52)

> alguien ha puesto *The blues with a feeling* y casi no se baila, solamente se está de pie, balanceándose, y todo es turbio y sucio y canalla y cada hombre quisiera arrancar esos corpiños tibios mientras las manos acarician una espalda y las muchachas tienen la boca entreabierta y se van dando al miedo delicioso y a la noche, entonces sube una trompeta poseyéndolas por todos los hombres, tomándolas con una sola frase caliente. (2007: 203)[10]

> [someone has put on *The Blues with a Feeling* and hardly anybody is really dancing, just standing up together, swaying back and forth, and everything is hazy and dirty and lowdown and every man is in a mood to tear off those warm girdles as his hands go stroking shoulders and the girls have their mouths half-opened and turn themselves over to delightful fear and the night, while a trumpet comes on to possess them in the name of all men, taking them with a single hot phrase.] (1966: 70)

They are passages, moreover, that echo lines from the earlier 'Louis, enormísimo cronopio', where, in his description of a Satchmo concert, Cortázar includes references to the musicians playing their instruments as if the latter were naked women (1970c: 17, cited in chapter 4). And they pre-empt the terms in which Cortázar refers to hot jazz in interview with Picon Garfield as 'una especie de música estática, música orgiástica como un climax [*sic*]; es un orgasmo en música' (1981: 128–29) [a type of static music, orgiastic music, like a climax; it's an orgasm in music].

Certainly from a modern perspective, these passages could be described as engaging in a facile, or hackneyed, machista eroticism. But we must also take care to consider the broader point being alluded to by such references, that is, the notion of the coupling or unifying of man and woman in the erotic act, with its implication of a collapsing of binaries into oneness. This is suggested more subtly in a further example cited in chapter 13, just before the passage from that chapter quoted above. Here, Armstrong's 'Don't Play Me Cheap' weaves and twists itself into the scene before us (and into the writing of it), awakening sexual and sensual feelings and contact between Ronald and Babs that, it is implied, would otherwise have remained dormant:

> Babs se retorcía en las rodillas de Ronald, excitada por la manera de cantar de Satchmo, el tema era lo bastante vulgar para permitirse libertades que Ronald no le hubiera consentido cuando Satchmo cantaba *Yellow Dog Blues*, y porque en el aliento que Ronald le estaba echando en la nuca había una mezcla de vodka y sauerkraut que titilaba espantosamente a Babs. (Cortázar 2007: 181)

> [Babs wiggled on Ronald's knees, excited by Satchmo's style of singing, the theme was vulgar enough to let her take liberties which Ronald would never condone when Satchmo sang the *Yellow Dog Blues*, and because in the breath that Ronald was blowing on the back of her neck there was a mixture of vodka and sauerkraut that aroused Babs fantastically.] (1966: 51)

The music provokes such contact, but the lines of connection are blurred and imprecise, further contributing to the sense that the effect and nature of jazz is not about simple cause and effect logic, but about the evocation and creation of something altogether less tangible and rational.

At times, this is also the case more widely in these chapters from *Rayuela*, as the scene laid before us — one centred around the playing of jazz records, let us not forget — is presented as bringing about a more general rapprochement with an essential and desired sense of being: in chapter 11, for example, Gregorovius comments that 'aquí todo respira, un contacto perdido se restab[l]ece; la música ayuda, el vodka, la amistad' (2007: 170) ('here everything breathes, a lost contact is established again; music helps, vodka, friendship', 1966: 42). Towards the end of this series of chapters, however, the role of jazz in bringing about such unity and contact is stated more explicitly. Thus, echoing the reference to breathing in the earlier, more nebulous depiction, Cortázar talks in chapter 16 of 'esa atmósfera donde la música aflojaba las resistencias y [t]ejía como una respiración común, la paz de un solo enorme corazón latiendo para todos, asumiéndolos a todos' (2007: 195) ('that atmosphere where the music was breaking down resistance and was weaving everything into a kind of common breathing, the peace of [a single] enormous heart beating for all, drawing them all into itself', 1966: 64), before the following chapter gives us the clearest and most sustained commentary on jazz's power and capabilities in Cortázar's *œuvre*. Here, a number of grand claims for jazz are made, with many being focused around this idea of a unity — a universality even — grounded in a centre which, like the 'solo enorme corazón' ('[single] enormous heart'), comes to determine and subsume everything and everyone. Jazz is:

la única música universal del siglo, algo que acercaba a los hombres más y mejor que el esperanto, la Unesco o las aerolíneas, una música bastante primitiva para alcanzar universalidad y bastante buena para hacer su propia historia [...], una música que permitía reconocerse y estimarse en Copenhague como en Mendoza o en Ciudad del Cabo, que acercaba a los adolescentes con sus discos bajo el brazo, que les daba nombres y melodías como cifras para reconocerse y adentrarse y sentirse menos solos [...]: una nube sin fronteras, un espía del aire y del agua, una forma arquetípica, algo de antes, de abajo, que reconcilia mexicanos con noruegos y rusos y españoles, los reincorpora al oscuro fuego central olvidado, torpe y mal y precariamente los devuelve a un origen traicionado. (2007: 202; 204)

[the [...] only [...] universal music of the century [...], something that brought people closer together and in a better way than Esperanto, UNESCO, or airlines, a music which was primitive enough to have gained such universality and good enough to make its own history [...], a music that could be known and liked in Copenhagen as well as in Mendoza or Capetown, a music that brings adolescents together, with records under their arms, that gives them names and melodies to use as passwords so they can know each other and become intimate and feel less lonely [...]: a cloud without frontiers, a spy of air and water, an archetypal form, something from before, from below, that brings Mexicans together with Norwegians and Russians and Spaniards, brings them back into that obscure and forgotten central flame, clumsily and badly and precariously [it] delivers them back to a betrayed origin.] (1966: 69; 70)

These are, unsurprisingly, amongst the most commented-on lines regarding jazz that Cortázar set out on paper, and they draw upon several aspects of the primary themes and concerns of his that I have analysed and in regard to which we have seen Cortázar's engagement with music to operate and, arguably, to be predicated. Perhaps most obviously, there is the clear focus on a more platonic version of the aforementioned erotic coming together. The universality depicted is one essentially built around the idea of community and solidarity: echoing the concerns of 'Soledad de la música', jazz here is described as making 'adolescentes' ('adolescents') feel 'menos solos' ('less lonely'), apparently by providing them — and people generally — with markers with which they can identify. And in this regard, Cortázar suggests, jazz is more successful than linguistic, political, and modern technological attempts at such a bringing together of people. Indeed, this characteristic of jazz's power is further suggested by the manuscript version of this passage, where in place of the word 'algo' ('something') in the line 'algo que acercaba a los hombres' ('something that brought people closer together'), Cortázar had originally written 'el santo y seña de una innegable fraternidad' (1982: 2) [the password to an undeniable fraternity].

Strongly bound up with this statement of unity and universality, that is, of a coming together of individuals in a sort of unified humanity, is the idea of the breaking of boundaries and barriers that bring about separation, here between both individuals and nations. The statements to this effect in the passage cited above are clear, but they must be understood not just as declarations of human identity and identification that go beyond national and ethnic lines, but as manifestations of Cortázar's wider concern for the collapsing of more abstract and theoretical boundaries that pertain to the issues of language and categorisation. Indications of this are found at several points in chapter 17, from the reference to 'una nube sin fronteras' ('a cloud without frontiers') to the descriptions of jazz as a 'saltabarreras' and a 'burlaaduanas' (2007: 204) ('roadblock jumper', 'smuggler', 1966: 70). This is a reinvocation and a reassertion of the claims made for jazz by Cortázar in 'Soledad de la música' and other early essays, where jazz collapses the barriers of linguistic (and other musical) expression.

Moving outside the confines of these particular passages, a closer look at certain aspects of both the *discada* scene in *Rayuela* and 'El perseguidor' discloses the importance of this 'jazz move' of dismantling or overcoming the divisions and barriers of language and, one might add, the norms of Western thought, reason, and logic (one recalls the persistent rejection of rational explanation found in these jazz-focused texts). One of the most notable sections of 'El perseguidor' is Johnny's discourse on his perception of reality and the world as full of holes, holes which are normally covered over and hidden by the operations of language found in words (and the same holes that we saw the author-narrator(s) of 'Tango de vuelta' to want to fill in as they constructed their narrative in chapter 3):

> no había más que fijarse un poco, sentirse un poco, callarse un poco, para descubrir los agujeros. En la puerta, en la cama: agujeros. En la mano, en el diario, en el tiempo, en el aire: todo lleno de agujeros [...]. [V]ienen las palabras... No, no son las palabras, son lo que está en las palabras, esa especie de cola de pegar, esa baba. Y la baba viene y te tapa. (Cortázar 1970d: 141; 143)
>
> [you only had to concentrate a [bit], feel a [bit], be quiet for a [...] bit, to find the holes. In the door, in the bed: holes. In the hand, in the newspaper, in time, in the air: everything full of holes [...]. [T]he words come... No, not words, but what's in the words, a kind of glue, that slime. And the slime comes and covers you.] (2013: 215; 216)

Such a description ties in with the notion of the barrier of words, the façade of reality that we have accepted and continue to accept as 'real', precisely the dividing wall, the 'muro de palabras' (Cortázar 2007: 531) ('wall [...] of words', 1966: 370) depicted in chapter 66 of *Rayuela*, which Cortázar wants to open gaps in and, potentially, dismantle.[11] And that *Johnny* is uttering this intrinsically ties such a discourse to jazz and its possibilities. Indeed, it is noteworthy in this respect that in chapter 13 of *Rayuela* we read of 'el silencio que ha[y] en toda música verdadera' (2007: 182) ('the silence there [is] in all true music', 1966: 52), a reminder of the important potential role of silence that we saw emerge from my discussion of Cortázar's early texts, itself bound up with the silent word to which poetry, *à la* Rimbaud, aspires. And whilst it may not be possible to conceive of 'una música sin sonidos' (1992: 291) [a music without sounds], these later discussions around jazz's potential nonetheless underline Cortázar's notion of silence in the essay 'Rimbaud' as 'el ápice que toca ya la música' (2006a: 142) [the zenith that music touches], clearly lending itself to an interpretation that calls upon the idea of the momentary glimpses (gaps, holes) that, according to Cortázar, jazz affords.

Perhaps more significant still in this regard is the appearance in both 'El perseguidor' and *Rayuela* of a key reference to vomiting. In the latter text, we are told at the end of chapter 12 that 'por lo común después de los discos le [a Oliveira] venían ganas de vomitar' (Cortázar 2007: 180) ('usually after [the records] he [Oliveira] would feel like vomiting', 1966: 50), whereas in the former, Bruno informs us that 'en el fondo *Amorous* me ha dado ganas de vomitar' (Cortázar 1970d: 149) ('[deep down], *Amorous* made me want to go vomit', 2013: 221). These two incidents can be seen to represent examples of the abject as developed by Julia Kristeva in her seminal work *Powers of Horror: An Essay on Abjection* (1982 [1980]). For Kristeva, the abject occurs where the distinction between subject and object falls away, 'where meaning collapses' (2); it is caused by 'what disturbs identity, system, order. What does not respect borders, positions, rules. The in-between, the ambiguous, the composite' (4); it is located prior to language and takes the individual back to before the entry into the Imaginary order, which is to say, prior to the mirror stage in Jacques Lacan's thought: 'abjection preserves what existed in the archaism of pre-objectal relationship' (Kristeva 1982: 10).[12] The response to this, which is also what constitutes the abject, is a repetition of the primal rejection, the moment when self separated from other, and vomiting is one of the principal ways in which Kristeva describes this as manifesting itself. Thus, the act of vomiting can be seen both as a moment where the boundary between inside and outside is dissolved, reflecting the general idea of the abject as having to do with the 'eras[ure] [of] borders' (4), and also as the rejection of that breakdown as the moment of separation is re-enacted. Seen through this framework, the two incidents of vomiting in 'El perseguidor' and *Rayuela* respectively serve to bind the jazz to which they are a response to precisely the sort of breakdown of meaning, collapse of differences, and pre-lingual operation that Cortázar sees this music as evoking and evincing. That is, whilst Kristeva sees great literature as 'unfold[ing] over [the] terrain' where '"subject" and "object" push each other away, confront each other, collapse, [...] at the boundary of what is assimilable, thinkable: abject' (1982: 18), Cortázar's texts here suggest that it is, rather, jazz where this is most strikingly the case.

Given these considerations, it is not surprising that the long passage cited above from chapter 17 of *Rayuela* should invoke references to the idea of origins ('forma arquetípica' ('archetypal form'); 'origen traicionado' ('betrayed origin')) and a centre ('oscuro fuego central olvidado' ('obscure and forgotten central flame')). Such terms underscore the extent to which jazz is being presented as a (re)engagement with the pre-linguistic, the semiotic — something emphasised by the sexual and erotic allusions —, or, to put it in more Derridean terms, with the sort of centre beyond the play of language, or *différance*, that I examined in relation to 'Clone'. This is explored in more detailed fashion in chapter 12, where the role of jazz in leading to such a location is brought to the fore, as we read of 'un centro, si era un centro, [...] excentrarlo [a Oliveira] así para mostrarle mejor un centro, excentrarlo hacia un centro sin embargo inconcebible' (2007: 180) ('a center, if it was a center, [...] to excentrate him [Oliveira] like this the better to show him a center, to excentrate him towards a center which was nonetheless inconceivable', 1966: 49–50). In pointing to both centre and origin, then, jazz is bound up with an end to separation and differences, and this is key to the association of this reality that jazz offers with freedom: it is a freedom from barriers, walls, and language. Indeed, this is stressed in the manuscript version of chapter 17, where this connection — under erasure — is rendered evident as we read of 'un origen donde la libertad traicionado' (Cortázar 1982: 2) [a betrayed origin where freedom].

Yet this link between freedom and the collapsing of linguistic, personal, and cultural differences also poses a challenge to Cortázar's engagement with jazz, in that it stands in contrast to the importance we have seen his work to give to the sociohistorical origins of the music and his insistence on black (improvisational) jazz as being 'true' or 'authentic' jazz. In short, these passages from *Rayuela* run the risk of writing out cultural difference and cultural identity *per se*, and are thus ethically somewhat problematic. Indeed, there is a striking explicitness about lines that talk of jazz as 'algo absolutamente indiferente a los ritos nacionales, a las tradiciones inviolables, al idioma y al folklore' (Cortázar 2007: 204) ('something completely beyond national ritual, sacred traditions, language and folklore', 1966: 70). One can only wonder how Satchmo, in reference to whom, at least in part, these words are written, would have responded to this suggestion, bearing in mind that this is the jazz artist who performed such profoundly socially and historically charged tracks as 'Go Down Moses' and '(What Did I Do to Be So) Black and Blue?'.[13]

This potential problem is signalled by Baraka in 'Jazz and the White Critic'. We have already seen how he talks of the need to understand the attitude and sociocultural philosophy and context of (black) jazz musicians, rather than 'strip[ping] the music too ingenuously of its social and cultural intent' (2010: 18), yet that is precisely the implication of the central presentation of jazz found in the *discada* chapters of *Rayuela*. Indeed, even in 'El perseguidor', although Cortázar brings in a number of biographical and socioeconomic details from the life story of Charlie Parker into this text,[14] Johnny's thought-contortions are the primary way in which Cortázar presents Johnny (Charlie) to us, and, whereas Parker was, as Mark Couture notes, a thoughtful, well-read man, with a 'relentless, obsessive curiosity' (2016: 8), the metaphysical considerations found in these passages in 'El perseguidor', concerning reality, life, and death, via discussions of holes in the fabric of reality (Cortázar 1970d: 141) or fields of burial urns filled with ashes (139–40), imply a similar overlaying of broad (Cortázarian) philosophical and universalising concerns onto Johnny's (Charlie's) jazz. Beyond the possiblity of this being construed as an example of the white appropriation of black American music, one bound up with an implicit sense of the broader, universal questions raised by Parker's music only being fully grasped by the white author (Cortázar), even if this is disavowed by placing such an idea in the story in the mouth of the ethically-challenged Bruno ('Johnny obsesionado por algo que su pobre inteligencia no alcanza a entender pero que flota lentamente en su música' (Cortázar 1970d: 130) ('Johnny obsessed by something that his [limited] intelligence was not equal to comprehending, but which floats slowly [in] his music', 2013: 206)), this aspect of 'El perseguidor' also opens up Cortázar to the plausible charge of engaging in what James O. Young terms 'subject appropriation', that is, where 'another culture *or some of its members*' (2008: 7, italics mine) are appropriated.

That being said, there is still a clear contrast between the central focus of the *discada* scene in *Rayuela* and that of 'El perseguidor' in regard to the way in which they present the potential of and possibilities for jazz. In broad terms, *Rayuela* focuses on the value of jazz as a universal and universalising force, marshalling a heady number of different jazz musicians and, to an extent, styles in the service of such a principle, and thus, in the process, giving further support to such a universalising ethos and sensibility; 'El perseguidor', on the other hand, whilst posing questions on a similarly overarching human level, is notable for its focus on the individual, not just in the sense that it concentrates on a single jazz musician, but also in formulating its broad questions as part of an individual search, be it that of Johnny or Bruno.[15] In short, the fundamental questions of being that go hand in hand with a notion of human brotherhood and solidarity in *Rayuela* are here depicted in the context of a personal struggle and questioning on the part of an individual human being. Indeed, the reference to Johnny's 'soberana indiferencia' (Cortázar 1970d: 139) [sovereign indifference] and to his being 'solo, completamente solo' (143) [alone, completely alone] render explicit the solitude and self-withdrawal that seep through the entire story.

And yet, despite this contrast, the different presentations found in the two pieces of Cortázar's fiction with which we are presently concerned can also be reconciled within the context of his fiction through a shared characteristic, in that both are bound up with the idea of totalisation, of an envisaged all-encompassing subsumption. That such a move is incorporated into *Rayuela*'s universalising jazz ethic is made particularly explicit in the reference to 'un solo enorme corazón latiendo para todos, asumiéndolos a todos' (2007: 195) ('[a single] enormous heart beating for all, drawing them all into itself', 1966: 64). In 'El perseguidor', on the other hand, it is connoted by the alignment of Johnny on the part of Bruno with Christ. This aspect of the story has been commented on by many critics,[16] and is a repeated feature of the text, from the early reference to how '[Johnny] tocaba como yo creo que solamente un dios puede tocar un saxo alto' (1970d: 102) ('[Johnny] played like I imagine only a god can play an alto sax', 2013: 184–85) to the description towards the end of how, as he was helping Johnny to his feet, people were looking at him 'como miraría la gente a alguien que se trepara a un altar y tironeara de Cristo para sacarlo de la cruz' (1970d: 160) ('as if they were looking at someone climbing up on the altar to tug Christ down from the cross', 2013: 229). This divine alignment clearly carries with it an allusion — inadvertent or not — both to the idea of an all-encompassing deity and to the more specifically Christian idea of the Christ-figure as the one who redeems and saves humankind and to whom each person must give him or herself. The latter point is further suggested in 'Louis, enormísimo cronopio', where Cortázar strongly implies a Christological understanding of Louis Armstrong, as he declares, notably in a tripartite structure, 'Louis cronopio, Louis enormísimo cronopio, Louis alegría de los hombres que te merecen' (1970c: 22) [Louis *cronopio*, Louis enormous *cronopio*, Louis joy of those who deserve you]. Moreover, if the divine and Christological allusions — with their implied pantheism — are not enough to convey the totalising nature of Bruno's depiction of Johnny, then we only have to note that the story is also replete with references to Johnny as a 'pobre diablo' (1970d: 180) [poor devil] too.[17] All bases are covered.

In an additional nod to this structural schematic of the central self envisaged as subsuming all that surrounds it, it is striking that 'El perseguidor' includes a series of more celestial references that are taken up in the later 'Reunión', 'Clone', and the essay 'Algunos aspectos del cuento'. Pre-empting the employment of star/planet imagery in 'Reúnión' and 'Clone' to describe a central (revolutionary, musical) figure in particular, in 'El perseguidor' we see two mentions of a star, each of which is associated with Johnny, either explicitly, as when Bruno expresses his desire for Johnny's demise in terms of being 'como una estrella que se rompe en mil pedazos' (1970d: 127) [like a star that bursts into a thousand pieces], or more implicitly, as with Johnny's citing of Revelation 8.11, when he repeatedly declares, 'el nombre de la estrella es Ajenjo' (167) [the name of the star is Wormwood], a star whose fall to Earth is occasioned when, we read in Revelation 8.10, 'The third angel blew his trumpet.' More significantly, though, and foreshadowing more neatly the imagery that would emerge in 'Clone', Bruno elsewhere talks of Johnny (and other such jazzmen) in planetary terms, where other people (women, Bruno himself) would be moons circling around him:

> Las mujeres se pasan la vida dando vueltas alrededor de Johnny y de los que son como Johnny. No es extraño, no es necesario ser mujer para sentirse atraído por Johnny. Lo difícil es girar en torno a él sin perder la distancia, como un buen satélite, un buen crítico. (Cortázar 1970d: 150–51)

> [Women spend their whole lives circling around Johnny and people like Johnny. It's not weird, it's not necessary to be a woman to feel attracted to Johnny. What's hard is to circle about him and not lose your distance, like a good satellite, like a good critic.] (2013: 222)

The difficult task described here is also one which is, applying the closest astronomical metaphor, ultimately a vain one: just as Earth's moon is destined to be subsumed into its planet's being, spiralling down to and fusing with its mass, so too does the image here act as a cipher for Johnny's subsuming pull.[18]

Although I have been talking in terms of the jazz figures at stake here, it is important to note that, just as proves to be the case with Gesualdo and his madrigals, it is as much the music that these jazzmen play which is portrayed in both the *discada* of *Rayuela* and 'El perseguidor' as being that which draws in all that surrounds it. In both cases, the jazz music that forms the basis of the narratives, as we noted briefly in relation to the erotic play between Ronald and Babs, imbues, infuses, and infects those narratives, on the level of plot, character, and the very nature and structure of the text we are reading. Thus, in the relevant chapters in *Rayuela*, the music from the records winds its way round the scenes being described, fusing with the events and feelings of the characters, intertwining with the very prose we are reading, and becoming one with the voice of la Maga, as we are told that Big Bill Broonzy 'les hablaría de otra barricada con la misma voz con que la Maga le estaría contando a Gregorovius su infancia en Montevideo' (Cortázar 2007:

191) ('would tell them about another barricade with the same voice that La Maga was using to tell Gregorovius about her childhood in Montevideo', 1966: 59).[19] And the extent to which the jazz imposes itself on and determines both the text and the narrative becomes increasingly apparent as titles and lyrics (in English) merge with and dominate the latter:

> Un blues, René Daumal, Horacio Oliveira, but you gotta die some day, you so beautiful but — Y por eso Gregorovius insistía en conocer el pasado de la Maga, [...] para fijarla en su propio tiempo, you so beautiful but you gotta, para no amar a un fantasma [...]. Y de golpe, con una desapasionada perfección, Earl Hines proponía la primera variación de *I ain't got nobody*, y hasta Perico, perdido en una lectura remota, alzaba la cabeza. (2007: 196)

> [A blues song, René Daumal, Horacio Oliveira, but you gotta die some day, you so beautiful but — And that's why Gregorovius insisted on knowing about La Maga's past, [...] so as to put her in her own time, you so beautiful but you gotta, so as not to love a ghost [...]. And suddenly with cool perfection, Earl Hines was giving his first variation of *I Ain't Got Nobody*, and even Perico, lost in some remote reading, lifted up his head.] (1966: 64–65)

Turning to 'El perseguidor', the creeping control of the text by the bebop jazz of Johnny Carter/Charlie Parker has drawn the attention of numerous critics.[20] On a basic level, the writing/jazz, self/other binary that the story apparently sets up is immediately problematised by the fact that the principal 'text' around which the story revolves, that is, Bruno's biography of Johnny, is entirely absent from the narrative in any direct form. What we have instead is what we might loosely, albeit unsatisfactorily, call the 'confessional' text by Bruno that we are reading, a text whose status and purpose is never clear and which is replete with logical aporia and inconsistencies, but whose 'jazz' nature has been frequently commented on.[21] Peris Blanes, for example, sees in this text the structure and characteristics of a bebop improvisation, arguing that, in the working and reworking of the same ideas, approached from different angles, the text's structure tries to 'traducir a la mecánica literaria el funcionamiento musical del *bebop*' (2011: 80) [translate the musical workings of bebop to the mechanics of literature].[22] Similar comments have been made by other scholars writing on the story, though often focusing more on textual details than overarching structure. Valentine, for example, comments on how, despite apparently representing and holding to a different perception of time from Johnny:

> Nevertheless, Bruno achieves success in duplicating the rhythms of jazz. Johnny is analyzed in a repetitious fashion throughout the story in a series of probings from different angles with new combinations of words, analogous to variations of the same theme in jazz, an application of Johnny's art to the story's form. (1974: 177)

Lanin A. Gyurko, meanwhile, notes that, like Johnny, Bruno displays fleeting moments of clarity and vision, where 'the supreme irony [...] is that the critic cannot sustain these moments, cannot translate them into meaningful action to remedy the distortion of Johnny that he is perpetuating' (1980: 219). The most sustained analysis along these lines, however, is found in Sommer's two similar articles from the late 1990s (1995; 1998). Her opening gambit lies in analysing the insistent use of the present perfect on the part of Bruno in the text we are reading as being 'a structural feature of [his] writing[,] [...] as if the writing refused to fit into time, the conventional grammatical time that opposes past to present in neat, mutually exclusive categories' (1995: 28). Clearly, given what we have examined in relation to the time thematic, this in itself hints at the notion of the jazzification of Bruno's writing, and Sommer goes on to develop this line, referring to how 'Bruno is also given to the kind of cramming, overpacking, and overloading so characteristic of bebop and of Johnny's particular speculations about music and time. [...] He squeezes words into his paragraphs like bebop squeezes notes into a melody' (35). In short, 'El perseguidor' constitutes the encroachment of jazz onto the very language and writing of the text before us. Indeed, the extent of this 'contamination' is evident in Bruno's reference to how 'cuando la marquesa echa a hablar uno se pregunta si el estilo de Dizzy [Gillespie] no se le ha pegado al idioma, pues es una serie interminable de variaciones en los registros más inesperados' (Cortázar 1970d: 124) [when the marquesa starts talking, you wonder if Dizzy [Gillespie]'s style has stamped itself on her language, it's such an interminable series of variations in the most unexpected registers]. Both within the text and on the level of the text, 'El perseguidor' presents a process whereby jazz appropriates, subsumes, and totalises the language of those who are putatively established as being in contrast to Johnny's flights of bebop improvisation.

Within the context of the ethical considerations signalled by the Barakian framework that I have been drawing upon, this appropriation of the text by jazz in both the *discada* in *Rayuela* and 'El perseguidor' lends itself to being seen as a move of resistance against the purloining of jazz by the white critic, or, in this case, the white author, in the interests of a universalising philosophical questioning that writes out the sociocultural specificity of the music. Conversely, it could also be considered to constitute — or to provide a potential model for — just the sort of transformation of literature Cortázar argued for in his early essays and texts, as I examined in the Introduction to this study, musicalising or poeticising the written, literary forms and language at stake. Again, the absence of the more 'normal' and putatively published text — the biography — in 'El perseguidor' would point towards such a contention. And yet, without precluding such readings, it is hard to ignore the ethically problematic nature and consequences of the apparently totalising move with which we are presented in these two Cortazarian works, pre-empting the disturbingly homogenising overtones of cloning invoked by the later 'Clone', even if it is the more affirmative jazz that is at the heart of this operation here. It is significant, then, that, as I shall now examine, a closer inspection of 'El perseguidor' reveals a resistance to such a move in Cortázar's writing.

As a number of critics have pointed out, the similarities between Johnny and Bruno in the story are not simply a question of, or reducible to, the latter's language, writing, and mind being taken over by the jazzistic questioning and improvisations of the former.[23] Certainly, Bruno, as well as writing in a manner that might be termed 'jazzistic', engages with and submits to a questioning of reality and himself that replicates that of Johnny, and much of our own insight into the latter's struggles and nature and the way in which these fit into Cortázar's broader philosophy comes from the biographer ('Johnny es [...] una realidad entre las irrealidades que somos todos nosotros' (Cortázar 1970d: 146) ('Johnny is [...] [a] reality among the unrealities that are the rest of us', 2013: 219)). Bruno grasps his and society's falseness and hypocrisy, whilst simultaneously displaying such characteristics:

> no puedo impedirme un mal gusto en la boca, una cólera que no va contra Johnny ni contra las cosas que le ocurren; más bien contra mí y la gente que lo rodea, la marquesa y Marcel, por ejemplo. En el fondo somos una banda de egoístas [...]. El fracaso de Johnny sería malo para mi libro. (1970d: 129–30)
>
> [I can't help having a bad taste in my mouth, anger, not against Johnny nor the things that happen to him; rather against the people who hang around him, myself, the marquesa and Marcel, for example. Basically we're a bunch of egotists [...]. If Johnny zonked it would be bad for my book.] (2013: 206)

And on occasion he reveals a stark alignment with the mindset and approach-to-being of the jazz saxophonist, not least in his rejection of understanding, such as when he states that 'no necesito buscarle explicaciones cuando lo siento tan claramente como puedo sentir la nariz pegada a la cara' (1970d: 151–52) ('I don't need to look for explanations when I can feel it as clearly as the nose on my face', 2013: 223). At the same time, however, the text is replete with Johnny's often lengthy expositions of his ideas and concerns, not just in language, but in a language that frequently exhibits a distinct and highly-developed use of rhetorical devices. An example in point is the passage to which I referred earlier, where Johnny is describing the holes in, or porosity of, reality (or of reality's façade), a porosity that, through convention, a refusal to challenge societal and human assumptions, and language, people fail to see:[24]

> no había más que fijarse un poco, sentirse un poco, callarse un poco, para descubrir agujeros. En la puerta, en la cama: agujeros. En la mano, en el diario, en el tiempo, en el aire: todo lleno de agujeros, todo esponja, todo como un colador colándose a sí mismo... (1970d: 141)
>
> [you only had to concentrate a [bit], feel a [bit], be quiet for a [...] bit, to find the holes. In the door, in the bed: holes. In the hand, in the newspaper, in time, in the air: everything full of holes, everything spongy, [everything] like a [strainer] straining itself...] (2013: 215)

Despite its implied rejection of orthodox and civilised façades, it is a passage which uses the rhetorical 'rule of three' to a significant degree: in the first sentence ('fijarse un poco, sentirse un poco, callarse un poco' ('concentrate a [bit], feel a [bit], be quiet for a [...] bit'), where we also see an effective use of asyndeton and epistrophe; in the further epistrophe of 'agujeros' ('holes'); and in the final sentence, which uses the last of the three 'agujeros' ('holes') as a fulcrum for the tripartite anaphora with which this cited passage ends. In addition, there is also the 'incremental' anaphora of 'en la/el' ('in the') (with, notably, three consecutive constructions of each gender) and the alliteration of the common-derivative pairing 'colador colándose' ('[strainer] straining itself'). Such linguistic flourish combines with what Sommer has noted regarding 'Johnny's capacity for intellectual speculation being more than equal to Bruno's' (1995: 32) in, for example, the fact that 'Johnny does more than merely quote lines from Dylan Thomas; he glosses them[,] [...] extrapolat[ing] on the general arbitrariness of signs' (32) to make clear that the story before us is working to bring the two protagonists together in more significant and complete ways than one might initially suspect. For Sommer, 'Cortázar is evidently deconstructing the difference between Bruno's intellectual work and Johnny's artistic genius' (31), but, with one eye on the way in which, as Robin William Fiddian demonstrates (1985), the story also brings together angels and devils, God and Satan, in its portrayal of *both* protagonists, we might expand such a conclusion to include a far wider range of aspects that are being (con)fused here: self/other, writer/musician, and, yes, language/jazz. What is more, it is, indeed, not just that the two terms of each binary are merged, but that, within each of their putative representatives (Bruno and Johnny, respectively), both terms are shown to coexist: Bruno and Johnny, it transpires, are each characterised as a cohabitation of what we might initially perceive as 'Bruno' and 'Johnny', these terms being substitutable by all of those just mentioned.

Evidently, then, not only is 'El perseguidor' very much not a text which posits a simple 'jazzification' of literature or writing; it is also one that, in a way that recalls my earlier discussion of the *figura* in 'Alguien que anda por ahí', constitutes a significant problematisation of and challenge to the idea of totalisation. Sommer comes closest to prising out the nature of this challenge when she contends that:

> The story [...] is not merely about the ultimate naiveté of binary oppositions. It is also — and most powerfully — about a refusal to overcome difference. [...] The fact that Bruno and Johnny overlap as personae and performances is no happy liberation from the tensions of difference. (1995: 37)

But I would suggest that what is ultimately at stake in 'El perseguidor' might be better encapsulated by borrowing and recasting a term used by Morelli in chapter 137 of *Rayuela* as he addresses how literature might be written in a new way, not seeking 'una suma', but 'una *resta* implacable' (Cortázar 2007: 708) ('a sum', 'an implacable *subtraction*', 1966: 526). Though usually interpreted in this context as a reference to a paring away, *resta* can also mean remainder, what is left over, surplus: an implacable surplus or remainder, then. And this gives us an indication of how 'El perseguidor', whose tensions work to frustrate a jazzistic totalisation, might be seen to offer its own particular 'take' on the relationship between writing and jazz.[25]

'El perseguidor': Translation and Tension

A starting point for exploring this 'take' is found in an element of 'El perseguidor' that has been commented on frequently but not, to my knowledge, given the centrality it deserves, namely the reiterated presence of translation. Three times in the narrative there is specific mention of the translation of Bruno's biography of Johnny into other languages. The first occurs immediately after Bruno has expressed his concern regarding the negative effect on his book should Johnny perform poorly in Paris, when the narrator informs us in an aside that '(de un momento a otro saldrá la traducción al inglés y al italiano)' (Cortázar 1970d: 130) [(any moment now the translation into English or Italian will be out)]. The third reference is found at the end of the story, as we are told that 'ya hablan de una nueva traducción, creo que al sueco o al noruego' (183) ('they're already talking of a new translation, into Swedish or Norwegian, I think', 2013: 247): with Johnny's death, the risk described earlier has dissipated, the book's success is assured, and the endless and comforting (textual) chain of language and commodified, consumerist Western society can continue. More notable, perhaps, because less commented on, is the second mention of the biography's life in translation. This arises in the context of Bruno's talking about the release of 'Amorous'. As discussed above, this event is contemporaneous with the second edition of Bruno's book's going to press, suggesting a synonymity of the essential nature of and processes involved in the production of records and texts. But the full passage here reads, 'Y *Amorous* acababa de salir en París, justo cuando la segunda edición de mi libro entraba en prensa y se hablaba de traducirlo al alemán' (1970d: 179) ('And *Amorous* had just been released in Paris, just as the second edition of my book went to press and they were talking about translating it into German', 2013: 244). What these lines point to, then, is a more significant reading of the role of translation in the story, as they hint at the inescapable presence of translation within and as part of those fundamental processes that pertain to any jazz recording or written text, and feasibly, beyond this, to any jazz or linguistic utterance *per se*. In this vein, a closer examination of 'El perseguidor' reveals a more pervasive allusion to translation, broadly defined. Gyurko remarks that, following Johnny's death, Bruno 'immediately translates the occurrence into an obituary notice for the new edition of his "biography"' (1988: 73), whilst Héctor Mario Cavallari and Graciela P. García draw attention to the text of Bruno's that we are reading as giving us a 'transcripción del lenguaje oral del músico' (1996: 275) [transcription of the oral language of the musician], that is, translating the oral 'balbuceo' (275) [babbling] into written form. On a wider scale, as Couture rightly points out, the entire text is itself a web of translation, in that 'we assume that Bruno is French [...]. We imagine that Bruno and Johnny converse in English. Bruno's biography would logically have been written in French [...]. And yet the text we are reading is in Spanish' (2016: 3). The text in our hands, that is, would be the Spanish translation of Bruno's French thoughts, Johnny's and his English dialogue, as well as the English of the various other characters and sources whom Bruno refers to and uses. One can also be reasonably sure that the English sources and conversations were first translated into French by Bruno before being translated into Spanish, assuming that it is Bruno who is writing the Spanish text before us, as opposed to some meta-translator who would possibly be an interlocutor of Bruno's in such a case. Taken in combination with the numerous languages into which the biography has been or is about to be translated, it is evident that this is a narrative defined in many ways by translation. Indeed, along these lines, and as Moran comments (2017: 1616), the use of the present perfect throughout almost the entire narrative, rather than constituting, as Sommer argues, a 'structural feature' (1995: 28) tied up with Johnny's own character and jazz, 'straddl[ing] between excess and inadequacy, too much time and too little' (28), may simply represent the literal translation into Spanish of the preference in spoken and non-formal written French for this verb tense over the preterite. Such a reading would fit in with the nature of this text as a less formal document than the biography, as well as going at least some way to explaining the delineation between the dialogue/inner monologue-driven body of the story and the final pages that narrate the period after Johnny's death, at which point the preterite imposes itself. More importantly, it helps draw attention to the question of the nature of translation(s): the inevitability of loss, the dangers/ consequences of loss, and the issue of what it is that the translation is most seeking to translate and transmit. In this case, is it that the translation is simply poor? Or is it that it was deemed more important to maintain the urgency of the present perfect than to adapt the French 'original' (or translation from the English) to a Spanish verbal code, an urgency that drops out with Johnny's demise?

The importance of these questions is found when we consider that the ultimate plane on which translation operates as a theme in 'El perseguidor' pertains not to languages, but to language itself, writing, and jazz. An indication of this is found in the only other appearance of a cognate of *traducir* [to translate] in the text, when Johnny complains that 'no se puede decir nada, inmediatamente lo traduces a tu sucio idioma' (Cortázar 1970d: 173) ('a man can't say anything, right away you translate it into your filthy language', 2013: 239). Discounting the possibility that Johnny has longstanding issues with the French language of which we are unaware, this line speaks of the translation of one type of language (Johnny's jazz-inflected speech) into another (Bruno's formal and 'correct' written biography). It also points towards the fact that the very nature of both the text in front of us and Johnny's reported speech within that text is, ultimately, a question of the apparent or attempted translation of (a) jazz (ethos) into writing. However, what is key here is to understand that it is not a question of jazz as the 'centre' which is somehow to be translated into the periphery that is language, the planet that the verbal satellite seeks to replicate (as we return once more to the sun/planets imagery of 'Clone'). Rather, it is about looking structurally and in broad terms — the story's own terms — at how writing and jazz are presented as elements bound up in translation. In other words, the story's extended consideration of translation, coupled with its stark, though uneasy, overlap — even blurring — between Johnny (jazz) and Bruno (writing), suggests that jazz and language (writing) are *both* to be seen as 'satellites'. And if this is the case, then, I would suggest, the centre emerges as being the implacable remainder or surplus that resists and is beyond totalisation or capture, the fleeting, unsustainable moment. (Johnny's) jazz is an attempt to translate this into music; writing — or the written text in front of us — is an attempt to translate jazz into language, where the most important element to be translated is precisely that centre that jazz glimpses, the central message, not the niceties of grammar: the writing seeks to replicate the translation that is jazz.[26] It may be, then, that the satellite of jazz is a 'better' translation than is writing, but we are reminded of Johnny's declaration that 'no es culpa tuya no haber podido escribir lo que yo tampoco soy capaz de tocar' (1970d: 171) ('it's not your fault that you couldn't write what I myself can't blow', 2013: 238).[27]

This equating of jazz and writing as examples and terrains of translation is further supported by several other lines in the story. Thus, having spoken of how Johnny's 'genio musical es como una fachada [...] que encubre otra cosa' (1970d: 131) ('musical genius is a façade [...] which conceals something else', 2013: 207), Bruno, who by this is apparently referring to Johnny's music itself as such a façade, underlines his own inability to get beyond this sonorous surface to what I have identified as the implacable remainder or, here, the *otra cosa* ('something else'), as he states that 'es fácil decirlo, mientras soy todavía la música de Johnny' (1970d: 131) ('it's easy to say it, while I'm still [...] Johnny's music', 2013: 207). Couture queries Bruno's assertion by arguing that 'Bruno, and by extension, his biography of Johnny, is not Johnny's music' (2016: 12), but I would contend that what we understand 'Bruno' to be is determined not by and as the biography that we never get to read, but by the text we are reading, with all the tensions and jazzistic overlaps by which we have seen him to be characterised. Music, (this) writing, Johnny, and Bruno are all joined together in their essential nature as façades which attempt to capture, or translate, that *otra cosa*. In this way, when Bruno, in defence of the need for critics, talks of how 'los creadores, desde el inventor de la música hasta Johnny pasando por toda la condenada serie, son incapaces de extraer las consecuencias dialécticas de su obra, postular los fundamentos y la trascendencia de lo que están *escribiendo* o *improvisando*' (Cortázar 1970d: 167, italics mine) ('the creators, from the [inventor of music] to Johnny, passing through the whole damned gradation, are incapable of extrapolating the dialectical consequences of their work, of postulating the fundamentals and the transcendency of what they're *writing down* or *improvising*', 2013: 234, italics mine), we might consider whether his words could be seen to be disclosing an equating of these two acts (writing and improvising), rather than discussing two distinct modes of creation. Indeed, moving outside of Cortázar's texts, the eminent jazz critic Larry Kart has suggested that jazz has engaged in the adoption (translation?) of certain literary forms, making specific reference to the sort of jazz/poetry connection — even synonymity — that Cortázar's work repeatedly intimates:

> the connection between jazz and literature might be that jazz has more or less spontaneously developed in the course of its life musical parallels to preexisting literary forms. I've always thought of the typical good jazz solo as being more or less a lyric poem. (Harper, Kart, and Young 1987: 133)

What all of this points towards is that the question posed, for example, by Couture, as to whether '"El perseguidor" [is] really something that can be called "jazz writing"' (2016: 2–3), or a 'jazz text' (12) is the wrong question to ask, missing the point of the text before us. The question is, rather: what does 'El perseguidor' tell us about jazz? On the surface, as it fuses, binds, and entwines language and music, 'Bruno' and 'Johnny', it appears to tell us, as we have seen, that writing, or linguistic and writing processes, are indeed involved in and bound up with jazz, and that jazz music and written text are in many ways coterminous. But the story, not least in the tension and irreducible difference between (or implacable remainder of) the different terms in play, principally for our present purposes those of jazz and writing/language, avoids a simplistic mapping or equivalency of the two. Crystalised in the example of 'Amorous', one way in which this difference plays itself out is in the persistent sense, if not affirmation, that, for all its similarities with writing and for all that it depends upon and is characterised by linguistic processes, jazz is, as I have argued, nevertheless a 'better' translation of that implacable remainder or surplus, that *otra cosa*, that it pursues but cannot sustain. And it is in this context that we can analyse how the story offers a further, and yet more profound, exploration of the nature of jazz. For in its presentation of jazz/Johnny and (and as) writing/Bruno, and writing/Bruno and (and as) jazz/Johnny, where the surplus or advantage of jazz emerges in those interstices of the text where language breaks down or in the references to Johnny's 'Amorous' performance to which the story cannot provide direct access, 'El perseguidor' offers itself as a model for the struggle and tension not just *between* jazz and writing, but as found *in* jazz itself, precisely, moreover, a characteristic of this musical genre that we have seen to be so pivotal to Cortázar's presentation and valorisation of it.

There are, I would suggest, two primary elements within the text that are helpful in illuminating this hermeneutic avenue: the mirror and the knife. Mirrors are mentioned several times in the course of the story, and, in both of the principal passages in which they appear, the mirror and one's mirror image are tied up with language. Johnny sees himself in the mirror and reacts with shock, surprise, and horror, declaring that 'realmente ese tipo no soy yo' (Cortázar 1970d: 143) ('[really], this guy's not me', 2013: 216). And yet people are taken in; they believe it is them that they see in the mirror, because the stuff of words — the condition and operation of language — convinces them of such: 'vienen las palabras... No, no son las palabras, son lo que está en las palabras, esa especie de cola de pegar, esa baba. Y la baba viene y te tapa, y te convence de que el del espejo eres tú' (1970d: 143) ('the words come... No, not words, but what's in the words, a kind of glue, that slime. And the slime comes and covers you and convinces you that's you in the mirror', 2013: 216). Further on, he describes both Bruno's book and writing (on jazz) in similar terms, stating that 'al principio yo creía que leer lo que escriben sobre uno era más o menos como mirarse a uno mismo y no en el espejo. [...], pero en realidad es como en un espejo' (1970d: 165) ('at first I thought that to read something that'd been written about you would be more or less like looking at yourself and not into a mirror [...], but in reality it's like in a mirror', 2013: 233).

It is not hard to see how these lines lend themselves to a Lacanian reading, understood through the idea of the mirror stage.[28] For Lacan, the identification with the specular image brings with it an aggressive tension, as the child is made aware of the difference between the whole image it sees and its own uncoordinated body, that is, the difference between the specular image and the subject. To resolve this tension, the subject identifies with the image, thus forming the ego (and, hence, alienating the subject from itself in the process). In Lacan's thought, this formation of the ego involves the notion of the ideal ego, which is and represents the promise of future wholeness.[29] Significantly, the mirror stage is also bound up with language. Deborah Caslav Covino, invoking Kristevan terminology, sees this as the stage when the child is introduced to the idea 'that persons and objects can be reflected back to her through representation[.] [...] [S]he begins to cross from the semiotic [...] into the symbolic' (2004: 19). Dylan Evans, however, underscores in more precise terms that the specular image (ego) is ultimately an imaginary formation that is 'structured by the symbolic order' (1996: 83). As he points out, for Lacan, language has both symbolic and imaginary aspects, where 'in its imaginary aspect, language is the "wall of language" which inverts and distorts the discourse of the Other' (83). The desire for (imaginary) wholeness, for an elimination of destabilising tension in one's conception of oneself, and the fact that this is all connected with the processes and veiling images of signification can all be read into the 'mirror lines' cited above. Johnny's rejection of the mirror (and of the text as mirror), that is, is a rejection of both language (the 'muro de palabras' (Cortázar 2007: 531) ('wall [...] of words', 1966: 370)) and illusory (and comforting) wholeness.[30, 31]

This reading is reinforced if we turn to the second motif, that of the knife. Immediately following his first discussion of mirrors, Johnny raises the issue of the act of cutting a piece of bread with a knife:

> O cortar un pedazo de pan con un cuchillo. ¿Tú has cortado un pedazo de pan con un cuchillo? [...] Y te has quedado tan tranquilo. Yo no puedo, Bruno. [...] Tienes el pan ahí, sobre el mantel [...]. Es una cosa sólida [...]. Algo que no soy yo, algo distinto, fuera de mí [...], pero lo toco con los dedos, lo siento, siento que eso es el mundo, pero si yo puedo tocarlo y sentirlo, entonces no se puede decir realmente que sea otra cosa [...]. Y yo me atrevo a tocarlo, a cortarlo en dos, a metérmelo en la boca. No pasa nada, ya sé: eso es lo terrible. [...] Cortas el pan, le clavas el cuchillo, y todo sigue como antes. Yo no comprendo, Bruno. (Cortázar 1970d: 143–44)

> [Or cut a hunk of bread with a knife. Have you ever cut a hunk of bread with a knife? [...] And you've stayed all that calm. Not me, Bruno [...]. [...] You have the loaf of bread there, on the tablecloth [...]. It's solid [...]. Something that's not me, something apart, outside me [...], but I touch it with my fingers, I feel it, I feel that that's the world, but if I can touch it and feel it, then you can't really say it's something else [...]. [...] And I dar[e] to touch it, to cut it in two, to put some in my mouth. Nothing happen[s], I know; that's what's terrible. [...] You cut the bread, you stick the knife into it, and everything goes on as before. I don't understand, Bruno.] (2013: 216–17)

A great deal could be said about this passage, but there are three elements on which I would wish to focus: the idea that what is cut, ostensibly the bread, is in fact an extension of the self; the astonishment on Johnny's part that this is not seen by people to be something significant and that it does not lead *per se* to any sort of change in the world or the self; and the act of ingesting the piece of bread that is cut off. To gloss these elements, Johnny is, in effect, describing the splitting of the self, where one part is simply ingested back into that self. What should, in Johnny's mind, be a rending apart of what is solid (here, the self), thus destabilising our very notion of self and being, instead results in a reaffirmation of the totalising coherence of that self, transmitted both in the world's reaction to the event and in the metaphor of the eating of the bread (noting the allusion here to the rites of Christian tradition and everything for which that acts as a metonym, in respect of the traditions and customs of Western society). *Plus ça change*. With Lacan's mirror stage in mind, this knife passage can therefore be seen to repeat the repudiation of a comforting and illusory sense of wholeness in the face of the evidence of a profoundly destabilised and split self.

The real value of these motifs in the reading I am advancing, however, only becomes fully apparent if we turn to the figure of Charlie Parker himself, and, specifically, to the way in which Réda talks of the saxophonist in his essay 'La coupure de Charlie Parker' (2010: 154–58) [Charlie Parker's Cut]. Réda describes Parker as a profoundly troubled and divided musician, primarily due to an other (*autre*), a 'puissance étrange' (155) [strange power] which inhabits him. Réda sees this *autre* as where the origins of Parker's creative instability is to be found, affirming that this instability 'est surtout en lui avec cet *autre* consubstantiel, énigmatique, qui se veut plus lui que lui-même, l'inconnu qu'il hésite à baptiser *moi* par un mélange d'étonnement, d'angoisse, d'orgueil ou de fierté' (155) [is above all in him with this consubstantial, enigmatic *other*, which claims to be more him than himself, the unknown one whom he hesitates to baptise *me* on account of a mixture of amazement, fear, pride or dignity]. On the one hand, this resonates with Johnny's rejection of himself as seen in the mirror (and text). Johnny certainly hesitates to call the image *moi* [me], and the reaction that leads up to that questioning hesitation matches that described by Réda. But something else is going on here, intimated by the idea that this other, this image wants to be 'plus lui que lui-même' [more him than himself]. That is, this other is not one where 'faltan cosas' (Cortázar 1970d: 165) ('things are missing', 2013: 237). Quite the contrary: here, there is too much, there is a surplus.

Key to understanding Réda's depiction of Parker here and its relevance to 'El perseguidor' are the lines that follow it, which invoke the second motif that I have highlighted, that of the knife. The knife, for Réda, plays a central role in comprehending Parker (and his music), in that the saxophonist's 'sonorité' (2010: 155) [sonority] is seen by the critic as a 'thing', an 'object', where 'cet objet n'est autre qu'un couteau' (156) [this object is none other than a knife]. And this knife — the entrance into sound, the release of sound by Parker — is, crucially, one 'dont la première tâche a été le partage de l'unité de Parker, coupé de soi et ne se ressaisissant que dans ce miroir à double face, dans la profondeur de la lame précisément' (156) [whose first job was the division of Parker's unity, cut off from himself and only coming together in this double-faced mirror, precisely in the depth of the blade]. Parker's 'sonority', that is, splits the unity of the self, sets up the self and its other in Réda's terms — the subject and the ego in Lacan's — both of which appear in the mirror that is this sonorous knife, one on each side, the knife that therefore splits and also brings the two sides together, without conjoining.

The effect of this figuration is to move beyond both Lacan's mirror stage and language (Bruno's text): *this* is the mirror stage as and through (Charlie Parker's) jazz, where the other (*autre*) is and demands excess, demands to be more. Parker's playing, according to Réda, cuts 'par une sorte d'éthique ou d'hybris du *toujours plus*, poursuivant la maîtrise de la maîtrise' (2010: 156, underscore mine) [via a sort of ethic or excessiveness of the *always more*, pursuing the mastery of mastery]. It is a line that describes precisely the pulsion and drive found in 'El perseguidor', both in the figure of Johnny and as a text which serves as a model for understanding how (Parker's/Carter's) jazz can operate. This other persists, wins out, its victory 'normalemente entendue comme l'expression du génie de Parker' (156) [normally understood as the expression of Parker's genius], but, in contrast to the acceptance of the mirror image of the whole self, this process does not lead, in the case of Parker's/Carter's jazz, to such comfort. Rather, it is accompanied by 'de désordres' (156) [disturbances], in the midst of which the jazz figure looks for 'non plus tant l'oubli du couteau, qu'un encouragement à rendre la coupure plus profonde, plus entière: irrémédiable' (157) [not so much the forgetting of the knife, as an encouragement to render the cut deeper, more complete: irremediable]. In other words, (Parker's/Carter's) jazz produces a split where the other is not a whole, but something more, and where the refusal to accept the idea of wholeness that this move entails also requires and is predicated upon a refusal ('l'activité d'un refus' (156) [the activity/act of a refusal]) to stop cutting: the excessive other, in order to be such, must be continually produced. And this is both what lies behind Johnny's confusion at the simple return to wholeness as the cut piece of bread is ingested or its importance ignored, and also what demonstrates how (his) jazz offers a radically different approach to this ontological self-mutilation, and to the very concept of the mirror image.

Of course, one might ask whether this determination to divide the self is not a repetition of the effect of language that Cortázar wishes to overcome (albeit one which refuses to believe the comforting façade of unity that people and society generally accept) and, attendantly, a repudiation of the notion of reconciliation between self and other, the potential for which Cortázar builds into his texts. Certainly, this conclusion ties in with the presentation that we have seen of jazz as being intimately bound up with writing and linguistic structures. But, through the framework offered by the concept of translation and the formulations of Réda's text, 'El perseguidor' also asks us to consider that at the heart of (Cortázar's) jazz lies both an understanding that this music is not, ultimately, able to capture the *otra cosa*, the implacable surplus or remainder, and yet also a belief that it can *produce* it, by continually splitting the self in order to create an irremediable tension between 'subject' (or 'civilised self') and that part of the self (the other) that seeks to exceed and resist totalisation. This is what Réda refers to when he talks of Parker's goal of the mastery of mastery, where the saxophonist's fundamental instability 'ne cessera de hanter cette maîtrise à la façon d'un refus' (2010: 155) [will not stop haunting this mastery in the manner of a refusal]. And this is what lies behind Johnny's 'acicate continuo' (Cortázar 1970d: 133) ('continual spur', 2013: 208) in 'El perseguidor'. It is also why the jazz that emerges from Cortázar's engagement with it is ultimately characterised by *and as* a self-perpetuating, relentless tension.

Notes to Chapter 5

1. There is not space to give an exhaustive list of studies of 'El perseguidor', but some of the more notable to which I shall be referring include (but are not limited to): Valentine (1974); Gyurko (1980; 1988); Fiddian (1985); Sommer (1995; 1998); Couture (2016); and Moran (2017). The most sustained analysis of chapters 10–18 of *Rayuela* is that found in Loyola (1994).
2. This point has been made by a number of scholars. Vaughn Anderson, for example, in discussing 'El perseguidor' comments that 'what interests Cortázar most in music is not an arrival at some revelatory state, but rather the pursuit of it. [...] "El perseguidor" characterizes both the performance and spectatorship of jazz as a "pursuit"' (2013: 121).
3. The crossed-out words 'una región' [a region] are not mentioned in the critical edition of *Rayuela* published in 1991.
4. In 'El perseguidor' Johnny also ruminates over the way in which he understands the verb *entender*, commenting to Bruno that 'yo empiezo a entender de los ojos para abajo' (Cortázar 1970d: 106) ('I begin to understand from the eyes down', 2013: 187–88). Noé Jitrik comments that this implies a form of understanding that is 'afectivo, intuitivo, que nada tiene que ver con el entender de los ojos para arriba, lo que sería el fundamento del entender racional' (1974: 352) [affective, intuitive, that has nothing to do with understanding from the eyes up, which would be the basis of rational understanding].
5. I am referring here to the basic concept of music as a 'temporal art [...] that requir[es] time in order to be realised' (Stambaugh 1964: 265).
6. The relationship of music to time as 'a complex structure of sounds whose different parameters can affect the perception of time' (Droit-Volet and others 2013: 1) is a substantial field of study in its own right. Although I am touching upon this area here, I do not intend to subject Cortázar's engagement with jazz and music generally to a thorough musicological examination in this regard, not least for lack of space. Nevertheless, a study that examines from such a detailed and technical perspective the extent to which the effect of music on one's perception of and relationship to time might be seen to play into and inform Cortázar's work would be potentially fruitful.
7. Shellac was generally used for records prior to the advent of vinyl in 1949.
8. The references here to the effect of the stylus and the scratched nature of the records recall a similar description by Cortázar of the tango records he would listen to and his idea, on which I dwelt in chapter 3, regarding the necessity of recreating the original listening conditions, thus bringing back those past moments (see Cortázar (1970b: 136)). However, the context and the significance of these elements in these two cases (tango and jazz) are very different.
9. This episode is based on the legendary Dial Session recording of 'Lover Man' on 29 July 1946. For contrast, see Woideck (1998: 129–30) for a much more downbeat account of this session.
10. The manuscript version of this passage has the words 'y sexual' (1982: 2) [and sexual] crossed out after 'canalla' ('lowdown'), underlining the overtly sexual nature of this description.
11. See chapter 2, n. 19 in relation to the presence of such a desire and idea in Buñuel and 'Las ménades'.
12. The mirror stage in Lacanian thought 'describes the formation of the ego via the process of identification; the ego is the result of identifying with one's own specular image' (Evans 1996: 115). I shall engage in more detail with these terms and ideas later on in this chapter.
13. 'Go Down Moses' is a Negro spiritual that uses the plight (and call for freedom) of the Israelites in the Biblical book of Exodus as a metaphor for that of black slaves in the USA. It dates back to the mid-nineteenth century and was recorded by Armstrong in 1958. '(What Did I Do to Be So) Black and Blue' is a jazz standard, first recorded by Armstrong in 1929.
14. See Borello (1980: 576–77) in particular.
15. In interview with Picon Garfield, Cortázar remarked, in the context of his engagement with jazz, 'Yo diría que prefiero al indivíduo en todo caso. No olvidando nunca la colectividad, soy tal vez demasiado individualista' (1981: 127) [I would say that I prefer the individual each time. Not ever forgetting the collective, I'm perhaps too individualistic].
16. Of particular note here is Fiddian (1985).
17. See Fiddian (1985: 151).

18. Gyurko (1988: 63–64) addresses the importance of this image in the story, reading it within the framework of what he sees as Bruno's 'elaborate defence mechanism' (63) against being subsumed by Johnny. More recently, Couture, though not specifically in reference to these lines, talks of Bruno's being an 'inconsequential periphery [...] to Johnny's center' (2016: 11).
19. Peiró comments on precisely this aspect of the *discada*, when he notes that 'las canciones citadas añaden comentarios a la acción, [...] los pensamientos de los personajes, la voz del narrador, la conversación y la música se entrelazan en el texto para dar sensación de coordinación entre todos los elementos' (2006: 60–61) [the songs that are cited add commentary to the action, [...] the characters' thoughts, the narrator's voice, the conversation and the music are woven together in the text to give a sense of coordination between all these elements].
20. See, for example, Valentine (1974), Gyurko (1988), Sommer (1995), Peris Blanes (2011), and Couture (2016).
21. See Moran (2017: 1615–16) for a more detailed exploration of the textual inconsistencies that call into question the nature of the text we are reading.
22. As Peris Blanes (2011: 80–81) recognises, in taking this approach he is leaning on the work of Eduardo Soren Triff (1991), who sets out in significant technical detail how certain theoretical models and descriptions of improvisation might be mapped onto, in particular, chapter 47 of *Rayuela*.
23. See, for example, Gyurko (1980), Cavallari and García (1996), and Sommer (1995; 1998).
24. I use the concept of porosity here, as an alternative way of envisaging the notion of holes in reality, not least in order to bring out a further way in which Cortázar himself talks of this idea. In 'Así se empieza', for instance, Cortázar comments that 'por el jazz salgo siempre a lo abierto, me libro del cangrejo de lo idéntico para ganar esponja y simultaneidad porosa' (1970b: 7) [through jazz I always come out into the open, I am freed from the crab of the identical and gain sponginess and porous simultaneity]. We might also recall the porous nature of certain delineations and barriers that underpin the narrative of 'Las ménades', as examined in chapter 2.
25. Chapter 137 of *Rayuela*, we might note in passing, is located between chapters 16 and 17, in the heart of the novel's jazz *discada*.
26. D. Emily Hicks, in her analysis of *Libro de Manuel* in which she maps a musical model onto the text, based on the Stockhausen piece *Momente* (1969), speaks of the premise on which she builds her study as being 'that the literary form and other forms of art such as photography, painting, and music are all separate discourses, not reducible one to another, and yet all share a common quality: all can be translated' (1991: 67). This is borne out by the present reading of 'El perseguidor'.
27. There is a certain parallel to be drawn here with the way in which Cortázar talks about the translation of his own stories. In interview with both González Bermejo and Picon Garfield, he underscores the importance of ensuring that the swing of his stories is translated into the new version. In the former, for example, he states, 'aunque la idea, la información esté perfectamente bien traducida, si no está acompañada de ese "swing", de ese movimiento pendular que es lo que hace la belleza del jazz, para mí pierde toda eficacia; se muere' (González Bermejo 1978: 103) [even if the idea, the information is translated perfectly well, if it's not accompanied by that 'swing', by that pendular movement that is what makes the beauty of jazz, then for me the translation loses all its effectiveness; it dies]. Given the elusive character and resistance to definition of 'swing', it does not seem too much of a stretch to align it with the 'central' implacable remainder or surplus in the present analysis.
28. This reading, as well as the importance of this mirror (stage) image, is reinforced by the reference in *Rayuela* to jazz as leading back to a 'mono mirándose en el agua el primer día del mundo' (Cortázar 2007: 179) ('monkey looking at himself in the water on that first day', 1966: 49), especially given that Bruno refers to Johnny as a 'mono en el zoo' (1970d: 118) ('monkey in the zoo', 2013: 197).
29. One of the key texts where Lacan sets out his idea of the mirror stage is Lacan (1977 [1949]).
30. Given that Bruno refers to Johnny as a chimpanzee on four occasions in the story (Cortázar 1970d: 110; 149; 154; 154), it is perhaps worth noting the details of the 'mirror test' precursor to

Lacan's development of the mirror stage: 'The "mirror test" was first described by the French psychologist and friend of Lacan, Henri Wallon, in 1931 [...]. The six-month-old child differs from the chimpanzee of the same age in that the former becomes fascinated with its reflection in the mirror and jubilantly assumes it as its own image, whereas the chimpanzee quickly realises that the image is illusory and loses interest in it' (Evans 1996: 115).

31. Along similar lines, Boldy describes mirrors in the story as either 'a tranquilizing confirmation of stable identity or, for Johnny, a terrifying encounter with his own unreality' (2005: 383).

CHAPTER 6

'More Than' Jazz

The analysis of *Rayuela* and 'El perseguidor' in the previous chapter focused on a number of key aporia and complexities in these texts, allowing us thus to nuance and extend our grasp of some of the broad areas and claims that pertain to Cortázar's jazz, as set out in chapter 4. Ultimately, this crystallised in a more detailed and profound understanding of the tension that we had seen to be so important to Cortázar's underlying valorisation of and fascination with this musical genre. But, perhaps appropriately, two elements or thoughts remain, hinted at but not captured by my analysis thus far. The first is based on the awareness that — as referenced earlier on — tension is built into Cortázar's engagement with other musical forms too, notably in relation to the rhythmic potential of *la música culta*. The second is that the notion of the implacable remainder, the *otra cosa* ('something else') that I contend is (at the heart of) the very essence of Cortázar's primary 'jazz texts' must surely have an application in respect of the other key elements of jazz (and the (surface) assumptions and claims made for them) that ground Cortázar's jazz theory and ethic. In short, if Cortázar's jazz is shot through with a surplus, an *otra cosa*, then on all levels there must be 'more than' what there appears to be (and what Cortázar describes there as being) in this music as it emerges in his work. Likewise, given that we can see the value and worth of jazz to dovetail with that found — albeit superficially to a lesser degree — in other musical forms that play a part in Cortázar's texts, then surely there is also 'more than' just jazz at stake in the 'more than' *of* jazz. This final chapter, then, will explore these two 'remainders' from the preceding sections of this study. In the process, it will move beyond the confines of a purely genre-based focus, and, accordingly, will proceed in a manner that reflects the more porous, less rigid underpinning that it identifies in Cortázar's engagement with jazz and music generally.

Jazz Fundamentals (Revisited)

Throughout the course of the preceding chapters, we have seen how Cortázar, in his texts and interviews related to jazz, frequently invokes swing and, above all, improvisation as he puts forward his vision of and claims for this music. And these aspects are the ones scholars have generally focused on, undoubtedly for this very reason. But, as we have also seen, there are problems and there is tension in regard to these two aspects of jazz, both in and of their own right and, in particular, in how they appear and operate in Cortázar's work. Moreover, even prior to such considerations, on a basic level we can say categorically that not only is Cortázar's jazz not just about improvisation and not just about swing, but that neither is it just a sum of these two elements (and the others related to them that I have examined): Cortázar's jazz is, to invoke the term once more, 'more than' the sum of its putatively key elements.

An exploration of this 'more than' in relation to the fundamentals of Cortázar's jazz theory, must, however, start with the very traits that Cortázar holds aloft but whose insufficiency is repeatedly intimated, whether consciously or not, even as they are lauded. The most problematic term in this respect is also the most central: improvisation, and it is here that I shall begin the process of re-examining the core elements of Cortázar's writing and thought on jazz, in order better to understand how they work together and, attendantly, potentially to identify what the 'more than' of Cortázar's overall presentation of this music might be.

Improvisation and Freedom

For all the emphasis on jazz improvisation as constituting, or at least glimpsing, a 'liberación profunda' (Cortázar 2006d: 209) [profound liberation], this is undoubtedly the most precarious and complex of the claims Cortázar makes for this aspect of jazz. The earliest of Cortázar's 'jazz texts', the poem 'Jazz' from *Presencia*, is, as noted in chapter 4, in sonnet form. López-Lespada comments that, in this sense, jazz is 'en desconcierto con [esta] forma poética' (1998: 108) [out of kilter with [this] poetic form], with the strict sonnet structure being 'lo más anti-jazz imaginable: es una forma oclusa y hermética, mientras que el jazz es la liberación y la apertura de la forma a las audacias de la experimentación y de la expresividad' (108) [the most anti-jazz thing imaginable: it is a closed and hermetic form, whilst jazz is freedom and the opening up of form to the daring possibilities of experimentation and expressivity]. However, subsequent essays by and interviews with Cortázar show that, on the contrary, the idea of underlying structure, order, and limits is an essential part of jazz and, specifically, jazz improvisation for the author. The examples are many: in interview with Prego, he talks of how 'hay una melodía que sirve de guía, una serie de acordes que van dando los puentes' (1985: 163) [there is a melody that serves as a guide, a series of chords that provide bridges]; speaking to González Bermejo, he describes how in jazz each musician creates his work 'sobre un bosquejo, un tema o algunos acordes fundamentales' (1978: 105) [on the basis of a sketch, a theme or some basic chords]; whilst, in conversation with Picon Garfield he reflects on the benefits of the time limitations of three-minute records, linking back indirectly to 'Jazz' as he affirms that 'los viejos discos se parecían a ciertas formas de poesía como el soneto, o la sonata musical. Hay que dar lo mejor en tres minutos' (1981: 128) [the old records were like certain forms of poetry like the sonnet, or the musical sonata. You've got to give your best in three minutes].[1] Turning back to the early essays that establish the fundamentals of Cortázar's vision of jazz, we see that such moulds and restrictions are set out in unequivocal fashion. In 'Soledad de la música', for example, we read of the unquestioned acceptance that the necessary starting point of the liberational jazz improvisations of which Cortázar speaks is that the jazzmen set their orchestras up 'sobre una melodía y un ritmo *conocidos*' (1992: 294, italics mine) [on a *known* melody and rhythm]. And in 'Elogio del jazz', where we find the most significant statements on this matter, Cortázar makes the case for this sense of stricture being a requirement for a 'true' attainment of the sort of freedom he desires, describing the jazzman as taking advantage of being subject to 'un esquema al cual [...] debe obediencia mientras improvisa' (2006d: 210) [a schema to which [...] he owes obedience while he improvises], viewing these underlying rules, like Valéry, as a 'trampolín para alcanzar una máxima libertad' (210) [trampoline for reaching a maximum of freedom], adding that 'la sujeción a un esquema armónico blues, o a cualquier melodía *hot*, da al *jazzman* una *seguridad previa* para su improvisación [...] que descansa en apoyos armónicos ya previstos como integrantes de la construcción' (211) [being subject to a blues harmonic scheme, or some hot jazz melody, gives the jazzman a *pre-existing safety net* for his improvisation [...] which [thus] rests on harmonic supports pre-planned as integral parts of the construction].[2] The terms of this line of argument are echoed explicitly in the *discada* scene in *Rayuela* some fifteen years later, where, in relation to a Bix Beiderbecke recording of 'I'm Coming Virginia', we read of how 'una corneta se desgajó del resto y dejó caer las dos primeras notas del tema, apoyándose en ellas como en un trampolín' (Cortázar 2007: 168) ('a cornet broke loose from the rest of the group and blew the first notes of the melody, landing [supporting itself] on them as on a [trampoline]', 1966: 40).[3, 4]

What Cortázar is describing here in broad terms is what Hartman has referred to as the relationship between improvisation and 'the given' in jazz (1991: 18). Hartman demonstrates how 'most jazz history has involved reducing the given' (18), from the importance of fidelity to composition of ragtime to the focus on melodic and then harmonic improvisation of hot jazz into the Swing Era, spearheaded notably by figures such as Louis Armstrong, and then onto the bebop era, where the extent and nature of improvisation was extended. In the post-bebop era, free jazz reduced 'the given' yet further, as form, structure, and chords were all themselves improvised, with Hartman drawing attention to Ornette Coleman's *Free Jazz: A Collective Improvisation* (1961) and John Coltrane's *Ascension* (1965) as albums which 'reduce the given almost to nothing' (20). Michael H. Zack (2000), in an illuminating article on extending the jazz metaphor to organisation and communication, neatly summarises some of the broad shifts in this relationship, bringing in the levels of intensity of improvisation suggested by the seminal jazz saxophonist Lee Konitz, and an adapted version of his graphical representation of this is given in Figure 1.

Despite the notable presence of free jazz figures such as Archie Shepp in 'Lugar llamado Kindberg' and Ornette Coleman in brief references in 'No hay peor sordo que el que' (1970b: 144) and 'Melancolía de las maletas' (1970c: 170) from *La vuelta al día en ochenta mundos*, there is generally little doubt as to where Cortázar stands on free/postbop jazz forms. In interview in 1981, for example, he states that 'je ne peux pas dire que le free jazz jouisse de toutes mes préférences [...]. [...] [C]ette bien belle idée de la liberté totale a, hélas, les risques de la liberté exercée d'une façon un peu anarchique' (Olivares 1981: 58) [I cannot say that free jazz is exactly my favourite

Music Genre	Extent of improvisation	Konitz's Stages
Classical	Minimal to none	Interpretation
Traditional jazz/Swing	Constrained within strong structure	Embellishment
Bebop	Extensive; harmony and basic tune structure can be modified	Variation
Postbop	Maximal; content and structure emerge	Improvisation

FIGURE 1. (Zack 2000: 232, adapted)

[...]. [...] [T]his beautiful idea of total freedom has, alas, the risks that come with freedom exercised in a manner that is a touch anarchic]. It is a stance that reiterates what he had said in an earlier interview with Picon Garfield, stating that 'en mi colección de discos no hay mucho "free jazz". [...] Hay momentos de una perfección absoluta y luego cacofonía. [...] [D]entro de un largo "take" de "free jazz", cinco minutos son buenísimos y lo demás es relleno' (1981: 129) [in my record collection there isn't much 'free jazz'. [...] There are moments of an absolute perfection and then cacophony. [...] In a long 'free jazz' take, five minutes are really good and the rest is filler]. Dizzy Gillespie, Miles Davis, and John Coltrane are, he says, the only (postbop) jazz musicians who impressed him after Charlie Parker (129).

Yet it is worth asking whether these putative reasons for largely rejecting free jazz do not simply represent a rejection of a greater (sense of) freedom. Certainly, it is hard to reconcile Cortázar's wariness of anarchic freedom and his focus on those passages of free jazz that are 'good' because they apparently conform to a more orthodox understanding of what 'good' music is (that is, not 'cacofonía' [cacophony]) with his desire elsewhere for a 'liberación profunda' (2006d: 209) [profound liberation]. Indeed, as we have seen, despite his disavowal of aesthetics as the principal aim and focus of art, these passages seem to dismiss free jazz because it is not aesthetically pleasing enough ('anarchique' [anarchic], 'cacofonía' [cacophony]). Either way, Cortázar's jazz preferences are evidently further towards the end of the jazz spectrum that gives a greater place to 'the given', and, whilst he refers to numerous figures from the bebop era in the course of his work and talks in particularly awe-struck terms about Charlie Parker, Clifford Brown, and Thelonious Monk,[5] ultimately his jazz heart lies in the hot tradition, that is, some way before these musicians and further away from the freer improvisation and schemas of their bebop jazz. Thus, as we have seen, he describes Jelly Roll Morton, Louis Armstrong, and Duke Ellington as 'mis predilectos' (Picon Garfield 1981: 127) [my favourites], and, in interview with Prego, declares more generally that 'el viejo jazz de New Orleans y el llamado jazz de Chicago en el fondo es mi jazz, y cuando llega la hora y tengo ganas de escuchar jazz, de tres veces dos saco a Duke Ellington, Armstrong, saco los viejos cantantes de blues' (1985: 165) [the old jazz of New Orleans and so-called Chicago jazz is, deep down, my jazz, and when the time comes and I want to listen to jazz, two out of every three times I get out Duke Ellington, Armstrong, I get out the old blues singers]. Of particular note here is the fact that he goes on to gloss these stated predilections by adding that 'ese tipo de música está muy ligado a tu vida personal, es imposible separar una serie de nostalgias y vivencias de otro tiempo' (165) [that type of music is very tied in with your personal life, it's impossible to separate [from it] a series of nostalgic memories and experiences from another time]. In other words, far from preferring this kind of jazz because the stronger presence of structure, of 'the given', allows a springboard for fuller freedom to be attained, Cortázar's leaning towards hot jazz and other, earlier forms, including the rigid structure of the blues, is tied up with the comforting and nostalgic links and sentiments that these pieces conjure up for him; hot jazz is, we recall, some of the first jazz Cortázar heard as an impressionable youth (González Bermejo 1978: 104). Casting our minds back to chapter 3 of this study, we thus see that, despite the apparent divides and contrasts that Cortázar sets up between them, jazz very much aligns itself with tango in terms of the draw it effects on him and the place it holds in his relationship with music. Indeed, continuing this encroachment on the terrain on which we saw tango to operate in his work, we might also note that the universalising claims Cortázar makes for jazz in the *discada* scene in *Rayuela*, where it is described as 'una música [...] primitiva' (2007: 202) [a primitive music] and as bound up with the idea of 'una forma arquetípica, algo de antes, de abajo, [...] un origen traicionado' (204) ('an archetypal form, something from before, from below, [...] a betrayed origin', 1966: 70), bear more than a passing resemblance to Boym's definition of the restorative nostalgic's desire for 'a return to the original stasis, to the prelapsarian moment' (2001: 49).

Bringing together all of the strands discussed here, we can thus appreciate, first, that the value of jazz as seen through Cortázar's own claims and preferences is not located only in the freedom from the known and from comforting structure that it is deemed to offer, but, simultaneously, and in a way that recalls his use of tango, in its *incorporation* of those very elements, and, secondly, that both of these aspects are found specifically in Cortázar's own (personal) relationship with jazz. Indeed, such a disclosure brings with it a way of understanding a story such as 'Lugar llamado Kindberg', where both free jazz and tango are present, personified in Lina and Marcelo, respectively. Moran has analysed this story in some detail from a Kristevan perspective, arguing convincingly that the tale's engagement with the free jazz of Archie Shepp undergirds an 'interplay between structure and force [which] corresponds to the distinction between and interpenetration of phenotext and genotext' (2000: 158), where Lina would be the marker of this textual dynamism 'in her "semiotic" traversal of the text' (159). Whilst agreeing with Moran's reading, I would add that it is also useful to take into account both Cortázar's ambivalence towards free jazz and his nostalgic leanings (in relation to both tango and jazz) when approaching this story. Despite the importance of Shepp and Lina, the heart of the story — and the character for whom the reader is made to care — is Marcelo, a figure tied in with tango in a key moment in the story in which, as we saw in chapter 3, he recasts the lyrics of Gardel's 'Mano a mano' as he reflects on how Lina's generation is no longer one of tango (as is his) but of free jazz (Cortázar 1974: 99). This is not a simple matter of Marcelo/tango constituting, or at least being aligned with, the phenotext 'pulveriz[ed]' (Moran 2000: 158) by Lina/

Shepp, but, rather, shows Cortázar not only necessarily countering the 'excessive' freedom of free jazz by incorporating a character bound up with nostalgia, the past, and 'concerned with clarity and coherence, order and consistency, and the security of the "inside"' (Moran 2000: 153), but making this character the focal point of the story. It may be, that is, that we are invited to dwell upon the regret at a life not lived more expansively, as Marcelo commits suicide at the text's end, but it is nonetheless the case that, in its focus on Marcelo, the story exhibits an insistent pull towards the nostalgic, the wistful, and the comfort of the safe and known. Given that this is one of the most explicitly jazz-based of Cortázar's fictions, such an insistence can thus be read as reinforcing the sense that such elements are, for Cortázar, an inescapable and necessary part of (his engagement with) jazz, which is to say, an inescapable part of Cortázar himself. (As an aside, we might note that, bearing in mind its dual musical focus, this text can be read as underscoring that the cohabitation of both progressive and regressive, novel and (restorative) nostalgic elements characterises both of these musical genres, as understood, felt, and used by Cortázar.)

A similar attitude to that found in relation to improvisation and 'the given' can also be detected in Cortázar's somewhat contradictory views on records and recording. In chapter 5, I examined the aspects of the record related to its nature as an inscription (a writing then read by the stylus) in *Rayuela* and 'El perseguidor' in particular, with records being seen to write out the (extra-linguistic) moments of plenitude supposedly found in jazz improvisation. But Cortázar's own take on the value of records is more equivocal. In fact, he often reiterates his gratitude for their existence, for the simple reason that they allow us to listen to the spectacular music produced by the jazz figures he mentions that would otherwise have been lost. In interview with Prego, for example, he talks of how 'desde el momento que se trata de una música improvisada, si eso no se graba la improvisación muere en el mismo minuto en que terminó' (1985: 164) [from the moment it's a question of an improvised music, if it isn't recorded, the improvisation dies the very minute it's finished], before referring to 'la aparición del disco [...] con su capacidad de conservar esas improvisaciones' (164) [the appearance of the record [...] with its capacity to conserve those improvisations]. Similarly, in an interview for *Le Monde de la Musique* in 1981, further revealing his predilection for hot jazz, he states that 'sans le disque la musique de tous les grands jazzmen des années 20, qui sont presque tous morts, serait morte avec eux' (Olivares 1981: 56) [without the record the music of all the great jazzmen of the 20s, who are almost all dead, would have died with them]. It is, however, in 'Elogio del jazz' that we find the most telling description of the effect of the record and one which segues into a hint of the more negative, or questioning, appraisal of the record explored earlier:

> Los discos, gracias a los cuales el mejor jazz quedó aprisionado para nosotros como las abejas en el ámbar, han mostrado [...] la formidable riqueza de la improvisación negra. Incluso los grandes *jazzmen* que se escuchaban a posteriori en el disco, elegían sus mejores improvisaciones y las aprendían, faltando a su propio deseo, para complacer comercialmente a públicos que deseaban oír otra vez el solo de Louis en *Mahogany Hall Stomp* o el ataque de Bix Beiderbecke en *I'm Coming Virginia*. (Cortázar 2006d: 211)

[Records, thanks to which the best jazz was imprisoned for us like bees in amber, have shown [...] the formidable richness of black improvisation. Even the great jazzmen who listened to themselves *a posteriori* on records, would choose their best improvisations and learn them, forgoing their own desire in order to be commercially pleasing for audiences who wanted once again to hear Louis's solo from 'Mahogany Hall Stomp' or Bix Beiderbecke's attack on 'I'm Coming Virginia'.]

The employment of terms of restriction and loss in this depiction of the record's conservation of jazz chimes with Cortázar's frequent references to the fleeting nature of those heights of jazz improvisation having value precisely *because* they are evanescent, as reflected by Johnny's reaction to the recording of 'Amorous' in 'El perseguidor'. As Hartman puts it, returning us to the problematic nature and effect of iterability, 'To value recordings for the wrong reasons — because what is repeatable is safely predictable and at our command — is indeed to lose the plenitude of jazz by fleeing its loss' (1991: 74). But this shackling also acts on the jazz musicians themselves, with Cortázar's comments here on the effect of recordings on jazzmen being backed up by Paul Berliner's analysis in his seminal *Thinking in Jazz: The Infinite Art of Improvisation* (1994) of how:

Record companies potentially wield additional power if they delineate idiomatic bounds within which improvisers work [...] as when [...] [they] persuad[e] performers to continue creating music that has proved itself commercially. Artists can become 'prisoners of their own success' in this regard. (482)[6]

Moreover, Cortazar's words in 'Elogio del jazz' are also explicitly reinforced in the decidedly pejorative reference in *Rayuela* to the repetitions of 'Mahogany Hall Stomp' in concert twenty years after its release as 'esos refritos' (2007: 183) ('that warmed-over stuff', 1966: 52).[7] Conversely, to take the other example specifically mentioned by Cortázar here, Beiderbecke's recording of 'I'm Coming Virginia' is listened to by the *Club de la Serpiente* and referred to in reverential terms in the text (2007: 168–69), an attitude that is, however, implicitly bemoaned in the unfinished story 'Bix Beiderbecke' — which also alludes to the track (Cortázar 2003: 1110) — when Bix states his hope that the story's protagonist does not end up as one of those fans who attends all his concerts, since seeing the same face in the audience makes him feel 'como si tuviera que repetir los solos que toqué ayer' (2003: 1113) [as if I had to repeat yesterday's solos], adding, 'vaya a saber si en una de ésas no empiezo a copiarme a mí mismo, no sería el primero' (1113) [who knows if one of these days I'm going to start copying myself, and I wouldn't be the first].

But if the record leads to jazz musicians' repeating past ideas and performances, it also, in the process, serves as a metaphor for a more fundamental way in which Cortázar's romanticised view of improvisation is undermined. Goialde Palacios is one of the few critics to have signalled this.[8] He states that, in his work, Cortázar 'idealiza la improvisación de este tipo de música' (2010: 485) [idealizes the improvisation of this type of music], with reality being somewhat different from 'la ilusión de la absoluta inspiración que parece proponer Cortázar' (485) [the illusion of absolute inspiration that Cortázar seems to propose], specifically in that 'en parte el improvisador jazzístico no hace sino ordenar de formas diferentes materiales estudiados y aprendidos previamente' (485) [to an extent the jazz improviser does nothing but order previously studied and learnt material in different ways].[9] The point is well made, and the extent to which (jazz) improvisation represents a complex play of quotation, dialogues, and precomposition is made clear by numerous jazz writers. Berliner, for instance, talks of how 'jazz improvisers continually explore the relationships of musical ideas, negotiating among a mixture of fixed elements, which derive from their storehouses, and fresh, variable elements, which present unique challenges and surprises' (1994: 221), going on to add, invoking notably linguistic terminology:

> As soloists call the figures repeatedly into action and redefine their relationships, [...] they sometimes find that the figures occur to them more frequently in some settings than others, interact more comfortably with certain other individual patterns, and even evolve increasingly consistent forms of usage with specialized syntactic functions. (227)

Indeed, it is worth noting that Charlie Parker, the epitome of the jazz improviser in Cortázar's work, is recognised to have had 'phrases and statements he often repeated' (Zack 2000: 230), building his solos around quotations from other musicians, songs, and solos, once meticulously quoting Louis Armstrong's 1928 introductory cadenza to 'West End Blues' in a performance of his song 'Cheryl', for example.[10] The most significant and famous example, though, is that of 'Ko-Ko', an early track recorded in 1945 for Savoy records. One of the landmark, throw-down-the-gauntlet tracks of bebop, with 'one of the greatest solos in the history of jazz' (Koch 1988: 66), it was described by Dizzy Gillespie as '"just perfect, man"' (cited in Rutkoff and Scott 1996: 93), whilst Miles Davis, a precocious nineteen-year-old at the time, stated, 'it's the damndest introduction I ever heard in my life' (1989: 75). But arguably its most striking element was precisely its use of quotation:

> In the midst of an inventive riff [...], Parker disclosed the tune of 'Tea for Two' imbedded in the pattern of his musical ideas. That remnant served as pun and evidence, a display of a reality that Parker's invention had displaced, a reminder that a representational world lay just beyond his music's abstraction. (Rutkoff and Scott 1996: 92–93)[11, 12]

Moreover, despite Cortázar's undeniable idealisation of jazz improvisation — akin to what Berliner describes as the flawed popular perception of improvisation as where the players '*must* perform spontaneously and intuitively' (1994: 2) — there are suggestions that he understood and appreciated, to an extent at least, the role played by quotation, not least when he has Bruno inform us in 'El perseguidor' that Johnny 'se ha divertido en citar muchas veces temas de [Charles] Ives en sus discos' (1970d: 164) [has had fun quoting [Charles] Ives's themes many times in his records].[13, 14]

Tying the threads of this discussion together, it is evident that the notion of improvisation as total or 'pure' freedom is repeatedly undermined both by Cortázar's texts and statements themselves and by the actual nature of (jazz) improvisation. The corollary of such a disclosure is, in turn, to bring into question whether Cortázar's entire discourse on and lauding of jazz (improvisation) is thus left undercut. In fact, it is not. Rather, we are led to approach the relationship between jazz and Cortázar in a different way, asking what it is about jazz (including jazz improvisation) that provides the pulsions and dynamics that actually inform and ground Cortázar's thought and work, *beyond and independent of* his statements on it. In order to do this, we need now to bring in and re-question other aspects of Cortázar's (claims for) jazz.

Notation, Performance, Voice

Along with freedom, one of the other principal advantages or advances of jazz over other music that is highlighted consistently by Cortázar is the idea of its resistance to notation. The general valorisation of a musical defiance to being 'written' is hinted at in *Teoría del túnel*'s concern for an undermining of literary language — concretely in the written form of the book — through poeticisation or musicalisation, but it is set down more starkly, and within the context of jazz, in 'Soledad de la música', as Cortázar talks of the genre's 'melodías viejas [...], jamás escritas porque la música no puede ser escrita' (1992: 294–95) [old melodies [...], never written because music cannot be written]. This jazz specificity is further entrenched by the time of Cortázar's much later declaration in interview with González Bermejo that music, again in the context of talking about jazz, communicates 'cosas que ningún lenguaje, ninguna escritura pueden comunicar' (1978: 107) [things that no language, no writing can communicate]. In line with the aspects of the genre that Cortázar highlights, this resistance to notation can be understood as a characteristic of swing, not only in its being elusive to definition, whereby 'nadie ha podido explicar qué cosa es el *swing*' (Prego 1985: 169) [no one has been able to explain what swing is], but in the sense that, as numerous writers on jazz have noted, given that swing is *felt* rather than mechanically reproduced, 'swing rhythms cannot be accurately notated on paper' (García 1990: 29). Talking about different performances of the jazz standard 'Bemsha Swing', for example, Steven Block comments that 'as in many jazz transcriptions, the element of swing is not provided by the notation' (1997: 208).[15] The underlying reason, to quote Denis L. Baggi, is that swing simply 'cannot be notated except by recording the improvised performance' (1990: 336). Of course, this moves us on to the relationship between improvisation and resistance to notation for Cortázar, reminding us that the link between the two subtends his entire discourse on the inscription of jazz improvisation on records — the inscription that Johnny rejects so vehemently in 'El perseguidor' —, and which serves only to destroy the essence of the improvisation.

However, my examination of the nature of improvisation, both in general and in regard to the type of improvisation that Cortázar favours, makes clear that, just as it fails to match the claims of absolute freedom that the author makes for it, in being tied in with elements ('the given', citation) that demand to be seen linguistically, as scripts to be read and reproduced, so, likewise, is improvisation not, in a straightforward way at least, an unproblematic candidate for being the mainstay of jazz's resistance to notation. Indeed, it is useful here to rejoin some of the more musicological arguments set forward by Hartman in this respect. Hartman is clear that the 'inaccessibility of jazz to notation' (1991: 71) is one of its key characteristics, and one which sets it apart from European music (that is, *la música culta*) (69; 71), but he goes on to show that it is not equatable with, or, at least, dependent upon, improvisation. Using the examples of Lee Konitz's 'highly literate improvisation' (73) in 'All the Things You Are' and Ornette Coleman's 'highly oral composition' (73) 'Lonely Woman', he argues that 'Konitz's solo is a complex piece of work, but not difficult to transcribe into standard musical notation; while Coleman's composed and reiterated bridge defies at least my pen' (73).[16] The Coleman piece is more composed, in the sense of being more guided and determined by Coleman himself as the track's 'author', but it is not composition understood in written terms: the piece's composition is found in its performance, our understanding of the word composition thus extending significantly beyond the idea of writing a score which is to be performed by being 'read'. As Hartman puts it, in this way, 'the line between composition and performance grows fuzzier', adding crucially, 'By the same token, the distinction between composition and improvisation loses importance' (68). In other words, following Hartman's line of argument, one might say that it is performance that occupies the central role in jazz and it is, thus, to performance — understood in a way that is very different from the performance of a score in *la música culta* exemplified by 'Clone' — that we must turn in order to understand more fully what it is about jazz that both defies, or resists, notation and challenges the putative binary of composition and improvisation, structure and supposed spontaneity in Cortázar's work.

Approached from this perspective, we start to appreciate to what extent performance, broadly understood, in fact underpins and characterises the principal engagements with jazz in Cortázar's *œuvre*. To pick just a few examples: three of the most overtly jazz-centred pieces in *La vuelta al día en ochenta mundos*, 'Así se empieza', 'Louis, enormísimo cronopio', and 'La vuelta al piano de Thelonious Monk', are all concerned with concert performances by Lester Young, Louis Armstrong, and Thelonious Monk, respectively; towards the 'end' of the unfinished 'Bix Beiderbecke', we find the suggestion that the cornettist considers the concert performance, rather than the record, to be where his jazz is to be met (2003: 1113); Cortázar's engagement with swing, itself an aspect of jazz that only emerges in and as performance, is described in terms of his own textual performance of such (Prego 1985: 169); the persistent focus on the unrepeatable, fleeting moments, supported by Johnny Carter's violent rejection of the recording of 'Amorous', underscores the primacy of the performance; and, along these lines, how to define what we are given by Johnny in 'El perseguidor' other than as a *tour-de-force* (verbal) performance? Beyond these examples, the way in which Cortázar presents and talks about jazz records — be it in pieces such as 'Clifford', where he refers to a 'dicha efímera y difícil, [...] un arrimo precario' (1970b: 109) [ephemeral and difficult happiness, [...] a precarious coming together] found at a particular point of Clifford Brown's 'I Don't Stand a Ghost of a Chance with You', or in the descriptions of the jazz emanating from the record player in the *discada* scene in *Rayuela*, of the sort where we are told of 'una perfecta pausa donde todo el swing del mundo palpitaba en un instante intolerable' (2007: 182) ('a perfect pause where all the swing of the world was beating in an intolerable instant', 1966: 52) — serves as a prime example of what Jed Rasula has in mind when he refers to how 'critics and historians have always used jazz records as primary sources, while pretending that what they are really talking about is something else, some putative essence of a "living tradition" that cannot be "captured" by the blatant artifice of technology' (1995: 135).[17] In short, even when he is talking about records, Cortázar is focusing on and presenting them as jazz performance.[18]

We have, in a sense, come full circle. In the Introduction, I argued that 'Soledad de la música' in particular identifies performance — understood as the unfurling of a piece of music in time — as a move away from an originary Music into linguistic operations, and as essentially lying at the heart of the problems of music. But, as we have seen, once we depart from viewing performance as the playing out of a score (or, at least, an Idea), as seen in 'Clone', it starts to take on more nuanced hues, hence the more politically and narratively challenging implications of the Chopin figure's new 'take' on (performance of) the *Revolutionary Étude* in 'Alguien que anda por ahí', the valorisation of the (reflective nostalgic, innovative, subversive) tango 'performance' that is 'Tango de vuelta', and the role of performance in allowing the emergence of epiphanic moments in the jazz improvisation of, for example, Johnny in 'El perseguidor'. With this in mind, the near-ubiquitousness of performance in Cortázar's presentation of jazz, together with Hartman's framework for understanding jazz in (such specifically) performative terms, thus suggests that performance asks to be understood as, in fact, one of the central tenets of Cortázar's engagement with jazz *tout court*. What is more, this (re)new(ed) focus on performance also provides — to reengage with those early texts — a different way of figuring the insistent, if not entirely consistent, pairing of jazz with poetry/poetism, in the sense that poetry is essentially (and originally) performative. Performance, that is, offers the link between the two that Cortázar often appears to be struggling to identify as he suggests their connection through, amongst other elements, improvisation (automatic writing) and a generalised and somewhat vague sense of musicalisation/ poeticisation, within which rhythm, metre, and, of course, more specifically swing can all be perceived to play a part. Indeed, such a link has been commented on by prominent jazz writers. Thus, Kart (Harper, Kart, and Young 1987: 131) makes reference to the way in which American poet Charles Olson recited his works, comparing it to Sonny Rollins, the jazz saxophonist, whilst Hartman, who also alludes briefly to the case of Olson (1991: 4; 45), analyses in some depth the example of American poet and performance artist David Antin, the primacy of whose improvised pieces is found more precisely in their performative nature. For Antin, 'performance is the first stage of composition' (Hartman 1991: 92) and, significantly, he once declared, 'I want it understood that my page is just that — a notation of some performance — which is the real work' (cited in Hartman 1991: 87). Moreover, the resonance with the idea of jazz's resistance to notation as it appears in Cortázar's work is made particularly striking in the light of Hartman's subsequent comment that 'Antin's talks make enough demands on printed language to render the visual blocks and regulated syntax of prose [...] inadequate to the task' (1991: 87–88).[19]

What is key here, however, is understanding what it is about (the nature of) performance — be it that of David Antin or Ornette Coleman — that permits it to resist, or be beyond, notation in this way and, attendantly, to occupy a space of potentiality that refuses a conceptualisation involving neat and naively understood categories of improvisation and composition. And, alongside swing (as we have seen), the answer lies in (the concept of) the voice. Thus, of Antin, Hartman states that 'what makes Antin's performances poetry [is] that at his best he attends so exactly to the what and the how of his speech at once' (1991: 85), whilst his description of Coleman's playing on 'Lonely Woman' is explicit in emphasising the importance of voice in setting this work apart from the more clearly improvised solos of Konitz and, in the process, crucially, in rendering it resistant to notation and resolutely focused on performance:

> Coleman's distrust of the tempered scale, his belief in expressive intonation, leads him sometimes into explicit vocal effects — horse laughs, wails, and so on. More continuously, it makes him adjust his pitch according to context, sliding up to one note, allowing another to sag halfway through, pushing at the boundaries of what formally defines a 'note'. (71)

Returning to Cortázar's work, we find, as we did with performance, that voice indeed retains an insistent — and largely overlooked — presence in his writing on and concerning jazz. Despite the emphasis he places on (male) jazz instrumentalists in his more theoretical essays and interview responses, and in the pieces from *La vuelta al día en ochenta mundos* mentioned previously, vocal performances, in particular female, abound: the music found in the early stories 'Llama el teléfono, Delia' and 'Retorno de la noche' from *La otra orilla* is described through such terms as 'aquella voz morena' (Cortázar 2004: 38) [that black voice] and 'la voz de la mujer negra' (71; 73; 78) [the voice of the black woman], as we have seen; the *discada* scene in *Rayuela* invokes the figures of Bessie Smith, Ma Rainey, and Ella Fitzgerald, three of the most important female jazz singers in the history of the genre; there are lengthy allusions to Satchmo's vocal performances in 'Louis, enormísimo cronopio' (Cortázar 1970c: 21); the horn instrument in the early poem 'Jazz' is referred to by talking of its 'boca de cobre y aluminio' (Denis 1938: 20) [mouth of copper and aluminium]; in *Un tal Lucas*, we recall, the song 'So You're Going to Leave the Old Home, Jim' is transformed when sung by Ethel Waters, a performance where '*sólo cuenta una voz* murmurando las palabras de la tribu, la recurrencia de lo que somos, de lo que vamos a ser' (Cortázar 1979b: 151, italics mine) [*the only thing that counts is a voice* murmuring the words of the tribe, the recurrence of what we are, of what we are going to be]; and the implementation of swing into Cortázar's writing is defined as 'una forma de respiración rítmica' (González Bermejo 1978: 102) [a form of rhythmic breathing]. Moreover, at the end of his interview with Picon Garfield, Cortázar is explicit in bringing out precisely the centrality of voice in jazz, alluding to several of the figures mentioned above and others (Bessie Smith, Cab Callaway, Ethel Waters, Ella Fitzgerald, Lena Horne, Billie Holiday, and Sarah Vaughan) as he asserts that 'creo que la voz humana es uno de los aspectos fundamentales del jazz' (1981: 132) [I think the human voice is one of the fundamental aspects of jazz]. This statement is often overlooked in favour of Cortázar's prioritising of improvisation elsewhere, but Cortázar's work can clearly be seen to back up the importance of the vocal factor in his engagement with jazz. Indeed, in this respect it is worth noting Michael Longley's contention, specifically referencing Bessie Smith and Ma Rainey, that 'backwoods keening, mainly by men, about sex and betrayal, money and hard times, was transformed by female singers with powerful voices into a universal lamentation, a sound that would encircle the globe' (1998: 95). Such a statement chimes with the universal(ising) claims made for jazz in *Rayuela* ('la única música universal del siglo' (Cortázar 2007: 202) ('the [...] only [...] universal music of the century', 1966: 69)), adding to our understanding of how voice — and the female voice in particular — fits into Cortázar's jazz ethic.[20]

Beyond this broad signalling of the centrality of voice and, more specifically, of the vocal inflections found in performance, Hartman's work is also important in highlighting that this element is, additionally, bound up with and determined by dialogue, in that '"voice," or at least "authentic voice," is never simply single, but arises out of dialogic relations among voices' (1991: 72). On the one hand, this has to do with the way in which any jazz musician's voice — their style, their improvisation, their approach — is, as we have seen, the result of learning, listening to, quoting, and refashioning other voices, whilst also being related to the interplay not just between 'the given' and improvisation, but also between the different musicians playing together in a particular performance. As Carlos Sampayo puts it, 'la creación jazzística necesita de los otros. Es un arte compartido desde el momento de su gestación' (2000: 178) [jazz creation needs others. It is a shared art from the moment of its gestation]. But it also has to do with the jazz musician's performance being in dialogue with the audience, with his or her listeners. Mikhail Bakhtin, whose ideas I am clearly channelling here, is insistent upon this double dialogic opening-up, stating, for instance, that 'there are no limits to the dialogic context (it extends into the boundless past and the boundless future)' (1986: 170), and frequently focusing, albeit in the context of speech, on the 'orientation toward the listener' (1981: 282), commenting, for example, that 'the word in living conversation is directly, blatantly, oriented toward a future answer-word: it provokes an answer, anticipates it and structures itself in the answer's direction' (280). As Hartman says, bringing us back to jazz, 'The self or voice is indefinable in isolation; it is born from a matrix of other voices' (1991: 47), and part of that is 'the musicians' dialogic relation to listeners' (73), whilst Don Bialostosky defines the 'authentic voice' in a way that brings these different dialogic aspects together in useful fashion:

> If voice ... is to be heard in the speaker's responsiveness to the voices of others who have spoken on the topic as well as to the voices of those who now listen but may yet speak, then an authentic voice ... would be one that vitally and productively engaged those voices. It would be *authentically situated*. (cited in Hartman 1991: 47)

This dialogic vocal framework helps us further reconsider what is at stake in Cortázar's presentation of jazz performance, in the broad terms I have set out above.

On a basic level, if swing underscores and symbolises the resistance to notation found in performance, then improvisation, 'rescued' from its falling short of the absolute or pure freedom mentioned by Cortázar, might find its value and power precisely in its melding and citation of different riffs, motifs, and voices, that is, in being essentially dialogic.[21] Moreover, Cortázar's work regularly foregrounds the way in which jazz performance, either in concerts or in his performance-focused depiction of recorded jazz, is concerned with a bringing together of musician and listener and the dialogue that emerges as a result, as, indeed, is intimated in the reference in the early poem 'Jazz' to the importance of the 'oído sensitivo' (Denis 1938: 19) [sensitive ear]. In the main jazz pieces from *La vuelta al día en ochenta mundos*, for example, 'Así se empieza' focuses on the impact of a Lester Young concert on the watching Cortázar, who enters into 'una participación que en esa noche de Lester era un ir y venir de pedazos de estrellas' (1970b: 7) [a participation that on that night with Lester was a coming and going of pieces of stars], 'La vuelta al piano de Thelonious Monk' is built around notions of the concert as a journey that musician and audience take together ('hay Thelonious capitán, hay rumbo por un rato' (1970c: 28) [there's Captain Thelonious, there's a course for a while yet]), 'Louis, enormísimo cronopio' talks of the audience — Louis's audience — as if they were the trumpeter's faithful congregation ('Louis alegría de los hombres que te merecen' (22) [Louis joy of those who deserve you]), and 'Clifford' reads as a personal paean to the jazz trumpeter in which listener and musician achieve a religious communion ('Cuando quiero saber lo que vive el shamán en lo más alto del árbol de pasaje, [...] escucho una vez más el testamento de Clifford Brown' (1970b: 109) [When I want to know what a shaman experiences in the highest part of the tree through which he is transported, [...] I listen once more to the screed of Clifford Brown]). As Ostendorf puts it, 'Jazz is dialogic, [...] in other words, it is highly interactionist' (1990: 46). More generally, over the course of his work, Cortázar repeatedly invokes the idea of playing records as a way of bringing the past and the present into dialogue, of presenting the (often now dead) jazz players in a new performance that constitutes the striking up of a conversation with the listener in the here and now. This is particularly evident in 'Bix Beiderbecke', whose main conceit is the dialogue, conversation, and interaction of Bix with the protagonist that is primarily constituted by, and then emerges either fantastically or, at least, in a psychologically and temporally disjointed fashion from, her playing his records. But it is also an accurate description of the way in which the records played in the *discada* scene in *Rayuela* engage with, and are engaged with by, the members of the *Club de la Serpiente*: the past playing out in front of them, performances — which are already dialogic in their own right — taking place in the presence of the group of assembled friends:

> Dos muertos se batían fraternalmente, ovillándose y desentendiéndose, Bix y Eddie Lang [...] jugaban con la pelota *I'm coming, Virginia,* y dónde estaría enterrado Bix, pensó Oliveira, y dónde Eddie Lang, a cuántas millas una de otra sus dos nadas que en una noche futura de París se batían guitarra contra corneta, gin contra mala suerte, el jazz. (2007: 168–69)

> [Two [dead men] sparred fraternally, clinching and breaking, Bix and Eddie Lang [...] played catch with *I'm Coming Virginia*, and I wonder where Bix is buried, thought Oliveira, and Eddie Lang, how many miles apart are their two nothings that one future night in Paris were [sparring], guitar against cornet, gin against bad luck, jazz.] (1966: 40)

> Y ahora una voz rota, abriéndose paso desde un disco gastado, proponiendo sin saberlo [...] un *carpe diem* Chicago 1929. (2007: 195)[22]

> [And now a cracked voice, making its way out of a worn-out record, suggesting unknowingly [...] a *carpe diem* from Chicago, [1929].] (1966: 64)

Moreover, the — often erotic — responses of the scene and club members to these performances, which I examined in chapter 5, can now be reinterpreted as dialogic responses to those musical voices, which, in turn, also act as responses to that scene. Indeed, at times the dialogic, conversational nature of the jazz being played is conveyed in explicit fashion, such as when we read of how Big Bill Broonzy 'les hablaría de otra barricada con la misma voz con que la Maga le estaría contando a Gregorovius su infancia en Montevideo' (2007: 191) ('would tell them about another barricade with the same voice that La Maga was using to tell Gregorovius about her childhood in Montevideo', 1966: 59).

This emphasis on performance and on performance as voice and voice as dialogic certainly stands in stark contrast to 'la soledad [de la música que] es presencia constante' (Cortázar 1992: 295) [the solitude [of music which] is a constant presence] from which Cortázar found he was unable to escape in 'Soledad de la música', and offers a way of understanding the trajectory that his work takes as it engages with jazz in a more developed and nuanced manner. More pointedly, this readjusting of our understanding of what Cortázar's work in fact signals as being most important about jazz, focusing more on the performative, vocal, and dialogic aspects of the genre rather than the more simplistic and idealistic, albeit more explicitly stated, notion of (improvisation as) 'freedom', for example, provides a more satisfactory explanation of Cortázar's declarations of jazz's unifying — if not universalising — potential than simply taking such statements at face value, with an apparent lack of concern as to why or how he can make them.

And yet, this turn to performance, voice, and dialogue also brings with it a more significant realisation. Hartman argues at one point that:

> While we attend to the players before us, the sense remains that we are being allowed to participate in something irreplaceable. Perhaps any music could give us that sense, heard in the way that jazz — through the intimacy among player and instrumental voice and the sound itself — *demands* to be heard. (1991: 74)

I would take this further. Certainly, jazz demands this, and jazz is, in this sense, a privileged form of music. Indeed, it is for this reason that it appears as such in Cortázar's thought and work: jazz is the locus where these performative, vocal, and dialogic elements emerge most insistently, not least in the way jazz improvisation and swing contribute and lend themselves to their production. But the importance of these three interlinked elements then also opens up the possibility that, as Hartman intimates, other forms of music can and do also lead, in their own way, to a similar engagement, to similar fleeting glimpses of individual and collective epiphany — of a voice 'authentically situated' — as jazz. And it is here, then, that we come to the crux of the matter. The early texts 'Soledad de la música' and 'Elogio del jazz' set up an apparent hierarchisation of music, where certain types of improvisational jazz are placed at the apex of the musical world. It is a hierarchisation that is repeated both in several later interviews and in written pieces such as 'Louis, enormísimo cronopio'. But, as the chapters of this study have shown, in practice, Cortázar's work both valorises and discloses the revolutionary, transgressive, and ontoexpressive potentialities of all types of music, from *la música culta*, to tango, to nostalgic as well as bebop jazz.[23] One way of squaring this circle is to see that the hierarchy can be ruptured by musicians and, in this case, by Cortázar transferring the locus of attention in regard to other forms of music onto performance, voice, and dialogue, including by showing how 'improvisation' and rhythmic effects, broadly understood, operate within these diverse musical genres. This is what emerges from the examples of more revolutionary and subversive (concepts of) performance in the tango and *música culta* texts to which I referred above, for example, but it is also evident from numerous other aspects of Cortázar's engagement with music that my discussions thus far have brought out: the presence of swing-like or polyrhythmic elements in several of the examples of *la música culta* with which Cortázar works in some of his key texts, often tied up with an attempted revolutionary move ('Reunión', 'Alguien que anda por ahí'); the foregrounding of the voice of the female tango singer in the engagement with this genre in 'Las puertas del cielo', bound up with the narrative's creation of a glimpse of redemptive possibility for its characters; the value of the dialogic bringing together of different musical pieces and genres in 'Alguien que anda por ahí', a text that works to counter any sense of teleology and to effect a refusal of easy identifications and definitions; a similar dialogic melding of multiple existing tango pieces in a number of Cortázar's texts, in particular 'Tango de vuelta', where it acts in the service of a narrative of subversive, transgressive challenge; and, more widely, the fact that improvisation, broadly understood, is found in tango, jazz, and — even if Cortázar does not acknowledge this explicitly — some of the main figures of *la música culta* to whom he refers (Bach, Mozart, Chopin), built around the distinctly comparable notions that I have identified: 'code and rupture', 'the given and improvisation', 'theme and variation', respectively.

In short, I am suggesting that performance, voice, and dialogue, to which improvisational and swing elements contribute, are the 'more than' of Cortázar's jazz and of jazz *per se*, but they also signal that the power and potential of music in Cortázar's work is about more than jazz.

A Case in Point

In support of this contention, I shall end this final chapter by bringing together two of the most famous musical engagements in Cortázar's fiction, each of which pertains to an apparently very different type of music (indeed, I have chosen them precisely for this reason): 'El perseguidor' and the Berthe Trépat scene from *Rayuela*;

bebop and, broadly speaking, *la música culta*. One of the near-constants in the existing commentary on 'El perseguidor', to which I referred in detail in chapter 5, is the sense that it is a story that sets out Cortázar's privileging of jazz in terms of its potential and possibilities. In contrast, the Berthe Trépat scene, a self-contained vignette occupying chapter 23 of *Rayuela*, in which Oliveira attends an avant-garde piano recital by Mme. Trépat before accompanying her home in the rain, is generally seen as an episode whose main elements are 'farcical and caricaturesque' (Standish 2001: 107), with Boldy, for example, focusing on the scene as Oliveira's 'attempt to destroy the absurd by conniving with it, becoming it' (1980: 59). When the episode is viewed within the specific context of Cortázar's engagement with music, however, not only does a more serious series of questions come to the fore, but several striking similarities with Johnny and his jazz in 'El perseguidor' emerge. In short, my assertion is that these two key texts are prime indicators of how Cortázar's writing destabilises his own apparent underlying musical hierarchy along the lines developed above. Accordingly, it is not my intention here to offer an exhaustive reading of the Berthe Trépat scene, plotting it in detail against what I have already said about 'El perseguidor', but, rather, to give a brief account that represents a template for the sort of comparative analysis that my argument suggests is invited by Cortázar's engagement with music. For this reason, I will additionally comment in passing on ways in which other texts referred to in the course of my study can also be seen to dialogue with the *Rayuela* episode.

The first thing to note about these two texts is the extent to which they both fit in with the elements that I have signalled as being key to the presentation and significance of music in Cortázar's work. For all the complexity of 'El perseguidor', it remains, amongst other things, a story about performance — both jazz and verbal — and about response, reaction, and dialogue between Bruno and Johnny. Likewise, the Berthe Trépat scene revolves around and focuses on a performance that is constituted not just by the music itself, but by listener response on the part of the audience present at the recital (and, more particularly, Oliveira) and by Trépat's response to those responses. Thus, for example, attention is drawn to reactions such as that of the 'señor de rotunda calva [que] se enderezó indignado, y después de bufar y soplar salió de la sala' (Cortázar 2007: 246) ('a man with a neat, round bald spot [who] got up indignantly and after snorting and huffing left the hall', 1966: 105), to Oliveira's detailed consideration of the performance, which is what constitutes the mainstay of the concert scene, and to how Trépat 'cada vez erraba más notas' (2007: 250) ('kept making more and more mistakes', 1966: 108) as she becomes aware of the stifled laughter of 'el señor de aire plácido' (2007: 250) ('the peaceful-looking man', 1966: 108). After the concert, the 'dialogue' is continued in verbal form between Trépat and Oliveira.

Beyond this shared characteristic, one which is also, we might add, found in 'Las ménades' and, to a lesser extent, 'Clone', it is, additionally, worth highlighting the similarities between the protagonists in each case. The two musicians are both largely misunderstood, unorthodox figures who occupy the margins of society and are portrayed as insular individuals. Regarding what he terms this 'loca encorsetada' (2007: 249) ('madwoman in a corset', 1966: 107), for instance, Oliveira says at one point that 'una artista como usted conocerá de sobra la incomprensión y el snobismo del público. En el fondo yo sé que usted toca para usted misma' (2007: 251) ('an artist like you must be aware of the lack of understanding and the snobbism of the public. Deep down I know that you [play] for yourself', 1966: 108). This chimes with many aspects of 'El perseguidor' that I examined earlier, both in terms of the aloofness and/or lack of understanding evident on the part of those who surround and listen to Johnny's music, and in terms of 'la sensación de que [Johnny] está solo, completamente solo' (1970d: 143) ('the feeling that [Johnny is] alone, completely alone', 2013: 217) that emanates insistently from the text. Meanwhile, in both scenes the role of audience and interlocutor is taken up, broadly speaking, by an intellectual character who acts as an observer and, either literally or mentally, note-taker and analyst: Bruno's biographer instincts become Oliveira's studious appraisal of the concert scene in which he participates, in a manner reminiscent of Dr Hardoy's scientific contemplation of Celine and Mauro in 'Las puertas del cielo'.

The most significant parallels, though, are found in the music itself. As noted in chapter 5, Johnny's performance of 'Amorous' and his demands for the recording of it to be destroyed stand out as the musical centrepiece of 'El perseguidor', crystallising everything that he and his jazz stand for. Turning to the Berthe Trépat scene, where the music is decidedly not a jazz improvisation, we nevertheless see indications of a similar underlining of and concern for the uniqueness of (the) performance. At the start of the scene, for example, we are told that the three pieces played by the pianist are 'los "Tres movimientos discontinuos" de Rose Bob (primera audición), la "Pavana para el General Leclerc", de Alix Alix (primera audición civil), y la "Síntesis Délibes-Saint-Saëns", de Délibes, Saint-Saëns y Berthe Trépat' (Cortázar 2007: 243) ('the *Three Discontinuous Movements* of Rose Bob (première), the *Pavan for General Leclerc*, by Alix Alix (first time for a civilian audience), and the *Délibes–Saint-Saëns Synthesis*, by Délibes, Saint-Saëns, and Berthe Trépat', 1966: 102). Although not mentioned initially, we learn later that the last of these is also a 'primera audición' (2007: 253) ('première', 1966: 111), and, after the concert, this overall point is reiterated, as Trépat says to Oliveira, 'Usted se habrá fijado en eso, que es fundamental: mi propia música. Primeras audiciones casi siempre' (2007: 254) ('You must have noticed that, it's [fundamental]: my own music. Almost always premières', 1966: 111). On the one hand, this could be taken as an indication of the poor quality — or poor reception — of Trépat's pieces, in that, in general, they simply do not receive more than one outing. But it can also be seen as an insistence on the primacy of the singular performance. Indeed, it is significant in this regard that the *Pavan*, the one work performed in this concert that is not a true première, in being a 'civil' première, is roundly criticised by Trépat, who informs Oliveira that 'no es en absoluto una pavana [...]. Es una perfecta mierda' (2007: 252) ('it isn't really a pavan at all [...]. [...] It's a piece of shit', 1966: 109). Of course, this focus on *primeras audiciones* marks Trépat's concert's difference from a number of other *música culta* performances referred to in Cortázar's texts, most notably in 'Las ménades', where the programme consists entirely of well-known and oft-repeated canonical classical pieces. And yet, further contributing to the forging of connections between apparently different musicians and musical types across Cortázar's work, and further emphasising the potential that his texts locate in even the most apparently staid musical scenarios, it is striking that the concerts of the avant-garde Trépat and the musically conservative *el Maestro* are linked in that they both come in the context of the artists' 'bodas de plata' (2007: 244; 1970a: 55) [silver anniversary] as composer and conductor, respectively.[24]

Returning to the music played by Berthe Trépat, just as Johnny implores that the recording of his unique performance of 'Amorous' be destroyed, so too do we find that the lack of repeated *future* performances of Trépat's pieces is also emphasised (albeit, unlike 'Amorous', not because this is the actual will of the musician in question). This is the logical conclusion, of course, of the notion that Trépat engages in premières, but is reinforced when the pianist talks of how:

> Germaine Tailleferre [...] había dicho que *Preludio para rombos naranja* era sumamente interesante y que le hablaría a Marguerite Long para que lo incluyera en un concierto.
> — Hubiera sido un éxito, señor Oliveira, una consagración. Pero los empresarios, usted lo sabe, la tiranía más desvergonzada, hasta los mejores intérpretes son víctimas... (Cortázar 2007: 259–60)
>
> [Germaine Tailleferre [...] had said that the *Prelude for Orange Rhombuses* was extremely interesting and that she would speak to Marguerite Long about it so she could include it in one of her concerts.
> 'It would have been a success, Mr. Oliveira, a triumph. But you know impresarios, little dictators, even the best artists are victims...'.] (1966: 116)

Everything conspires, that is, against her pieces being performed again.[25] And if both past and future performances are written out in the Berthe Trépat scene, it is also notable that, despite the clearly composed nature of the pieces she plays,[26] none of them is known to us, as readers, beforehand: the first two are works whose existence is invented by Cortázar, as is the third, even if it is made up of 'real' works by the composers Léo Delibes and Camille Saint-Saëns. In other words, these three pieces of music exist only in their performance in *Rayuela*.

Beyond this, parallels with the claims for both jazz improvisation and rhythm/swing made by Cortázar, many of which, as we have noted, are portrayed as pertaining to Johnny Carter's/Charlie Parker's jazz, are also perceptible in the style and nature of the pieces played by Trépat. In regard to the music's rhythmic traits, for example, Trépat's *Synthesis* stands out as a work that clearly plays with and is built around the multiple different metres and rhythms found in — and formed by the bringing together of — the at least nine alternating, intercalated pieces of which it consists (2007: 250). The improvisational resonances are even starker. The 'infinitas variaciones' (247) [infinite variations] of the three themes that form the central motifs of the *Pavan* and the recontextualisation of diverse themes that constitutes the *Synthesis*, for instance, are reminiscent of Parker's improvisational *modus operandi*, built to a significant extent around the repurposing and refashioning of citations and melodic themes, as commented on earlier; they also resonate, we might add, with Cortázar's practice of reworking old tango lyrics and themes in his texts. Meanwhile, with respect to the compositions of both Trépat and Rose Bob, one of her students, we are told that the announcer:

> podía resumir su estética en la mención de *construcciones antiestructurales*, es decir, células sonoras *autónomas*, fruto de la *pura inspiración*, concatenadas en la intención general de la obra pero *totalmente libres* de moldes clásicos, dodecafónicos o atonales. (244, italics mine)

> [[could] sum up their art by mentioning *antistructural constructions*, that is to say, *autonomous* cells of sound, the result of *pure inspiration*, held together by the general intent of the work but *completely free* of classical molds, dodecaphonic or atonal.] (1966: 103, italics mine)

These lines suggest that this music's aesthetic might go beyond even the atonal improvisational structures of free jazz greats such as Miles Davis and John Coltrane.

In short, on numerous levels, the two texts, (sets of) performances, and types of music are brought together, with the (putatively non-iterable) performative aspects of (Carter's/Parker's) jazz in particular not only being present in the Berthe Trépat scene, but brought to the fore and insisted upon. Moreover, the corollary of this is that a number of the effects of Johnny's jazz, effects bound up with what Cortázar sees as the theoretical and practical advance and possibilities represented by jazz generally, are also identifiable in relation to Trépat's performance. As we saw in chapter 5, one of the most significant parts of 'El perseguidor' in this regard is when Johnny talks about the presence of holes in the fabric of language, traditions, laws, and 'reality'. These are the holes that we cover up, that we refuse to see, because they would rupture our comforting understanding of the world. And it is therefore significant that similar references are also found at several points in the Berthe Trépat scene. In the music itself, the first movement of the Rose Bob piece played by Trépat is, for example, full of 'holes', in that it consists of 32 chords separated by silences of different lengths. Similarly, of the *Pavan* we are informed that Trépat's performance of it is 'con agujeros y zurcidos por todas partes' (Cortázar 2007: 247) ('with holes and [darning] everywhere', 1966: 105), the reference to *zurcidos* [darning] hinting (in a way echoed subsequently by 'Tango de vuelta') at the music's role in simultaneously trying to sew up such holes. Meanwhile, beyond these musical examples, there are numerous references in this chapter to rainwater having seeped into Oliveira's shoes (through holes, one imagines), with one such allusion occurring shortly after a description of the pianist's unleashing 'una lluvia de acordes' (2007: 247) [a shower of chords] and coinciding with Oliveira's realisation that, despite himself, he had developed 'cierta simpatía por Berthe Trépat' (249) ('a certain sympathy for Berthe Trépat', 1966: 107). Building upon this, such a coincidence of the reference to holes and an implied dismantling of a social/interpersonal barrier is repeated twice more, in the temporal hole opened up at the end of the concert, the 'segundo sin término, algo desesperadamente vacío entre Oliveira y Berthe Trépat solos en la sala' (2007: 250) ('an interminable second, something desperately empty between Oliveira and Berthe Trépat alone in the hall', 1966: 108) and in Oliveira's description of the prospect of sharing a drink with

Trépat and Valentín, the pianist's partner, as 'como un camino que se abriera de golpe en mitad de la pared: [...] abrirse paso por la piedra, [...] salir a otra cosa' (2007: 264) ('like a path suddenly opening up in the middle of the wall: [...] open a path through the stones, [...] come out into something else', 1966: 118), lines that bring to mind the 'muro de palabras' (2007: 531) ('wall [...] of words', 1966: 370) in which Morelli (and Cortázar) seek to open up a hole. Indeed, it is thus notable that, in one highly significant moment of the scene, we are told that Oliveira 'se sentía como un vómito' (2007: 254) ('felt like a mouthful of vomit', 1966: 111). Superficially an allusion to Oliveira's awareness of his insincerity at this point towards Trépat, it is a line which, more pointedly, echoes both his own reaction to the jazz sessions of the *Club de la Serpiente*, when 'por lo común después de los discos le venían ganas de vomitar' (2007: 180) ('usually after [the records] he would feel like vomiting', 1966: 50), and Bruno's informing us that 'en el fondo *Amorous* me ha dado ganas de vomitar' (Cortázar 1970d: 149) ('[deep down], *Amorous* made me want to go vomit', 2013: 221), on which I commented in chapter 5. It is a line, that is, that binds the effect on Oliveira of this scene of dialogic avant-garde classical performance with precisely the breakdown of boundaries and collapse of differences or categories that, through a Kristevan analysis, we saw the jazz of both 'El perseguidor' and the *discada* scene in *Rayuela* to evoke.

The parallels between these two well-known pieces of Cortazariana are, then, highly suggestive and of considerable importance to the current study. In sketching them out, I am not suggesting that the differences between Johnny Carter's jazz and Berthe Trépat's avant-garde *música culta* are dissolved. But what they demonstrate is that, just as each of them signals, in some way at least, an unrepeatable performative moment in which barriers and divisions, associated with language and a Western, 'inauthentic' sense of personal and societal being, are dismantled, so, taken together, do they render porous the boundary that separates them from each other.[27] And in this sense, they are indicative of both the nature and the effect of Cortázar's musical engagement in general. For, as well as the hierarchisation of value to which I referred earlier, Cortázar also engages, as we have seen, in a process of division, categorisation, and classification of music into la *música culta* (/classical music), tango, and jazz, but then also into descriptive and non-descriptive *música culta*, old (New Guard/Golden Age) and new tango, Swing jazz, bebop, free jazz, black jazz, white jazz. And yet such categorisation of jazz, for example, apparently blind to the essence of jazz *per se*, is mocked by Oliveira when he comments that he will never enter into the 'game', as Ronald does, for whom 'sería bueno o malo, hot o cool, blanco o negro, antiguo o moderno, Chicago o New Orleans, nunca el jazz, nunca eso que ahora eran Satchmo, Ronald y Babs' (2007: 182) ('[it would be] good or bad, hot or cool, white or black, old or modern, Chicago or New Orleans, never jazz, never what was now Satchmo, Ronald, and Babs', 1966: 51). What my brief comparison of 'El perseguidor' and the Berthe Trépat scene demonstrates and symbolises, then, is that, just as Cortázar's work ends up disturbing, if not dismantling, the hierarchy of musical types in 'value' terms, so too do his musical engagements destabilise the musical categories themselves. The points of commonality that link

'El perseguidor' and the Berthe Trépat scene, that is, signal how Cortázar's own texts work simultaneously on several levels to deconstruct the musical barriers that the author himself erects in those very texts. Music in Cortázar's work is indeed about more than jazz, then: it is about the overarching sense that in the musical experience *per se*, in the moment of performative dialogue and mutual epiphany involving music(ian) and listener, something essential can be met.

Notes to Chapter 6

1. See Chanan (1995: 47–50) for a discussion of how the three-minute record can be seen to constitute a limitation which in fact led to greater freedom.
2. Seeking to differentiate the nature of these subjugations in jazz from their *música culta* counterparts, Cortázar argues that those found in jazz 'carecen de la obligada servilidad que un concertista *debe* a sus déspotas' (2006d: 215) [lack the obligatory servitude that a concert player *owes* to his/her despots].
3. Along similar lines, the American jazz pianist Bill Evans stated that 'there is no freedom without it being in reference to something. You take this form, this strict form, and you find some way to get away from it, and that gives it a meaning [...]. When I play, I'm playing everything I play against the strict squareness of the original form' (2005 [1966]).
4. An alternative view with regard to the effect of the underlying structures and conventions of jazz is set out by Adorno in 'On Jazz' (1989 [1936]). Adorno's essays on jazz have been largely pilloried, with Eric Hobsbawm famously declaring that they include 'some of the stupidest pages ever written about jazz' (1993: 300). But more recent scholarship has, without trying or wishing to excuse or explain away some of the more head-scratching or racially problematic elements, sought to show that what Adorno is doing that is of value in these essays is not so much tackling jazz *per se* (not least because the music to which he was exposed scarcely qualifies as such), as, as Gunther Kodat puts it, addressing 'the culture industry['s] *packaging* of jazz as African American music, and the degree to which this packaging disguises some of the ideological uses to which the music is put' (2003: 3). In addition to this, 'On Jazz' also wrestles with the extent to which the claims of freedom made on behalf of jazz — notwithstanding the caveat regarding the music to which he was referring with this term — are undercut by the reliance of the music on certain structural and musical characteristics: 'The stimulation and the artistic piece, the new color and the new rhythm are merely inserted along with the banal — just as the jazz vibrato is inserted into the rigid sound, and syncopation in the basic meter. This element of interference in jazz is accomplished by the arrangement of the composition. But its contours remain the old ones. The schema can still be heard, even through the most digressive breaks in the arrangement. He who is reproducing the music is permitted to tug at the chains of his boredom, and even to clatter them, but he cannot break them. Freedom in reproduction is no more present here than in "artistic" music' (Adorno 1989: 56). Such an outlook is also found among Cortázar's writings, in particular in *Libro de Manuel*, where Andrés reflects on the fundamental way in which *lo viejo* is simply always present: 'Es así, a pesar de tantos años de música electrónica o aleatoria, de *free jazz* [...], lo mismo el hombre viejo sigue vivo y se acuerda [...]: [...] del piano puede nacer la serie menos pianística de notas o de acordes pero el instrumento está ahí reconocible, el piano de la otra música, una vieja humanidad' (1973a: 25–26) [That's how it is, despite so many years of electronic or random music, of free jazz [...], still the man of old remains alive and remembers [...]: [...] from the piano can emerge the least piano-esque series of notes or chords, but the instrument is there, recognisable, the piano of the other kind of music, an old humankind]. As an aside, it should be noted that Robinson (1994) is the seminal work in this important revision of Adorno's writing on jazz.
5. On Charlie Parker, see, for example, Picon Garfield (1981: 128); on Clifford Brown, see 'Clifford' (Cortázar 1970b: 109); on Thelonious Monk, see 'La vuelta al piano de Thelonious Monk' (Cortázar 1970c: 23–28).

6. An additional consideration here is found when we move on from the hot jazz and Swing Era examples Cortázar gives in the lines cited to the case of bebop. Although bebop is, as I have examined, often seen, in part at least, as a move of black liberation from the white commercial exploitation of the Big Band Era, it is erroneous to suggest that bebop did not, in turn, also become a terrain for commercialisation and commodification. As Gunther Kodat argues, there was in bop 'a movement, among the musicians themselves, to take "advantage of the disadvantages" by refashioning the pre-existing non-commercial jam session into a profitable commodity' (2003: 11), and Scott DeVeaux refers keenly to the 'commodification of bop' (1997: 298). That said, the example of 'Amorous' in 'El perseguidor', as with the real-life 'Lover Man' incident on which it is based, constitutes an instance of continued commercial exploitation of the black musician (Johnny Carter and Charlie Parker respectively) on the part of white producers and managers. Relatedly, it is also worth noting free jazz's distinctly non-commercial nature. In a telling analysis, Gunther Kodat links this failure of free jazz to sell with its 'near-complete erasure [...] from the jazz canon' (2003: 13).
7. 'Mahogany Hall Stomp' was, according to Cortázar, the first Louis Armstrong record he bought (1970c: 22).
8. Couture (2016: 12) also makes gestures in this direction.
9. That said, 'Soledad de la música' demonstrates that Cortázar was at least partially aware of the hyperbole of his writing on jazz: he takes care to state in a footnote that 'no se trata aquí de sobreestimar el *jazz*, cuyas limitaciones son evidentes' (1992: 297) [it's not a question here of overestimating jazz, whose limitations are evident], although it is certainly the case that, Swing Era jazz aside, his 'jazz texts' rarely bring up its limitations in any obvious way.
10. Owens (1974) has analysed how Parker's improvised solos are constructed from a set of around a hundred 'motives'.
11. 'Tea for Two' was a jazz standard that had initially appeared in the musical *No, No, Nanette* from 1925.
12. This quotation demonstrates that this repetition and reformulation of previous material is not to be seen negatively, but, rather, as part of 'bebop's process of criticism and engagement through musical quoting' (Borshuk 2004: 279), through which it questioned and subverted previous musical composition and sensibilities. For more details on this and other versions of 'Ko-Ko', including earlier ones where Parker cited other tunes, see Woideck (1998: 115–17).
13. Charles Ives (1874–1954) was an American modernist composer who made innovative use of numerous techniques, including polyrhythm.
14. Gioia's writing on improvisation also underscores the extent to which Cortázar's vision of jazz spontaneity and inspiration is somewhat distant from the reality, not least in underplaying the time, effort, and concentration needed not just to master an instrument but to be able to improvise in an adequate way: 'Anyone who has performed jazz can attest to the immense powers of concentration required in improvisation [...]. Such concentration on the music is [...], in fact, quite essential: the necessity that jazz be *improvised* — the requirement of spontaneity — increases rather than decreases the demands on the artist. Put simply, the creation of jazz requires more than mere visceral energy' (1988: 47–48). Couture (2016: 12), writing on 'El perseguidor', gestures towards this point in highlighting that, as well as Cortázar himself, critics such as Lois Parkinson Zamora place too much emphasis on what the latter calls the 'passionate transcendence' (1999: 98) of jazz improvisation.
15. 'Bemsha Swing' was written by Thelonious Monk and Denzil Best. It was first recorded by Monk in 1952.
16. 'All the Things You Are' (1939) was composed by Jerome Kern. The version by Konitz (1927–) referred to here dates from 1953 and was included on the album *Lee Konitz Plays with the Gerry Mulligan Quartet*. Mulligan and Konitz are both associated (though not exclusively) with the cool jazz era. 'Lonely Woman' is a track from Coleman's *The Shape of Jazz to Come* album, released in 1959. Coleman (1930–2015) was a saxophonist and key figure in the free jazz movement.
17. One might say that this constitutes a third take on the role and nature of records in Cortázar's work, in addition to the two already discussed.
18. In interview with Jacques Chesnel in 1977, Cortázar states that, in contrast to his early years

in Argentina, in Europe he preferred records to the concert hall. However, this appears to be due more to his frustration with concert goers than to anything else, and it is notable that he continues to recognise the superiority of the jazz concert, in that 'évidemment [...] il n'y a rien de mieux que la présence en plus de la musique' (10) [evidently [...] there is nothing better than presence/being present in addition to the music].

19. On the centrality of performance to the early poetic traditions (Ancient Greece, Occitan troubadours) from which more modern traditions evolved, see Nagy (1996).

20. More could certainly be made of the fact that the voice is so often conceived of as the female voice in jazz, both generally and in Cortázar's work. A case could quite easily be made, for example, for it to be seen as an alignment of Cortázar's jazz with the role played by female figures such as la Maga in *Rayuela*, offering an alternative to the staid and structured intellectualism of Oliveira (and, thus, more broadly, the structures and strictures of language and (Western) society). There is no space to engage with this question here, but it is worth noting in passing the end of the Picon Garfield interview, where Cortázar's response to the interviewer's pointing out that 'en el jazz los músicos generalmente son hombres mientras los cantores son mujeres' (1981: 132) [in jazz the musicians are generally men whilst the singers are women] is a simple 'sí' (132) [yes]. One wonders whether this reveals a certain disinterest on Cortázar's part in this observation, or whether, coming at the end of what was clearly a long and exhausting interview, he was simply in desperate need of a *vin rouge*.

21. The identification of improvisation as dialogic is far from novel. As Panagiotis A. Kanellopoulos sums up, 'improvisation is dialogic exactly because it creates a very special sense of interaction, which is characterized by unfinalizability and openness' (2011: 113). We might also comment here on the way in which jazz *per se* is dialogic in its emergence from the meeting of diverse musical genres which were themselves the result of sociocultural and social mixing, as I examined in chapter 4.

22. This coming together of present and past in the playing of old jazz records resonates both with the role of the tracks heard by Jiménez in the hotel bar in 'Alguien que anda por ahí' and with Cortázar's relationship with and discourse on old tango records. However, it is notable that the focus here is not on a wistful nostalgia, as in the former instance, nor on a restoration of the past listening context, as in the case of tango records, but on a bringing of the past into (dialogue with) the present.

23. In interview with Guillermo Schavelzon, Cortázar repudiates the idea that he sees music in hierarchical terms, in respect of his enjoyment of different forms of music at least, referring to his musical taste as one of 'eclecticismo' (1980: 2) [eclecticism].

24. An additional nod to 'Las ménades' might be found in the description of Trépat's 'zapatos tan de hombre que ninguna falda podía disimularlos' (Cortázar 2007: 245) ('men's shoes, incapable of disguise by any skirt', 1966: 104). The bringing together of male and female here recalls the dual gender identification of Teiresias, upon whom the blind man in the earlier story appears to be based.

25. This also pre-empts 'La isla a mediodía', where any attempt by Marini to repeat his sighting of the island of Xiros at any time other than when he passes over it at midday is put off or frustrated (see chapter 1, n. 14).

26. It is worth remarking, however, that some of Trépat's compositional methods are far from conventional and recall the operations of the poet in 'Para una poética' that I examined in the Introduction, in particular when we are told that the compositional technique of the *Synthesis* 'entroncaba con las fuerzas más primitivas y esotéricas de la creación' (Cortázar 2007: 245) ('was based on the most primitive and esoteric forces of creation', 1966: 103).

27. In this respect it is significant that Charlie Parker himself 'was interested in studying classical music composition with a goal of writing new pieces of his own' (Woideck 1998: 212), an element of the saxophonist's practice that Cortázar alludes to in 'El perseguidor' in the references to Johnny's knowledge of and desire to play the music of Vivaldi, Bach, and Ives (1970d: 163–64).

CONCLUSION

In formulating a conclusion to this study, there are few more apt places to start, and indeed finish, than the text 'Para escuchar con audífonos' [To Listen Through Earphones] from the posthumous *Salvo el crepúsculo* (2009 [1984]: 33–40).[1] It is a text that serves a variety of purposes in the light of my analysis over the preceding chapters. For one, it rejoins the discussion of music (and poetry) found in Cortázar's early texts such as *Teoría del túnel*, 'Soledad de la música', and 'Elogio del jazz', thus acting together with them as the respective bookends to the music-infused literary production that I have been exploring in these pages. It hence also seems appropriate to bookend the present study in the same way. But its usefulness goes beyond that of structural neatness, in that it takes up numerous tropes, metaphors, and issues from those early treatises, sometimes repeating them in a way similar to that found in those early discussions, at other times recasting or even rewriting them in a stark manner. In the process, 'Para escuchar con audífonos' also alludes to and brings itself to bear upon the different ways in which music and the questions and potential solutions Cortázar sees it as offering up are allowed to develop and operate in the course of his intervening work. Scarcely surprising, then, that it should do so in a way that also responds to some of the key findings and debates to surface from the chapters that I have dedicated both to those early texts and to that intervening body of work.

As set out in the preceding chapter and, more implicitly, in the way in which I have shown Cortázar to deal with the different forms of music on which I have focused, despite an at-times concerted and robust attempt at delineating neatly between *la música culta*, tango, and jazz — and between different types and examples of these — ultimately all of these musical forms and genres emerge from Cortázar's work both celebrated and bemoaned, both capable of resisting, in different ways, the traps and problems of language and being from which Cortázar seeks an escape, and yet also susceptible of falling foul of them. Peiró notes the broad appreciation of different musical types on Cortázar's part, and, likewise, rejects the idea that the author constructs a hierarchy of musical genres, concluding that 'la preferencia de Cortázar es la síntesis de todas las músicas, el universo musical en conjunto, no un estilo en concreto' (2006: 105) [Cortázar's preference is for the synthesis of all types of music, the musical universe together, not one particular style]. But a synthesis of genres of music, creating some totalising, universal musical form is very much not what Cortázar desires; indeed, he often speaks in decidedly negative terms of projects such as Third Stream music, aimed at bringing together, in this instance, classical music and jazz in some sort of fused, hybrid form.[2]

At the end of chapter 6, I advanced the idea that, in fact, one could infer from Cortázar's work a valorisation of music *per se*, effectively returning us to *Teoría del túnel*'s talk of music loosely defined and without specific referent; 'Para escuchar con audífonos', at the other end of Cortázar's production, in many ways takes up this baton and provides support for and a way of developing the aforementioned inference. In the course of this late essay, several musical forms and artists are mentioned: Orlando Gibbons's *Royal Fantasies*, Schubert's lied 'Du bist die Ruh', sung by Elisabeth Schumann, a Mozart quartet, the French composer Edgard Varèse, the Italian composer Luigi Nono, the Polish composer Witold Lutoslawski, Cat Anderson, a jazz trumpeter who played with Duke Ellington's band, and a Béla Bartók quartet. More generally, Cortázar talks of listening to 'jazz y música de cámara' (2009: 35) [jazz and chamber music]. On the one hand, this points to the fact that, unlike in *Teoría del túnel*, the later Cortázar maintains discrete categories of music, as he has done throughout his intervening production. Indeed, the range of types of music referred to is extensive, from the seventeenth-century polyphonic composer Gibbons, through a wide spectrum of forms and composers of, broadly, *la música culta*, to jazz. But, within the context of the essay, the detailed enumeration of these musical figures and genres proves to be secondary to the primary consideration, which is the experiencing of music *per se* through earphones.

At the heart of 'Para escuchar con audífonos' in this regard lies an almost page-long, near-parodically detailed description in which Cortázar sets out the journey by which an 'estructura sonora' (2009: 37) [sonorous structure] invented by Bartók arrived at the earphone-wearing Cortázar's 'laboratorio central' (37) [central laboratory] (brain). Following the tortuous route taken by the piece of music, involving myriad forms of inscription and reading (score, recording onto disc, reading of disc by stylus, and so on), it is an exposition that recalls and takes up in exaggerated fashion the numerous references found in Cortazarian texts over the decades to the problematic barriers between ('original') music and listener that are raised by such processes of musical production, with the focus in *Rayuela* on the stylus as it reads the grooves of the discs' surface coming most readily to mind. And yet, precisely in its exaggeration, it is a description that undercuts the idea that these putative barriers actually represent a problem; its aim appears more simply to marvel at the complexity of what lies behind listening to music through earphones, 'como si fuera la cosa más sencilla de este mundo' (38) [as if it were the simplest thing in this world].

This essay, then, sends up a concern for the minutiae both of musical identification and of the decidedly linguistic, and formerly highly problematic, processes of musical production, playfully indicating that neither is, ultimately, that important. This is not, though, a facile dismissal of either the differences between musical genres and pieces, or the issues surrounding their creation and transmission. Rather, it speaks of a grounding concern for and desire to focus here on the fundamental, underlying question of the musical experience itself. And one of the key aspects of this late text in this respect is the primacy it gives to the listener or 'receiver' of music, a figure who has been a persistent, if often inconspicuous, presence in Cortázar's work, not just in being invoked by the essential dialogism of music as performance and voice that I discussed in chapter 6, but also in its emergence as central to Cortázar's presentation of music *per se*. Thus, Cortázar, as we have seen, repeatedly talks of his *own* response and relationship to music of all types, and often bases his fictional texts concerned with both *la música culta* ('Reunión', 'Las ménades', the Berthe Trépat concert scene in *Rayuela*) and tango ('Las puertas del cielo', *Rayuela*) around those 'receiving' or experiencing the music in question. Beyond this, the musicians he alludes to are open to be understood as listeners too: the numerous composers and performers in 'Clone' draw upon the music that they have heard from or by others; the tangos penned by Cortázar (including tango-poems and the story 'Tango de vuelta') and those performed in stories such as 'Las puertas del cielo' are implicitly built upon those composers'/performers' listening to and engaging with previous tangos; and Charlie Parker's inventively citational style tells of a man who was an attentive musical 'listener', a trait reflected in Cortázar's presentation of Johnny in 'El perseguidor'.

In many ways, then, 'Para escuchar con audífonos' serves to tie these more hidden strands together and to underline their collective importance. Indeed, the essay's focus on the listening to, rather than the production of, music is clear, a notable example being the way in which Cortázar draws particular attention in the text to the semantic difference between the Spanish, English, and French words for loudspeaker (*altoparlante*, loud-speaker, *haut-parleur*) and earphones (*audífonos*, earphones, *casques d'écoute*). Although putatively focusing on the fact that the terms for the former have to do with language more than music ('centra[n] su función en la palabra más que en la música' (2009: 36) [they focus their function on the word more than on the music]), whilst those for the latter have a broader meaning that includes, it is implied, the full range of elements that pertain to 'la reproducción sonora' (36) [the reproduction of sound], in fact, what is at least as stark — and relevant — is the more general move here from speaking to listening, from production to reception. But this focus on listening goes further, as signalled in the section of the essay written in the form of poetic verse. Here, we read that 'la música no viene del audífono, es como si surgiera de mí mismo, soy mi oyente' (39) [the music does not come from the earphone, it is as if it were surging up from myself, I am my listener]. To understand the significance of this line we must go back over four decades to 'Soledad de la música', where Cortázar states that 'la Música debe surgir, pura porque *nuestra*, desde el centro mismo de cada hombre. Cada uno debe ser *su Músico*' (1992: 295) [the Music must surge up, pure because it is *ours*, from the very centre of each man. Each person must be *his or her Musician*]. The late text answers the challenge of its predecessor with an affirmation, but one which recasts this success as the subject in question becoming his or her own listener, rather than his or her own musician.

The first thing to note when analysing this shift is that 'Para escuchar con audífonos' re-engages with the titular concern of 'Soledad de la música'. As in that essay, the invocation of solitude, here in the form of the isolation from the world that results from putting on and using earphones, appears initially somewhat negatively, as he talks of feeling 'bruscamente tan aislado del exterior' (Cortázar

2009: 35) [abruptly so cut off from the outside world]. However, again as is the case with 'Soledad de la música', this soon gives way to a more affirmative stance being assumed, in this instance where Cortázar perceives the isolation of earphones as affording a far greater musical experience, one described in terms that emphasise a more intimate connection with the music: outlining the emotions he sees on the face of a woman listening to music through earphones, for example, Cortázar writes of 'esa pequeña noche interior, [...] esa intimidad total de la música y sus oídos' (36) [that small interior night, [...] that total intimacy of the music and her ears]. But where 'Para escuchar con audífonos' differs from 'Soledad de la música' is, as I have indicated, that, whereas the latter's affirmation of solitude is built precisely around eschewing the idea that we are passive receivers of someone's interpretation of the music, seeing us instead as the 'musicians' producing these sounds, in this late text, the positive turn has to do entirely with experiencing the music as listener. Mapping these two texts onto each other in this way, I would contend that this shift does three inter-related things: it reaffirms the listener's role and value *qua* listener; it challenges the conception of the nature and origin of music advocated at the end of 'Soledad de la música'; and it, thus, suggests an alternative to that essay's insistence upon the isolation of the musical experience. What is more, on each of these three points, which I shall now discuss, 'Para escuchar con audífonos' effectively works to bring together and crystallise the implications of Cortázar's career-long engagement with music in all its forms.

An initial reading of the later essay might lead one to conclude that, as at the end of 'Soledad de la música', music is conceived of here as being produced by and from within the individual who (subsequently) hears it. This is implied, for instance, by the repeated mention of the 'silencio interior' or 'silencio previo' (38) [interior silence; silence before], recalling the unrung bell in the cathedral that we are called to build within ourselves in the earlier essay. These references culminate in the lines:

> [...] un silencio fosfeno
> hasta que estalla la primera nota o un acorde
> también adentro, de mi lado, la música en el centro del cráneo de cristal. (38)
>
> [[...] a phosphene silence
> until the first note or a chord explodes
> also within, on my side, the music in the centre of the crystal skull.]

The suggestion seems to be that, as in 'Soledad de la música', the music is indeed experienced as coming directly from the individual. And it is a reading that is further enhanced towards the end of the essay, where ideas from both 'Soledad de la música' and *Teoría del túnel* are taken up again. The first of these instances occurs when we are returned to the problem of communication, literature, and language, in that, in a story or a novel, Cortázar affirms, 'el sistema de comunicación se mantiene ligado al de la vida circundante, la información sigue siendo información por más estética, elíptica, simbólica que se vuelva' (2009: 39) [the system of communication remains tied to that of surrounding life, the information is still information, however aesthetic, elliptic, symbolic it becomes]. Following this, the essay then restates the more affirmative presentation of poetry that we saw in *Teoría del túnel*, in contrast to that found in 'Soledad de la música' and 'Para una poética', declaring:

> En cambio el poema *comunica el poema*, y no quiere ni puede comunicar otra cosa. Su razón de nacer y de ser lo vuelve interiorización de una interioridad, exactamente como los audífonos que eliminan el puente de fuera hacia adentro y viceversa para crear un estado exclusivamente interno, presencia y vivencia de la música que parece venir desde lo hondo de la caverna negra. (39)

> [By contrast, the poem *communicates the poem*, and neither wants nor is able to communicate anything else. Its reason for being born and for being turns it into the interiorisation of an interiority, just like earphones which eliminate the bridge from the outside towards the inside and vice versa to create state that is exclusively internal, the presence and experience of the music that seems to come from the depths of the black cave.]

Poetry and music are brought together once more in this paean to interiority and isolation that again brings to mind the cathedral image from 'Soledad de la música': the 'interiorización de una interioridad' [interiorisation of an interiority] describes aptly the bell within the cathedral constructed within us that is posited at the end of that essay.

But two elements of 'Para escuchar con audífonos' serve to undermine the text's own putative stance here. The first of these is the discussion earlier in the essay of the phenomenon of the pre-echo, the faint appearance of the music one is about to hear when listening to a gramophone record as the needle plays the silent block that precedes the track. A technician friend explained the reasons for this phenomenon to Cortázar, but the author scarcely hides his disinterest in such rational explanations, as he declares that 'yo seguí sin entenderlo y poco me importó' (34) [I still didn't understand it and I didn't really care].[3] What is more important for Cortázar is to focus on the pre-echo as an indicator of and a metaphor for the relationship between music and people as found at the experiential level. And it is here that we find the most important implications for our own understanding of this relationship, including at a broader, theoretical level. For the pre-echo not only breaks the 'physical' silent buffer that precedes the putative beginning of the music on the disc, but also entails the revision within Cortázar's presentation of music of the more abstract silence from which he posits music to emerge: the pre-echo, that is, comes to metaphorise the idea of the pre-existence of the music prior to its (perceived) emergence from the individual listener (or, more specifically, from the ringing of the internal bell).

The second element of 'Para escuchar con audífonos' to which I wish to draw attention is the use made by Cortázar at the end of the essay of tree imagery to describe the surging up of music (and poetry) through the individual. Cortázar makes a number of allusions to the first of Rainer Maria Rilke's *Sonnets to Orpheus* (1946 [1923]) here, including what we might see as a nod to his earlier bell/cathedral image in his reference to Rilke's description of '[la] creación interior' (Cortázar 2009: 40) [[the] interior creation] as the raising up of 'un templo en el oído' (40) [a temple in the ear]. However, Cortázar's principal interest is in the line 'Orfeo canta. ¡Oh, alto árbol en el oído!' (39) [Orpheus sings. Oh, tall tree in the ear!], which he sees as a perceptive description of the experience of listening to (Orphic) music, an experience enabled by earphones, and one which he glosses, more precisely, as the rising up (growth) of an 'árbol interior' (39) [interior tree].[4] Indeed, the final line of the essay replaces the temple image by this organic alternative, as Cortázar ends by referring to 'el altísimo árbol en el oído interior' (40) [the exceedingly tall tree in the interior ear], in the process signalling the replacement of his bell/cathedral conceptualisation from 'Soledad de la música' by this tree image.

The significance of this move, however, is found not in the visual image of the tree itself, but in its (subterranean and subtextual) ramifications: a tree has roots, which spread outside of and beyond the isolated space of the (visible) tree. In other words, bringing the two elements together, I am suggesting that the pre-echo and the tree are to be seen as disturbing the silence and the isolation, respectively, of the essay's portrayal of music's emergence in each individual listener, opening up this depiction of the experiencing of music to a different, rupturing reading.

Importantly, the key to such a reading lies in mapping the two concepts onto each other. Thus, the pre-echo, understood *as* the music (a Mozart quartet, a track by Charlie Parker, a tango by Carlos Gardel), which is to say, as the origins and source of the music's emergence in the individual, comes to be seen as coterminous with the tree's roots. Moreover, and crucially, these roots in turn demand to be understood specifically as a rhizome, in that they are essentially characterised as and constitute a latent, all-connecting (tunnel-like?) root system from which each tree (each individual experiencing of that music) grows. (It should, incidentally, come as no surprise that we have ended up with a schema that combines both rhizome and arborescence, rather than one which rejects one of those two, usually antagonistic, systemic concepts.) We can thus appreciate the nature of the disruption of the listener's isolation that is conveyed by the replacement of the image in 'Soledad de la música' of the cathedral, which — note the active voice — '[c]ada uno debe levantar' (Cortázar 1992: 296) [each person must construct], by that of the tree that grows in 'Para escuchar con audífonos': it is a move that maintains the sense of music as individually experienced and formed, whilst also insisting that it shares a common underlying provenance that goes beyond and precedes that individual experiencing and formation. In the process, then, it both replaces the idea of the individual as perceiving him/herself as the producer of the music with that of an inner production that emerges from an initial — and central — *listening*, and, attendantly, recasts the communicative nature of music: it is not that it *communicates* any intention or message from any one person to another; rather, in communicating itself in this way, it constitutes a means by which individuals might *commune* through the same rhizomatic musical 'root', chiming thus with the quasi-religious communion involving jazz musician and listener glimpsed in texts such as 'Clifford' and 'Louis, enormísimo cronopio'. In short, if the cathedral/bell image, 'resonating' with Hegel's *Klang*, pointed to the need for the harnessing of the unrung, silent potentiality of Music, whilst underlining the apparent impossibility of squaring this with the attendant need for that Music to be communicated, then the recasting of that early image through that of the tree and the concept of the pre-echo offers a potential solution for a successful envisaging of this dual necessity.

But the pre-echo and the tree/rhizomatic roots motifs, understood expansively and figuratively, also do more than this, offering new ways of seeing other, more specific strands that emerge from Cortázar's work. Thus, they provide a visualisation of understanding as *entender* [tending-in] rather than *inteligir* [making sense, reading], as advocated by Oliveira in *Rayuela*, and, recalling the presentation of musicians as listeners to which I referred earlier, they give us a way of formulating the idea that both musicians and listeners are operating in the same way. As jazz saxophonist Pharoah Sanders put it, in a line that numerous musicians have (pre-)echoed down the ages, 'the music speaks through me [...] and I just try to bring it out' (Prestianni 2003): composing/improvising music is also about listening to the silence and hearing the pre-echo, the pre-echo of the music that one is called to produce. Indeed, the extent to which the pre-echo in particular responds to and illuminates a number of the findings of this study becomes apparent if one ponders Cortázar's own judgment in this late essay that, technical explanations aside, the idea of hearing the echo of what one is about to listen to prior to the sound being produced 'en buena y sana lógica temporal me parecía imposible' (2009: 34) [in all good and sane temporal logic seemed impossible to me]. This reversal of the logic of cause and effect, and of the (associated) temporal flow appeals to Cortázar because it ties in with exactly the sort of rupture in the accepted order of things that he desires,[5] and, metaphorised, it enables a suggestive recasting of numerous elements that underpin the role and nature of music in his work: the *pre*-echo implies once more the problem of *la música culta*'s only ever being a version or iteration of a putative original, but in being a pre-*echo* it renders each playing or experiencing of the music an 'original', even as it accepts the inevitability of iterability; as *pre*-echo it can be seen as a way of imaging how music from one's back-history (tango, for example) inevitably filters into one's (present) consciousness, ensuring a persistent anchoring in the past, or where listening to it would be, at heart, a(n attempted) restoration of that past, but, again, as pre-*echo* it implies that that posited past can be perceived in reflective nostalgic, creative terms as a future to be striven towards; relatedly, then, it also serves as a metaphor for improvisational jazz citation, where cited passages both pre-exist the improvisation (*pre*-echo) and — simultaneously — exist as a new creation in it (pre-*echo*).[6]

At the end of this study, then, we can, with some confidence, affirm that not only are the central issues and ideas of Cortázar's writing played out on the terrain of music in his work, but that music offers news ways of seeing and potentially resolving some of the binds and concerns with which the author wrestles. This is not, moreover, necessarily a result of conscious planning by Cortázar. Indeed, there is an overarching sense that music, unleashed in his texts, works in its own ways to destabilise, disturb, and resist *both* the elements that Cortázar seeks to destabilise *and* Cortazar's own, often problematic, presentation of music and diverse musical types. Music is, in this sense, not simply a topic that literature and Cortázar 'engage with'; rather, it is a challenge to literature's nature and meaning, not least in challenging what that literature and its author apparently say and do — including what they say about and do with music. Cortázar's texts and themes, that is, emerge differently when music acts upon them; and music, in turn, in its incorporation into Cortázar's texts, also emerges differently, both from the way in which Cortázar envisages and presents it, and, quite possibly, from how we ourselves may have understood and experienced it previously.

Indeed, in this respect, and cognisant of the return to poetry at the end of 'Para escuchar con audífonos', it seems apposite to end this study by turning to our own role as readers, for it is we as readers and critics of Cortázar's texts who are at least in part responsible for *allowing* music to act on them. And Cortázar's persistent, underlying engagement with music requires us to do so: it requires that we allow music to challenge our existing interpretations of his work and of its music, that is, that we allow *music* to determine, above the claims of the author, how we read his texts, their operations, and the role of music in them. The preceding chapters have shown how, perhaps most fundamentally, this means becoming aware of the extent to which, where we see constraint, comfort, and rules in those texts and in that music, there is also freedom, revolution, challenge; and where we see freedom, revolution, and challenge, there is also constraint, comfort, rules. And maybe, crucially, and with all that that entails as both a restriction and a liberation, it means ensuring that when we read Cortázar's literature, we always hear its music.

Notes to the Conclusion

1. Although 'headphones' often appears a more likely translation of *audífonos* than 'earphones', I am using the latter term in part because it is the one adopted by Cortázar himself, and because, for reasons that will become obvious, it is important to retain the auricular reference found in the Spanish word.
2. In interview with Picon Garfield, for instance, Cortázar rejects Third Stream music, stating that 'la música clásica no gana nada con unirse al jazz y el jazz aún menos. El jazz perdería todo' (1981: 132) [classical music gains nothing from combining with jazz and jazz even less. Jazz would lose everything].
3. The cause of the pre-echo is the stylus detecting the faint outlines of the ridges cut into the disc's grooves on the other (track) side of the silent block.
4. Cortázar had previously engaged with this line from Rilke's poem in relation to music and poetry in the essay 'Para una poética' (1994b: 281).
5. The temporal 'reversal' implied by the pre-echo chimes with Réda's depiction of jazz swing as constituting a similar reversal of cause and effect (2010: 20).
6. Reinforcing this, and showing the relevance of this point beyond just jazz and tango, Berthe Trépat in *Rayuela* insists that what she plays is 'mi propia música' (Cortázar 2007: 254) ('my own music', 1966: 111), even as the example of her music that we are given — the 'Síntesis Délibes–Saint-Saëns' (Cortázar 2007: 243) ('*Délibes–Saint-Saëns Synthesis*', 1966: 102) — is made up of nothing but citations and passages from pre-existing works by other composers.

BIBLIOGRAPHY

Works from the same year are ordered alphabetically, with the exception of the texts found in Cortázar's *Obras completas VI* (2006). As these are all from the same work, they are ordered, in the first instance, in order of their writing, and then alphabetically where they were written in the same year.

Where necessary or useful for the purposes of this study, the date of first publication (in the original language in the instance of translated texts) or, in the case of several of Cortázar's works, the date of writing, where known, is put in square brackets.

ADORNO, THEODOR W. 1989 [1936]. 'On Jazz', trans. by J. Owen Daniel, *Discourse*, 12.1: 45–69

AJURIA IBARRA, ENRIQUE. 2005. 'Fantasía y compromiso social en los relatos de Juan Rulfo y de Julio Cortázar' (unpublished doctoral thesis, Universidad de las Américas Puebla)

ALIAU, MAGDALENA. 1997. '"Las ménades": transmutación del arte', in *Cortázar 1994: estudios críticos: Actas de las Jornadas de Homenaje a Julio Cortázar, 2, 3 y 4 de noviembre de 1994* (Buenos Aires: Academia del Sur), pp. 19–24

ÁLVAREZ-SCHÜLLER, VIVIANA. 2008. *Der Tango im Werk Julio Cortázars: Eine Tangoreise durch seine Literatur* (Hamburg: Diplomica Verlag GmbH)

ANAD, GUILLERMO. 2004. 'Presencia de los tangos en la poesía de Julio Cortázar', in *The Space of Culture: Critical Readings in Hispanic Studies*, ed. by Stewart King and Jeff Browitt (Newark: University of Delaware Press), pp. 110–17

ANDERSON, VAUGHN. 2013. 'Unfrozen Music: Disrupted Synaesthesia in Julio Cortázar's Paris', *Hispanic Journal*, 34.1: 115–29

ANDREA, PAT and JULIO CORTÁZAR. 1982a. *La puñalada/Le tango du retour* (Brussels: Elizabeth Franck)

—— 1982b. *La puñalada/Tango op zijn retour* (Brussels: Elizabeth Franck)

—— 2002 [1984]. *La puñalada/El tango de la vuelta* (Buenos Aires: Centro Cultural Recoleta)

ARCHETTI, EDUARDO P. 1999. *Masculinities: Football, Polo and the Tango in Argentina* (Oxford: Berg)

ARGYLE, RAY. 2009. *Scott Joplin and the Age of Ragtime* (Jefferson: McFarland & Company)

ARNOLD, DENIS. 1984. *Gesualdo* (London: BBC)

ARTAUD, ANTONIN. 1964. *Œuvres complètes*, vol. IV (Paris: Gallimard)

—— 1993 [1938]. *The Theatre and Its Double*, trans. by Victor Corti (London: Calder Publications)

AZZI, MARÍA SUSANA. 1995. 'The Golden Age and After: 1920s–1990s', in *¡Tango! The Dance, the Song, the Story*, ed. by Simon Collier (London: Thames and Hudson), pp. 114–60

—— 2002. 'The Tango, Peronism, and Astor Piazzolla during the 1940s and '50s', in *From Tejano to Tango*, ed. by Walter Aaron Clark (New York: Routledge), pp. 25–40

BAGGI, DENIS L. 1990. 'Neurswing: A Connectionist Workbench for the Investigation of Swing in Afro-American Jazz', in *Proceedings of the 23rd Asilomar Conference: Signals, Systems, and Computers*, vol. I (Los Alamitos: CS Press), pp. 336–41

BAIM, JO. 2007. *Tango: Creation of a Cultural Icon* (Bloomsbury: Indiana University Press)
BAKHTIN, MIKHAIL. 1981 [1975]. *The Dialogic Imagination: Four Essays by M. M. Bakhtin*, ed. by Michael Holquist, trans. by Caryl Emerson and Michael Holquist (Austin: University of Texas Press)
—— 1986. *Speech Genres and Other Late Essays*, ed. by Caryl Emerson and Michael Holquist, trans. by Vern W. McGee (Austin: University of Texas Press)
—— 1993. *Toward a Philosophy of the Act*, trans. and notes by Vadim Liapunov (Austin: University of Texas Press)
BALDWIN, BROOKE. 1981. 'The Cakewalk: A Study in Stereotype and Reality', *Journal of Social History*, 15.2: 205–18
BARAKA, AMIRI. 2010 [1963] 'Jazz and the White Critic', in Leroi Jones (Amiri Baraka), *Black Music* (New York: Akashic Books), pp. 15–26
BARAKA, AMIRI and AMINA BARAKA. 1987. 'The Great Music Robbery', in *The Music: Reflections on Jazz and Blues* (New York: Morrow), pp. 328–33
BARCHINO PÉREZ, MATÍAS. 2002. 'Libros con música: jazz en las misceláneas de Julio Cortázar', in *Literatura y música popular en Hispanoamérica: IV Congreso de la Asociación Española de Estudios Literarios Hispanoamericanos*, ed. by Ángel Esteban, Gracia Morales, and Álvaro Salvador (Granada: Método Ediciones), pp. 493–99
BAUDRILLARD, JEAN. 1983 [1981] *Simulations*, trans. by Paul Foss, Paul Patton, and Philip Beitchman (New York: Semiotext(e))
BELFIGLIO, ANTHONY. 2008. 'Fundamental Rhythmic Characteristics of Improvised Straight-ahead Jazz' (doctoral thesis, The University of Texas at Austin)
BERLINER, PAUL. 1994. *Thinking in Jazz: The Infinite Art of Improvisation* (Chicago: University of Chicago Press)
BERG, WALTER BRUNO. 2000. 'Julio Cortázar y el tango (*Rayuela y Trottoirs de Buenos Aires*)', in *'¡Bailá! ¡Vení! ¡Volá!' El fenómeno tanguero y la literatura: actas del coloquio de Berlín 13–15 de febrero de 1997*, ed. by Michael Rössner (Madrid: Biblioteca Iberoamericana), pp. 233–49
BIVINS, JASON C. 2015. *Spirits Rejoice!: Jazz and American Religion* (New York: Oxford University Press)
BLOCK, STEVEN. 1997. '"Bemsha Swing": The Transformation of a Bebop Classic to Free Jazz', *Music Theory Spectrum*, 19.2: 206–31
BOLDY, STEVEN. 1980. *The Novels of Julio Cortázar* (Cambridge: Cambridge University Press)
—— 2005. 'Cortázar's Controllers', *Bulletin of Spanish Studies*, 82: 375–86
BORELLO, RODOLFO A. 1980. 'Charlie Parker: "El perseguidor"', *Cuadernos Hispanoamericanos*, 364–66: 573–94
BORGE, JASON. 2011. 'Dark Pursuits: Race and Early Argentine Jazz Criticism', *Afro-Hispanic Review*, 30: 63–80
BORGES, JORGE LUIS. 1955. 'Historia del tango', in *Evaristo Carriego* (Buenos Aires: Emecé Editores), pp. 141–64
BORGES, JORGE LUIS and SILVINA BULLRICH. 1968. *El compadrito* (Buenos Aires: Compañía General Febril Editora)
BORSHUK, MICHAEL. 2004. '"So Black, So Blue": Ralph Ellison, Louis Armstrong and the Bebop Aesthetic', *Genre*, 25: 261–84
BOYM, SVETLANA. 2001. *The Future of Nostalgia* (New York: Basic Books)
—— 2007. 'Nostalgia and its Discontents', *The Hedgehog Review*, 9.2: 7–18
BRENES REYES, JAIME. 2010. 'Improvisation and Writing: Julio Cortázar's "El Perseguidor" and the Pursuit for Freedom', *Improvisation, Community and Social Practice Research Collection*: 1–5 <http://www.improvcommunity.ca/research/improvisation-and-writing-julio-cortazars-el-perseguidor-and-pursuit-freedom> [accessed 18 September 2018]

BROWN, MAURICE J. E. 1972. *Chopin: An Index of His Works in Chronological Order* (London: Macmillan)
BROYLES, MICHAEL. 2011. *Beethoven in America* (Bloomington: Indiana University Press)
BUTTERFIELD, MATTHEW W. 2011. 'Why Do Jazz Musicians Swing Their Eighth Notes?', *Music Theory Spectrum*, 33.1: 3–26
CANTARERO DE SALAZAR, ALEJANDRO. 2014. 'Caracteres psicológicos míticos insertos en la narrativa breve de Julio Cortázar', *Estudios griegos e indoeuropeos*, 24: 281–307
CARÁMBULA, RUBÉN. 2005. *El candombe* (Buenos Aires: Ediciones del Sol)
CARPENTIER, ALEJO. 1984 [1946]. *La música en Cuba*, 2nd edition (Mexico: Fondo de Cultura Económica)
CASLAV COVINO, DEBORAH. 2004. *Amending the Abject Body: Aesthetic Makeovers in Medicine and Culture* (Albany: New York Press)
CAVALLARI, HÉCTOR MARIO and GRACIELA P. GARCÍA. 1996. 'Escritura y desfetichización: En torno a "El perseguidor", de Julio Cortazar', *Revista de Crítica Literaria Latinoamericana*, 22.43–44: 267–77
CELLIER, LAURENT. 1926. 'Les préludes de Chopin', in Frédéric Chopin, *24 Préludes Op. 28, Édition de Travail*, ed. by Alfred Cortot (Paris: Éditions Maurice Senart), n.p.
CHANAN, MICHAEL. 1995. *Repeated Takes: A Short History of Recording and its Effects on Music* (London: Verso)
CHESNEL, JACQUES. 1977. 'Le fantastique du quotidien et le jazz', *Jazz Hot*, 337: 8–14
COLLIER, JAMES LINCOLN. 1978. *The Making of Jazz: A Comprehensive History* (Boston: Houghton Mifflin Co.)
COLLIER, SIMON. 1995. 'The Tango is Born: 1880s–1920s', in *¡Tango! The Dance, the Song, the Story*, ed. by Simon Collier (London: Thames and Hudson), pp. 19–64
COMES PEÑA, CLAUDIA. 2002. 'Cortázar: el túnel del jazz', in *Literatura y música popular en Hispanoamérica: IV Congreso de la Asociación Española de Estudios Literarios Hispanoamericanos*, ed. by Ángel Esteban, Gracia Morales, and Álvaro Salvador (Granada: Método Ediciones), pp. 217–23
COOPER, GROSVENOR W. and LEONARD B. MEYER. 1960. *The Rhythmic Structure of Music* (Chicago: University of Chicago Press)
CORBATTA, JORGELINA. 1994. 'El tango: letras y visión del mundo', *Hispanic Journal*, 15.1: 63–72
CORTÁZAR, JULIO. 1948. 'Muerte de Antonin Artaud', *Sur*, 163: 80–82
—— 1953. 'Gardel', *Sur*, 223: 127–29
—— 1962. *Historia de cronopios y famas* (Buenos Aires: Minotauro)
—— 1964. 'Reunión', *Revista. Universidad de México*, 14–17
—— 1965. 'Reunión', *El escarabajo de oro*, 6.26–27: 1–17
—— 1966. *Hopscotch*, trans. by Gregory Rabassa (New York: Pantheon Books)
—— 1970a [1956]. *Final del juego* (Buenos Aires: Editorial Sudamericana)
—— 1970b [1967]. *La vuelta al día en ochenta mundos*, vol. 1 (Mexico: siglo xxi editores)
—— 1970c [1967]. *La vuelta al día en ochenta mundos*, vol. 2 (Mexico: siglo xxi editores)
—— 1970d [1959]. *Las armas secretas* (Buenos Aires: Editorial Sudamericana)
—— 1970e [1949]. *Los reyes* (Buenos Aires: Editorial Sudamericana)
—— 1970f [1966]. *Todos los fuegos el fuego* (Buenos Aires: Editorial Sudamericana)
—— 1971. 'Policrítica en la hora de los chacales', *Casa de las Américas*, 67: 41–52
—— 1972. *Prosa del observatorio* (Barcelona: Editorial Lumen)
—— 1973a. *Libro de Manuel* (Buenos Aires: Editorial Sudamericana)
—— 1973b [1969]. *Último round*, vol. 1 (Mexico: siglo veintiuno editores)
—— 1973c [1969]. *Último round*, vol. 2 (Mexico: siglo veintiuno editores)
—— 1974. *Octaedro* (Madrid: Alianza Editorial)
—— 1977. *Alguien que anda por ahí* (Madrid: Alfaguara)

—— 1979a. *All Fires the Fire and Other Stories*, trans. by Suzanne Jill Levine (London: Marion Boyars)
—— 1979b. *Un tal Lucas* (Madrid: Alfaguara)
—— 1980. *Queremos tanto a Glenda* (Mexico: Nueva Imagen)
—— 1981a [1960]. *Los premios* (Barcelona: Club Bruguera)
—— 1981b. *Queremos tanto a Glenda* (Madrid: Ediciones Alfaguara)
—— 1982. *Julio Cortázar Literary Manuscripts* (Austin: Benson Latin American Collection, The University of Texas at Austin)
—— 1984. *We Love Glenda So Much* and *A Change of Light*, trans. by Gregory Rabassa (New York: Vintage Books)
—— 1991. *Rayuela*, critical edition, coord. by Julio Ortega and Saúl Yurkievich (Madrid: CSIC)
—— 1992 [1941]. 'Soledad de la música', in *Cartas desconocidas de Julio Cortázar: 1939–1945*, ed. by Mignon Domínguez (Buenos Aires: Sudamericana), pp. 290–97
—— 1993a [1951]. *Bestiario* (Madrid: Ediciones Alfaguara)
—— 1993b [1980]. 'Un gotán para Lautrec', *Mapocho: Revista de Humanidades y Ciencias Sociales*, 34: 227–39
—— 1994a. *Obra crítica / 1*, ed. by Saúl Yurkievich (Madrid: Alfaguara)
—— 1994b [1954]. 'Para una poética', in *Obra crítica / 2*, ed. by Jaime Alazraki (Madrid: Alfaguara), pp. 265–85
—— 1995 [1950]. *Diario de Andrés Fava* (Madrid: Alfaguara)
—— 2003. *Obras completas I*, ed. by Saúl Yurkievich (Barcelona: Galaxia Gutenberg)
—— 2004 [1945]. *La otra orilla* (Madrid: Suma de Letras)
—— 2006a [1941]. 'Rimbaud', in *Obras Completas VI*, ed. by Saúl Yurkievich (Barcelona: Galaxia Gutenberg), pp. 140–46
—— 2006b [1941]. 'Soledad de la música', in *Obras completas VI*, ed. by Saúl Yurkievich (Barcelona: Galaxia Gutenberg), pp. 135–40
—— 2006c [1947]. *Teoría del túnel*, in *Obras completas VI*, ed. by Saúl Yurkievich (Barcelona: Galaxia Gutenberg), pp. 45–125
—— 2006d [1948]. 'Elogio del jazz: carta enguantada a Daniel Devoto', in *Obras completas VI*, ed. by Saúl Yurkievich (Barcelona: Galaxia Gutenberg), pp. 204–16
—— 2006e [1948]. 'Muerte de Antonin Artaud', in *Obras completas VI*, ed. by Saúl Yurkievich (Barcelona: Galaxia Gutenberg), pp. 201–03
—— 2006f [1963]. 'Algunos aspectos del cuento', in *Obras completas VI*, ed. by Saúl Yurkievich (Barcelona: Galaxia Gutenberg), pp. 370–86
—— 2006g [1969]. 'Literatura en la revolución y revolución en la literatura: algunos malentendidos a liquidar', in *Obras completas VI*, ed. by Saúl Yurkievich (Barcelona: Galaxia Gutenberg), pp. 399–422
—— 2006h [1970]. 'Viaje alrededor de una mesa', in *Obras completas VI*, ed. by Saúl Yurkievich (Barcelona: Galaxia Gutenberg), pp. 422–39
—— 2007 [1963]. *Rayuela* (Madrid: Cátedra)
—— 2009 [1984]. *Salvo el crepúsculo*, definitive edition (Madrid: Alfaguara)
—— 2012a. *Cartas 1937–1954*, vol. 1, ed. by Aurora Bernárdez and Carles Álvarez Garriga (Buenos Aires: Alfaguara)
—— 2012b. *Cartas 1955–1964*, vol. 2, ed. by Aurora Bernárdez and Carles Álvarez Garriga (Buenos Aires: Alfaguara)
—— 2012c. *Cartas 1977–1984*, vol. 5, ed. by Aurora Bernárdez and Carles Álvarez Garriga (Buenos Aires: Alfaguara)
—— 2013. *Blow-Up and Other Stories*, trans. by Paul Blackburn (New York: Pantheon Books)
CORTÁZAR, JULIO and HERMENEGILDO SÁBAT. 1980. *Monsieur Lautrec* (Madrid: Ameris)

COULSON, GRACIELA. 1985. 'Orfeo y el orfismo en la obra de Cortázar', *Revista chilena de literatura*, 25: 101–13
COUTURE, MARK. 2016. 'Does Julio Swing?: Writing on Jazz and Jazz Writing in Cortázar's "El perseguidor"', *Hispanic Studies Review*, 1.1: 1–14
DALEN, BRENDA. 1989. '"Freundschaft, Lieve, und Welt": The Secret Programme of the Chamber Concerto', in *The Berg Companion*, ed. by Douglas Jarman (Boston: Northeastern University Press), pp. 141–80
DANIELS, DOUGLAS HENRY. 2006. *One O'Clock Jump: The Unforgettable History of the Oklahoma City Blue Devils* (Boston: Beacon Press)
DAVIS, MILES. 1989. *Miles: An Autobiography*, with Quincy Troupe (New York: Simon and Schuster)
DELEUZE, GILLES and FÉLIX GUATTARI. 1987 [1980]. *A Thousand Plateaus: Capitalism and Schizophrenia*, trans. by Brian Massumi (Minneapolis: University of Minnesota Press)
DENIS, JULIO. 1938. *Presencia* (Buenos Aires: El bibliófilo)
DERRIDA, JACQUES. 1982 [1972]. *Margins of Philosophy*, trans. by Alan Bass (Chicago: University of Chicago Press)
—— 1986 [1974]. *Glas*, trans. by John P. Leavey, Jr and Richard Rand (Lincoln: University of Nebraska Press)
—— 1997 [1967]. *Of Grammatology*, trans. by Gayatri Chakravorty Spivak (Baltimore: The John Hopkins University Press)
—— 2001 [1967]. *Writing and Difference*, trans. by Alan Bass (London: Routledge Classics)
DEVEAUX, SCOTT. 1991. 'Constructing the Jazz Tradition: Jazz Historiography', *Black American Literature Forum*, 25.3: 525–60
—— 1997. *The Birth of Bebop: A Social and Musical History* (Berkeley: University of California Press)
DEVOTO, DANIEL. 1950 [1948]. 'El jazz y la música moderna', in *Las hojas (1940–1949)* (Buenos Aires: Losada/Aldabahor), pp. 14–21
DINZEL, GLORIA and RODOLFO DINZEL. 2000. *Tango: An Anxious Quest for Freedom* (Stuttgart: Editorial Abrazos)
DROIT-VOLET, SYLVIE and OTHERS. 2013. 'Music, emotion, and time perception: the influence of subjective emotional valence and arousal?', *Frontiers in Psychology*, 4: 417
DUMAS, ALEXANDRE. 1871 [1859]. *Les mohicans de Paris*, new edition (Paris: Michel Lévy frères, éditeurs)
—— 1889 [1864]. *Théâtre complet*, vol. XXIV (Paris: Michel Lévy frères, éditeurs)
EURIPIDES. 2016. *Bacchae*, trans. by Kenneth McLeish and Frederic Raphael (London: Bloomsbury)
EVANS, BILL. 2005 [1966]. *The Universal Mind of Bill Evans*, dir. Louis Carvell (Discovery Records)
EVANS, DYLAN. 1996. *An Introductory Dictionary of Lacanian Psychoanalysis* (London: Routledge)
FIDDIAN, ROBIN WILLIAM. 1985. 'Religious Symbolism and the Ideological Critique in "El Perseguidor" by Julio Cortázar', *Revista Canadiense de Estudios Hispánicos*, 9.2: 149–63
'Fourscore — Add to Friends'. 2008. Schott <https://en.schott-music.com/shop/fourscore-add-to-friends-no235146.html> [accessed 18 September 2018]
FRALASCO, HÉCTOR. 2005. *Julio Cortázar y el tango* (Buenos Aires: Edición del autor)
FRANCO, JEAN. 1998. 'Comic Stripping: Cortázar in the Age of Mechanical Reproduction', in *Julio Cortázar: New Readings*, ed. by Carlos J. Alonso (Cambridge: Cambridge University Press), pp. 36–56
FRIBERG, ANDERS and ANDREAS SUNDSTRÖM. 2002. 'Swing Ratios and Ensemble Timing in Jazz Performance: Evidence for a Common Rhythmic Pattern', *Music Perception: An Interdisciplinary Journal*, 19.3: 333–49

GALLEGO, ISABEL. 2002. 'Cortázar, *Rayuela* y el blues', in *Literatura y música popular en Hispanoamérica: IV Congreso de la Asociación Española de Estudios Literarios Hispanoamericanos*, ed. by Ángel Esteban, Gracia Morales, and Álvaro Salvador (Granada: Método Ediciones), pp. 247–52

GANTZ, TIMOTHY. 1993. *Early Greek Myth: A Guide to Literary and Artistic Sources* (Baltimore: John Hopkins University Press)

GARCÍA, ANTONIO J. 1990. 'Pedagogical Scat', *Musical Educators Journal*, 77.1: 28–34

GARCÍA PÉREZ, DAVID. 2015. 'Representación de las *Bacantes* en Cortázar y Carpentier: la relectura de un mito griego', *Nova tellus*, 32.2: 271–87

GIDDINS, GARY. 1998. *Visions of Jazz: The First Century* (New York: Oxford University Press)

GILLESPIE, DIZZY. 1979. *To Be or Not... To Bop: Memoirs*, with Al Fraser (Garden City: Doubleday & co.)

GIOIA, TED. 1988. *The Imperfect Art: Reflections on Jazz and Modern Culture* (New York: Oxford University Press)

—— 1997. *The History of Jazz* (New York: Oxford University Press)

GIVAN, BENJAMIN. 2010. 'Swing Improvisation: A Schenkerian Perspective', *Theory and Practice*, 35: 25–56

GOIALDE PALACIOS, PATRICIO. 2010. 'Palabras con "swing". La música de jazz en la obra de Julio Cortázar', *Musiker*, 17: 483–96

GONZÁLEZ BERMEJO, ERNESTO. 1978. *Conversaciones con Cortázar* (Barcelona: Editora y Distribuidora Hispano Americana)

GONZÁLEZ RIQUELME, ANDRÉS. 2003. 'La máquina musical en "El perseguidor" de Julio Cortázar', *Acta Literaria*, 28: 33–44

GORDON, SAMUEL. 1980. 'Algunos apuntes sobre crítica y "jazz", en la lectura de "El perseguidor"', *Cuadernos Hispanoamericanos*, 364–66: 595–608

GOYALDE PALACIOS, PATRICIO. 2001. '"Las Ménades" de Julio Cortázar: mito clásico y recreación literaria', *Faventia*, 23.2: 35–42

GREENBERG, ROBERT. 2004. *The Chamber Music of Mozart. Part I* (The Teaching Company) <http://www.stonedcoder.org/~aestetix/chamber/Chamber%20Music%20of%20Mozart.PDF> [accessed 18 September 2018]

GUEVARA, ERNESTO CHE. 1963. *Pasajes de la guerra revolucionaria* (La Habana: Unión de Escitores y Artistas de Cuba)

GUNTHER KODAT, CATHERINE. 2003. 'Conversing with Ourselves: Canon, Freedom, Jazz', *American Quarterly*, 55.1: 1–28

GYURKO, LANIN A. 1980. 'Artist and Critic in Cortázar's "El perseguidor": Antagonists or Doubles?', *Ibero-amerikanisches Archiv*, 6.3: 205–38

—— 1988. 'Quest and Betrayal in Cortázar's "El perseguidor"', *Hispanófila*, 93: 59–78

HARPER, MICHAEL S., LARRY KART, and AL YOUNG. 1987. 'Jazz and Letters: A Colloquy', *Tri-Quarterly*, 68: 118–58

HARRISON, MAX. 1980. 'Jazz', *The New Grove Dictionary of Music and Musicians*, vol. 9, 6th edition, ed. by Stanley Sadie (London: Macmillan), pp. 561–79

HARTMAN, CHARLES. 1991. *Jazz Text: Voice and Improvisation in Poetry, Jazz, and Song* (Princeton: Princeton University Press)

HEGEL, GEORG WILHELM FREIDRICH. 1970. *Philosophy of Nature*, vol. II (London: George Allen and Unwin)

HEIDEGGER, MARTIN. 2001 [1971]. *Poetry, Language, Thought*, trans. by Albert Hofstadter (New York: Harper & Rowe)

HERNÁNDEZ Y CASTILLO, ANA. 1981. *Keats, Poe, and the Shaping of Cortázar's Mythopoesis* (Amsterdam: John Benjamins)

HICKS, D. EMILY. 1991. *Border Writing: The Multidimensional Text* (Minneapolis: The University of Minnesota Press)

HINSON, MAURICE. 1993. *Music for Piano and Orchestra: An Annotated Guide*, enlarged edition (Bloomington: Indiana University Press)

HOBSBAWM, ERIC. 1983. 'Introduction: Inventing Traditions', in *The Invention of Tradition*, ed. by Eric Hobsbawm and Terence Ranger (Cambridge: Cambridge University Press), pp. 1–14

—— 1993. *The Jazz Scene* (New York: Pantheon Books)

HODEIR, ANDRÉ. 1956. *Jazz: Its Evolution and Essence*, trans. by David Noakes (New York: Grove Press)

—— 1959. 'Perspective of Modern Jazz: Popularity or Recognition?', *Down Beat*, 26.17: 40–42

—— 2001 [1959]. 'Monk or the Misunderstanding', in *The Thelonious Monk Reader*, ed. by Rob van der Bliek (New York: Oxford University Press), pp. 118–33

HUICI, ADRIÁN. 2009. 'Borges y Cortázar: entre Apolo y Dionisos', *Studi Ispanici*, 34: 285–302

HUXLEY, ALDOUS. 2001 [1932]. *Brave New World* (London: HarperCollins)

HWANGPO, M. CECILIA. 2009. 'El compadre: un tipo porteño liminal y espacial', *Revista de crítica literaria latinoamericana*, 35.70: 257–72

IRVING, JOHN. 1998. *Mozart: The 'Haydn' Quartets* (Cambridge: Cambridge University Press)

JARMAN, DOUGLAS. 1979. *The Music of Alban Berg* (Berkeley: University of California Press)

JITRIK, NOÉ. 1974. 'Crítica satélite y trabajo crítico en "El perseguidor" de Julio Cortázar', *Nueva Revista de Filología Hispánica*, 23.2: 337–68

JORDAN, RUTH. 1978. *Nocturne: A Life of Chopin* (London: Constable)

JUVENAL. 2014. *Satire 6*, ed. by Lindsay Watson and Patricia Watson (Cambridge: Cambridge University Press)

KADIR, DJELAL. 1973. 'A Mythical Re-Enactment: Cortazar's *El perseguidor* [*The Pursuer*]', *Latin American Literary Review*, 2.3: 63–73

KALLBERG, JEFFREY. 2001. 'Chopin and the Aesthetic of the Sketch: A New Prelude in E♭ Minor?', *Early Music*, 29.3: 408–22

KANELLOPOULOS, PANAGIOTIS A. 2011. 'Freedom and Responsibility: The Aesthetics of Free Musical Improvisation and Its Educational Implications — A View from Bakhtin', *Philosophy of Music Education Review*, 19.2: 113–35

KEIL, CHARLES. 1966. 'Motion and Feeling Through Music', *Journal of Aesthetics and Art Criticism*, 24: 337–49

KENNEDY, RAYMOND F. 1987. 'Jazz Style and Improvisation Codes', *Yearbook for Traditional Music*, 19: 37–43

KERR, LUCILLE and OTHERS. 1974. 'Interview: Julio Cortázar', *Diacritics*, 4.4: 35–40

KING, A. HYATT. 1945. 'Mozart's Counterpoint: Its Growth and Significance', *Music & Letters*, 26.1: 12–20

KING, JOHN. 2005. 'The Boom of the Latin American novel', in *The Cambridge Companion to the Latin American Novel*, ed. by Afraín Kristal (Cambridge: Cambridge University Press), pp. 59–80

KOCH, LAWRENCE O. 1988. *Yardbird: A Compendium of the Music and Life of Charlie Parker* (Bowling Green: Bowling Green State University Popular Press)

KRISTEVA, JULIA. 1982 [1980]. *Powers of Horror: An Essay on Abjection*, trans. by Leon S. Roudiez (New York: Columbia University Press)

LACAN, JACQUES. 1977 [1949]. 'The Mirror Stage as Formative of the Function of the I', in *Écrits: A Selection*, trans. by Alan Sheridan (London: Tavistock), pp. 1–7

LACHMAN, KATHRYN. 2014. *Borrowed Forms: The Music and Ethics of Transnational Fiction* (Liverpool: Liverpool University Press)

LAMBERT, PHILIP. 1993. 'Berg's Path to Twelve-Note Composition: Aggregate Construction and Association in the Chamber Concerto', *Music Analysis*, 12.3: 321–42

LEVITIN, DANIEL J., PARAG CHORDIA, and VINOD MENON. 2012. 'Musical Rhythm Spectra from Bach to Joplin Obey a 1/f Power Law', *PNAS*, 109.10: 3716–20

LITWEILER, JOHN. 1985. *The Freedom Principle: Jazz After 1958* (Poole: Blandford)

LOMAX, ALAN. 1973 [1950]. *Mister Jelly Roll: The Fortunes of Jelly Roll Morton, New Orleans Creole and 'Inventor of Jazz'*, 2nd edition (Berkeley: University of California Press)

LONGLEY, MICHAEL. 1998. 'A Perpetual One-Night Stand: Some Thoughts on Jazz and Poetry', *Writing Ulster*, 5: 91–99

LOPES, PAUL. 1999. 'Diffusion and Syncretism: The Modern Jazz Tradition', *The Annals of the American Academy of Political and Social Science*, 566: 25–36

LÓPEZ, TERESA. 1998. 'La música clásica en los relatos de Julio Cortázar', in *Poéticas argentinas del siglo XX: literatura y teatro*, ed. by Jorge Dubatti (Buenos Aires: Editorial de Belgrano), pp. 119–26

LÓPEZ-LESPADA, MARTA. 1998. '"Jazz" poema de Julio Cortázar"', *Revista de Literatura Hispanoamericana*, 36: 105–16

LOYOLA, HERNÁN. 1994. 'El jazz en Cortázar: la discada del club de la serpiente', *Casa de las Américas*, 194: 61–74

LUENGO, ANA and KLAUS MEYER-MINNEMAN. 2004. '(Des)enmascaramiento de "Las Ménades" y "La escuela de noche" de Julio Cortázar', *Hispamérica*, 33.98: 19–36

MACADAM, ALFRED. 2001. 'Julio Cortázar and Music', *Review: Literature and Arts of the Americas*, 34.63: 43–50

MAGEE, JEFFREY. 2005. *The Uncrowned King of Swing: Fletcher Henderson and Big Band Jazz* (New York: Oxford University Press)

MALL, JAMES P. 1979. 'Glas: What Is Derrida Doing?', in *French Literature Series: Authors and Philosophers. Vol. 6. Authors and Philosophers*, ed. by A. Maynor Hardee (Columbia: University of South Carolina), pp. 95–100

MANUEL, PETER (ed.). 2009. *Creolizing Contradance in The Caribbean* (Philadelphia: Temple University Press)

MARTIN, HENRY. 2001. *Charlie Parker and Thematic Improvisation* (Lanham: Scarecrow Press)

MATTAX MOERSCH, CHARLOTTE. 2009. 'Keyboard improvisation in the Baroque period', *Musical improvisation: Art, Education, and Society*, ed. by Gabriel Solis and Bruno Nettl (Urbana: University of Illinois Press), pp. 150–70

MAZZUCCHELLI, ALDO. 2006. 'El Modernismo en el tango', *Revista de crítica literaria latinoamericana*, 32.63/64: 25–45

MCKINNEY, LOUISE. 2006. *New Orleans: A Cultural and Literary History* (Oxford: Signal)

MEIER, MARILYN ANNE. 1993. 'Chopin Twenty-Four Preludes Opus 28' (unpublished doctoral thesis, University of Wollondong)

MERCER, SAMUEL. 1949. *The Religion of Ancient Egypt* (London: Luzac and co.)

MESA GANCEDO, DANIEL. 2002. 'Los arrabales de la escritura. Cortázar, *gotán* y poesía', in *Literatura y música popular en Hispanoamérica: IV Congreso de la Asociación Española de Estudios Literarios Hispanoamericanos*, ed. by Ángel Esteban, Gracia Morales, and Álvaro Salvador (Granada: Método Ediciones), pp. 421–31

MILLER, MARILYN G. 2016. 'Sardonic Recurrence and Barking Dogs in Julio Cortázar's Library of Tangos', *Hispanic Review*, 84.1: 1–23

MILTON, JOYCE. 1996. *Tramp: The Life of Charlie Chaplin* (New York: HarperCollins)

MIRKA, DANUTA. 2009. *Metric Manipulations in Haydn and Mozart: Chamber Music for Strings, 1787–1791* (Oxford: Oxford University Press)

MITCHELL, W. J. T. 2011. *Cloning Terror: The War of Images, 9/11 to the Present* (Chicago; London: Chicago University Press)

MONTANARO, PABLO. 2001. *Cortázar: de la experiencia histórica a la Revolución* (Rosario: Homo Sapiens Ediciones)
MOORE, ROBIN. 1992. 'The Decline of Improvisation in Western Art Music: An Interpretation of Change', *International Review of the Aesthetics and Sociology of Music*, 23.1: 61–84
MORA VALCÁRCEL, CARMEN DE. 1979. 'Julio Cortázar: "Alguien que anda por ahí"', *Anales de literatura hispanoamericana*, 8: 169–82
MORAN, DOMINIC. 2000. *Questions of the Liminal in the Fiction of Julio Cortázar* (Oxford: Legenda)
—— 2017. 'Straight from *The Horse's Mouth*? On the Origins of Cortázar's "El perseguidor"', *Bulletin of Spanish Studies*, 9.9: 1601–22
'Música: entrevista a Antonio Zimmerman'. 2007. 'Una ópera que contaba Cortázar', *Clarín*, 6 July 2007 <https://www.clarin.com/espectaculos/opera-contaba-cortazar_0_SygZDDgJRtl.html> [accessed 9 September 2018]
NAGY, GREGORY. 1996. *Poetry as Performance: Homer and Beyond* (New York; Cambridge: Cambridge University Press)
NIELSEN, CHRISTINE S. and JUAN GABRIEL MARIOTTO. 2006. 'The Tango Metaphor: The Essence of Argentina's National Identity', *International Studies of Management & Organization*, 35.4: 8–36
OLIVARES, EDUARDO. 1981. 'Julio Cortázar: écrire comme Parker, comme Mozart', *Le Monde de la Musique*, 31: 55–58
ORLOFF, CAROLINA. 2013. *The Representation of the Political in Selected Writings of Julio Cortázar* (Suffolk: Boydell and Brewer)
OSTENDORF, BERNDT. 1979. 'Minstrelsy & Early Jazz', *The Massachusetts Review*, 20.3: 574–602
—— 1990. 'The Afro-American Musical Avant-Garde: Bebop Jazz', *Angol Filológiai Tanulmányok / Hungarian Studies in English*, 21: 45–57
OWENS, THOMAS. 1974. 'Charlie Parker: techniques of improvisation' (unpublished doctoral thesis, University of California at Los Angeles)
—— 1996. *Bebop: The Music and its Players* (New York: Oxford University Press)
PARKINSON ZAMORA, LOIS. 1999. 'Art and Revolution in the Fiction of Julio Cortázar', in *Critical Essays on Julio Cortázar*, ed. by Jaime Alazraki (New York: G. K. Hall), pp. 92–114.
PEAVLER, TERRY. 1990. *Julio Cortázar* (Boston: Twayne)
PEIRÓ, JOSÉ VICENTE. 2006. *Las músicas de Cortázar* (Valencia: Institució Alfons el Magnànim)
PÉREZ-ABADÍN BARRO, SOLEDAD. 2010. *Cortázar y Che Guevara: Lectura de 'Reunión'* (Bern: Peter Lang)
PÉREZ-MUKDSI, ANDREA. 2015. 'On Rhizomatic Bridges in Cortázar's Musical "Clone"', *SUNY Buffalo Romance Studies Journal*, 3.1: 1–18
PERIS BLANES, JAUME. 2011. '*El perseguidor*, de Cortázar, entre la figuración de la vanguardia y la emergencia de una nueva subjetividad', *Revista de Crítica Literaria Latinoamericana*, 37.74: 71–92
PEYRATS, PILAR. 1999. *Jazzuela: Julio Cortázar y el jazz* (Barcelona: La Autora)
PICON GARFIELD, EVELYN. 1975. *¿Es Julio Cortázar un surrealista?* (Madrid: Gredos)
—— 1981 [1978]. *Cortázar por Cortázar* (Xalapa: Universidad Veracruzana)
PLANELLS, ANTONIO. 1975. 'Narración y música en "Las ménades", de Julio Cortázar', *Caravelle, Cahiers du monde hispanique et luso-brésilien*, 25: 31–37
PLEASANTS, HENRY. 1969. *Serious Music and All That Jazz: An Adventure in Music Criticism* (New York: Simon & Schuster)

PLISSON, MICHEL. 1987. 'Un genre musical du Nord-Ouest argentin: la baguala', *Journal de la Société des Américanistes*, 73: 219–42

PONIATOWSKA, ELENA. 1975. 'La vuelta a Julio Cortázar en (cerca de) 80 preguntas', *Plural*, 44: 28–36

PONIATOWSKA, IRENA. 2009. *Fryderyk Chopin: The Man and His Music, 1810–2010* (Warsaw: Multico)

POOLE, GEOFFREY. 1991. 'Alban Berg and the Fateful Number', *Tempo*, 179: 2–7

PORTER, LEWIS, MICHAEL ULLMAN, and ED HAZELL, 1993. *Jazz: From Its Origins to the Present* (Englewood Cliffs: Prentice-Hall)

PREGO, OMAR. 1985. *La fascinación de las palabras: conversaciones con Cortázar* (Barcelona: Munchnik)

PRESTIANNI, SAM. 2003. 'The Sharing of Pharoah', *SFWeekly*, 30 July 2003 <https://archives.sfweekly.com/sanfrancisco/the-sharing-of-pharoah/Content?oid=2148902> [accessed 20 September 2018]

PRIESTLY, BRIAN. 2005. *Chasin' the Bird: The Life and Legacy of Charlie Parker* (London: Equinox)

PRÖGLER, J. A. 1995. 'Searching for Swing: Participatory Discrepancies in the Jazz Rhythm Section', *Ethnomusicology*, 39.1: 21–54

PULEO, ALICIA H. 1990. *Cómo leer a Julio Cortázar* (Madrid: Júcar)

RAMOS RUIZ, ANUCHKA. 2015. 'Estudio de tres colecciones de cuentos de Cortázar: *Alguien que anda por ahí*, *Queremos tanto a Glenda* y *Deshoras*' (unpublished doctoral thesis, Universidade de Santiago de Compostela)

RASULA, JED. 1995. 'The Media of Memory: The Seductive Menace of Records in Jazz History', in *Jazz Among the Discourses*, ed. by Krin Gabbard (Durham and London: Duke University Press), pp. 135–62

RÉDA, JACQUES. 2010 [1990]. *L'improviste: une lecture du jazz* (Paris: Éditions Gallimard)

REICH, WILLI. 1963. *Alban Berg*, trans. by Cornelius Cardew (New York: Harcourt, Brace and World)

RENFREW, ALASTAIR. 2015. *Mikhail Bakhtin* (London; New York: Routledge)

RILKE, RAINER MARIA. 1946 [1923]. *Sonnets to Orpheus: Written as a Monument for Wera Ouckama Knoop* (London: Hogarth Press)

ROBERTS, NICHOLAS. 2009. 'Subverted Claims: Cortázar, Artaud, and the Problematics of Jazz', *Modern Language Review*, 104.3: 730–45

—— 2013. 'Variations on a Theme: Scored Music and Language in Julio Cortázar's "Clone"', *Bulletin of Spanish Studies*, 90.6: 1011–34

ROBINSON, J. BRADFORD. 1994. 'The Jazz Essays of Theodor Adorno: Some Thoughts on Jazz Reception in Weimar Germany', *Popular Music*, 13.1: 1–25

RODRÍGUEZ-LUIS, JULIO. 1983. '"Alguien que anda por ahí": ¿encrucijada o paradero?', *Sin nombre*, 13.2: 7–23

ROMANO, EDUARDO. 1991. *Las letras del tango. Antología cronológica: 1900–1980* (Rosario: Editorial Fundación Ros)

ROUSSEAU, JEAN-JACQUES. 1779. *A Dictionary of Music*, trans. by William Waring (London: J. French)

RUSCH, RENÉ, KEITH SALLEY, and CHRIS STOVER. 2016. 'Capturing the Ineffable: Three Transcriptions of a Jazz Solo by Sonny Rollins', *Music Theory Online*, 22.3: 1–20 <http://mtosmt.org/issues/mto.16.22.3/mto.16.22.3.rusch.html> [accessed 18 September 2018]

RUSSELL, ROSS. 1959. 'Bebop', in *The Art of Jazz: Essays on the Nature and Development of Jazz*, ed. by Martin T. Williams (New York: Da Capo Press), pp. 187–214

RUTKOFF, PETER and WILLIAM SCOTT. 1996. 'Bebop: Modern New York Jazz', *The Kenyon Review*, 18.2: 91–121

SÁBATO, ERNESTO. 1968. *Tango: discusión y clave* (Buenos Aires: Losada)
SAGER, DAVID. 2002. 'History, Myth and Legend: The Problem of Early Jazz', *The Cambridge Companion to Jazz*, ed. by Mervyn Cooke and David Horn (Cambridge: Cambridge University Press), pp. 270–85
SALZMAN, PATRICIA and ELEONORA TOLA. 1996. 'El camino órfico en la literatura argentina. Texto e intertexto en J. Cortázar y H. Costantini', *Praesentia*, 1: 295–308
SAMPAYO, CARLOS. 2000. 'Jazz en literatura, literatura en jazz', *Litoral*, 227/228: 176–79
SAMSON, JIM. 1985. *The Music of Chopin* (London: Routledge & Kegan Paul)
SASSOON, HUMPHREY. 2003. 'JS Bach's Musical Offering and the Source of Its Theme: Royal Peculiar', *The Musical Times*, 144.1885: 38–39
SAVIGLIANO, MARTA E. 1995. *Tango and the Political Economy of Passion* (Boulder: Westview Press)
—— 1997. 'Nocturnal Ethnographies: Following Cortázar in the Milongas of Buenos Aires', *Etnofoor*, 10.1/2: 28–52
SCHAVELZON, GUILLERMO. 1980. 'Julio Cortázar y la música', *Sábado (unomásuno)*, 144: 2
SCHOLZ, LÁSZLÓ. 1977. *El arte poética de Julio Cortázar* (Buenos Aires: Castañeda)
SCHULLER, GUNTHER. 1986 [1968]. *The History of Jazz. Vol. 1, Early Jazz: Its Roots and Musical Development* (New York: Oxford University Press)
—— 1989. *The Swing Era: The Development of Jazz, 1930–1945* (New York: Oxford University Press)
SCRUTON, ROGER. 1997. *The Aesthetics of Music* (Oxford: Clarendon Press)
SEGAL, CHARLES. 1997. *Dionysiac Poetics and Euripides'* Bacchae (Princeton: Princeton University Press)
—— 2001. 'Introduction', in Euripides, *Bakkhai*, trans. by Reginald Gibbons (Oxford: Oxford University Press), pp. 3–32
SERRA SALVAT, ROSA. 2002. 'Presencia del tango en la obra de Julio Cortázar: *Con tangos y Tango de vuelta*', in *Literatura y música popular en Hispanoamérica: IV Congreso de la Asociación Española de Estudios Literarios Hispanoamericanos*, ed. by Ángel Esteban, Gracia Morales, and Álvaro Salvador (Granada: Método Ediciones), pp. 307–16
SHIPTON, ALYN. 1999. *Groovin' High: The Life of Dizzy Gillespie* (New York: Oxford University Press)
SILVA-CÁCERES, RAÚL. 1997. *El árbol de las figuras. Estudio de motivos fantásticos en la obra de Julio Cortázar* (Santiago: Lom)
SMOIRA COHN, MICHAL. 2010. *The Mission and Message of Music: Building Blocks to the Aesthetics of Music in Our Time* (Newcastle upon Tyne: Cambridge Scholars)
SOMMER, DORIS. 1995. 'Grammar Trouble: Cortázar's Critique of Competence', *Diacritics*, 25.1: 24–45
—— 1998. 'Pursuing a Perfect Present', in *Julio Cortázar: New Readings*, ed. by Carlos J. Alonso (Cambridge: Cambridge University Press), pp. 211–36
SOPHOCLES. 2006. *Oedipus Rex*, ed. by R. D. Dawe (Cambridge: Cambridge University Press)
SOREN TRIFF, EDUARDO. 1991. 'Improvisación musical y discurso literario en Julio Cortázar', *Revista Iberoamericana*, 155–56: 657–63
SOSNOWSKI, SAÚL. 1973. *Julio Cortázar: una búsqueda mítica* (Buenos Aires: Ediciones Noé)
STAMBAUGH, JOAN. 1964. 'Music as a Temporal Form', *The Journal of Philosophy*, 61.9: 265–80
STANDISH, PETER. 2001. *Understanding Julio Cortázar* (Columbia: University of South Carolina Press)
STOWE, DAVID W. 1994. *Swing Changes: Big-Band Jazz in New Deal America* (Cambridge, Mass.; London: Harvard University Press)

TAYLOR, JULIE M. 1976. 'Tango: Theme of Class and Nation', *Ethnomusicology*, 20.2: 273–91

TEACHOUT, TERRY. 2009. *Pops: A Life of Louis Armstrong* (Boston: Mariner)

TERRAMORSI, BERNARD. 1997. '"Alguien que anda por ahí": le spectre de la Révolution en marche', *América. Cahiers du CRICCAL*, 17: 153–64

THAUT, MICHAEL H., PIETRO DAVIDE TRIMARCHI, and LAWRENCE M. PARSONS. 2014. 'Human Brain Basis of Musical Rhythm Perception: Common and Distinct Neural Substrates for Meter, Tempo, and Pattern', *Brain Science*, 4.2: 428–52

THOMPSON, ROBERT FARRIS. 2005. *Tango: The Art History of Love* (New York: Vintage Books)

TOSSOUNIAN, CECILIA. 2016. '*Milonguitas*: Tango, Gender and Consumption in Buenos Aires', *E.I.A.L.*, 27.2: 29–45

TROIANO, JAMES. 1984. 'Theatrical Technique and the Fantastic in Cortazar's "Instrucciones para John Howell"', *Hispanic Journal*, 6.1: 111–19

TYLER, JOSEPH. 1996. 'Cortázar: Jazz y literature', *Inti: Revista de literatura Hispánica*, 43: 147–55

VALENTINE, ROBERT Y. 1974. 'The Creative Personality in Cortázar's "El perseguidor"', *Journal of Spanish Studies: Twentieth Century*, 2.3: 169–91.

VÁZQUEZ, CARMEN. 1986. 'La función de la música en "Alguien que anda por ahí"', in *Coloquio International: Lo lúdico y lo fantástico en la obra de Julio Cortázar: Centre de Recherches Latino-Americaines, Université de Poitiers* (Madrid: Editorial Fundamentos), pp. 125–33

VERNE, JULES. 2003 [1874]. *A Fantasy of Doctor Ox*, trans. by Andrew Brown (London: Hesperus)

VILADRICH, ANAHÍ. 2006. 'Neither Virgins nor Whores: Tango Lyrics and Gender Representations in the Tango World', *The Journal of Popular Culture*, 39.2: 272–93

WARD, JAMES F. 1995. *Heidegger's Political Thinking* (Amhurst: University of Massachusetts Press)

WATERS, KEITH. 1996. 'Blurring the Barline: Metric Displacement in the Piano Solos of Herbie Hancock', *Annual Review of Jazz Studies*, 8: 19–37

WATKINS, GLENN. 1991. *Gesualdo: The Man and His Music* (Oxford: Clarendon Press)

WATTS, ISAAC. 1799. *Hymns and Spiritual Songs, in Three Books. I. Collected from the scriptures. II. Composed on divine subjects. III. Prepared for the Lord's Supper* (York: Printed for Thomas Wilson and Robert Spence)

WEISS, JASON. 1991. *Writing at Risk: Interviews in Paris with Uncommon Writers* (Iowa City: University of Iowa Press)

WILHELM, KATE. 1976. *Where Late the Sweet Birds Sing* (New York: Harper & Row)

WOIDECK, CARL. 1996. *Charlie Parker: His Music and Life* (Ann Arbor: University of Michigan Press)

YAHNI, ROBERTO. 1969. 'Los conciertos de Cortázar', *Sur*, 319: 56–59

YOUENS, FREDERICK. 1964. Sleevenotes to JOHANNES SEBASTIAN BACH, *The Musical Offering*, BWV 1079, realisation by Millicent Silver, London Harpsichord Ensemble (Saga, XID 5237)

YOUNG, JAMES O. 2008. *Cultural Appropriation and the Arts* (Malden: Blackwell)

YU, FRED. 2009. 'Études', ourchopin.com <http://www.ourchopin.com/analysis/etude.html> [accessed 12 September 2018]

YURKIEVICH, SAÚL. 2003. 'Julio Cortázar: sus bregas, sus logros, sus quimeras', in *Julio Cortázar, Obras completas I*, ed. by Saúl Yurkievich (Barcelona: Galaxia Gutenberg), pp. 9–37

ZACK, MICHAEL H. 2000. 'Jazz Improvisation and Organizing: Once More from the Top', *Organization Science*, 11.2: 227–34

Music (recordings and scores)

BACH, JOHANNES SEBASTIAN. 1964. *The Musical Offering*, BWV1079, realisation by Millicent Silver, London Harpsichord Ensemble (Saga, XID 5237)

COLEMAN, ORNETTE. 1959. *The Shape of Jazz to Come* (Atlantic, SD 1317)

—— 1961. *Free Jazz: A Collective Improvisation* (Atlantic, SD 1364)

COLTRANE, JOHN. 1965. *Ascension* (Impulse!, A-95)

CORTÁZAR, JULIO, EDGARDO CANTÓN, and JUAN CÉDRON. 1980. *Trottoirs de Buenos Aires* (Polydor, 2473 114)

DEBUSSY, CLAUDE. 1983 [1909]. *Three Great Orchestral Works in Full Score* (Mineola: Dove Publications)

GESUALDO, CARLO. 1958 [1611]. *Sämtliche Madrigale für fünf Stimmen*, vol. V (Hamburg: Ugrino Verlag)

KONITZ, LEE and GERRY MULLIGAN. 1953. *Lee Konitz Plays with the Gerry Mulligan Quartet* (World Pacific, LPM 2054)

MOZART, WOLFGANG AMADEUS. 1941 [1784]. *String Quartet 'The Hunt' B♭ Major K.V. 458* (London: Boosey & Hawkes)

ROLLINS, SONNY and COLEMAN HAWKINS. 1963. *Sonny Meets Hawk!* (RCA Victor, LPM-2712)

INDEX

abject 196
Adorno, Theodor 179 n. 27, 235 n. 4
aesthetics 3–4, 6, 8, 12, 27–28, 72–73, 76–77, 84, 87, 151, 163, 217, 233, 242
Aieta, Anselmo 128
  see also 'Mariposita'
Ajuria Ibarra, Enrique 101 n. 41
Aliau, Magdalena 65
Álvarez-Schüller, Viviana 128, 136, 137, 146 nn. 40 & 43, 147 nn. 47 & 50, 148 n. 58
Anad, Guillermo 119
Anderson, Cat 240
Anderson, Vaughn 211 n. 2
Andrea, Pat 106, 131, 143 n. 12
Antin, David 224–25
Apollinaire, Guillaume 81
Apollo 65–66, 68, 70, 71, 99 n. 9 & 16
Armstrong, Louis 149, 155, 159, 173, 174, 176, 177 n. 5, 179 n. 23, 181 n. 44, 189, 190, 192, 193, 197, 198, 211 n. 13, 216, 217, 221, 223, 225, 227, 234, 236 n. 7
  'Don't Play Me Cheap' 189, 190, 192, 193
  'Mahogany Hall Stomp' 219–20, 236 n. 7
  'West End Blues' 221
  'Yellow Dog Blues' 193
  see also 'Go Down, Moses' ('Oh! Let My People Go') *and* '(What Did I Do to Be So) Black and Blue'
Arnold, Denis 47
Artaud, Antonin 154–57, 165, 168–69
Avalos, Maria d' 31
Azzi, María Susana 145 n. 28

Bacchae 57
Bach, Johann Sebastian 53 n. 20, 54 n. 28, 229, 237 n. 27
  The Musical Offering 39–44, 49, 50, 52 n. 8 & 17, 53 n. 18, 20, 21 & 24, 100 n. 32
Baggi, Denis L. 222
baguala 148 n. 61
  see also improvisation
Bahr, Carlos 128
  see also 'Tanto'
Bakhtin, Mikhail 47, 54 n. 32, 226
Baraka, Amiri 159, 164–65, 180 n. 28, 197, 201
Barbieri, Gato 115, 117, 144 n. 25
Barchino Pérez, Matías 176
Baroque 30, 40, 53 n. 18

Bartók, Béla 240
Basie, Count 173, 180 n. 39
Baudrillard, Jean 19
Beethoven, Ludwig van 1, 19, 26, 51 n. 1, 59–60, 172
  Symphony No. 5 in C minor (Op. 67) 63, 71, 99 n. 5
Beiderbecke, Bix 179 n. 26, 181 n. 44, 227–28
  'I'm Coming Virginia' 216, 219–20, 227–28
Belfiglio, Anthony 77
'Bemsha Swing' 222, 236 n. 15
Berg, Alban 53 n. 20
  Chamber Concerto for Piano and Violin with 13 Wind Instruments 53 n. 20
Berg, Walter Bruno 119–20, 142 n. 2
Berliner, Paul 220, 221
Best, Denzil 236 n. 15
  see also 'Bemsha Swing'
Bialostosky, Don 226
Bible:
  Revelation 199
Bivins, Jason C. 188
Blake, William:
  'The Sick Rose' 21–22
Bley, Paul 187
blues 106, 157, 158–59, 173, 175, 178 n. 17, 178–79 n. 19, 179 n. 21 & 22, 216, 217–18
Boldy, Steven 2, 10, 45, 46, 49, 81, 129, 146 n. 41, 147 n. 49, 213 n. 31, 230
Borello, Rodolfo A. 23 n. 1
Borge, Jason 162–64
Borges, Jorge Luis 122, 132, 134, 146 n. 35
Borshuk, Michael 236 n. 12
Boulez, Pierre 51 n. 1
Boym, Svetlana 111, 113–21, 125, 129, 134, 135, 136, 137, 144 n. 24, 146 n. 44, 148 n. 59, 218
Brahms, Johannes 67
Brenes Reyes, Jaime 186
Broonzy, Big Bill 199, 228
Brown, Clifford 156, 181 n. 44, 217, 227, 235 n. 5
  'I Don't Stand a Ghost of a Chance with You' 223–24
Brückner, Anton 67
Bullrich, Silvina 122
Buñuel, Luis 68, 71, 99–100 n. 19, 211 n. 11
Butterfield, Matthew W. 171, 173, 174

cakewalk 158, 179 n. 22
  see also improvisation

Callaway, Cab 225
candombe 112, 144 n. 21
Cantarero de Salazar, Alejandro 65
Casa de las Américas 23 n. 6, 83
Caslav Covino, Deborah 208
Castro, Fidel 73, 83, 88
Cavallari, Héctor Mario 204
Chanan, Michael 235 n. 1
Chaplin, Charlie 17
Chopin, Frédéric 19, 26, 51 n. 1, 88, 89–92, 93, 94, 96–97, 98, 101 n. 42, 101–02 n. 45, 102 n. 46 & 48, 108, 224, 229
  Revolutionary Étude (Op. 10 No. 12) 90, 92, 93, 94, 96–97, 98, 101 n. 44, 224
  Tristesse (Op. 10 No. 3) 91, 96
Chordia, Parag 76, 77
classical music 14, 23 n. 2, 26, 28, 29, 51 n. 1 & 3, 56, 58, 59, 61, 62, 67, 74–75, 76, 77, 79, 83, 84, 85, 100 n. 25 & 30, 104, 144 n. 27, 152, 153, 173, 217, 231, 234, 237 n. 27, 239, 246 n. 2
  see also *música culta, la*
Cœuroy, André 175
Cole, Cozy 163
Coleman, Ornette 216, 223, 225, 236 n. 16
  Free Jazz: A Collective Improvisation 216
  The Shape of Jazz to Come 236 n. 16
  'Lonely Woman' 223, 225, 236 n. 16
Collier, Simon 145 n. 28, 145–46 n. 35, 146 n. 37
Coltrane, John 217, 233
  Ascension 216
Comes Peña, Claudia 23 n. 10
Corbatta, Jorgelina 112, 113, 116, 144 n. 23
Cortázar, Julio:
  'Alguien que anda por ahí' 30, 56, 57, 71, 73, 88–98, 99 n. 1, 101 n. 41, 102 n. 50, 108, 140, 145 n. 33, 147 n. 55, 148 n. 59, 203, 224, 229, 237 n. 22
  'Algunos aspectos del cuento' 52 n. 12, 72, 89, 199
  'Anillo de Moebius' 11, 57, 60, 171
  'Las armas secretas' 11, 24 n. 19, 58, 60
  'Así se empieza' 167, 177 n. 3 & 9, 212 n. 24, 223, 227
  'Las babas del diablo' 11
  'La banda' 30
  'Bix Beiderbecke' 149, 177 n. 2, 179 n. 26, 220, 223, 227
  'Las caras de la medalla' 30, 177 n. 3
  'Carta a una señorita en París' 177 n. 3
  'Casa tomada' 24 n. 17
  'Clifford' 156, 177 n. 3, 223, 227, 235 n. 5, 244
  'Clone' 29–50, 51 n. 8, 52 n. 9 & 15, 53 n. 18 & 22, 54 n. 28 & 29, 54 n. 32, 54–55 n. 35, 56, 57, 84, 87–88, 93, 100 n. 3, 120, 124, 128, 130, 135, 141, 147 n. 53 & 55, 148 n. 60, 171, 196, 199, 201, 205, 223, 224, 230, 241
  'Continuidad de los parques' 78

  'Cristal con una rosa adentro' 81
  'Del cuento breve y sus alrededores' 100 n. 31
  Diario de Andrés Fava 28, 105, 142 n. 8, 177 n. 3
  'Elogio del jazz: carta enguantada a Daniel Devoto' 5, 8, 17, 21, 23 n. 12, 26, 27–28, 51 n. 1, 72, 84, 149, 150, 151–52, 154, 157, 159, 162, 163, 164, 165, 166, 167, 169, 172, 173, 174–75, 177 n. 8, 189, 215, 216, 217, 219–20, 229, 235 n. 2, 239
  'Gardel' 105, 110, 114, 118, 125, 143 n. 14 & 16, 177 n. 1, 211 n. 8
  'Historia con migalas' 171
  Historia de cronopios y famas 153–54
  'Instrucciones para John Howell' 44
  'La isla a mediodía' 52 n. 14, 57, 58, 185, 237 n. 25
  'Lejana. Diario de Alina Reyes' 26, 30, 185
  Libro de Manuel 30, 156, 177 n. 3, 180 n. 30, 212 n. 26, 235 n. 4
  'Literatura en la revolución y revolución en la literatura' 2–3, 89
  'Llama el teléfono, Delia' 157–58, 225
  'Louis, enormísimo cronopio' 27, 100 n. 25, 153, 155, 163, 177 n. 3, 179 n. 23, 189, 192, 198, 223, 225, 227, 229, 236 n. 7, 244
  'Lugar llamado Kindberg' 23 n. 2, 118, 149, 177 n. 2, 216, 218–19
  'Melancolía de las maletas' 34, 168, 170, 177 n. 3, 216
  'Las ménades' 11, 30, 56, 57–71, 72, 73, 75, 77, 85, 93, 97, 98, 99 n. 1, 3, 9 & 12, 100 n. 25, 121, 129, 130, 140, 145 n. 33, 153, 155, 211 n. 11, 212 n. 24, 230, 231–32, 237 n. 24, 241
  'Mudanza' 177 n. 3, 178 n. 18
  'Muerte de Antonin Artaud' 154
  musical tastes 29, 56, 60, 75, 106–09, 112, 118, 144 n. 22, 146 n. 35, 149–50, 159, 172, 176, 177 n. 6, 179 n. 23, 180 n. 40, 211 n. 15, 216–18, 219, 222, 237 n. 23, 239, 246 n. 2
  'No hay peor sordo que el que' 24 n. 15, 25 n. 26, 177 n. 3, 216
  'La noche de mantequilla' 105
  'Orientación de los gatos' 177 n. 3
  'Para una poética' 5, 8, 9, 12, 21, 24 n. 16, 28, 159, 237 n. 26, 243, 246 n. 4
  'El perseguidor' 30, 61, 66, 99 n. 6 & 19, 145 n. 34, 149, 156, 164, 166, 169, 176–77, 177 n. 2 & 16, 179 n. 25, 180 n. 28, 182–84, 185–89, 190–92, 195–96, 197–210, 211 n. 1, 2 & 4, 212 n. 18, 26, 28 & 30, 213 n. 31, 214, 219, 220, 221, 222, 223, 224, 229–35, 236 n. 6 & 14, 237 n. 27, 241
  'Policrítica en la hora de los chacales' 89
  Los premios 24 n. 17, 81, 95, 105, 118
  Presencia [Julio Denis] 6–7, 14, 24 n. 14, 24–25 n. 21
    'Jazz' 6, 159–62, 179 n. 24, 215, 225, 227; 14; 'Música' 6–7, 14; 'Música II' 6–7, 'Músicas' 6; 'La Presencia en la Música' 6, 14
  Prosa del observatorio 86, 96

'Las puertas del cielo' 24 n. 17, 66, 104, 105, 106,
    117, 121–32, 133, 134, 135, 136, 137–39, 140,
    142 n. 2 & 7, 144 n. 21, 146 n. 38, 40 & 43,
    147 n. 49, 50 & 51, 162, 229, 231, 241
Rayuela 11, 15, 23 n. 10, 24 n. 17 & 19, 30, 53 n. 20,
    81, 100 n. 24, 101 n. 36, 105, 106, 111, 142 n. 2
    & 5, 143 n. 20, 145 n. 31, 149, 156, 165–66,
    173, 174–75, 176–77, 177 n. 2, 178 n. 17,
    179 n. 25 & 26, 180 n. 30, 182, 183–85, 189,
    190, 192–98, 199–200, 201, 203, 208, 211 n. 1
    & 3, 212 n. 19, 22, 25 & 28, 214, 216, 218, 219,
    220, 223–24, 225, 226, 227–28, 234, 237 n. 20,
    240, 241, 245
    Berthe Trépat scene 100 n. 25, 229–35, 237 n. 24
        & 26, 241, 246 n. 6
'Retorno de la noche' 157–58, 225
'Reunión' 23 n. 2, 30, 56, 57, 71, 73–88, 92, 95,
    96, 97, 99 n. 1, 100 n. 22 & 32, 101 n. 38, 120,
    145 n. 33, 147 n. 55, 148 n. 59 & 63, 199, 229,
    241
Los reyes 24 n. 17
'Rimbaud' [Julio Denis] 21, 25 n. 29, 195
Salvo el crepúsculo 103, 106, 119, 131, 141–42 n. 1,
    147 n. 52, 148 n. 59
    'El agua entre los dedos...' 141 n. 1
    'La camarada' 141 n. 1; 'Java' 141 n. 1
    'Con tangos' 103, 107, 110, 113, 118–19, 142 n. 1
        & 2
        'Milonga' 142 n. 1; 'La mufa' 142 n. 1;
        'Rechiflao en mi tristeza' 109, 119; 'Las
        tejedoras' 133, 147 n. 54; 'Veredas de
        Buenos Aires' 142 n. 1
    'Para escuchar con audífonos' 239–46
    'Razones de la cólera' 111, 119, 143 n. 19
    '1950 Año del Libertador, etc.' 119
'Silvia' 177 n. 3
'Soledad de la música' 5–6, 7–8, 12–22, 23 n. 11, 26,
    27, 28, 30–31, 34, 43, 45, 52 n. 12, 74, 93–94,
    100 n. 25, 103, 104, 106, 149, 151–53, 157, 159,
    162–63, 167, 168, 184, 185, 189, 191, 194, 195,
    215–16, 222, 224, 228, 229, 236 n. 9, 239,
    241–44
'Tango de vuelta' 104, 105, 121, 131–41, 142 n. 6,
    147 n. 53, 54, 55 & 56, 148 n. 59, 60 & 61, 195,
    224, 229, 233, 241
    History of 143 n. 12
Teoría del túnel 3–5, 6, 7–8, 9–10, 12, 15, 16, 18, 20,
    21, 22, 23 n. 10, 27–28, 44, 54 n. 31, 72–73,
    75–76, 77, 151, 159, 222, 239, 240, 242–43
'Torito' 105, 118, 142 n. 6, 145 n. 29
Trottoirs de Buenos Aires 103, 106, 108, 119, 120, 131,
    141 n. 1 & 2
    'La camarada' 141 n. 1; 'La Cruz del Sur' 119,
    141–42 n. 1; 'Java' 141 n. 1; 'Medianoche
    aquí' 141 n. 1; 'Tu piel bajo la luna' 141 n. 1;
    'Veredas de Buenos Aires' 141–42 n. 1

'Un gotán para Lautrec' 106, 111, 119, 131, 143 n. 10
Un tal Lucas 29, 30, 51 n. 3, 75, 177 n. 3, 178 n. 19,
    225
'Viaje alrededor de una mesa' 2–3, 89
'Vientos alisios' 177 n. 3
'La vuelta al piano de Thelonious Monk' 177 n. 3,
    223, 227, 235 n. 5
Cortot, Alfred 91
Coulson, Graciela 99 n. 10
counterpoint 47, 54 n. 33, 74, 77–78, 80, 82, 94–95,
    100 n. 28 & 30
Couture, Mark 197, 204, 206, 212 n. 18, 236 n. 14
cross-rhythms 94–95, 102 n. 47, 171, 174, 176
'Cuando tú no estás' 143 n. 20
Cuban Revolution 2, 72, 73, 79–80, 83, 85, 87, 88–89,
    94, 96, 98, 101 n. 40
    see also revolution

Daniels, Douglas Henry 180 n. 39
danzón 90, 94, 102 n. 49
Daumal, René 200
Davis, Miles 176, 217, 221, 233
Davis, Virginia 158
    'My Heart is Anchored in the Lord' 158
Debussy, Claude 71
    La mer (L. 109) 62, 99 n. 5
'Deep River' 158
Delaunay, Charles 164
Deleuze, Gilles 86
Delibes, Léo 231, 232
Derrida, Jacques 6, 7, 18, 20, 31–32, 88, 168–69, 172,
    180 n. 32, 189, 191, 196
Des Prés, Josquin 31, 87–88
DeVeaux, Scott 236 n. 6
Devoto, Daniel 151
différance 31, 81, 191, 196
Dinzel, Gloria 117
Dinzel, Rodolfo 117
Dionysus 57, 64–66, 68, 70, 71, 77, 85, 99 n. 9
Droit-Volet, Sylvie 211 n. 6
Dumas, Alexandre 54 n. 29
    Les mohicans de Paris 54 n. 29
Dunne, Irene 90, 91, 101 n. 43
Dupree, Champion Jack:
    'Junker's Blues' 190

'Eche veinte centavos en la ranura' 143 n. 20
Ellington, Duke 149, 172, 173, 174, 176, 177 n. 5, 217,
    240
    'The Blues with a Feeling' 192
    'Hot and Bothered' 180 n. 30
Euripides:
    Bacchae 65, 66, 70
Evans, Bill 180 n. 31, 235 n. 3
Evans, Dylan 208, 211 n. 12, 213 n. 30
existentialism 10–13, 29, 44, 72, 159

Fiddian, Robert William 203
figura 81–83, 85–88, 95–97, 101 n. 35, 203
Fitzgerald, Ella 225
Flaubert, Gustave 3
'Flor de fango' 111, 142 n. 3
Fralasco, Héctor 105, 110, 117, 118, 124, 127, 142 n. 2
Franco, Jean 146 n. 40, 147 n. 51
Frederick II 39, 40, 44, 52 n. 17
Friberg, Anders 173

Gallego, Isabel 178 n. 17
García, Antonio J. 222
García, Graciela P. 204
García Jiménez, Francisco 128
  see also 'Mariposita'
García Pérez, David 61, 64, 65, 99 n. 3 & 9, 100 n. 21
Gardel, Carlos 1, 107, 108, 110, 114, 118, 124, 125,
  143 n. 13, 14, 16 & 18, 144 n. 22, 244
  'A la luz del candil' 124, 127–28, 129, 138, 146 n. 43
  'Anclao en París' 143 n. 20
  'Cuando tú no estás' 143 n. 20
  'Flor de fango' 111, 142 n. 3
  'Mano a mano' 118–19, 218
  'Mi noche triste' 143 n. 20, 144 n. 22
Gesualdo, Carlo 31, 32–33, 34, 35–39, 41–44, 47–49,
  50, 51 n. 1, 52 n. 15, 54 n. 32, 55 n. 35, 87–88,
  124, 128, 147 n. 55, 199
  'O voi, troppo felici' 48, 54 n. 34
  'Poichè l'avida sete' 41, 48, 53 n. 27, 54 n. 34
Gibbons, Orlando:
  Royal Fantasies 240
Gillespie, Dizzy 77, 156, 178 n. 14, 188, 201, 217, 221
Gioia, Ted 158, 159, 178 n. 17, 179 n. 27, 236 n. 14
Givan, Benjamin 175
'Go Down, Moses' ('Oh! Let My People Go') 159,
  197, 211 n. 13
Goialde Palacios, Patricio 64–65, 99 n. 3, 167, 168,
  170, 180 n. 31, 220–21
Goodman, Benny 174
Goyalde Palacios, Patricio *see* Goialde Palacios, Patricio
Graettinger, Bob 156
Greenberg, Robert 80, 87
Guattari, Félix 86
Guevara, Ernesto 'Che' 73, 84
Gunther Kodat, Catherine 179 n. 27, 235 n. 4, 236 n. 6
Gyurko, Lanin A. 200, 204, 212 n. 18

habanera 90, 94, 102 n. 49, 112, 144 n. 21
Hampton, Lionel 173
Handel, George Frideric:
  Six fugues or voluntarys for organ or harpsichord 53 n. 23 & 24
Harrison, Max 180 n. 31
Hartman, Charles 16, 18, 165, 216, 220, 223, 224–25,
  226, 228–29
Hawkins, Coleman 1, 183, 184, 187

Hegel, Georg Wilhelm Friedrich 20
  and *Klang* 20–21, 244
Heidegger, Martin 15, 21
Henderson, Fletcher 172, 180 n. 37
Hicks, D. Emily 212 n. 26
Hines, Earl:
  'I Ain't Got Nobody' 51 n. 3, 200
Hobsbawm, Eric 113, 114, 121, 235 n. 4
Hodeir, André 164, 166, 173, 176, 189
Hölderlin, Friedrich 15, 21
Holiday, Billie 225
Horne, Lena 225
Huici, Adrián 64, 100 n. 21
Huxley, Aldous 54 n. 31
  Brave New World 46, 54 n. 31
Hwangpo, M. Cecilia 116, 122

'I Know the Lord Laid His Hands on Me' 158
improvisation 39, 44, 212 n. 22, 229, 237 n. 21, 245
  and the *baguala* 148 n. 61
  and the cakewalk 179 n. 22
  and jazz 6, 51 n. 5, 75, 78, 104, 150, 165–71, 172,
    175, 176, 178 n. 14 & 17, 180 n. 31, 183,
    187, 188–90, 191, 197, 200, 201, 206, 214–17,
    219–23, 224, 225, 226, 227, 228–29, 231, 232,
    236 n. 10 & 14, 245
  and *la música culta* 39, 52–53 n. 18, 60, 101–02 n. 45,
    229
  and poetry 224–25
  and ragtime 179 n. 21
  and tango 104–05, 115, 117, 144 n. 25, 144–45 n. 27,
    145 n. 28, 229
interpretation 14–18, 21–22, 23–24 n. 13, 25 n. 16, 26,
  27, 30–31, 34–40, 42–44, 48–50, 51 n. 1, 57, 68,
  93–94, 97, 104–05, 117, 152, 155, 174, 217, 232, 242
Irving, John 74, 80
iterability 32, 168–69, 180 n. 32, 189–90, 191, 220,
  233, 245
Ives, Charles 221, 236 n. 13, 237 n. 27

jazz 2, 8, 16, 22, 23 n. 2, 4 & 10, 23–24 n. 13, 27, 29,
  34, 51 n. 3 & 5, 75–76, 77–78, 100 n. 29, 30 &
  31, 103, 104, 105, 106, 108, 115, 144 n. 27, 149–77,
  177 n. 3, 4, 5 & 6, 178 n. 17 & 18, 180 n. 30 &
  31, 182–210, 211 n. 2 & 8, 212 n. 28, 214–35,
  235 n. 2 & 4, 236 n. 9, 237 n. 20, 21 & 22, 239,
  240, 244, 245, 246 n. 2 & 6
  bebop 166, 174, 175–76, 177 n. 2, 178 n. 14 & 15,
    180 n. 39, 186, 187, 188, 200, 201, 216, 217,
    221, 229, 230, 234, 236 n. 6, 236 n. 12
  Big Band jazz 84, 166, 171, 172–73, 174–76,
    177 n. 5, 180 n. 35, 36, 37, 38 & 39, 216, 234,
    236 n. 6 & 9
  cool jazz 166, 234, 236 n. 16
  free jazz 115, 166, 177 n. 2, 187, 216–17, 218–19,
    233, 234, 235 n. 4, 236 n. 6

history of 150, 158–59, 160, 162, 164, 165, 166–67, 171, 172–75, 176, 178 n. 17, 179 n. 20, 21 & 22, 180 n. 29, 40 & 41, 188–89, 197, 216–17, 225, 237 n. 21
hot jazz 166, 173, 174, 176, 177 n. 5, 180 n. 40, 188, 192, 216, 217–18, 219, 234, 236 n. 6
and race 150, 157–65, 174–75, 178 n. 18, 178–79 n. 19, 179 n. 26 & 27, 183, 197, 201, 211 n. 13, 219–20, 236 n. 6
resistance to notation of 222–25, 227
swing 76, 77, 100 n. 30, 101 n. 36, 150, 171–72, 173–76, 179 n. 22, 180 n. 30, 187, 189, 212 n. 27, 214–15, 217, 222, 223, 224, 225, 227, 228, 229, 232, 246 n. 5
Swing Era jazz *see* Big Band jazz
takes 34, 168, 170, 171
see also improvisation
Jitrik, Noé 211 n. 4
Jordan, Ruth 101 n. 44
Judaeo-Christian tradition(s) 15, 19, 33, 198–99, 209
Juvenal:
  Satire 6: 54 n. 29

Kadir, Djelal 188, 189
Kallberg, Jeffrey 101–02 n. 45
Kanellopoulos, Panagiotis A. 237 n. 21
Kansas City Six 173, 180 n. 39
Kart, Larry 206, 224
Keats, John 19
Keil, Charles 173
Kennedy, Raymond F. 180 n. 31
Kern, Jerome 236 n. 16
Koch, Lawrence O. 221
Konitz, Lee 216–17, 223, 225, 236 n. 16
  Lee Konitz Plays with the Gerry Mulligan Quartet 236 n. 16
  'All the Things You Are' 223, 236 n. 16
Kristeva, Julia 196, 208, 218, 234

Lacan, Jacques 196, 207–10, 211 n. 12, 212 n. 29, 213 n. 30
Lachman, Kathryn 52 n. 16, 53 n. 21
Lang, Eddie 227–28
Lauder, Sir Harry 178 n. 19
Laurenz, Pedro 110, 143 n. 17
Levitin, Daniel J. 76, 77
Litweiler, John 156
logocentrism 44, 98
Logos 5, 7, 19, 31–32, 33, 88, 161
London, Jack 84, 101 n. 38
Longley, Michael 226
Lopes, Paul 172
López, Teresa 65
López-Lespada, Marta 160–61, 162, 179 n. 24, 215
Loyola, Hernán 154
Luengo, Ana 99 n. 2 & 4

Lutoslawski, Witold 240

Maenads 57, 64–65, 68
Mall, James P. 20
Mallarmé, Stéphane 19, 20–21
Manzi, Homero 112
Marenzio, Luca 47
'Margo' 147 n. 47
Mariotto, Juan Gabriel 112, 117
'Mariposita' 128, 131, 132, 133, 137–38
Mazzucchelli, Aldo 114, 117
McKinney, Louise 166
Mendelssohn, Felix:
  A Midsummer Night's Dream (Op. 21) 99 n. 5
Menon, Vinod 76, 77
Mesa Gancedo, Daniel 142 n. 1 & 2, 145 n. 32
Meyer-Minneman, Klaus 99 n. 2 & 4
Miller, Glenn 172, 174, 180 n. 36
  'Serenade in Blue' 172, 180 n. 36
Miller, Marilyn G. 120, 142 n. 2
milonga (music/dance) 112, 144 n. 21
milonga (tango club) *see* tango
Minotaur 11
minstrelsy 178 n. 17
Mirka, Danuta 74–75, 76, 77
Mitchell, Red 187
Mitchell, W. J. T. 32
Monk, Thelonious 181 n. 44, 189, 217, 223, 227, 235 n. 5, 236 n. 15
  see also 'Bemsha Swing'
Monteverdi, Claudio 31, 47, 87
Moore, Robin 53 n. 18
Mora Valcárcel, Carmen de 98, 101 n. 41
Moran, Dominic 2, 23 n. 6, 24 n. 20, 81, 86, 96, 147 n. 55, 204–05, 218–19
Morton, Jelly Roll 149, 158, 174, 177 n. 5, 217
Mozart, Wolfgang Amadeus 29, 51 n. 1, 3, 4 & 5, 75, 76–78, 100 n. 28–29, 171, 176, 190, 229, 240, 244
  String Quartet No. 17 in B♭ major (K.458) (*The Hunt*) 73–74, 78–87, 96, 100 n. 32, 101 n. 33 & 37
Mulligan, Gerry 236 n. 16
  see also Konitz, Lee
'Muñeca brava' 118, 119, 142 n. 3
música culta, la 2, 22, 26–50, 51 n. 1, 2, 5 & 6, 52–53 n. 18, 56–98, 99 n. 1, 100 n. 25 & 32, 103, 104, 108, 109, 120, 121, 135, 140, 141, 145 n. 33, 147 n. 53, 149, 150, 151, 153, 164, 168, 171, 172, 173, 176, 177 n. 1, 214, 223, 229, 230, 231, 234, 235 n. 2, 239, 240, 241, 245
  see also classical music *and* improvisation
musicalisation (of language) 8, 12, 21, 24 n. 16, 56, 71, 75, 77, 159, 165, 201, 222, 224
  see also poeticisation (of language)
musicology 17, 23 n. 2, 76, 142 n. 2, 150, 151, 154, 164–65, 171, 172, 174, 211 n. 6, 223
'My Heart is Anchored in the Lord' 158

myth 11, 24 n. 17 & 18, 57, 64–65, 69–70, 99 n. 3 & 9, 102 n. 50, 179 n. 27
see also Apollo, Bacchae, Dionysus, Maenads, Orpheus, Pentheus, and Theseus

Negro spirituals 158–59, 178 n. 17, 179 n. 22
Neruda, Pablo 7
Nielsen, Christine S. 112, 117
Nono, Luigi 240
nostalgia 19, 89, 91–93, 95, 99 n. 1, 101 n. 42, 102 n. 46, 107, 108–21, 123–29, 131, 133–35, 136, 137, 140, 141, 142 n. 2, 144 n. 21, 22 & 23, 145 n. 31, 146 n. 36 & 44, 192, 218–19, 224, 229, 237 n. 22, 245

Olson, Charles 224
ontology 1, 2–3, 10, 22, 27, 43, 51 n. 3, 56, 81, 83, 108, 109, 121, 150, 157, 159, 174, 182, 185, 189–90, 210, 229
Orloff, Carolina 23 n. 5
Orpheus 11, 64–65, 99 n. 9 & 10, 243–44
Ortiz Oderigo, Néstor 163, 227
Ostendorf, Berndt 178 n. 17
Owens, Thomas 175

Padilla, Heberto 88–89, 101 n. 40
Panassié, Hugues 164, 179 n. 27
Parker, Charlie 156, 164, 177 n. 2, 178 n. 14, 180 n. 28, 181 n. 44, 188, 189, 197, 200, 209–10, 217, 221, 232, 233, 235 n. 5, 236 n. 6, 10 & 12, 237 n. 27, 241, 244
  'Cheryl' 221
  'Ko-Ko' 221, 236 n. 12
  'Lover Man' 190, 211 n. 9, 236 n. 6
Parkinson Zamora, Lois 236 n. 14
Parsons, Lawrence M. 76, 84
Peavler, Terry 44
Peiró, José Vicente 28, 105, 111, 130, 142 n. 8, 145 n. 31, 153–54, 178 n. 17, 212 n. 19, 239
Pentheus 65–66, 70
Pereyra, Teresa:
  Tango canyengue 146 n. 37
Pérez-Abadín Barro, Soledad 73–74, 80, 82, 84, 91, 98
Peris Blanes, Jaume 185, 187–88, 200, 212 n. 22
Petit de Murat, Ulises 162, 163
Peyrats, Pilar 183
Piazzolla, Astor 117, 120, 144–45 n. 27
Picasso, Pablo 81
Planells, Antonio 61, 63
Plisson, Michel 148 n. 61
poeticisation (of language) 8, 75, 151, 222, 224
  see also musicalisation (of language)
poetism 9–12, 18, 21, 71, 72–73, 87, 98 n. 19, 159, 224
poetry 1, 2, 5–8, 9–10, 12, 14, 16, 18–19, 21–22, 24 n. 14 & 16, 24–25 n. 21, 27, 28, 105, 108, 118–20, 144 n. 21, 150, 151–52, 153, 159–60, 195, 206, 224–25, 237 n. 19 & 26, 239, 243, 246 n. 4
see also improvisation
polyrhythms 94–95, 102 n. 47, 174, 175, 176, 179 n. 22, 229, 236 n. 13
Poniatowska, Irena 101 n. 42
Poole, Geoffrey 53 n. 20

ragtime 158, 173, 177 n. 5, 179 n. 21 & 22, 216
see also improvisation
Rainey, Ma 225, 226
Ramos Ruiz, Anuchka 53 n. 21 & 25, 54 n. 29, 54–55 n. 35
Randal, Elías 128
see also 'Tanto'
Rasula, Jed 224
Re 33
Réda, Jacques 187, 209–10, 246 n. 5
Renfrew, Alastair 54 n. 32
revolution 1, 2–3, 4, 56–57, 68, 70, 71, 72–73, 76, 77–80, 83–89, 94, 95–98, 99 n. 1, 100 n. 32, 101 n. 41, 102 n. 48 & 50, 103, 108, 109, 126–27, 144 n. 27, 148 n. 59, 153, 155, 199, 229, 246
see also Cuban Revolution
rhizomatics 86, 87, 96, 244–45
rhythm 48, 75–78, 82–83, 84, 87, 90, 94–97, 100 n. 30, 31 & 32, 101 n. 36, 108, 117, 145 n. 28, 147 n. 55, 152, 156, 158, 167, 171–76, 178 n. 17, 179 n. 22, 180 n. 30 & 31, 187, 189, 200, 214, 216, 222, 224, 225, 229, 232, 235 n. 4
see also counterpoint, cross-rhythms, polyrhythms, and syncopation
Rilke, Rainer Maria 243, 246 n. 4
Rimbaud, Arthur 7, 21, 195
Rivero, Edmundo:
  'Amablemente' 36
Rodríguez-Luis, Julio 97
Rollins, Sonny 187, 224
  Sonny Meets Hawk! 187
  'All the Things You Are' 187
Romanticism 4, 94, 97, 98
Rusch, René 187
Russell, Ross 175, 176
Rutkoff, Peter 172, 173, 175, 221

Sábat, Hermenegildo 106, 119, 143 n. 12
Sábato, Ernesto 112
Sager, David 178 n. 17, 179 n. 21
Saint-Saëns, Camille 232
Salley, Keith 187
Sampayo, Carlos 226
Samson, Jim 101 n. 42, 102 n. 46
Sanders, Pharoah 245
Sartre, Jean-Paul 153, 154
Sassoon, Humphrey 53 n. 23 & 24

Savigliano, Marta E. 117, 122–23, 126–27, 129, 137, 139, 140, 142 n. 2 & 7, 144 n. 26, 146 n. 36, 38, 39 & 40
Schaeffner, André 175
Scholz, László 23 n. 8
Schönberg, Arnold 51 n. 1
Schubert, Franz:
  'Du bist die Ruh' 240
Schuller, Gunther 77, 174, 180 n. 31
Scott, William 172, 173, 175, 221
Scruton, Roger 76
Serra Selvat, Rosa 117–18, 133, 134, 136–37, 148 n. 62
Shaw, Arvell 163
Shepp, Archie 118, 177 n. 2, 216, 218–19
Silver, Millicent 39–40, 41, 42–43, 44, 49, 50, 53 n. 21
Smith, Bessie 183, 225, 226
  'Baby Doll' 190
  'Empty Bed Blues' 190
Smoira Cohn, Michal 77
'Smoke Gets in Your Eyes' 89, 91, 92, 94, 95, 98
'So You're Going to Leave the Old Home, Jim' 178 n. 19, 225
socialism 2–3, 9, 89
Sommer, Doris 166, 201, 203, 205
Soren Triff, Eduardo 212 n. 22
Stambaugh, Joan 211 n. 5
Standish, Peter 2, 23 n. 5, 30, 44, 66, 73, 230
Stockhausen, Karlheinz:
  Momente 212 n. 26
Stover, Chris 187
Stowe, David W. 77
Strauss, Richard:
  Don Juan (Op. 20) 59, 62, 99 n. 5
Stravinsky, Igor 17, 26
Sundström, Andreas 173
surrealism 10, 23 n. 8, 154, 169–70, 180 n. 34
syncopation 77–78, 87, 90, 94, 100 n. 27, 28 & 30, 162, 171, 173, 174, 175–76, 235 n. 4

tango 1, 2, 14, 22, 23 n. 2 & 4, 26, 35–36, 37, 38, 103–41, 142 n. 2, 3, 4, 5, 7 & 8, 143 n. 10, 11, 13 & 18, 143–44 n. 20, 144 n. 23, 145 n. 31, 32 & 33, 147 n. 52 & 53, 148 n. 59, 60 & 61, 149, 162, 177 n. 1, 211 n. 8, 218, 224, 229, 232–33, 234, 237 n. 22, 239, 241, 244, 245, 246 n. 6
  compadre 122–23, 145–46 n. 35
  compadrito 116, 122–23, 130, 136, 137, 138, 145–46 n. 35, 146 n. 37 & 38, 147 n. 57
  dance 106, 108, 116, 117, 121, 122, 123, 124, 126–27, 136–37, 141, 143 n. 12, 144 n. 22 & 26, 146 n. 37, 148 n. 58
  Golden Age 116, 144 n. 22, 145 n. 28, 234
  history of 112–13, 116, 117, 138, 143 n. 13 & 15, 144 n. 21 & 22, 145 n. 28, 146 n. 35 & 36
  milonga (tango club) 106, 121–24, 125–27, 128, 129, 130, 131, 137, 140, 146 n. 39, 40 & 41

milonguita 116, 117, 122–23, 126, 137, 138
New Guard 112, 116, 117, 123, 126, 144 n. 22, 145 n. 28, 146 n. 36, 147 n. 57, 234
niño bien 122–23, 130, 146 n. 38
nuevo tango 120, 144 n. 27, 234
Old Guard 117, 138, 144 n. 22, 145 n. 28, 146 n. 35 & 36, 147 n. 57
  see also improvisation
'Tanto' 128, 131, 132, 133, 138
Taylor, Julie M. 112, 116, 143 n. 16, 146 n. 37
'Te aconsejo que me olvides' 147 n. 47
'Tea for Two' 221, 236 n. 11
Teiresias 65, 66, 69, 70, 99 n. 12, 237 n. 24
Terramorsi, Bernard 96, 98, 101 n. 41, 102 n. 50
Thaut, Michael H. 76, 84
Theseus 11
Third Stream music 239, 246 n. 2
Thomas, Dylan 203
Thompson, Robert Farris 108, 111–12, 144 n. 21, 144–45 n. 27, 145 n. 28
Tossounian, Cecilia 122, 126
Toulouse-Lautrec, Henri de 106
Trimarchi, Pietro Davide 76, 84

'Un tropezón' 146 n. 43

Vaccarezza, Alberto:
  La comparsa se despide 123
Valentine, Robert Y. 185, 188, 200
Valéry, Paul 5, 7, 152, 216
Varèse, Edgard 240
Vaughan, Sarah 225
Vázquez, Carmen 90, 94–95
Verne, Jules:
  A Fantasy of Doctor Ox 99 n. 7
Viladrich, Anahí 138
Vivaldi, Antonio 237 n. 27
voice 14, 49, 79, 85, 107, 110, 122, 125, 140, 143 n. 16, 157–58, 159, 160, 161, 164, 178–79 n. 19, 190, 199–200, 212 n. 19, 225–29, 237 n. 20, 241

Wallon, Henri 213 n. 30
Ward, James F. 21
Waring's Pennsylvanians 190
Waters, Ethel 178–79 n. 19, 225
Waters, Keith 178 n. 17
Watkins, Glenn 37, 47
'(What Did I Do to Be So) Black and Blue' 197, 211 n. 13
Whiteman, Paul 174–75
Wilhelm, Kate:
  Where Late the Sweet Birds Sang 46, 54 n. 31
Woideck, Carl 237 n. 27

Yahni, Roberto 60
Youens, Frederick 41, 44

Young, James O. 197
Young, Lester 167, 181 n. 44, 223, 227
Young, Trummy 163
Yu, Fred 91–92, 94, 96

Yurkievich, Saúl 171

Zach, Michael H. 216–17, 221
Zimmerman, Antonio 40

www.ingramcontent.com/pod-product-compliance
Lightning Source LLC
Chambersburg PA
CBHW080541090426
42734CB00016B/3171